SOUNDTRACK OF THE REVOLUTION

Stanford Studies in Middle Eastern and Islamic Societies and Cultures

SOUNDTRACK OF THE REVOLUTION

THE POLITICS OF MUSIC IN IRAN

NAHID SIAMDOUST

STANFORD UNIVERSITY PRESS
STANFORD, CALIFORNIA

Stanford University Press
Stanford, California

©2017 by Nahid Siamdoust. All rights reserved.

Printed in the United States of America on acid-free, archival-quality paper

Library of Congress Cataloging-in-Publication Data

Names: Siamdoust, Nahid, author.
Title: Soundtrack of the revolution : the politics of music in Iran / Nahid Siamdoust.
Other titles: Stanford studies in Middle Eastern and Islamic societies and cultures.
Description: Stanford, California : Stanford University Press, 2017. |
    Series: Stanford studies in Middle Eastern and Islamic societies and
    cultures | Includes bibliographical references and index.
Identifiers: LCCN 2016020201 (print) | LCCN 2016020972 (ebook) |
    ISBN 9780804792899 (cloth : alk. paper) | ISBN 9781503600324 (pbk. : alk.
    paper) | ISBN 9781503600966 (ebook)
Subjects: LCSH: Music—Political aspects—Iran—History. | Iran—Politics and
    government—1979-1997. | Iran—Politics and government—1997-
Classification: LCC ML3917.I7 S49 2017 (print) | LCC ML3917.I7 (ebook) |
    DDC 780.955/09048—dc23
LC record available at https://lccn.loc.gov/2016020201

Typeset by Bruce Lundquist in 10/14 Minion Pro

In memory of my father, Mir Ali Akbar Seyed Siamdoust

Dedicated to my mother, Hamideh Seraj Ansari

And my beautiful daughters, Delara & Leili

Join our path, dear one
Join our path, dear one
Don't remain alone with this pain
Because this shared pain
Never will be
Separately cured

> —Mohammad Reza Shajarian's new encore *"Razm-e moshtarak"*
> (Common Battle), on his concert tour following the 2009 election un-
> rest, a song that he first sang at the time of the revolution in 1979

Only words of steel remain
Public trust has been shattered
 . . .
One day, though, the money you usurp
Shall choke you in your throat
I said it to the door
But the walls take note, word for word

> —Alireza Assar's *"Khiābān-khābhā"* (Street-Sleepers),
> released in 2001 but reused by Green Uprising supporters
> over footage of government repression in 2009

You are the most beloved wife of God
So much so that he even divorced Mohammad for you

—Mohsen Namjoo's "homage" to Supreme Leader
Ayatollah Ali Khamenei, titled "*Gelādiyātorhā*" (Gladiators), 2009

After all this rain of blood
Finally, a rainbow will shine
The sky won't appear cloudy from all the stones
The aqueducts won't turn red like tulips
Muezzin, call to prayer

—Hichkas's "*Yeh ruz-e khub miyād*" (A Good Day Will Come),
released online as he boarded the plane to leave
Iran indefinitely, following the 2009 unrest

CONTENTS

SOUNDTRACK OF THE REVOLUTION

THE POLITICS OF MUSIC

ON ONE OF MY FIRST EVENINGS back in Iran after a long absence, my parents treated me to a meal at the garden restaurant of Tehran's Hyatt Hotel—called Azadi (Freedom) following the 1979 revolution—where they had occasionally taken me and my three siblings as children. It was 1996, and I had been away from my home country for ten years, going to school in Germany. When my siblings and I were growing up in the revolutionary and war-torn Iran of the nineteen-eighties, this was one of the biggest treats my parents would afford us during the city's hot summers. I remember that at least once, at one of those dinners, one of the adults pushed us kids into the large swimming pool for fun. Although it was kept fairly clean, the pool had become off-limits to all guests since the 1979 revolution, since the public exhibition of semi-clothed bodies was forbidden under the new Islamic regime.

As a returning teenager, I instantly recognized the place. Everything looked the same, just more faded and dilapidated: a retro hotel of former glory. Formally dressed but sloppy-looking waiters attended to customers in an uninterested manner. But then I noticed something that jarred with my memory of those strict earlier years. There was a black grand piano next to the pool, and a male pianist was playing Persian and Western classical music on it. Still, the atmosphere was quite somber. After the pianist finished each piece, patrons remained unmoved. Clearly, they knew that they must not clap. Although in the late nineteen-nineties President Akbar Hashemi Rafsanjani's policies had led to a loosening in the social sphere, the expression of joy by means of clapping in public was still not acceptable. I commented to my parents that it seemed as though sadness had enveloped Iran, and happiness was a sin.

Fifteen years later, in March 2011, on the last night of my penultimate research trip to Iran, I attended a pop concert that would have been utterly unimaginable in 1996, just as the restaurant piano would have been unimaginable a decade before that. The teen-idol crooner Benyamin, looking suave in his black outfit and trendy glasses, was moving about on a stage drenched in red light and smoke and singing "I've fallen in love" (*āsheq shodam*) to fast rhythms and a pounding beat. His fans, revealed by flickering stage lights that panned over the audience, were moving along rhythmically and could barely stay attached to their seats; they sang along with every single word. Throughout, guards were running around frantically to admonish audience members to lower their arms or stop dancing with their upper bodies.

There had been a sea change in Iran's musical scene from 1996—when just about enough time had passed since the end of the war in 1988 to allow for a slightly more relaxed atmosphere—to 2011, when the government no longer stood in the way of dance-pop concerts. Of course, the waning of the revolutionary government's zeal, as well as the chronological distance from the revolution itself and from the war years, had led to a general easing up of the public atmosphere. But while Benyamin was allowed to croon about adolescent love to hordes of Iran's majority-youth population, many other artists who attempted to sing about socially or politically sensitive subjects were stopped in their tracks.

After initially banning all music, following the 1979 revolution, the Islamic Republic's leaders bowed to the need to allow some music. Nevertheless, they have stifled music that does not serve their political and ideological interests, banned music that they perceive as threatening those interests, and facilitated a popular but shallow musical culture while an officially impotent but lively subculture thrives mostly outside of the official public realm. Since 1979, both state-approved and banned musicians have to varying degrees contested and critiqued the state's official rhetoric. Throughout these years, music has served as an important alternative political, societal, and ideational space, and Iranians, music producers and consumers alike, have imbued it with great significance. The soundtrack of revolutionary Iran tells the story not just of the matters that have lain at the center of the people's and policy makers' negotiations about politics, religion, and national identity, but also the story of the evolution of the Islamic Republic itself.

Music was one of the first official casualties in 1979. When the revolutionaries overthrew the shah's regime and established the Islamic Republic, their new, "pure" society was not going to allow for music. In their view, music had been complicit in the moral corruption of youth. But only months after the revolution, music was "revived." When Ayatollah Morteza Motahhari, one of the dearest protégés of the revolutionary leader Ayatollah Ruhollah Khomeini, was assassinated in May 1979, musicians who were loyal to the regime wrote a song to commemorate him. They presented the song to the Imam himself, and (as I describe in greater detail in chapter 4) Khomeini was so moved that he vowed to support this "beautiful music committed to the revolution."

After that, music of a certain kind was green-lighted for broadcast on the radically conservative state media. Indeed, the state made heavy use of music for its revolutionary propaganda and during the long Iran-Iraq war, which broke out soon after the revolution and raged from 1980–1988. But it repressed other kinds of music, often punishing people who made, traded in, and consumed them. Even makers of Persian classical music, which the revolutionaries viewed as unadulterated by Western influences and as "authentically" Persian, were at first severely restricted in their art. Eventually, however, Khomeini's views and a later postwar edict, in 1988, opened the floodgates to music, and in the years since, every major genre of music has been practiced to varying degrees of official or underground reception. Throughout these changing circumstances, female musicians have suffered the most. Women's voices were deemed un-Islamic soon after the revolution, and so some of Iran's most famous musicians of all time were forced into what seemed to be permanent silence.[1] This silence, this nearly total absence of the female voice in postrevolutionary Iranian music production, is glaring, all the more so because it stands in stark contrast to the soundscape of Pahlavi-era Iran. The solo female voice remains officially banned to this day.

Music has played an important role in Iran's political upheavals since the Constitutional Revolution of 1905–1911, when Iranians rose up against the Qajar-dynasty ruler Mozaffar al-Din Shah to demand a constitution, which led to the establishment of Iran's first majles, or parliament. This period produced some of Iran's most enduring freedom-seeking songs, a repertoire that was kept alive throughout the 1979 revolution and revived yet again at the height of the Green Uprising in 2009. In the social realm, music has been important for at least that long as a way to relay critiques and to broach taboo subjects, often using playful, innocent-sounding folk songs that belie their sharp edges. And in the years since the Pahlavi monarchy was toppled in 1979, the children of the revolution have come of age and expressed their critiques of political and social conditions on a wide musical scale, continuing a tradition that links the many Iranian generations who have sought political freedom for over a century.

THE ISLAMIZATION OF IRANIAN POLITICS

Still in the throes of its own revolutionary genesis, the newly formed government of the Islamic Republic set out in 1979 to create a vast series of laws and institutions to Islamize the country's politics as well as its polity.[2] This affected everything from the regulation of the public sphere and the creation of media content to the formulation of school curricula, as well as more personal matters like dress and alcohol consumption.[3] When the constitution of the Islamic Republic of Iran came into being in December 1979, it stipulated in its Article 4 that:

> All civil, penal, financial, economic, administrative, cultural, military, political, and other laws and regulations must be based on Islamic criteria. This principle applies absolutely and generally to all articles of the Constitution as well as to all other laws and regulations, and the fuqahā of the Guardian Council are judges in this matter.[4]

In his first New Year's address as Iran's leader in March 1979, Ayatollah Khomeini emphasized above all that a "fundamental cultural revolution all over" Iran was necessary. In subsequent speeches and decrees, Khomeini reiterated the goals of this policy:

> Exiting the ill-formed western culture, and replacing it with the Islamic-national educational culture and the cultural revolution in all fields across society, demands such an effort that we should strive for long years to materialize it and fight [against] the deeply-rooted penetration of the West.[5]

In order to determine the outlines of this revolution, Khomeini decreed that a Cultural Revolution Headquarters be created, and it was established and in force by early 1981. It was also legally stipulated that the state be established on Islamic foundations, but due to the position of moral and religious supremacy the new regime had adopted, it set out on a somewhat ambiguous objective not merely to regulate the public aspects of its citizens' lives, but also to enforce correct Islamic behavior in the private sphere. In the first decade after the 1979 revolution, the state—through its mobilized masses of volunteers, the *basij*—undertook aggressive incursions into people's private lives.[6]

The importance of universities and student activism in Iran's 1979 revolution was amply clear, and so the first task of the Cultural Revolution Headquarters was to Islamize universities, which were shut down for three years during these operations. The universities were purged of about twenty thousand professors who either espoused other political convictions, such as Marxism or liberalism, or were not believed to be sufficiently revolutionary. Within this new political context, being revolutionary meant believing in and practicing Islam and fully supporting the state's new ideology and political system, which were based on the "guardianship of the jurist," the Supreme Leader. Other tasks involved training new professors, purging universities of nonrevolutionary students, and revising textbooks.[7]

In December 1984, the new Supreme Council for Cultural Revolution replaced the old Cultural Revolution Headquarters, and its tasks became more formalized and all-encompassing. This new body was now in charge of Islamizing all aspects of society, not just the universities. Khomeini soon decreed that "the declarations and directives issued by the esteemed Supreme Council of the Revolution must be enforced."[8] The body was declared the highest instance for the determination of the country's policies in all spheres of culture and education, and while it is not a legislative body, its decrees carry legal power.

With the success of the revolution, Iranians were for the first time witnessing a state that claimed to be the official protector and promoter of Islam, although for centuries Iranian kings had claimed legitimacy on a two-pronged basis: national and Islamic. In fact, it had been the clergy's very lack of involvement in, or even oppositional stance towards, former governments that had caused many Iranians to trust the clergy. And now, after the victorious revolution, many believed that Khomeini would retreat to the religious seminary town of Qom. Many (mostly middle-class) Iranians who regarded themselves as believing Muslims, but whose religious beliefs and practices were not as strict as the version that was officially propagated, felt alienated and disenfranchised by the government's discourse. Not surprisingly, the vast reach of state-imposed Islam has rendered the interpretation of what exactly Islam means and where its place is in Iranian society one of the most contested matters for recent cultural production, including music.

The mainstays of Islamic Republic ideology, as projected in regime speeches, policies, and material culture, have remained fairly consistent over more than three decades. They include immense devotion to Islam, the Prophet Mohammad, and the twelve Shia imams. It is not enough to be inwardly committed to Islam; one's piety is to translate into ideological allegiance and must be out-wardly visible. (This is why during the strictest postrevolutionary years, clean-shaven men or men sporting Western neckties were punished. A man could be an observant Muslim, as indeed many clean-shaven, necktie-sporting men were, but if he did not grow an "Islamic" beard or if he appeared to support Westernization through his attire, he was suspected of not supporting the revo-lution.) Another hallmark of this ideology is indebtedness to a long series of martyrs who sacrificed their blood for the potential or actual Islamic Republic, from martyrs of prerevolutionary eras, who agitated for a strict Islam and were later lionized by the Islamic Republic, through martyrs of the revolution and the Iran-Iraq war and beyond.[9] Other elements of this ideology include an aver-sion to vanity and earthly joys, strong anti-Western sentiments, and pride in independence. As the revolutionary leader Khomeini had avowed, the motto of the new Iran was to be "*na sharqi, na gharbi*," neither Eastern nor Western. An important component of Shi'ism and hence a pronounced part of the new ideology is also fervor for the twelfth imam, Mahdi, the hidden messiah. And finally, full commitment to the political system of the *velāyat-e faqih* (the rule of the jurist) and subservience to the "Guide of the Revolution" (the Supreme Leader) are indispensable elements of this ideology. In his theoretical treatise on the *velāyat-e faqih*, Khomeini concludes that religious jurists have "the same authority as the Prophet and the imams, . . . in other words, disobedience to the religious judges [is] disobedience to God."[10]

Guided by their benevolent leader, Iranians were promised a truly Islamic society that would be the exact opposite of the corrupt, Western Pahlavi puppet regime. This new Iran "would be free of want, hunger, unemployment, slums, inequality, illiteracy, crime, alcoholism, prostitution, drugs, nepotism, corrup-tion, exploitation, foreign domination, and yes, even bureaucratic red tape. It would be a society based on equality, fraternity, and social justice."[11] The dis-crepancy between these lofty promises and the inevitable unfolding of reality has not ceased to offer substance for critique in cultural productions.

MUSIC AND ISLAM IN THE REVOLUTIONARY REPUBLIC

In July 1979, the all-powerful new leader Ayatollah Khomeini shared his views on music in a speech to state radio employees:

> One of the things that intoxicate the brains of our youth is music. Music causes the human brain, after one listens to it for some time, to become in-

active and superficial and one loses seriousness. . . . Of course music is a matter that everyone naturally likes, but it takes the human being out of the realm of seriousness and draws him toward uselessness and futility. . . . A youth that spends most of his time on music becomes negligent of life issues and serious matters, and becomes addicted—just like someone who becomes addicted to drugs, and a drug addict can no longer be a serious human being who can think about political issues. . . . Now you must take these issues seriously, and turn away from jokes and light matters. . . . There is no difference between music and opium. Opium brings a sort of apathy and numbness and so does music. If you want your country to be independent, from now on you must transform radio and television into educational instruments—eliminate music.[12]

In the new Islamic Republic, then, music was to be neglected, if not eliminated altogether. Most kinds of music were soon prohibited on radio and television, music schools were shut down, and musicians, especially female singers, were badly treated. Soon the new state prohibited the importing of foreign cassette and video tapes and recorders. The state regularly deployed its forces, at the time known as the *komiteh* or just *basij* ("committee" or "volunteers"), to confiscate such equipment from cars and homes, punishing the owners with lashes or fines.[13] In the first decade of the Islamic Republic, when thousands of young men were falling in the Iran-Iraq war, the only tunes broadcast on state television were marches, patriotic hymns and songs, and religious lamentations (*noheh-khāni*).[14]

The permissibility of music in Islam has always been a matter of interpretation, and views have ranged from a total ban to permission for all music and instruments, including dance.[15] Since the ultimate authority in Islam, the Qur'an, does not mention music explicitly, and the sunnah—traditions of the practices and sayings of the Prophet Mohammad as recorded through hadiths—offer little clarity on the subject, Muslim scholars and authorities have interpreted various verses in the Qur'an according to their own points of view.[16] Most of the Islamic discussion has revolved around three Qur'anic verses where abstention from "*lahw al-hadith*" (idle talk) is advised, which conservative Islamic scholars have interpreted to mean music, espousing the view that music is "futile folly."[17] However, some of the most important and influential Islamic theoreticians on music, including Al-Ghazali, Al-Farabi, and Avicenna—all of whom happened to be of Persianate origin—viewed music favorably.[18] Ghazali's work on music, which many other scholars followed as a model, concluded that both "statutory and analogous evidence indicate the admissibility of music."[19] A major point in his argumentation, which has since been replicated by authorities within the Islamic Republic, is that the impression that music leaves on the heart "follows the rule of what is in the heart," meaning in effect that it is the intention of the listener that determines his or her reception of a piece of music.[20]

Despite Khomeini's harsh pronouncement on music at the beginning of his reign, his views on music actually turned out to be closer to those expressed in Ghazali's writings.[21] One of the main architects of the constitution of the Islamic Republic and a close ally of Khomeini, Ayatollah Mohammad Beheshti, had laid out this view clearly in speeches made at the Iranian mosque in Hamburg, Germany, almost a decade before the revolution. In response to questions about the legality of music, he had responded, "Not all singing is haram [forbidden in Islam], not all instrument-playing is haram; those kinds of singing and instrumental music are haram that draw listeners or the audience in a gathering toward sin. . . . That is considered *lahw* [idle entertainment/play], which makes the human being heedless of God's remembrance."[22]

But how is it decided what type of effect a kind of music has? Here, Khomeini's view again overlaps with Ghazali's, namely, that "the nature of music's influence depends on the basic intentions of the listener and the purpose for which it is used."[23] Khomeini's position manifested itself best shortly after the Iran-Iraq war, when the conservative mullah Ayatollah Mohammad Hassan Qadiri criticized a television series called *"Pāyiz-e sahar"* (Dawn's Autumn) for showcasing a female actress whose neck was exposed, and also took exception to the music used in the series. Khomeini responded that if someone feels excited by watching a certain image, he should prevent himself from watching that image, and that the same applied to music.[24] In effect, it appears that Khomeini placed responsibility for discerning the effect and hence permissibility of different kinds of music on the individual, at least within the already regulated framework of the Islamic Republic. Furthermore, in response to numerous *esteftā'* (religious questions) on music, most ulama (clerics)—including the current Supreme Leader Ayatollah Ali Khamenei—have responded in line with Ghazali and Beheshti. Often ulama have further explained that it is *'orf*—meaning custom or convention—that determines which music distances one from God and which does not.

It is not practical, however, in an authoritarian political system, to act based on statements that music's effects can be judged by the listeners themselves, on the basis of custom or convention, if we are to take the term *'orf*, or custom, at face value. The state officially controls music and does not leave judgment on that music up to each listener. Nor, in the absence of a free public sphere and solely democratically elected bodies, can truly popular customs, conventions, or laws be debated and established. For that matter, nor have the highest ulama ever unanimously agreed on one custom or convention to apply to all. That is not the job of the ulama, who study a life long in order to lend their own interpretations to the original texts. As for the state and governmental bodies that regulate the production and distribution of music, they too have to make do with these ambiguous edicts, and so the field of music regulation remains a Kafkaesque labyrinth that causes a great deal of frustration and consternation for most artists. This interpretational ambivalence, as well as a lack of resolve or action on the part of the country's highest leaders, has created an atmosphere of uncertainty regarding music in postrevolutionary Iran. Not surprisingly, the most repeated plaintive expression in conversations about music is *"taklif-e musiqi roshan nist"* (music is in limbo).

THE STATE, IDEOLOGY, AND PERFORMATIVITY

Despite the theological explication above, which is useful for an understanding of the Islamic concerns at hand, it is of course important to remember that as a governing body, the Islamic Republic, in setting its music policy, is not solely concerned with Islamic permissibility. In this ideologically driven state, with its initially expressed intent to reform its citizens from prerevolutionary heathens into postrevolutionary believers, music as a site of state control is important for the performativity of the state's professed values and principles and the aesthetic and acoustic expressions thereof: in short, its identity.

Although I will be referring to "state ideology" throughout this text, I do not intend this term to be understood in monolithic or static terms. While the basics of the Islamic Republic's projected ideology have remained surprisingly consistent over the past decades, the parameters of action within it have changed with shifting social and historical contingencies and have, overall, expanded considerably. Furthermore, I hope to show a more nuanced picture of the relationship between official stance and practical action, on the part of both artists and the state. Nevertheless, it is analytically productive to discuss the state as an entity and to locate artists' positions and discourses with respect to an official state ideology, because the state encroaches on all aspects of Iranians' lives. However, inasmuch as Iranians, including Iranian artists, validate the state's existence and authority by the very expression of their discontent with it, they also lend the state variation and nuance through their multifarious representations of it in the substance and practice of their productions, artistic and otherwise.

All this is not to say that Iranian artists are locked in a binary conflict with the state. Michel Foucault has written that he finds the notion of ideology difficult to use, in part because it always posits an opposition to "something else which is supposed to count as truth."[25] I do not, however, oppose ideology to some implicit truth; instead, my notion of ideology here is based on Louis Althusser's understanding of a socially constructed worldview that aims to govern our perceptions and actions and to reproduce the legitimacy of a dominant power. Consequently, there can be competing worldviews, all of them socially constructed, but in the Iranian case the official ideology carries tremendous weight because the state attempts to enforce it both through its ideological apparatuses (including schools, the media, and the cultural field) and its disciplinary apparatuses (such as the judiciary, security forces, police, and prisons).[26]

Within the context of the Islamic Republic, the function of the state ideology is to rule or subjugate on the basis of "Islam" and to reproduce the legitimacy of the leadership of its clerical caste. This reproduction is enacted performatively, through discourse and practice, as evidenced in the many political and religious speeches as well as rites and rituals of the Shi'ism that stands at the center of this ideology. Considering the deep and widespread roots of religious belief and practice in Iranian society, it is useful to remember Foucault's refusal of the notion of repression, which he finds problematic because "what makes power hold good, what makes it accepted, is simply the fact that it does not only weigh on us as a force that says no, but that it traverses and produces things, it induces pleasure, forms knowledge, produces discourse."[27] And indeed, the human body is a main site for the manifestation of the state, whether it embodies the state by wearing prescribed attire (in the Iranian case, the hijab), reciting national anthems in schools, bearing the flag in military service and war, or simply abiding by the given laws; "one's life and death are continual performances of discursive practices that delimit one's society, culture, and State."[28]

The notion of performativity (in this case, the definition of identity by speech acts and other communicative expressions) is key to understanding the works of the musicians discussed here. "Performativity," as Judith Butler has argued, "is not a singular 'act,' for it is always a reiteration of a norm or set of norms," or it would have no traction or power within the environment in which it functions.[29] This kind of performativity then relies on citationality, referencing fragments of traditions, cultures, discourses, and communal memories. To perform alternative subjectivities or discourses, Iranians draw on various traditions and repertoires of contention.[30] Some of the most potent reservoirs of signification are rooted in the country's defining cultural sources and anxieties, such as pre-Islamic Persian culture and its traditions, Islam in its various Iranian configurations, political tyranny, Westoxification (imitation of the West, loss of Iranian identity), modernity, the discourses of freedom, and the forces of globalization, to name only the most significant. The various instances of performativity of these and other citations, in the public sphere more broadly and in the musical sphere more specifically, allow for overlapping interpretations of the past and an engagement in a national discourse about the future.

It is in part because the state transgresses into people's most personal spheres that they resist those transgressions with minute and personal subversive acts. Here Michel de Certeau's notion of the "weapons of the weak," formulated in everyday practices and tactics, will be useful in analyzing the ways in which both the producers of music and the "other producers," namely the consumers, write themselves into the public space that the state aims to control.[31] On a similar plane there is Asef Bayat's useful concept of "quiet encroachment," by which he too means the behavior of (in our context) politically and culturally repressed people whose everyday acts keep expanding their territory into the spheres of state power.[32] Bayat also explains how in order to assert their identities, the young often utilize what look like accommodating strategies, using dominant norms and institutions to "creatively redefine and subvert the constraints of those codes and norms."[33] This he calls "subversive accommodation," such as when the young turn austere Muharram processions into "Hossein parties" in Iran.[34] When musicians and their audiences insert themselves into and traverse the space between what James C. Scott has termed the "public transcript" (authorized by the dominant power) and the "hidden transcript" (critique of power spoken behind its back) and increasingly widen the parameters of the "public transcript," it is often through such subtle subversive acts of creating new meanings.[35] However, as I hope to show in my discussion of music, there is no binary process of domination and resistance, and no singular "hidden" or "public" transcript. Rather, transcripts—like other social constructs—are multiple and their forms and content depend on the given contexts. Nonetheless, I do use the term "public transcript" to invoke that which is propagated or permitted by the state, and "hidden transcript" to point to all that which is not officially approved or is disapproved.

In such performative acts, people often enlist what Pierre Bourdieu has called cultural capital, along with the affects—or expressions of emotion—that are rooted in the traditions being cited.[36] Within the Iranian symbolic market (where social and cultural goods contain varying degrees of prestige and honor), this concept works well on the ideological register. So, for example, the greatest goods are those that subtly or clearly—depending on the official legitimacy of that good— signify where the allegiances of their possessors lie: on what stretch of the spectrum between diehard pro-*velāyat-e faqih* (Supreme Leader) and secular anti-regime. There are of course various shades all along the way, from religious but anti-regime to secular but vaguely in support of the status quo if not the regime, drawing on various strands of the three main romanticized identities (rooted in either traditionalist conceptions of Islam, Islamic reformism, or a secular modernist outlook) within postrevolutionary Iran.[37] Using Bourdieu's analogy, culture or cultural signifiers are in effect being used as currency for the performativity of identity: for the expression of a political, social, or cultural stance.

To give an example, in my later discussions of pop music I will argue that both musicians and concert audience members employ the affect of joy as a subversive act.[38] The state puts great human and financial resources into controlling any joy and self-expression that take place outside of its power paradigm. Such expressions are tolerated within the context of celebrations of the revolution's anniversary, for instance, but they can be punished if they are spontaneous or occur outside of official frameworks. As recently as ten years ago, governmental monitoring bodies that oversaw public gatherings, including concerts, did not tolerate enthusiastic clapping, and as I have mentioned, minders still monitor all concert audiences to make sure no one gets up to dance or becomes too enthusiastic in other ways. The enforcement of public piety and solemnity is one way in which the Islamic Republic performs its official culture. Shi'ism—its holy persons and commemorative days and its rites and rituals— are held paramount over all competing sources of national identity. Iran's often joyous pre-Islamic holidays are therefore not promoted, and some clerics even call for their complete elimination. Shi'ism itself is used by the state largely within its capacity as a religion of mourning. That is not to say that participants don't find joy in Shi'i rituals and gatherings, or that *ta'ziyeh* performances (Shi'i passion plays) are bleak affairs—quite the contrary—but the most important holidays are held to commemorate the death of holy persons and involve black banners and clothes and a lot of weeping, real or pretended.[39] There are many sacred mourning days that Shi'is must observe, culminating in the ultimate holiday of 'Āshurā when the favored hero, Imam Hossein "the oppressed," is slaughtered. In fact, there are only very few joyous holidays, including the birth of the Prophet Mohammad and the Mahdi as well as the main Islamic Eids, such as Eid-e Fitr (the end of Ramadan), Eid-e Qorbān (the Sacrifice Feast), and Eid-e Ghadir, when according to Shia lore the Prophet appointed Imam Ali as his successor.[40] Even Ramadan is a somewhat solemn affair in Iran, whereas in some Sunni countries it can often be a month of joyous gatherings.[41] Hence, in politically enforcing a familiar and deeply ingrained culture of Shi'ism, the Islamic Republic is able to use grief both to perform and assert its identity, and as a powerful tool of subjugation. The disciplinary nature of this performativity reinforces the state's paternalistic relationship to its subjects, and it does so by intruding into a very personal sphere of its subjects, namely their feelings and expressions of joy.

In Iran's authoritarian polyarchy, legitimacy is drawn from Islam as well as from the state's genesis in the vastly popular 1979 revolution.[42] The Iranian government does not merely rely on Iranians' verbal expressions of their obedience to reproduce its authority; its power is ubiquitously inscribed into the physical public space and onto people's bodies. Posters and murals of senior religious figures and martyrs cover most cities. Mechanisms such as the obligation to wear Islamic dress to which all women (and to a lesser degree, men) are subjected, or the fact that until recently Iranians had to live in public spaces that often evoked war, death, loss, and mourning as well as the state's constant reiteration of the sacrifices of the revolution, inherently reinforce the state's self-projected legitimacy and authority.

Needing to submit to circumstances imposed from the outside is part of what Bourdieu calls "symbolic violence,"[43] in which people, motivated by a host of factors, often voluntarily subject themselves to restrictions. In submitting to Iran's government-regulated public space, as they are required to varying degrees to do, Iranians must act according to the "public transcript" authorized and promoted by the state. Depending on their situation (for example whether they are enrolled in state universities or hold government jobs), they are subject to varying forms of symbolic violence. For my purposes here, this notion expands to include the realm of cultural production and music. Within this sphere, musicians have to dissimulate and submit to official regulations, often against their beliefs and choices, in order to obtain permits for publications and performances.

AN ALTERNATIVE PUBLIC SPHERE

Music is present in the lives of most Iranians, whether they listen to it in its officially approved form on state media; tune in to foreign-based Persian satellite television channels for both foreign and homegrown productions; or listen to a random assortment of music on public transport such as shared taxis, where drivers play music to their heart's delight, from prerevolutionary pop to current hip-hop. Music is more accessible to Iranians than film or theater, both of which require, at a minimum, dedicated time for their viewing, whereas music can be listened to throughout the day and alongside other activities. Crucially, however, as far as the political nature of the musical sphere is concerned, music concerts allow for a communal sharing of critical views between perfect strangers, and consequently a critical discursive community that is unavailable elsewhere in the official sphere, short of direct political protests.

Music's greatest power lies in its ability to create publics, the deliberate coming together of strangers, engaged with each other through mere attention to certain texts (in this case music) and involved in poetic (i.e. imaginary and aspirational, as opposed to real) world-making.[44] These publics can manifest as simply as in their shared attention to certain music. Listeners who purchase or download a song and appreciate its content constitute a public because they are partaking in the same discourse. Such a public can come face-to-face with itself virtually, in online forums; or actually, in concerts or protests, lending substance to its world-making. No other form of cultural production makes this possible with quite such ease. In order to be part of a public that appreciates certain literature, for example, one must invest time in studying that literature. In order to be part of the Tehran Friday prayer public, to cite another example, one should, ideally, attend the sermon, because physical presence and participation in its rituals, such as the chanting of slogans and communal *namāz* (prayer), are important aspects of this public. But to belong to a public around music, all one needs is to have heard a song and identified with its sentiments. Music allows for socially constructed imagined communities that exist purely on the level of discourse.[45] Importantly, these publics built around music, or even just a couple of lines from a song, can become activated and come to the fore at times of heightened political or social tension. It is at such times that members of such a public are able to communally express their common interest and investment in a certain text and world-making, manifesting the extent and power of their public. This was the case during both the 1979 revolution and the 2009 Green Uprising, when perfect strangers came together to express shared sentiments through popular songs.

What forms of "publicness" are available to Iranians, and what do we mean specifically when we use the term "public sphere" in the Iranian context? Jürgen Habermas's coinage of the term "public sphere" referred to the reasoning public of eighteenth-century Enlightenment Europe engaged in rational-critical discourse, in a space free from the infringements of official authority.[46] In using the term for the contemporary Iranian situation, we have to dislodge it from these earlier associations, but it is still a useful concept for examining the ways in which people can come together as a public and express their views. Especially if we draw out the nuances of the German word Habermas uses for the public sphere—*Öffentlichkeit*, rooted in the German word "*offen*" (open)—we can come closer to an understanding of the kinds of publicness that state bodies allow to be performed openly.

Throughout the nineteen-eighties, the state monopolized public spaces like streets, squares, and halls for the exhibition and performativity of its Islamic-revolutionary ideology and fervor. As Roxanne Varzi writes in her observation of the public space:

> By the time the generation of youth born at the beginning of the revolution was fully cognizant of its environment, Tehran was already transformed into an Islamic revolutionary space: Islamic covering for women was fully enforced; old monuments were replaced by revolutionary ones; and billboards of Muslim clerics and other Islamic visuals covered the city.[47]

The public sphere was so restricted that people organized events that would otherwise have been public affairs, such as poetry readings and photo exhibits, in private spaces such as basements and garages. With the end of the war and the election of the somewhat more moderate president Akbar Hashemi Rafsanjani, the "reconstruction" government launched a program in the nineteen-nineties to create public spaces for leisure, and some of these formerly "private" public events surfaced in the newly created public spaces. But cultural events that were outside of the state's permitted parameters—such as rock music concerts, readings of works by banned authors, or photo and art exhibits that did not conform to norms of official morality—continued to take place either within these "private" public spaces or in spaces that were legally outside of government control, such as the places of worship of minority groups or foreign embassies.

The parameters of the official public sphere—of what amount of openness and what kind of conversation are officially tolerated—are fairly well delineated, though not static, and the boundaries of the permissible are more or less known to most Iranians. Two very powerful promulgators of official norms are the state media and the Friday prayer leaders, not to mention the Supreme Leader Ayatollah Ali Khamenei himself. The pronouncements and policies of the sitting president, his ministers, and members of the majles (parliament) can also function as purveyors of the acceptable, but more often such guidelines come from the more powerful hard-line or conservative governments, ministers, or parliamentarians whose views are closer to those of the Supreme Leader. So, for example, criticism of the Supreme Leader or showing unveiled Iranian female actors is unthinkable on state television.[48] However, both of these things, and many others that would be unacceptable to the Islamic Republic, regularly occur on expatriate satellite TV channels that are watched by millions of Iranians inside Iran. This points us to another, parallel, public sphere in Iran.

Since about 2005, new communication technologies—mainly mobile phones, satellite television, and the Internet—have provided an alternative to the approved public sphere, one that is much less susceptible to state control. When examining the discourses and debates taking place within the Iranian "public sphere," it is therefore necessary to define that space to include both the internal, state-controlled public sphere and the expansion afforded to it by the large expatriate community abroad and the new media technology. While there are no accurate statistics for Internet and satellite TV use in Iran, the Internet World Stats research group, which tracks Internet usage worldwide, puts the number of Internet users in Iran for the year 2015 at 46.8 million, or 57.2% of the population.[49] By 2014, Iran had 88 mobile phones per 100 inhabitants of all ages.[50] This affects the perspectives available even to those who do not personally participate in the Internet and satellite TV mediascape, as interesting occurrences on these freer channels are sometimes reported in conventional media and often talked about in the informal channels of talk and gossip, even between perfect strangers. This increasingly widespread access to new media and satellite television over the last decade has led to the expansion of the space wherein critique can be mounted against religious and political authorities, to a degree that was previously impossible.[51]

This alternative public sphere is almost like a big national private sphere, where conversations can take place on a mass level, on mobile phones, satellite TV programs, and the Internet, and off the state's approved register. The state security apparatus understands the significance of this alternative public sphere and tries to shut down communication channels at times of heightened political crises by disrupting mobile phone networks and satellite TV broadcasts and cutting off the Internet.

Within this larger, multifaceted public sphere, which encompasses both state-controlled and uncontrolled spaces and media, music plays a particularly important role in allowing for a national conversation outside of official parameters. Music is essential to the creation of these alternative discursive spaces, as well as to the construction and performance of identity among Iranians, young and old. There are several reasons for this.

For one thing, the Islamic government's fraught relation to music has imbued this particular art form with greater political significance, so that often its presence alone, or one's participation in particular forms of it, can project certain meanings, indicate a certain attitude, and construct a social or political position.[52] In the first postrevolutionary decade, people were regularly arrested, fined, and lashed for having music tapes in their cars, as I have mentioned, and musicians carrying their instruments in public often saw them confiscated or broken. Hence, one's very association with or support for music could signal opposition to the draconian measures of the early Islamic Republic. More specifically, partaking in the discourse of a particular musician by quoting certain lines from his or her work could and still can readily signal a political association, depending on the context. "Imposing" in one's taxi the music of a prerevolutionary pop diva, on the one hand, or Qur'anic recitation, on the other, can signal a particular political and religious alignment, although these markers are of course not necessarily permanent. Identity and subjectivity are fluid and can take on different forms depending on all sorts of variables, including the social and political context. A taxi driver who drinks arak at night and listens to the music of the sexy Los Angeles bombshell Sepideh will do neither of those things even in the privacy of his own home when a religious relative is visiting, and is likely to switch the music off in his car if he happens to pick up a passenger who looks like a diehard regime supporter with the potential to cause trouble.

As the state's stance toward music—and hence the official musical space—has evolved over the decades, the meanings of this participation have also evolved. Whereas some families once considered it haram, forbidden by Islamic law, to attend any live music concerts or listen to recorded music at all, now their attendance at a state-approved singer's concert might signify support for an evolved official state ideology, while a youngster's attendance at an underground rock concert signifies more open attitudes that diverge from the officially propagated framework on a whole range of issues.

The very nature of the musical medium is also a main contributing factor to its flexible and multifarious use by cultural producers and secondary producers alike (following de Certeau's designation of consumers as the "other" producers, discussed above[53]). Because of "music's location between the real and fictional, serious and sarcastic, musical mediation provides a wider space for expression than even verbal discourse or behavior."[54] Music can express a sentiment at a lower risk than could, for instance, explicit verbal communication.

At the presidential candidate Mir-Hossein Mousavi's largest campaign event, on 23 May 2009 in Azadi Stadium, "Āftābkārān" (literally "Sun-Workers"), a song with communist connotations, was revived: in great part to project hopefulness, as the song augurs the end of winter. A few seconds into the song, Maryam, a journalist in her mid-thirties who was seated next to me, burst into tears. She said, "It tells you that Mousavi is ready to move beyond old animosities, to put those dark days behind us and work together for a better Iran."[55] It signaled a sort of "let bygones be bygones," even towards the Islamists' archenemies, the communists; and it was something that no politician could have actually said in so many words, but that music could communicate subtly.

Furthermore, and this is quite important, among the arts, music is the most inclusive and salient communal discursive space, because, as already mentioned, it is present in most Iranians' lives in multiple forms and forums, and unlike theater or film, can be consumed while other life activities are going on. Music is also more affordable. For a thousand toman (approximately one dollar), you can buy a CD containing more than a hundred MP3 tracks from a street peddler, some of whom function as disc jockeys for the neighborhood or the entire town and choose and burn the selections themselves.[56] Increasingly, though, people now simply download their music online for free, from sites such as Radio Javan.

As for the political nature of the musical sphere, music concerts allow for a communal sharing and performativity of critical views and consequently a critical discursive community that is unavailable elsewhere in the official public sphere. Walter Benjamin points out (comparing painting and film) that "painting simply is in no position to present an object for simultaneous collective experience"; more than any other art form in Iran, music does allow that kind of experience.[57] Similarly, Walter Ong notes that "sight isolates, sound incorporates. Whereas sight situates the observer outside what he views, at a distance, sound pours into the hearer," allowing for a kind of communion between performers and audiences as well as among audiences in a way that no other art form really does in this intrinsic, sonic form. Hence, "by contrast with vision, the dissecting sense, sound is thus a unifying sense."[58] This is not to negate sound's (and, by extension, music's) multisensory dimension, nor its necessarily social construction.[59] I am simply arguing that music, more than any other art form in Iran, is able to allow for a popular, collective experience. The public concert in contemporary Iran (along with theatrical performances, though to a lesser extent) is the only type of event that brings together a self-organized public and allows for the spontaneity of live action both onstage and within the audience. Gatherings around music are also potent because they are based on Iran's long-standing cultural engagement with the embodied sense of sound, rooted in its cultivation of poetry as the master sonic form. Poetry, meanwhile, finds its strongest form of mass mediation through music, which is able to magnify its social reach and impact.

What is also important is that musical mediation is possible within the small spaces over which people have direct control, even within officially overseen public spaces: the small spaces that flow into and expand the alternative public sphere, such as shops, taxicabs, and even the very personal space that can be colored through the humming of a controversial tune or lyric. Blaring the song "Āftābkārān" out one's car windows in the period after the 2009 elections, for example, a time of great political contention, was a way to create a very clear political positioning.

Last but not least, while on the one hand we invest music with this great capacity to relate universal truths, on the other hand, paradoxically, we deny it the kind of weight or importance that we accord to other forms of political communication, such as political speeches, newspaper editorials, or actual street demonstrations. Hence, music is somewhat unburdened and, as such, freer to function in important ways, while because of the attributes discussed above, it can never be truly controlled by any governing body.

PERSIAN MUSIC

There is material evidence that music has been played in Iran for over five thousand years. The Greek historians Herodotus and Xenophon wrote about both religious and military uses of music at the time of the Achaemenid Empire, and Ferdowsi's *Shāhnāmeh* (*Book of Kings*) is replete with references to the musical preferences of Iranian kings.[60] However, there is still too little material for it to be possible to weave a comprehensive history of music in Iranian lands reaching any further back than about a thousand years.[61] Most scholars who have studied the history of Persian classical music believe that the foundation of this music, the *radif* (a series of modal scales and melodies that must be memorized, which I describe in detail below), was only reified as a system about two hundred years ago, although its components have existed and evolved for centuries, possibly even millennia.[62]

It will be useful at this point to talk a little bit about the somewhat complicated subject of Persian classical music and its foundation, the *radif* repertoire, which I will be referring to again at various points in this book. In Persian, this classical music is usually referred to as *musiqi-ye asil-e Irāni* (authentic Iranian music) or *musiqi-ye sonnati-ye Irāni* (traditional Iranian music), and in English it is variously called Iranian or Persian classical, traditional, or art music. This tradition is regarded as a quintessential Persian heritage. In this musical system, there are twelve principal modal categories, which are divided into seven *dastgāhs* (loosely, "modes") and five *āvāzes* (loosely, "lesser modes"), not to be confused with "*āvāz*" in its definition as free-metered vocals within Persian classical music, about which I write in chapter 2. The *dastgāhs* are more complete and complex musical modes and contain a greater number of *gushehs* (melodic units). Strictly speaking, however, the European term "musical mode" does not adequately capture the term *dastgāh*, as each *dastgāh* also exhibits a certain melodic character. So, for example, the *shur dastgāh*—which is the basis of many folk songs—is characterized by burning and yearning for the beloved, while the *chāhārgāh*—which is used for the musical accompaniment of the heroic epic *Shahnameh* (*Book of Kings*)—has qualities of heroism and grandeur.[63] Furthermore, each *dastgāh* is actually a collection of several modes but gains its name from the mode in which it begins, a mode that is repeated as a theme throughout. The *radif* repertoire includes the totality of all the *gushehs*, categorized as they are within the tonal spaces of the various *dastgāhs* and *āvāzes*. Depending on the source of the notation of the *radif*, there may be as many as eight hundred *gushehs*. The most canonical repertoire is one recorded by Mirza Abdollah Farahani (1843–1918), which contains two hundred and fifty *gushehs*. Each *gusheh* can belong to one or more *dastgāhs* and play roles of varying importance. I should also note that Persian music contains a quarter tone, a pitch halfway between the semitones in the usual twelve notes of a chromatic scale. Memorization and improvisation are such integral parts of Persian music that until Mirza Abdollah recorded his encyclopedic knowledge of the *radif*, no such written notation existed. And to this day, different sources still give varying accounts of the number of *gushehs*—and even *dastgāhs*—depending on the definitions they use. For that matter, the *radif* has never been static and its *gushehs*, *dastgāhs*, and *āvāzes* have been continually transformed through the myriad interpretations of its practitioners.

The best record of the state of Iranian music in the first half of the twentieth century was compiled by Ruhollah Khaleqi, himself a musician and music educator. Khaleqi's work offers a unique and indispensable musicological and sociopolitical account of Iranian music from the constitutional period onward, with profiles of musicians, stories about concerts, texts of songs, and his own insider perspective on the significance of it all.[64] There is little else that was written about music during this period. But based on the available writings, we know that the great jolt to Persian music—leading to the many divisions and schisms over its value and place in Iranian culture and education that continue to this day—happened in the nineteen-twenties, early on in Reza Pahlavi's reign. In his great zeal to modernize Iran, the newly minted Pahlavi king devalued Persian music as unscientific and invited European educators to Iran to teach his people Western music. Reza Pahlavi's regime actively promoted the *sorud*—a marchlike anthem genre informed by Western military music that is also a favorite genre of the Islamic Republic's—over the homegrown *tasnif*, a lighter, more rhythmic genre that had often been used for songs of freedom since the Constitutional Revolution of 1905–1911.[65] While the *sorud* filled the official national soundscape, other more popular, grassroots musical forms, such as *ruhowzi* (social theater often performed in house courtyards, offering a comical commentary on daily life) and *pish-pardeh-khāni* (adopted from the French "avant-scène," literally "before-scene performance," short pieces, often politically infused, inserted between the acts of a play but thematically independent of the play), occupied alternative, semipublic places in the absence of the *tasnif*.

MUSICAL EDUCATION

During the Islamic Golden Age (generally regarded to be the period from the beginning of the Abbasid caliphate in 750 until the Mongols' siege of Baghdad in 1258), the great Persian scholars considered music as a field of knowledge, ranked among the theoretical and empirical sciences. Scholars such as Ghazali, Farabi, Avicenna, Eshshaq Movaseli, and Safi al-Din Armuyi wrote treatises on music and taught music to their pupils, just as they taught them other sciences such as medicine and philosophy. For the renowned Iranian musician Hossein Alizadeh, this was the first of five phases of the history of musical education in Iran.[66]

Over the course of the next phase, during the Safavid Dynasty (1501–1722), music lost its grand status. The Safavids institutionalized Shi'ism as the land's religion, and music was repressed to such an extent that many musicians emigrated to neighboring countries. Those who remained practiced in secrecy. Officially, music and the other arts were promoted only within a religious framework.

During the Qajar dynasty (1789–1925), royal courts started supporting music once again, and this trickled down to an increased practice of music in society at large. Alizadeh calls this the period of practical reconstruction, in which teachers emphasized practical training. Music continued to be at the service of religious, literary, and dramatic expression, and the Arabic *maqām* repertoire was slowly replaced by the Persian *radif*, which was compiled by Mirza Abdollah, as we have already seen, and taught orally. The teacher played an all-important role in this phase; learning took place by imitation.

But in 1868, a Frenchman by the name of Alfred Jean-Baptiste Lemaire came to Iran and established the "State Music School" as a branch of the *Dār al-Fonun*—Iran's first European-style polytechnic school, founded in 1849—to train state bands to accompany royal occasions.[67] On his first visit to Europe in 1873—in fact the first European visit of any Iranian monarch—the Iranian king Naser al-Din Shah Qajar became so impressed with the ceremonial march music he heard there that he asked the French government to send more experts to teach this military music to Iranian soldiers. This is when the words *muzik*, *muzikchi* and *muzikānchi* first came into use.[68] Lemaire composed Iran's first national anthem in 1873 and formed its first royal orchestra and several Western-style marching music bands. Following his death, one of his best students established the Music School in 1918, where uniformed military students could train to play in marching bands for official occasions, while civilian students studied Western classical music.[69]

The next phase, the modern period, spanned the Pahlavi dynasty (1925–1979), when Iran was dominated by Western culture. The belief in Western supremacy was so absolute in some circles that people even debated eliminating the quarter tone from Iranian music. In 1923, Ali-Naqi Vaziri, a military man whose dexterity on the *tār* was legendary and who had just returned from five years of musical education in France and Germany, opened the Music Academy, which was a counterpart to the Music School. He also started a musical club, a "*klāb musikāl*," where an orchestra comprised of students and Vaziri himself performed a weekly program for members of the all-male club.[70] In his school, however, Vaziri received unprecedented official permission to run two classes for young girls, which his own daughter Badri attended.[71] About one hundred students formed the inaugural class, studying both Western and Iranian music and instruments. Unlike the Music School, which neglected Persian music in favor of Western music, Vaziri's Music Academy was dedicated to promoting Persian music, but via "scientific" methods. This basically meant using Western-style notation and a teaching method far removed from the Iranian one-on-one master-apprentice model, which relied on memorization and improvisation. Fifteen years earlier, Vaziri had spent eighteen months with Mirza Abdollah as well as some of his students and notated the seven *dastgāh* (the principal musical modalities described above) of classical Persian music, which had not existed on paper until that point.[72] In an unprecedented move, Vaziri taught his students the *dastgāh* by teaching them to read written music, rather than through imitation. Out of Vaziri's school was born a genre of music called *musiqi-ye melli* (national music), which still thrives today. It is Iranian music performed with Western instruments and regimented in a way that classical Persian music is not. Iran's alternate (unofficial) national anthem, "*Ey Iran*" (O Iran), is an example of this. Vaziri's school produced some of the most important musicians of its time, including Ruhollah Khaleqi himself, the composer Javad Ma'rufi, the songwriter and composer Hossein Gol-Golab, and the violin virtuoso Abolhasan Saba. Due to disagreements between the founders of the different schools about the value of Persian music, the schools were eventually completely divided: by 1948, the Music School—by then renamed the Higher Academy for Music—was only teaching Western music, and the Academy of National Music, the successor to Vaziri's Music Academy, established in 1949, taught only Persian music.

Both academies continued their activities until 1978, when the revolution disrupted schools across the country. While these were the most important institutions for official musical education in Iran, there were also a series of other, smaller private schools that blossomed in the middle decades of twentieth-century Iran; music was coming out of the proverbial closet and into the open in an increasingly modern Iran, where the state protected and promoted such ventures.[73] After its foundation in 1934, Tehran University, Iran's oldest modern institution of higher education, also added a faculty of fine arts in 1941; music theory and composition were taught in a more systematic fashion as of 1965. It was also during these years that the younger Pahlavi, Mohammad Reza Shah, took some steps toward the preservation of Iranian music by establishing the Foundation for the Protection and Promotion of Music (which still exists today), centers for the documentation of ancient artifacts, and festivals for the display of Persian classical music (most notably the Shiraz Festival).

With the revolution of 1979, all music schools and departments were shut down. Many musicians with whom I have talked believe that the government's repression of music in this period actually led to a wider circulation of music in society. Ten years after the revolution, musical education was able to begin again legally. For decades prior to the revolution, music had been taught exclusively according to Western models in official settings, which meant that explicitly and implicitly, Western music was accorded greater value, while indigenous forms and methods were for the most part ignored. In response to this Westernization, Alizadeh believes, a form of extreme traditionalism emerged that reacted strongly against any creativity or novelty in classical Persian music, which has contributed to a sort of stagnation, decried by both musicians and critics, that has caused great chagrin to some Persian classical musicians. Many of the music students and teachers that I have talked to over the years have complained about the lack of a clear foundation or mission for musical education in Iran today and blamed it on the ambivalence of the music community of the preceding decades toward the value of Persian music.

Throughout the nineteen-eighties, a few music classes were held in secret, mostly in Tehran. But following a fatwa by Imam Khomeini in 1988, the gates to music opened up more publicly and the Ministry of Culture and Islamic Guidance (commonly called *Ershād*) even set up classes itself, through its cultural centers and branches in the provinces. Tehran University's College of Performing Arts and Music began taking students again in late 1988. At the time of the revolution, five arts colleges and academies, including the two abovementioned music academies with their respective Western and Iranian emphases, had been united under the umbrella of a University of the Arts, but while other faculties at this university started accepting students in 1983, its music college only reopened in 1994. In 1989, Tehran's Azad University established an Arts and Architecture College, where music is also taught. The universities of Karaj, Gilan, and, more recently, Shiraz offer music degrees as well. Other colleges and centers where music is taught include the Sureh University, a subsidiary of the Islamic Development Organization's Arts Domain, *Howzeh-ye honari.* There are many opportunities for the young to pursue studies in music in Iran today, though the prospects for professional and economic success are rather grim. This situation is compounded by the uncertain status of music, which came to light again in 2010 when the Supreme Leader stated that while music was not haram per se, the promotion of music and musical education were not compatible with the highest values of the Islamic Republic.[74]

THE POLITICS OF MUSIC IN IRAN

This book presents a sort of soundtrack for Iran's tumultuous postrevolutionary decades. I trace the evolution of music and music policy in Iran through four periods, highlighting one genre of music within each period and, within each genre, one musician—a giant of Persian classical music, a government-supported pop star, a rebel rock and roller, and an underground rapper—each with markedly different political views and relations with the state. The chapters are organized in pairs, with the first providing the necessary historical, political, and social context in each case, and the second delving deeper into a discussion of the music and, in particular, of the work of the highlighted musician.

Chapters 2 and 3 offer insight into the status of music before and in the immediate years after the revolution and then go on to highlight the life and work of Iran's preeminent vocalist of Persian classical music, Mohammad Reza Shajarian, a highly revered and sometimes polarizing figure whose career has spanned the reign of Mohammad Reza Shah Pahlavi and the entirety of the Islamic Republic so far. Islamic Republic officials have often admitted that Shajarian's work "aided the aims of the revolution," and his vocalization of a Ramadan prayer was until 2009 the official overture on all state media to the broadcast for the breaking of the fast, but he has since been recategorized by conservative state mouthpieces, from a "treasure" of the revolution to a "traitor." Shajarian claims that throughout his long career, he has attempted to remain outside of politics by following a path that he calls *"mardomi"*—which trans-lates as "popular" but has historical connotations of "democratic" in Iran—all the while producing some of the most "political" songs of the past decades.

Shajarian has arrived at his art by undergoing the traditional process of the "heart-to-heart" apprenticeship, and he utilizes Persian poetry in a socially and politically active capacity. The tradition of using a typical trope of Persian literature—*"gol o bolbol"* (the rose and the nightingale)—to signify loss and mourning, not for the lover but for a political struggle, is rooted in Iran's Con-stitutional Revolution, when it represented a turn in the use of Persian poetry and song. Shajarian creates a language that links itself to this freedom-seeking repertoire of a century ago, when music was first used as a medium of protest.

It was also during the Constitutional Revolution, in early-twentieth-century Iran, that the musical concert crystallized as an important venue where, ac-cording to music historian Khaleqi, those who attended came to share a "hid-den secret." Persian classical music retained its subversive cachet throughout Iran's prerevolutionary period of the nineteen-sixties and nineteen-seventies, when this music was set up by supporters as the "authentic" counterpart to the "Westoxified" music of the so-called cabarets, where pop music often reigned and the Iranians who mingled there looked no different from Parisians or Lon-doners. This cabaret scene was regarded as the epitome of Iran's Westernization and was one of the revolution's very first casualties, with the cabarets being shut down and vandalized.[75] Many of the creators of pop music then moved to Los Angeles, where they established an elaborate and professional expatriate music scene with studios, concert halls, and satellite television channels that eventu-ally broadcast their music back into Iran. (Los Angeles has such a large Iranian population that Iranians call it Tehrangeles.)

In Iran itself, it seemed as though pop music had been eliminated for good. But restrictions eased up eventually, and chapters 4 and 5 narrate the process through which a few officials within state television, in the mid-nineteen-nineties, opened the floodgates to pop music for the first time in nearly twenty years. Secure in their revolutionary credentials, these officials yielded to the en-thusiasm of several young musicians who had been pushing for the inclusion of pop music, deciding to support them in order to stem the unidirectional flow of expatriate Iranian pop music from Los Angeles into Iran. These chapters, based on interviews with Islamic Republic officials at the heart of policy mak-ing, examine this process and highlight some of the most popular music of that time, with a focus on the work of Alireza Assar.

Interestingly, most of the first-generation postrevolutionary pop singers were clean-shaven, wore jeans, and imitated famous Iranian voices from Los Angeles (called *los anjelesi*).[76] The heavily bearded Assar, however, had a unique style and sang in a somber manner about heavenly love and heroism, drawing on Shi'ite themes that resonated with a public that had only recently been through the traumatizing experience of the Iran-Iraq war. While the conventional wisdom has been that the popularity of religious pop music such as Assar's is a result of government backing, this independent, trendy religiosity actually competed with the state's promotion of dogmatic religiosity and offered an attractive alternative for postwar youth.[77]

The turn of the millennium was an important juncture for politics and music in postrevolutionary Iran, a period that I describe in chapters 6 and 7. Nearly two decades after the revolution, President Mohammad Khatami's reformist government eased restrictions on the public sphere and allowed for openings in the intellectual, artistic, and physical realms. Simultaneously, the Internet was spreading in Iran. This opening allowed the first wave of alternative and rock musicians in Islamic Iran to surface. What many consider to be the first underground rock concert in postrevolutionary Iran, a concert by the band O-Hum at Tehran's Russian Orthodox Church, took place in 2001, and this is also the period in which the alternative music scene's enfant terrible, Mohsen Namjoo, was developing his unique style of music in Mashhad. Before the advent of Namjoo's iconoclastic attitude and music, it was unthinkable that a musician would be able to ridicule the Supreme Leader, Ayatollah Khamenei, in the most offensive terms, and even deny the existence of God. Namjoo's absurdist nihilism resonated with many members of his generation who had come of age during some of the Islamic Republic's strictest years and rejected everything religious or ideological. But his gripe is not just with the state; he has also broken the mold of the permissible within Persian classical music by combining it with rock and other genres and, what is for some the most sacrilegious, fusing doglike howls with lines from Rumi.

New media fundamentally transformed the framework for the production, distribution, and consumption of music in Iran. With music software and home studios at everyone's fingertips, musicians no longer needed permits from the state, allowing for unprecedented freedom in lyrics and musical styles. Chapters 8 and 9 discuss the turn in music due to new media, the much-hyped phenomenon of underground music that it facilitated, and the highly popular genre of *Rap-e Farsi*—Persian rap. Hichkas, the so-called godfather of Persian rap, whose work I look at closely here, came of age about ten years after Namjoo. In his formative years, he did not experience the worst of the repression, the way the generation before him did. More importantly, he grew up in a post-9/11 world, in which his identity as an Iranian was denigrated in the global media and his existence placed directly under the threat of military attack from the United States. Hichkas's work is particularly attractive to young Iranian men because it offers an alternative approach to the old Iranian ethic in which honor is paramount. Hichkas places the responsibility for protecting that honor on Iran's youth, assigning them the role of upholding Iran's flag and even manning its army, both core elements of modern nationalism.[78]

The political unrest following the 2009 presidential elections—commonly called the Green Movement or Uprising—involved the greatest political and social upheaval in Iran since the 1979 revolution and represented a pivotal moment for the musicians I showcase here. Each of the four artists utilizes a particular discursive strand anchored within Iranian culture and society to lend relevance to his work and find resonance with his audience. In drawing out some of the ways in which each artist deals with the state, I show how they all face restrictions on their creativity as well as the communication of their messages, and how each of them adopts a unique strategy in order to function within the given parameters while still retaining and projecting a sense of authenticity and integrity. As all of the artists put it to me, in slightly different ways, "lying is the death of the artist." The momentous events following the 2009 elections forced all but one of these artists to take clear positions, jeopardizing their artistic futures within the Islamic Republic yet securing their credibility with their audiences.[79] Throughout the upheavals, musicians and consumers revived old political songs to highlight the Green Movement's connection to previous political struggles and created new songs to fit the spirit of the new movement.

LINES IN THE SAND

As will become apparent over the course of this book, many of the red lines drawn by the Islamic Republic on the subject of music have shifted over time, as the once-revolutionary state evolves in response to internal and external developments, such as the youth bulge or advancing media technologies. Thus, it has lifted the unwritten bans on musical education, the import and sale of musical instruments, and even, eventually, pop music. However, while a faint tendency towards liberalization in cultural policy can be seen over the now nearly-forty-year arc of the Islamic Republic, many of the shifts in policy and occasional transgressions of the boundaries actually appear rather erratic, caused by temporary fluctuations in the political climate, infighting among cultural bodies with counterintuitive results, or some individual in charge somewhere deciding to take matters into his own hands. So, for example, the Khatami era (1997–2005) initially allowed for a cultural openness that has not been witnessed since; one of the first postrevolutionary pop stars was allowed to publish an album in 1999 that contained songs using the illicit 6/8 beat (as I will explain, this is traditionally a dance-inducing rhythm within Iranian music) before he was banned from appearing on state media and emigrated to Los Angeles; the cultural arm of the conservative Islamic Development Organization (*Howzeh-ye honari*) published an album in 2007 that the otherwise more liberal Ministry of Culture rejected; and every now and then—though very rarely—state television has aired programs in which musical instruments can be seen.

Still, despite such anomalies, one could argue that the only prohibitions that have remained fairly constant are the ones applied to the female solo voice; the exhibition of musical instruments on state television (except for the marching band during the Sacred Defense Week commemorating the Iran-Iraq war of 1980–1988); extensive use of the 6/8 beat; and, of course, political criticism of or insult to Islam, the Islamic Republic, or its officials. Some of these uncrossable red lines, such as political criticism or insulting the Supreme Leader, are self-evident. No musician would dream of submitting an album with such content to the Ministry of Culture (*Ershād*) for review. But when I first started researching music in Iran, it was a question for me as to how people in charge knew what was permitted and what was not. After all, there seemed to be no booklet with guidelines, let alone any laws that spelled out the boundaries. In my conversations with officials working in state television and radio, as well as governmental organizations regulating cultural production, every now and then I would hear phrases like, "oh yes, there was a directive on the ban on 6/8, but it's somewhere in my files, I'll try to find it for you," and of course, I would never see any such piece of paper.

Slowly, I came to understand that specific policy was set in a fairly organic, and mostly unwritten way. For example, the Supreme Leader would give a talk to a small circle about some aspect of music, or the Supreme Council for Cultural Revolution would have a meeting (whose minutes are not public) on music. The heads of state broadcasting and other cultural arms would be present, or they would be informed later about the content of these meetings. Subsequently, those directors would hold meetings with their managers and relay the substance of these talks, or at least the points that mattered as far as practice was concerned. Sometimes these directors would also issue directives to their managers, though in my conversations I found no one who had compiled these directives into organized volumes of any sort. They all appeared to be hidden in piles of paper somewhere. (In 2011, for the first time, I heard of an actual manual, which had been distributed within state television and radio with a series of dos and don'ts that managers could refer to. I managed to acquire a copy of this manual, which I discuss in more detail in chapter 4. The rules do not clear up all of the ambiguities and gray areas that existed before, but they do present a basis for practice, black on white, for what seems to be the very first time.[80])

Probably the greatest rupture in Iranian music following the revolution was caused by the new religious state's ban on the female voice, one of the most stringently applied prohibitions over the last decades. This imposed silence is beautifully captured in Newsha Tavakolian's photographic series called "Listen," where she features close-ups of six professional female singers against sparkly set designs, with their eyes closed, drowning in the passion of singing. But of course, we don't hear their voices because they have been banned. One of those photographs, picturing the singer Maral Afsharian, is on the cover of this book.[81] In the opening of her exhibition, Tavakolian accompanied her photographs with fictional album covers and empty CD shells for each singer. This silence is also palpable throughout the present book, featuring as it does musicians whose work was produced inside Iran and was able to create a national conversation on social and political matters within the internal musical public sphere. The ban on the solo female voice in postrevolutionary Iran meant that women singers were unable to release songs that could have brought about the kinds of conversations and publics that I examine here.

FEMALE SINGERS

Those who are familiar with the cultural history of Iran know that some of the country's all-time most popular singers have been female, beginning with Qamar-ol-Moluk Vazirizadeh (known simply as Qamar), whose groundbreaking performance at the Tehran Grand Hotel in 1924 marked an unprecedented feminist gesture. Qamar appeared unveiled in front of a mixed-gender audience and began her concert with a song composed to the famous anti-veiling poem by Iraj Mirza:

> Her radiance melts the heart right through her mask
> If she had none, God's help we'd have to ask.[82]

A few decades later, the cabaret performer and singer Mahvash was so popular that when she died in a car crash at the age of forty, in 1961, her funeral processions were reportedly the largest Tehran had ever seen. Many of the greatest singers of prerevolutionary Iran were women, including Delkash, Marzieh, Susan, Parisa, Hayedeh, Mahasti, and Homeyra, not to mention Googoosh, Iran's most prolific and famous pop star of all times.[83] Googoosh (born Faeqeh Atashin) remained in Iran after the revolution and kept silent for twenty years. In 1999, she managed to leave the country, gave concerts the world over, joined the expatriate Iranian music scene in North America, and restarted her career. Hers was an astonishing—and astonishingly strong—rebirth.[84] Her Googoosh Music Academy—a musical talent television show launched in 2010 that ran for three seasons—provided a platform for young musicians to present their work outside of the restrictions of the Islamic Republic. Importantly, her show became a venue for female singers (many of them recent emigrées from Iran) to air their voices to thousands of viewers—inside and outside of Iran—who watched the program on the Persian expatriate satellite channel *Manoto*.

However, while expatriate female singers like the ones mentioned above maintained their popularity with fans inside Iran, and younger singers like the classical singer Shakila and the Shakira-esque pop singer Sepideh joined their ranks in Los Angeles, their music was not produced from within the social and political contexts that prevailed inside Iran. As for female musicians inside Iran, the two female members of the important Chavosh group (a group I discuss in detail in chapter 3), Hengameh Akhavan and Sima Bina, were prohibited soon after the revolution from collaborating with the collective. Bina, a highly accomplished Persian classical musician, pursued her passion for Iranian folk music and is today perhaps the leading expert on and performer of Iranian folk music, though her solo concerts to mixed audiences only take place abroad. Other prominent singers like Simin Ghanem, Pari Zanganeh, and Pari Maleki, who stayed in Iran, eventually started giving occasional concerts to all-female audiences two decades after the revolution. Still other musicians, such as the composer and folk singer Maliheh Saeedi, have succeeded in publishing albums in postrevolutionary Iran by employing the multi-vocal method, in collaboration with other female singers. Some younger vocalists, like Mahsa Vadat, who live in Iran and have created a following through private concerts, unofficial CDs, and concerts abroad, still refuse to perform to all-female audiences on principle, however. Within the official pop genre, the highly popular band Arian drew attention in the first decade of the millennium for incorporating female vocalists, the sister duo consisting of Sahar and Sanaz Kashmari. The government organizes an all-female music festival every year, the Jasmine festival, where female musicians perform for all-female audiences.[85] I have seen several performances at Jasmine festivals over the years, including, in 2008, the band Orkideh, which has been the most visible attempt at nurturing a self-sufficient all-female band, including instrumentalists and vocalists. However, while the band members' skills may have improved in the years since then, at that time, their lack of exposure and competition, given the prohibitions they were subject to, was reflected in the low quality of their music. I should add that solo female vocalists are not just prohibited from performing to mixed-gender audiences, they are also entirely prohibited from selling records.

The lasting impact of this government-imposed silence became evident when young musicians started contributing to the burgeoning of an underground music scene that was not dependent on government approval. Underground musicians were for the most part unbound by government policies, as they distributed their music in unofficial networks and, later, online and performed, if at all, in the unregulated underground. And yet, as this music scene slowly developed, and even a decade or so later, when underground hip-hop music attracted a vast following in Iran, there emerged no vastly popular female vocalists who matched groups or singers like O-Hum, Namjoo, or Hichkas in significance. In fact, female performers were few and far between. The absence of the female voice in the public realm for the entirety of these young women's lives, as well as the higher social and political risks involved for women in this field, may go a long way towards explaining the dearth of female musicians even in the underground scene.

The first female rock band to have a real following—not to mention sophisticated reggae-rock-pop crossover music and, often, sociopolitically critical lyrics—is the Iranian-born Swedish sister duo Abjeez, who grew up and formed their band outside of Iran. And there are many other Iranian female musicians abroad who have built successful careers outside of Tehrangeles as solo singers in Persian—such as Rana Farhan, Sara Naini, Eendo, and 25band, to name just a few—but the focus of this book is specifically musicians who have developed their music in Iran. Within the rap genre, Salome MC, Iran's first female rapper, was also for a very long time Iran's only female rapper of note, though there are now a few others.[86] Around the year 2000, tracks sung by the underground musician DJ Maryam in the style of prerevolutionary pop, but with an electro twist, were often played at parties and have found interest among young and old. Otherwise, in the underground music scene, there is a very limited number of female acts with any renown; in 2010, a singer by the name of Mehrnoosh became famous with her sweet, mellow pop song "Cheshmāt" (Your Eyes), which was broadcast many times a day on expatriate radio and television channels, with a colorful video that is clearly produced abroad. However, few know that the song (and in fact the whole album) was arranged and produced in Iran, which would make her one of the few widely known female "underground" singers, except that she resides in the US. Two other newish "underground" singers are Melanie and Madmazel, whose soulful songs and artful videos are produced inside Iran and broadcast on satellite channels. But it would be amiss to say that they were widely known.

However, over the years since the revolution, many girls have taken up the study of music and musical instruments—mainly in the Persian classical genre—and they have now started to appear more frequently in musical performances. For the most part, female vocalists like the ones portrayed in Tavakolian's series "Listen" have had to make a living appearing as background singers (usually to male singers), as part of large ensemble choirs, dubbing children's voices for television and film, or lending their voices to commercials. The only semi-public mixed-gender occasions at which some female singers have been able to perform solo are probably events at foreign embassies in Tehran, where the rules of the Islamic Republic do not apply.

Much more recently, on very rare occasions, one has even been able to hear short passages by female solo vocalists at mixed-sex concerts in Iran. One musician who has taken it upon himself to promote women is the composer and tār player Majid Derakhshani, a member of the Chavosh collective and a collaborator of Mohammad Reza Shajarian's. Derakhshani formed the almost-all-female Khorshid ensemble, as well as the Māh ensemble with its female vocal soloist, and it was in a performance by Māh that the female singer Mahdiyeh Mohammadkhani sang solo at a concert in October 2014 in Tehran's Tālār-e Vahdat (Unity Hall), an unprecedented act in the history of the Islamic Republic.[87] However, by the spring of 2015 there seemed to be a backlash against female musicians, even instrumentalists, with repeated instances of women being asked to leave the stage by security forces. But today there is a large and formidable cadre of well-trained young female vocalists and instrumentalists in Iran, a fact that the Islamic Republic's policy makers will have to face sooner than later.

THE SOUNDTRACK OF THE REVOLUTION

My work is informed by research spanning a period of five years in Tehran. Prior to and overlapping with this period, I worked as a journalist for American, German, and Qatari print publications and television networks, which also involved my spending periods of several months at a time in Iran. This enabled me to undertake extensive participant observation, attending music practice sessions, talks and lectures on music, and concerts and music festivals, as well as participating in insider conversations in various contexts. However, the central pillar of my methodology has been interviews, with the main artists discussed in my work as well as with other knowledgeable sources in the field of music. I met and interviewed each of the four principal artists treated in this study several times, often in different countries, and placed the information and knowledge they generously shared with me within the context of my other interviews as well as of my research in Persian- and English-language primary and secondary sources. I was able to meet and talk about music with a wide range of people active in the field, from masters of Persian classical music to popular artists in pop, rock, and rap, and from government officials working for conservative state radio and television in various capacities to independent producers, songwriters, instrumentalists, and journalists. My research also involved interviews with other concert attendees, close listening to audio and video recordings, and a great deal of research online on Persian music sites and YouTube.

Most of my interviews were semi-structured, which meant that I had prepared certain topics of conversation and questions, but allowed the interviews to be led in directions determined by the material that was produced as the interviews proceeded. I often found that interviewees in official positions, in particular, warmed up over the course of our interviews, providing better insights into their work and experience the longer we talked. I often had to corroborate information given to me by one interviewee with other sources, and I often remained unable to weave one definitive narrative about a given topic. Due to the various sensitivities regarding music in Iran, where a person's job can depend on one's religious or political position on any topic, it was sometimes hard to ascertain the real position of an interviewee on a given topic. Where necessary, the book reflects these ambiguities.

The most difficult aspect of my interview-based research over the past years has been keeping a critical distance to subjects whose work I admire and being able to place their generously offered insights into the context of my other research. The breadth of material that resulted from my participant observations, interviews, and eyewitness research was too vast to fit into any book, but has fully informed what I present here.

CHAPTER TWO

THE NIGHTINGALE REBELS

THE END OF ALMOST EVERY Mohammad Reza Shajarian concert unfolds similarly, in what by now has become a ritual: Shajarian intones the last notes of his performance, often in a crescendo, and finishes the show to ecstatic applause. But then, whether in Tehran, London, or New York, the imploring audience soon calls out for him to sing an encore, and always the same one: the song "Bird of Dawn" (*Morgh-e sahar*). With his right hand on his heart, the iconic septuagenarian bows down and, without much hesitation, indulges the audience's request. As he sings in his familiar plaintive tenor, he embodies the pained bird, dramatizing in music and verse the epic struggle of a people. Set to classical Persian music in the upbeat *māhur* scale, "Bird of Dawn" is a song that urges the bird to summon its powers and, as it progresses with its swinging rhythm and rolling crescendo, urges the bird to build up the resolve to break free from its cage and fill the air with tunes of freedom:

> Bird of dawn, start your lament, relight my anguish
> Break this cage with your scintillating sighs and turn it upside down
> Wing-tied nightingale, emerge from the corner of the cage
> Compose the song of freedom for humankind
> And with your breath fill the arena of this people's land with sparks
> The cruelty of the oppressor, the callousness of the hunter, have destroyed
>   my nest

An enraptured audience eagerly joins in on the lyrics that call on the powers of the universe to bring about the metaphorical dawn, expressing their desire for freedom from tyranny. And on the prayerlike refrain, the audience members raise their voices:

> Oh God, oh Heavens, oh Nature, turn our dark night into morning again!

Shajarian first performed "Bird of Dawn" publicly on his 1990 United States concert tour, in commemoration of the song's main composer, Morteza Ney-Davud, who had just passed away.[1] The timing was hardly accidental. Iran was very slowly emerging from the devastating Iran-Iraq war, which had ended in 1988 after nearly eight years, making it the twentieth century's longest conventional war. Bolstered internally, as governments tend to be by war, the Islamic Republic had consolidated its grip on power in the nineteen-eighties, ruling through a politically and socially repressive culture of death and martyrdom. Shajarian's "Bird of Dawn" quickly became a celebrated, if subdued, protest song, so much so that his early concerts became one of the very rare public settings in which, by joining in with this song, people could express their protest against the prevailing conditions. This was of great significance in the pre-Internet and pre-satellite-TV era, when no other forms of communal anti-government communication could take place without grave repercussions. The poem "Bird of Dawn" dates from the nineteen-twenties, when the poet-educator-politician Malek o-Sho'ara Bahar[2] wrote it in apparent criticism of the newly crowned Reza Shah's increasingly authoritarian rule. The exact year of the poem's creation is not known, but it first appeared in print in the magazine "Nāhid" in 1927, without attribution.[3] In the many decades since then, artists as varying in style as the pioneering female vocalist Qamar and the prerevolutionary folk-rock singer Farhad Mehrad have performed their own renditions of this song, attesting to its continuing appeal.[4]

In his own words, Shajarian reached for this particular song because he knew it would resonate with his audience:

> "*Morgh-e sahar*" is a very social-political *tasnif* [rhythmic song] . . . and I felt that I should sing it again in a way that creates a lot of attention, [so I] waited for a moment in which the conditions in society required it. . . . People like to hear these words from their artists and so I sang it and everywhere that we've had a concert they always ask for "*Morgh-e sahar*." I still always tell my group to prepare "*Morgh-e sahar*" because it's a rallying cry, a form of protest that must be repeated over and over again, which says, "we still have this protest, we still feel the same way."[5]

By choosing to revive this particular song, Shajarian was plugging into a nearly-century-old freedom discourse, encapsulated in the lyrics of the song. In every one of the Shajarian concerts that I have attended—New York in 2002; London in 2005, 2008, and 2011; Tehran in 2007; and Beiteddine (near Beirut) in 2010—the ending scene described above has been played out. Usually the audience is largely of Iranian origin, though outside of Iran there are also a good number of non-Iranians at Shajarian's concerts. He is, after all, Iran's preeminent vocalist of Persian classical music and has performed on the international stage since 1987. The Iranian crowds in his audiences—both inside and outside of Iran—tend to be from diverse social and economic backgrounds. When Shajarian went on a world tour following Iran's contested 2009 elections and the ensuing uprisings, Iranian audiences accompanied his singing of "Bird of Dawn" by flashing V for victory signs and shouting *Marg bar diktātor*, "Death to the dictator," making the song's implicit message explicit.

Mohammad Reza Shajarian came of age in the nineteen-fifties and was trained by celebrated old-school teachers like Abdollah Davami (1891–1980) and Faramarz Paivar (1933–2009). He belongs to a generation of art singers, the best of whom were trained in the arts of Qur'anic recitation and religious singing before vocalizing Persian poetry in the form of *āvāz*—the classical singing of traditional Persian poems and texts. He was born in 1940 in Mashhad, in the northeastern Iranian province of Khorasan that is home to the country's most sacred Shia site—the shrine of Imam Reza—as well as some of Persian-ate culture's most illustrious thinkers, writers, poets and scientists of the past, including Avicenna, Khayyam, Ferdowsi, and Rumi. The first of six children, Shajarian grew up in a traditional and religiously conservative household under the tutelage of his father, Mehdi Shajarian, who spent a great deal of his time in Qur'an recitation circles and about whom Shajarian has remarked, "My father was fanatical in his beliefs: for him faith was more important than anything."[6] From an early age, Shajarian accompanied his father to Qur'an readings, and by the time he was six years old he was joining in the readings, which he attended regularly until he left his hometown at the age of nineteen to work as a teacher in a small village close by. In remembering those years, Shajarian says: "To put it simply, my father loved to show off with me as his child. . . . Everyone in Mashhad knew me then already for my Qur'an recitation. No one could match me in Mashhad, I was [my father's] greatest hope."[7]

In Shajarian's own view, his traditional background and religious upbringing slightly disadvantaged him and impeded the progress of his career during the buzzing cosmopolitanism of the later Pahlavi period of the nineteen-sixties and nineteen-seventies. However, his Qur'anic training has certainly contributed to his stature as a masterful artist (*ostād*) who has gravitas and is worthy of respect.[8] In all the main Persian texts on Shajarian's life and work, he highlights his early training as a Qur'an reciter, thus positioning himself within the discourse of authenticity, obviously aware of the significations within Iranian society of this particular cultural capital. There are several old photographs of a small, then pubescent, and later adolescent Shajarian gazing out quite seriously from among rows of suited and turbaned adult men, stacked vertically, with the front row kneeling in front of huge Qur'ans. Remembering the education he received from his father, Shajarian recounts: "Throughout puberty, my father would wake me up very early in the morning and encourage me to recite the Qur'an loudly so that I could overcome my pubescent vocal problems. The foundation of the successes that I have attained in this path lies in this fatherly attention and training."[9]

Shajarian excelled at Qur'an recitations. At age eleven, he was invited by Radio Khorasan to recite the Qur'an on air, and in 1978, shortly before the revolution, he ranked first in Iran's national Qur'an competition. As the country's best Qur'an reciter, he would ordinarily have represented Iran at the 1978 International Qur'an Reading Competition in Malaysia, but despite his impeccable background, conservative clerics, protesting that Shajarian could not represent Iran as its voice of the Qur'an because of his reputation as a singer of musical *āvāz*, prevented him from participating.[10] As much as his *āvāz* singing disadvantaged him in this episode, however, his reputation as a Qur'an reciter, along with his pro-revolutionary stance during the early stages of the revolution, saved him from direct persecution in the new Islamic Iran.

Shajarian's love for *āvāz* had remained latent as long as he was in his parental home, and it was only once he moved away for work that he was able to exercise his voice on texts other than the Qur'an. After high school, in the nineteen-fifties, Shajarian trained as a teacher and was then employed by the government and dispatched to a village called Radkan, a few hours from his family home. There, away from the confines of his home environment, he was able to practice singing: "As long as I was in Mashhad . . . I was reciting the Qur'an and participating in religious gatherings. That's why when I was pulled toward music, there were many who were upset with me. My moving to Radkan really was an opportunity for me to practice and dedicate myself with ease to something that I loved. Sometimes I would sing so much I could barely speak."[11]

The religious mentality that pervaded Shajarian's upbringing, in which music was frowned upon as an art form that deviated from God's path, had been the cultural norm for many Iranians, at least in urban areas. Philosophical treatises on music—reaching back from the works of 'Abdolqader Maraghi in Timurid Iran (in the fourteenth to fifteenth centuries) to Safi al-Din Urmavi (thirteenth century), Ghazali (eleventh century), Farabi (tenth century), and all the way back to Barbad (sixth century: "the first great name of music that was wholly Iranian, preceding the Islamic era"[12])—indicate music's high standing in Persianate courts throughout the centuries. However, while the philosophers and theoreticians of music were often influential polymaths in the courts, those who practiced music for a living did not have a high social standing and often constituted a class of their own, isolated from society at large:

> In urban areas they often were drawn from non-Moslem minority groups such as the Jewish and Armenian communities. In rural areas, musicians constituted a kind of "caste" group. They were endogamous, and passed on their traditions within family groups. In tribal regions one often finds lineages of musicians who perform for weddings and other ceremonies but who do not intermarry with the rest of the tribe.[13]

The canonization of Persian art (classical) music in the late nineteenth century, attributed to Ali-Akbar Farahani under Naser al-Din Shah's patronage, and later its notation by Farahani's son Mirza Abdollah, along with the formal bifurcation of music into "art" music and "popular" music (variously called "*mardomi*," "*motrebi*," "*kucheh-bāzāri*," or "pop," depending on the kind of music and the period) and the teaching and practice of this music outside of the courts appears to have opened the field to people who were neither genius polymaths nor necessarily from musician families nor of low status—people such as Shajarian.

Shajarian first heard classical Persian music on the radio. Throughout his three years in Radkan, he would stay up until the wee hours every night to listen to the radio and imitate the old songs he heard. "It was thanks to radio's *Golha* program that I became enamored with Iranian music, and my first teacher was this very radio,"[14] he once noted, referring to the popular radio program that first aired in 1956 and continued until 1979, broadcasting what many consider to be the best of Persian classical music, poetry, and literary commentary.[15] Soon, Shajarian was making a few a cappella recordings for Radio Mashhad—"spiritual and love songs"—until the radio deputy, a certain

Dr. Sharifi, told him he was too good for Mashhad and recommended that Shajarian attempt a test at the music council of Radio Tehran.

In 1966, Shajarian went to Tehran for a few weeks to try his luck at Radio Tehran. After singing in front of the music council, which included some of the era's great names in music, Shajarian remembers being enthusiastically praised and then asked: "Do you also sing *tarāneh*?" As opposed to *āvāz*, which is the art of singing classical poetry to art music, *tarāneh* is the lighter art of singing more rhythmic, modern, less vocally demanding pieces. In the late nineteen-sixties, around the same time as Shajarian made that trip from the more conservative, provincial Mashhad to the more cosmopolitan capital of Tehran, various factors, including mass media, urbanization, and Mohammad Reza Pahlavi's vision for Iran, were propelling the country toward greater modernization. This was reflected in the field of music, where lighter pop music that appealed to the greater masses was promoted over the more complicated, classical Iranian variant.[16] Shajarian was told that he was very talented, but not suited for radio.[17]

PERSIAN "ART" MUSIC VERSUS POPULAR FORMS

The distinction between art music (along with some of its lighter derivatives) and other forms of music in Iran is fairly evident, both in musical form and in vocal style, and I think it is safe to say that practitioners of music outside the art music categories are still often viewed with social condescension by some older Iranians. Shajarian, however, is regarded as one of the foremost living masters, if not the single foremost living master, of *āvāz*, generally considered to be the highest form of Persian vocals. *Āvāz* draws on classical Persian *ghazals* (lyrical verse)[18] and is sung to music based on the *radif*. Within these parameters, *āvāz* entails segments of improvisation on the part of the singer, including skillful vibratos, which can last up to twenty minutes or more. Although the history of *āvāz* is not well recorded, "the tradition of sung poetry in Iran and West Asia is very ancient, indeed archetypal," and shares a heritage with ancient folk and bardic traditions.[19] The Persian classical musical repertoire—the *radif*—has absorbed melodies from these traditions, which is reflected in the names of regions given to many of its melodic segments, or *gushehs*. It has also been noted that sung poetry and the art of Qur'an recitation have deeply influenced one another, with Iranian Qur'an recitation displaying "some striking relationships to *āvāz* in terms of both structure and performance practice."[20] However, the existing sources appear to indicate that *āvāz* crystallized into its systematized form as we know it today only in the late nineteenth century and not before, a view that Shajarian also holds.

The shorter, fixed-meter, composed vocal genre of the *tasnif* (or its more modern version, the *tarāneh*, which is what the radio executives asked Shajarian to perform) can last just a few minutes and is more rhythmical, usually accompanied by the Persian goblet drum (*tonbak*), which provides the rhythm. In the words of the historian of music Ruhollah Khaleqi, a *tasnif* is a "short song always accompanied by lyrics, which may treat events and happenings of the day, sometimes in a critical light."[21] Singers of *āvāz* generally did not attribute much value to singing *tasnifs*, considering it beneath them. This sentiment is still current among classical musicians and is often intertwined with traditionalist discourses of authenticity, according *āvāz* a sort of ancient, more "authentic" status. Similarly, the goblet drum that usually accompanied *tasnifs* was seen as a lesser instrument, so that in the nineteen-fifties Khaleqi wrote that some "still do not consider the *tonbak* to be a musical instrument and when it is mentioned, they do not value or appreciate the instrument itself or its player."[22] However, while the art of *āvāz* allowed Shajarian to engage in the most respectable form of singing, "Shajarian has sung and become identified with some of the most emblematic, significant and politically charged tasnifs of the past decades[. . .]and it is quite likely that his widespread fame among the majority of Iranians is more a result of these tasnifs than his avaz."[23]

Indeed, shorter strophic songs have a long history in Iran, and the musical term *tasnif* itself has been in use since the fourteenth century, although what the term refers to has undergone some degree of change.[24] Khaleqi sees a relationship between regional and folk songs and the *tasnif*, and says that like the "simple rhythmical tunes" of the former, *tasnifs* "are produced quickly and circulate orally, are sung in the street and bazaar, and disappear quickly."[25] Entertainment groups called *motrebi* (from the Arabic *tarab*, amusement)[26] were the usual purveyors of such songs, along with skits and dances, both in Qajar households and among the wider, non-elite public. Strands of this music were eventually dubbed *ruhowzi* ("on top of the pool"), because they were usually performed on a makeshift stage that consisted of a plank placed on top of the little pool in the center of the inner courtyard found in traditional houses. The songs that these *motrebi* troupes performed were humorous and often dealt with issues within everyday society, such as conflict or rivalry between the genders.

Hence, the usage of the term *asil* (authentic) for Persian classical music, setting up other kinds of music as "real" Persian music's dialectical other, is historically not warranted. In fact, until the Constitutional Revolution (1905–1911), Persian classical music was played almost exclusively in the royal courts and households, the homes of aristocrats, and Sufi lodges.[27] In contrast, folk music and other lighter forms were more widely and deeply rooted among people of various backgrounds. One could understand "authentic music" to refer to music that is more widespread among common people, or to music that is more exclusive and based on the classical regimentation of melodies thought to hail from centuries ago, so depending on that understanding, either form of music could be regarded as more authentic than the other.

From the nineteen-forties onward, the *ruhowzi* music of the common people even found its way into places called "joy-making kiosks" (*dakkehhā-ye shādmāni*), which were set up specifically for the performance of this kind of music, interspersed with skits. Soon thereafter, *motrebi* performers and their songs entered the public sphere even further with performances in cafés, where their music became known as *kāfei*, and included both comical folk songs and the more Arabized form called *kucheh-bāzāri* (literally, songs of the streets and bazaar).[28] With the advent of television and the greater prevalence of cinemas, the "joy-making kiosks" faded away, but performers of the proto-popular urban music attracted large audiences in restaurant cafés, where one could drink, smoke, order food, and be entertained. These restaurant cafés brought their owners significant income, and over time many converted these spaces into so-called *kāfeh-kābāreh* (cabarets or music clubs), building stages and upgrading the interior design to give them more pizzazz.

At first, these were places on Tehran's famous Lalehzar Street, where the music was mostly "the music that the underprivileged of society . . . wanted, lust-arousing melodies with texts that were erotic and sometimes transgressed moral boundaries: both a vehicle for the alleviation of repressed desires and a sort of making faces at the existing moral codes of society."[29] With time, however, there developed a very wide range of cabarets, from ones that, like the original ones, were frequented by working-class men and where female performers sometimes stripped, to others that were very exclusive and where the clientele consisted of Iran's mixed-gender elite, sporting the latest European fashions. Some of Iran's most highly regarded singers performed at the more upscale of these venues. Traditional society, however, did not look favorably on any part of this cabaret nightlife, where patrons consumed alcohol and the genders mixed freely. They considered the whole "cabaret scene" as devilish and haram at worst, lowly and degenerate at best.

While Shajarian himself also looked down on this scene and says he never performed at a cabaret, another singer of higher standing at that time, Ali Akbar Golpaygani (commonly and affectionately referred to as Golpa), did perform in cabarets, to an immense reception. However, he was regarded disparagingly by some in the classical music community, and banned by the Islamic Republic from public musical activity for nearly two decades due to his association with this scene. He is still not permitted to give concerts in Iran, though he has gone on frequent tours abroad and released his first officially permitted album, "*Mast-e eshq*" (Drunk for Love), in 2003.[30]

SHAH-ERA POP MUSIC

Some of the early entertainment celebrities of modern Iran emerged from this burgeoning cabaret scene. Mahvash, the female entertainer of the nineteen-fifties mentioned earlier, was a sex symbol who in her urban *kāfei* or *kuchehbāzāri* music articulated the everyday problems of the lower classes and attracted their loyalty at cabarets like Kristal, Pars, and the legendary and reputedly oldest cabaret, Shokufeh-ye Now, in Tehran's red-light district, Shahr-e Now (literally "new city"). This area in south-central Tehran also housed brothels and cheap hotels in addition to the theaters, cafés, and music venues. Other immensely popular singers of this first generation of mass-mediated urban music were Susan and Aghasi, who similarly catered to a less dogmatically religious South Tehran clientele and sang about love and heartbreak in an accessible manner.[31] Aghasi was from Dezful in Iran's culturally Arab south and infused the region's *bandari* music into this urban genre, which to this day is very popular across Iran. Also around the mid-century and into the nineteen-sixties, there were other equally, if not more widely, popular singers whose musical styles presented a cross between this popular music and Persian classical music. Singers in this "elevated" genre included singers like Delkash, Pouran, Elaheh, and, later, Hayedeh, whose music was described as the "mainstream style" of the nineteen-sixties in Iran, with singers consisting mostly of "women with full, sensuous voices,"[32] not unlike other Middle Eastern metropolises, where Egypt's Umm Kulthum and Beirut's Fairuz ruled ears and hearts. There were of course also famous male artists, such as Vigen, whose moniker was "The Sultan of Jazz" (until not long ago, and among older Iranians to this day, "jazz" is used to mean simply "pop") and who was among the first to introduce the guitar into Iranian music in the late nineteen-fifties; and slightly later, Aref, the "Golden Throat" who often sang sentimental pieces of romance with opera-style vocals.

By the late nineteen-sixties and into the nineteen-seventies, younger stars were moving away "from the dominance of styles seen broadly as 'eastern' to that of what is generally seen as a 'westernized,' smooth Persian pop style."[33] This music continued to take in Eastern (including Indian, Arabic, and Turkish) influences, but trends and sounds coming from the increasingly internationalizing force of the rock and pop music scene in the West were tipping the music in that direction. This more "modern" or "cosmopolitan" type of pop music was increasingly performed in the top cabarets like Bakara, Mayamey (Miami), and Moulin Rouge, and had taken over radio and television programs. Even youths who did not frequent these clubs due to their traditional or religious family backgrounds listened to the music of the likes of Ramesh, Aref, Googoosh, Hayedeh, Mahasti, Sattar, Dariush, Shohreh Solati, Ebi, Leila Forouhar, and Shahram Shabpareh, to name just a few of the best-known stars of the time. Television, which was launched in Iran in 1959 but only began broadcasting programs in earnest once it was nationalized in 1967, played an important role in spreading this varied pop music, which, while it was more upbeat and frequently employed "Western" instruments like the guitar or electronic and psychedelic elements, still had a uniquely Iranian sound.

Spread by attractive and much-watched television shows as well as flashy pop culture magazines full of the latest photographs of the hair, clothing, and lifestyles of these celebrities, there emerged in the Iran of the nineteen-sixties and seventies a youth culture that idealized popular singers and famous actors. Because of this mass mediation, the figure of the celebrity had become accessible and relatable, and many young people aspired to perform their own sense of being modern by imitating these stars. Every time one of the most beloved pop stars, Googoosh, would change her hairstyle, for example, young women would flock to hair salons and ask for the *Googooshi* haircut. In addition to live performances on television, there were also talk shows and variety shows that featured these singers and introduced new ones. One of the most popular shows of those decades was "The Silver Carnation," moderated by the flamboyant Fereydun Farrokhzad, brother of Iran's groundbreaking modernist poet Forough Farrokhzad.[34] This live-audience show, which was watched by millions, was a combination of Farrokhzad's own talk and performances with the showcasing of popular singers.[35] The trend of Westernization was evident in Farrokhzad's remarks on his programs, where he would, for example, coolly denigrate the exaggerated "traditional" Iranian politeness called *tārof*, or comment that he was "personally against songs that have Afghani, Indian, or Pakistani rhythms, because I love Iranian music and I love contemporary pop music, which is the same all over the world. What I sing over here is sung in France, just like it is in Russia and America. . . . I prefer that if we imitate, we imitate the works of countries that are more progressive than countries like Afghanistan, for example."[36]

Although this pop musical style dominated the mainstream in the late nineteen-sixties and nineteen-seventies, the more intrepid, alternative music of the time had cosmopolitan aspirations that looked to both East and West.[37] While Fereydun Foroughi and Kourosh Yaghmayi were creating works that combined Iranian vocals with blues and psychedelic rock tunes, Abbas Mehrpooya was fusing "Ananda Shankar-style funk with Fela Kuti-inspired Afrobeat,"[38] Farhad Mehrad blended Iranian folk with rock, and other bands were busy making garage rock and beat music. Some of the most successful Persian pop stars who are still continuing their careers out of Los Angeles today came from this scene, including Shahram Shabpareh, Siavash Ghomeyshi, and Ebi, who were members of the beat band the Rebels. Tehran of the nineteen-seventies boasted a truly vibrant music scene, which even attracted foreign musicians like the Dia Prometido band, a Chilean guitarist and Iranian percussionist duo who incorporated the Iranian *tār* (lute) and created crossover music; or Erik, the Frenchman of African origin who arranged music for various artists and acted as Googoosh's live band leader and was the diva's arranger anytime she wanted a "funk, soul or samba feel in a recording."[39] In recent years, international music collectors have gone back to dig out many of the most coveted tracks of the nineteen-sixties garage rock and nineteen-seventies psychedelic-funk fusion scene in Iran and compile them into new records, drawing renewed attention to this progressive music scene of the Iran of the nineteen-seventies.[40]

RADIO BREAKTHROUGH FOR SHAJARIAN

Considering the cultural and musical atmosphere of Tehran in the nineteen-sixties and nineteen-seventies, it is perhaps not surprising that radio managers rejected Shajarian several times because of what he understood them to see as the "too traditional" nature of his singing.[41] Frustrated by the response he received in his encounters with the radio officials, Shajarian decided to bring a tape of his singing to Davud Pirnia, the creator of the widely celebrated radio show *Golha*. Pirnia had recently launched a more mystical branch of the *Golha* program, called *"Barg-e Sabz"* (Green Leaf), and invited Shajarian to record a piece for it. Impressed with what he heard, Pirnia then broadcast Shajarian's voice for the first time on Radio Iran, but the stigma of appearing on radio as a *khānandeh* (singer) at that time was such that Shajarian used the artist name "Siavash Bidkani." The *Golha* phenomenon had made listening to music in public acceptable even in more conservative society, which until that time had only done so behind closed doors, due to the anti-music bias of traditional Islamic thought. Shajarian chose an artist name to make himself less readily identifiable; as he explained, "For my father it was a real disgrace to see me working in music, because he had strong religious beliefs and thought music was haram. He didn't like me to pursue music, so out of respect for him I didn't use his name."[42] Every now and then, Islamic Republic officials use the fact that Shajarian first sang under a different name as a reason to attack his character, accusing him of duplicity and opportunism, though in fact it is easy to understand the explanation that Shajarian gives.

Shajarian has recounted that it was very difficult for him to enter radio and remembers that at the time of his first recording, other musicians complained that his singing was different, because of his provincial background, and refused to accompany him. Within Iran's highly centralized geosocial structure, which is so culturally valorized that it is still socially acceptable to denigrate dialects and customs that are not from Tehran, anything provincial lacks the kind of cool or cosmopolitan cachet that the norm aspires to. Hence, it appears that the initial obstacles Shajarian faced were in part due to his provincial, traditional background. In the many old photographs of Shajarian, he does not look much different from the other dandies of his time, all sporting cosmopolitan airs: tight suits with broad lapels, bell-bottoms and broad neckties, large-framed glasses and whopping hairdos. Indeed, Shajarian looks like a well-dressed man in modern attire even in photographs dating back to his teenage years. The fact that Shajarian hardly looked any different from his counterparts in Rome or New York is due to Tehran's aspiring cosmopolitanism of the time, the sartorial parallel to the musical trend that rejected *āvāz* in favor of *tarāneh*. However, while the young Shajarian dressed in trendy ways, his more traditional cultural background was presumably evident to his more up-to-date contemporaries in other ways; unlike Shajarian, they may have exhibited trendier mannerisms or been more inclined to socialize with women or attend the cabarets of the time. This may have been the "provincialism" that his radio colleagues detected in him, in addition to the remnants of his Mashhadi accent.

Shajarian highlights his encounter with the revered Pirnia and his entry into *Golha* through the very creator of the program that was so crucial to giving Shajarian's voice the kind of exposure he received. Participation in the program is an indispensable line item on the résumé of an artist of Shajarian's age and reputation. To this day, musicians, historians, and laypeople alike refer to the *Golha* program with near-reverence as an "exemplar of excellence"[43] and "the best in the musical history of Iran."[44] Even Islamic Republic state radio, which was sitting on the program's archives but abstained from airing them for two decades, eventually started broadcasting them and now replays them frequently.

Still, while Shajarian studied industriously with the famous memorizer and vocalist of the Persian classical musical *radif* repertoire, the master Abdollah Davami, and while the three main "biographical" volumes on Shajarian include dozens of photographs showing him together with all the great musicians of his time,[45] he told me that he did not have any one main mentor who took him on and showed him the ropes of the music business in Tehran: "I had no one when I came to Tehran. I rented a small room with my wife and two children and was all on my own. I learned some *gushehs* from my *ostāds*, but nothing about style or anything else."[46] Although Shajarian does not emphasize the point too much, it is clear that he takes pride in the self-made nature of his trajectory: from a Qur'an reciter and teacher in the provinces to appearances on national radio in the capital, and then on to the most luminous stages in the world. (The "self-made" narrative is an important marker in Shajarian's narrative of authenticity and is, in general, more prevalent in Shajarian's generation, an age cohort that felt empowered to reach its goals, than it is today. Iran's postrevolutionary generations more often conceive of their lives in much less empowering narratives, as devoid of opportunities and wasted by bad government and fateful geography, i.e. having had the misfortune of being born in Iran.

Soon after his first radio broadcasts, Shajarian was transferred by the Ministry of Natural Resources to Tehran, to teach and carry out research into radio and television, and he continued to record programs for radio for about ten years. For the first four to five years, he continued to use his artist name. Shajarian's work in radio raised his profile, and from 1968 onwards, for ten consecutive years, he participated in Iran's international Shiraz Arts Festival, *Jashn-e*

Honar-e Shiraz.[47] At some point in the early nineteen-seventies, when Shajarian was invited to sing for a program on television, he finally decided to appear under his real name, explaining, "My father fully believed that if I went into music I would fall for alcohol and drugs, which the music scene at the time unfortunately entailed. But when he saw that I was treading the right path, bit by bit, he was all right with me doing my work, although he always continued to tell me that I should try to protect my faith and know God."[48]

EVOLVING FORMS OF POETIC PROTEST

Poetry has long played an important role in the Persian language for expressing critique and discontent of a social or political nature. However, until the modern period, this kind of poetry was mostly confined to the unofficial or more informal spheres. The classical poet Omar Khayyam openly criticized the hypocrisy of clerics and preachers[49] a millennium ago, as did Hafez three hundred years later,[50] but the recorded history of Persian poetry suggests that there was little by way of critical poetry between the giants of almost a thousand years ago and the "awakened" poets of the early twentieth century.[51] A revealing and much-repeated anecdote says that the nineteenth-century Qajar chief minister Amir Kabir—often referred to as "Iran's first reformer"—severely admonished the court's poet laureate, Habib Allah Qa'ani, after the poet recited a panegyric qasida in the minister's honor. Recent authors speculate that Amir Kabir grew angry because he could not tolerate the hypocrisy of the court poet, who had previously, in a dozen similar qasidas, praised "the very man he was now disparaging as cruel and unjust."[52] Amir Kabir's reaction was significant because that sentiment heralded an early turning point in "the long and eventful project of poetic modernity in Iranian culture."[53] Soon after this episode, however, court intrigues led to Amir Kabir's dismissal and later assassination in 1852. It would be several more decades before the first generation of socially aware or politically critical and freedom-seeking poetry appeared in the works of writers like Ali Akbar Sheyda, Malek o-Sho'ara Bahar, and Abolqasem Aref Qazvini. Some of the most enduring Iranian songs of all time were written by these poets or originated in their works.

But we do have other, older anecdotes about socially or politically conscious or critical rhyme in informal communication. One of the earlier accounts of such a "popular" poem dates back to 1807, in Edward Scott Waring's *A Tour to Sheeraz, by the Route of Kazroon and Feerozabad*, where he describes a song that people sang at the beginning of the Qajar dynasty to commemorate the escape and death of the well-liked Lotf-Ali Khan Zand.[54] Later in that century, in his *Year Amongst the Persians*, the famous orientalist E. G. Browne also remarks on the currency of "popular" lyrics that Iranians recite or sing during leisure and work, which reflect on their current social and political conditions, but states that "their authors are not known and prefer to remain anonymous."[55] Abdollah Mostofi, a prominent man of politics whose memoirs are considered an indispensable guide to the social history of the end of the Qajar period and the first three decades of the Pahlavi era,[56] records several such lyrics in his memoirs, among them a song of protest over Naser al-Din Shah's pilgrimage to Karbala in Iran's years of famine:

> The Shah with the funny hat / Is gone to Karbala / Bread is expensive/
> Several kilos a whole qerān/ We've become captives / To the vizier /
> Oh, the vizier![57]

Still, these "popular/folk" (*mardomi*) lyrics were never recorded as part of Iran's cultural heritage or body of literature, as happened with folk culture in much of the rest of the world, in part because they were usually short and short-lived, their authors unknown, and print and audio recording technologies were either nonexistent or much more limited than they are today. And more generally, historically, "traditional popular music—mardomi, ruhowzi, or motrebi music—was disparaged and excoriated because of the perceived low class of its performers and its contents, contexts, and consumers."[58]

During the years of Iran's Constitutional Revolution (1905–1911), the number of these spontaneous *mardomi* rhymes incorporating social and political critique multiplied, as noteworthy events quickly led to rhymes that circulated in society.[59] The *Mashruteh*, as the Constitutional Revolution is called in Persian, was the culmination of a people's movement to put an end to the Qajar dynasty's tyrannical rule and reckless mismanagement of the country, as well as foreign (mostly British and Russian) domination. Following widespread protests, the then king Mozaffar al-Din Shah Qajar was forced to sign Iran's first constitution—and indeed, the first constitution in the Middle East—in 1906. In the absence of mass or broadcast media, which today facilitate the existence of a public sphere, these *mardomi* songs were used to relay news about events as well as people's sentiments about those events.[60]

But around this time, works of formal poetry also turned political. As calls for a constitution gained momentum, several prominent and often politically active poets lent their voices to this nascent movement.[61] Their poetry is full of talk of freedom. In fact, that is where the enunciation of the word freedom (*āzādi*) in a way synonymous with notions of Western democracy emerged for the first time.[62] Also around this time—spurred on by several nineteenth-century intellectuals and aided by the printing press—the modern notion of a nation-state was cultivated, whereby people in a specified geographical region actively imagined themselves as citizens of a community with a widely shared language and culture. All of this of course brought forth a changing relationship between the poet and his or her social context, and the flourishing of politically conscious poetry early in the twentieth century is a reflection of these processes.

Although politically barbed proverbs and poems seem to have existed for a very long time, at least in informal spheres, it was only at the turn to the twentieth century that poetic protest took on a musical form and became more widespread, thanks to the forums of salons, concerts, and later, gramophone technology. The poet and singer Aref Qazvini is often recognized as the one who lent form to the short, rhythmic *tasnif*. The music historian Ruhollah Khaleqi credits Aref with being the first to cloak criticism of the circumstances of his time in the mantle of song and music and to turn music into a publishing and advertising medium for his revolutionary beliefs and liberal opinions.[63] Khaleqi says that Aref should be considered the inventor of this genre, which he describes as an artful, authored format that combined "effective words" with "expert rhythms."[64] Over the course of the first decade of the twentieth century, the *tasnif* became a vehicle for mobilizing the supporters of the constitutionalist cause.[65]

It was also during these years that the public concert, in the form in which we know it today, emerged. At first, concerts were held in private homes and gardens, but over the course of the nineteen-twenties, musicians began performing concerts in hotels and other halls that were open to the public via ticket sales. The public performance of music transformed it into a socially and politically significant medium through which people shared ideas and showed political allegiance to certain attitudes. This was unprecedented, as Aref himself relates in his memoir: "At the time when I started composing *tasnifs* and made national and patriotic songs, people thought songs were meant to be made for the courtesans or 'Babri Khan,'" (the cat of the long-reigning nineteenth-century Qajar ruler Naser al-Din Shah).[66] Within this new context, the shorter, more message-laden *tasnif* gained more currency.

Aref became very popular for imbuing his compositions with sociopolitical meaning, and he created some of the century's most enduring songs.

The invention of recording technology at the turn to the twentieth century brought significant changes to musical forms. In Iran, however, the "creation" and popularity of the politically inflected *tasnif* genre seems to have had only tangentially to do, at first, with the age of recording and the medium of the gramophone, and more to do with the popularity of the concert as a medium. The invention of the gramophone (or phonograph) dates to 1877, but the first period of Iranian gramophone recording only began in 1906 and was put to rest by 1915, when World War I caused a decade-long interregnum in productions and recordings in Iran. The adverse effects on Iran of World War I (1914–1918), continuing British and Russian imperial machinations, and the ineffective rule of the young Qajar king Ahmad Shah (official reign 1909–1925) led to great political instability in Iran during that decade, not to mention agricultural devastation, famine, and an economy in shambles. This may well explain the absence of recording technology for a decade, while in other countries in the region, such as Egypt, recording was thriving again by 1919.[67] For that first phase of recording technology in Iran, most of the existing archives consist of recordings of the master vocalists and instrumentalists of the courts of Naser al-Din Shah Qajar (reigned 1848–1896) and Mozaffar al-Din Shah Qajar (reigned 1896–1906), interspersed with military marches, hymns for kings and the country, *ta'ziyeh* (passion play) recordings commemorating Imam Hossein's martyrdom, recordings of theatrical plays, and some farcical pieces that treat issues of gender, ethnicity, and religion.[68]

While there are recordings of other vocalists singing some of Aref's less political *tasnifs*,[69] Aref's own reportedly likeable voice has not been preserved. It seems that the record companies cared mostly about recording the masters of the time, and while Aref was a very popular performer, his art was not so much in the virtuosity of his performance as in the socially and politically critical content of his songs and the communal expression of that content. And when other masters covered Aref's *tasnifs*, they were disinclined to record the overtly political ones, not least because of their own associations with the royal court, but also due to fear of repercussions in general. This attitude is best exemplified by an anecdote relayed by the *radif* master Abdollah Davami. On a recording trip to Tbilisi in 1911, Aref accompanied Davami and the master *tār* player Darvish Khan. In the studio, Aref asked Davami to play a *tasnif* of his called "Shustar," in homage to the pro-constitutionalist American treasurer-general of

Persia, William Morgan Shuster.[70] Barely a few seconds into the piece, Darvish Khan excused himself from the recording due to the song's political nature, so that Davami was forced to choose a different, nonpolitical song.[71] The relative permanence of a song, once recorded on a gramophone disc, meant that artists often abstained from relaying political content on recordings. In contrast, the ephemeral nature of the songs performed at a live, unrecorded gathering meant that attendance at concerts was indispensable to partaking in this alternative public sphere, where people used music as a language of critique and dissent.

The concert was also a more important medium for the exchange and distribution of music than the gramophone in the first decades of the twentieth century because in its various public and private forms, the concert was more accessible to a wider strata of Iranians than was the expensive gramophone technology. In the gramophone's first phase in Iran (1906–1915),[72] and even for a while subsequently, only the wealthiest strata of society could afford to own the machines. Still, people who could not afford their own gramophones could often hear recorded music in cafés and restaurants that had acquired the device for entertainment.

It was not until several years after the 1921 coup d'état against the last Qajar government, by a general of the Persian Cossack Brigade by the name of Reza Khan, that relative stability allowed for trade and technology to begin flourishing again and the gramophone became more affordable and widespread, around 1925. Indeed, the scarcities of 1906–1915 and then the absence of any recording technology or infrastructure for dissemination in Iran throughout the decade from 1915 to 1925 seem to have contributed even further to the importance and popularity of concerts.[73] In the absence of technological mass mediation, concerts contributed to the popularity of the political *tasnif* and of accolades crediting Aref with being its "creator."[74] Relative stability also allowed for the establishment of cultural institutions and schools and so the early nineteen-twenties were a sort of golden era of the concert, with frequent performances in the salons of Tehran's Grand Hotel and other newly established public venues. In his memoirs, the music historian Khaleqi describes the impact of a concert:

> It was enough for Aref to perform a song about social conditions of the time in one or two places, and it would travel from mouth to mouth and reach everyone; it would even travel from town to town.[75]

Inspired by the example of Turkey, the new ruler initially planned to establish a republic. Aref, the era's most "political" musician, was elated over Reza

Khan's plans for a republic, and his prolific artistic activity mirrored his en-
thusiasm. But as early as 1923, when an adolescent Khaleqi attended an Aref
concert, the new ruler had already curtailed free political talk, and Khaleqi's father told him, "Don't forget Aref's *tasnifs*; you may never hear their like again."
When the son naively asked why, the father responded, "His tongue may be
tied!"[76] Khaleqi later wrote about his concert experience:

> At that time I still didn't fully grasp the real reasons behind the power of
> the song-maker. But I understood this much: that the majority of audience
> members had a hidden secret in their hearts, and without revealing it, when
> they would see others of the same mind, with one look alone, would share
> that secret. That same secret that wasn't expressed in front of strangers, but
> in burning hearts lit a luminous fire.[77]

Due in great part to the clergy's opposition to a republic, Reza Khan finally
crowned himself Reza Shah Pahlavi in 1925, became increasingly intolerant of
criticism, and banned all talk of republicanism. Aref, on the other hand, had
composed several songs celebrating republicanism and even performed one
very explicit song in 1924, named "Republic," in which he decried the evil of
monarchies and called the people the legitimate holders of power. As the political page turned, Aref chose silence; he spent the rest of his life in the Moradbek
Valley of Hamedan in solitude and misery.[78]

Until the nineteen-twenties, either political instability, repression by ruling
kings, or chaos resulting from the meddling of the great powers in Iran had
meant that no unified policy for music existed. But following Reza Shah's take-
over in 1925, the new modernizing state devised policies based on a utilitar-
ian attitude toward music. The political *tasnif* receded into the background as
the state promoted the patriotic *sorud*—a combination of march, hymn, and
anthem that was often taught in schools and expressed pride in one's country,
history, and flag.[79] In line with Reza Shah's grand policy of modernization, the
state regarded Iran's traditional music as backward and neglected it in its official institutions. Instead, it promoted the Western musical canon and provided
the means for teaching Western music and musical instruments in schools.
When Iran launched radio in April 1940, for example, the first programs offered a preponderance of European music, in combination with news, talk,
and Iranian music. The shah-appointed, foreign-educated director of Iran's Organization for the Cultivation of Thoughts (*Sāzmān-e Parvaresh-e Afkār*) and
of Iran's Music Bureau (*Edāreh-ye Musiqi*), Gholam-Hossein Minbashian, had

little regard for Persian music and completely eliminated it from the curriculum of Iran's Higher Academy of Music (*Honarestān-e 'Āli-ye Musiqi*) when he took over its management in 1938. He then formed Iran's first European orchestra, consisting of Czech masters and Iranian students, which performed European music several nights a week on Iranian radio.[80]

Throughout the nineteen-thirties and nineteen-forties, Iranian music continued in a variety of platforms, including private gatherings as well as organized concerts. The folksier, popular *motrebi* and *kucheh-bāzāri music* was offered by bands that performed at weddings and other private occasions and later in cafés, restaurants, and eventually cabarets. But immense repression—especially in the nineteen-thirties—suppressed all open or even lightly disguised social or political critique in songs.

In 1941, when the Allies occupied Iran and forced Reza Shah to abdicate because of his strong ties and sympathies with Nazi Germany, Minbashian was dismissed and the highly influential reformist music educator Ali-Naqi Vaziri once again took over the administration of the Music Bureau and the Higher Academy of Music, which he had founded as the Music Academy in 1923. Soon thereafter, he also formed an orchestra on Iranian radio that gave greater prominence to Iranian music and featured, among other virtuosos, Iran's all-time master violinist, Abolhasan Saba.[81]

During the nineteen-forties a kind of performance art called *pish-pardeh-khāni* ("before-scene performance," the short political pieces already briefly mentioned in chapter 1) became significant for airing critique. This genre consisted of skits that were performed in the interludes between acts, and combined song and play to express social and political criticism. One music historian writes that this form became so popular during those mid-century decades of silence and censorship that theaters without *pish-pardeh* lost audiences.[82] This was a generally chaotic period, when state institutions were weak and lacked clear direction as far as cultural policy was concerned. At the same time, recording technology meant that Western, Arabic, and Turkish influences began to shape the course of Persian music in particular and Iranian popular culture in general.[83] An outcry arose from the literati and musicians, who in numerous magazine articles expressed their concern over the course of their national music (*musiqi-ye melli*), lamented its decadence and decline, and criticized the lack of support for the development of music, as well as the interference, from the Ministry of Culture.[84]

Much of the political critique at this time was directed at the misdoings of the Allied forces and the negative impact of foreign influence on Iran. Musically, these sentiments culminated in the era's most lasting patriotic song, "*Ey Iran,*" which to this day remains Iran's de facto national anthem, though it was never the official one.[85] Its genesis story is fitting, as the poet who wrote its lyrics did so in reaction to witnessing the maltreatment of Iranian civilians by English soldiers on the streets in 1944, when Iran was under occupation by Allied forces.[86] This anthem-like song declares a love for Iran and its many virtues and a readiness to sacrifice one's life for the homeland. "*Ey Iran*" still maintains its quality of protest and is often intoned at political gatherings.[87] It begins with the verses:

> O Iran, o land full of jewels
> O, your soil the wellspring of the arts

and then goes on to profess eternal love for the land's many beauties, ending with:

> In your cause, when would our lives matter?
> May the land of Iran be eternal

In a country where history has long been told through a prism that pits people and state against one another, this song is able to override this binary and express a patriotic love for the land independent of politics.[88] This goes a long way toward explaining its immense popularity through various decades and governments.

By the early nineteen-fifties, foreign interventions and Prime Minister Mohammad Mosaddeq's attempts to nationalize Iranian oil had created a highly politicized atmosphere. This period continues to have a significant impact on Iranians' understanding of their own history and current political predicament, as well as on Iran's foreign relations. Surprisingly, the only widely popular song from this period is a heartfelt, passionate ballad titled "*Marā bebus*" (Kiss Me), characteristic of "political" songs under repressive conditions in that at first, it hardly sounds political at all. However, it projects a feeling that those who were privy to the political environment of that era could instantly decode.[89] "*Marā bebus*" is sung by a man who asks his lover for a last kiss because "our spring is over," emanating a sense of desperation over dashed hopes. Following Mosaddeq's removal from office in the British-American coup d'état of August 1953, a student activist and member of the National Front (Mosaddeq's party) by the name of Heydar Reqabi wrote the lyrics to this song on the night of his departure into exile.[90] It was immortalized in the voice of Hasan Golnaraqi and is still broadcast by Persian-language radio stations abroad.[91] However, even before the Golnaraqi version was recorded in 1957, there was high demand for an earlier, less popular version. One observer, who lived through these times and wrote about them several decades later, notes: "I remember Tehran radio [in 1955], which had a policy of not repeating a song on the same day, bowing to popular demand and playing *"Marā bebus"* 16 times in one day."[92] Another person recounts: "Two generations of our society wept over their pain and sorrow and heartache and defeat and death to the song *"Marā bebus"* with Hasan Golnaraqi's voice."[93] There may be various, as yet unstudied, reasons for the fact that no record exists of any other "political" songs from this highly contested period in recent Iranian history, but the stark political repression of that era is sure to be one of the reasons.[94]

I have already mentioned the importance to Shajarian's career of Davud Pirnia and the fabled *Golha* radio program. In the late nineteen-fifties, Pirnia, who was already a distinguished civil servant, launched *Golha*, which he reportedly conceived of in order to "combat the increasing corruption of classical Persian music."[95] This was a groundbreaking program that (re-)introduced Persian poetry and music to a wider public. It did not serve as a channel for political opposition, since its content was artistic rather than political. The *Golha* program featured the best of Persian music and literature in relatively short, palatable segments, enlisting the finest voices and musicians of its time. The programs "marked a watershed in the appreciation of music in Persian culture, leading to the enhanced respectability of musicians and their art."[96] *Golha* revived the works of a wide range of Iran's greatest poets and composers (including Aref), many of whose names and work had receded from the public's knowledge at the time, but the program also exhibited the best of the country's living talents. Considering its popularity and its reach into all parts of Iran, due to the prominence of the medium of radio in those days, the *Golha* program, for more than ten years, practically amounted to a national education in Iran's own literature and music.

But *Golha* was an exception for its time. In the nineteen-sixties and seventies, radio and television played a growing role in bringing Western cultural productions into Iranian homes. Then, as (ironically) now, an economic and cultural obsession with all things *farangi* (foreign, read Euro-American) had a tendency to place Western goods, customs, and values above Iranian ones. Paradoxically, the shah's Ministry of Culture and National Iranian Radio and Television (NIRT) were the two most important cultural and financial supporters of Persian classical music at that time, as Shajarian himself testifies, in a way,

when he names state radio and its *Golha* program as his first and most important teacher.[97] Still, even though the state was investing in Iran's native arts, the
general tide of Westernization in the nineteen-seventies created an atmosphere
within which Shajarian perceived the state to be giving greater value to "cabaret" music. His understanding of the state's value system is part and parcel of
his narrative of why he eventually quit state radio:

> I was really active—out of 201 "*Golhā-ye Tāzeh*" (Fresh Flowers), I per-
> formed about 67, although there were four or five other singers—so I could
> see what was happening from the inside. . . . After Davud Pirnia's departure
> from radio and television, Mr. Ebtehaj took over . . . and I could see that
> they were really making his life difficult; they wouldn't broadcast the pro-
> grams properly and the colleagues working in recording and production
> were less at our service. One night we were recording a television program
> with the Sheyda group, with Mohammad Reza Lotfi and so on, and a light-
> bulb burned out and we had to interrupt our session and wait for someone
> to replace the bulb. We had another hour left to record, but our produc-
> tion team had left and no one changed the bulb, and after a while we real-
> ized everyone had gone into a bigger studio to watch a "cabaret" show that
> was being recorded, instead of recording our program! Our role as active
> *Golha* performers had become so small, and the role of the new café-cabaret
> singers had become so big, that I realized radio and television were no lon-
> ger a place for me. After that I said good-bye.[98]

Shajarian perceived those in power as favoring these newer musical trends,
which in his view borrowed from foreign influences, over Iran's own cultural
heritage, a widely shared grievance that contributed to the growing discontent
with the shah's regime and eventually helped to bring it down a few years later.
Mohammad Reza Lotfi, the Sheyda group member mentioned by Shajarian in
the anecdote above, also described this lack of esteem for traditional Iranian
culture, and says he felt the discrimination was systematic:

> For example, the income of the foremost *kamāncheh* [Iranian bowed string
> instrument] maestro, Ostād Bahari, was 140 toman, but then the salary of
> the conductor of the Tehran Symphony Orchestra was 12000 toman. There
> was no correlation, no balance. If you had a "Western" project proposal,
> they would give you a big budget, but if you had a project for maintaining or
> reviving old Iranian art, the budget was very small or nonexistent.[99]

This perceived systematic discrimination against traditional arts was in part also a product of cosmopolitan and early globalizing forces. Shajarian had already stopped performing for radio in 1976, before the revolution had gained any momentum, because of what he saw as the cabaret owners' control of state media programming: "Radio and television cared more about *tarāneh* [light rhythmic songs] and the cabaret-type singers, who would last just a couple of years and sing hit songs that were sometimes broadcast seven to eight times in one day! Radio was no longer a place for our music."[100]

While the cafés, cabarets, and television sets were blaring with joyous pop songs and dance music—many influenced by Arabic and European rhythms—political discontent was brewing among the wider population. By the early nineteen-seventies, the first "mainstream" political songs appeared, sung by Farhad, Fereydun Foroughi, and Dariush. While in the nineteen-sixties many specifically leftist political songs were produced, in the nineteen-seventies political songs were more general and all-encompassing, expressing themes of grief, poverty, and misery. To work around state censorship, themes of extreme sadness—such as blood pouring instead of rain on Fridays in Farhad's "*Jom'eh*" (Friday); the poor hands and deprived eyes of a lone man with thirsty lips in his "*Mard-e tanhā*" (Lonesome Man); the chained fairies in Dariush's "*Pariyā*" (Fairies); or hearts as bloody as poppy flowers in his "*Shaqāyeq*" (Poppy Flower)—were used as metaphors of protest against the reigning conditions of extreme disparity. By the mid-nineteen-seventies, there was a prevalence of sadness both in the themes and the melodies of popular songs, so much so that the shah reputedly complained to his minister of culture about this trend and asked for countermeasures to be taken.[101]

Although the soundscape of that time was filled with songs of a political or oppositional bent, classical Persian music had yet to partake of the spirit of the times. In fact, it was criticized for its conservative nature and condemned as being removed from contemporary circumstances, a state of affairs that critics blamed on its practitioners' strict adherence to traditional forms. But in the late 1970s a cadre of young musicians of Persian classical music that included Shajarian were beginning to transform the genre from bazmi (banquet style) to what another one of its leaders, Hossein Alizadeh, called "razmi" (militant). A performance that foregrounded this direction happened at the 1977 Shiraz Art Festival, where, as Ramin Sadighi and Sohrab Mahdavi write, Shajarian sang the constitution-era *tasnif* "All night sleep doesn't come to my eyes / Oh, you who are asleep / In the desert those who are thirsty die / While water is being carried to ostentatious palaces."[102] And after a political watershed moment in September 1978, these young musicians finally brought Persian classical music to the fore and revealed for the first time since the Constitutional Revolution its potential for containing politically and socially critical messages. Earlier in the century, Reza Shah's authoritarian government had suppressed the "libertarian and patriotic" *tasnif* in favor of the "nationalistic and monarchist" *sorud*, which was a reflection of the authoritarian turn that Iranian politics took after World War I.[103] By the same token, the return of the *tasnif* in the nineteen-seventies— when these songs were once again resurrected and adapted to the political situation of 1979—signaled a return to the political spirit of the constitutional era. The resurgence of Persian classical music at that time, as well as its continued popularity to this day, is an expression of the nativism that was part and parcel of the dominant ideals of the 1979 revolution.

CHAPTER THREE

THE MUSICAL GUIDE

MOHAMMAD REZA SHAJARIAN

IN THE MONTHS leading up to the 1979 overthrow of the shah, one particular day is often identified as a turning point for the revolution. This day was, in addition, probably *the* turning point for Persian classical music. In early September 1978, following days of protests (including one that numbered around half a million people, the largest protest to that date), the shah's government declared martial law. Nevertheless, on the next day, 8 September 1978, thousands mounted a demonstration in central Tehran's Zhaleh Square. After repeated warnings, troops opened fire on demonstrators, killing sixty-four people in the square and twenty-four elsewhere in Tehran. The day was called "Black Friday," and at the time it happened and for more than twenty years thereafter, people believed that thousands had been gunned down at the event, exponentially magnifying the tragedy and, in turn, the political significance of the event.[1] Following Black Friday, Iran's most accomplished classical musicians quit radio in protest. The resignation letter was written in Shajarian's handwriting.[2]

Soon afterwards, the "Chavosh Culture and Arts Society"—founded a few months earlier by the *tār* virtuoso Mohammad Reza Lotfi and young musicians such as Hossein Alizadeh, Parviz Meshkatian, Shahram Nazeri, and Shajarian, under the spiritual guidance of the prominent poet Houshang Ebtehaj[3]—sprang into action and started producing some of the most enduring revolutionary songs of the period. Lotfi, the main founding member, described the necessity of Chavosh and its creations in the following words:

When the revolution was happening, I realized that everyone was in the streets and there was an affectionate warmth and excitement going around everywhere. People were no longer interested in the music of that time, neither the pop music of that time nor any other music.[4]

This may very well have been Lotfi's perception, situated as he was within the conservative realm of classical music. Nevertheless, his comment throws open some questions, considering that some of the pop music of that period was highly political and led to the exile or internal silencing of its creators, including Dariush, Farhad Mehrad, and Fereydun Forughi. But several factors complicated pop music's capacity for taking on the mantle of revolutionary music, leading up to 1978 and 1979, the way that the creations of the Chavosh group did. For one thing, pop music's inherent associations with "Westernization"—the "curse" that Iran's most popular intellectuals of the time had singled out as being at the core of the country's problems—meant that, as a genre, it was not a natural vessel for protest, while Persian classical music, with its connotations of Iranian authenticity, was at the opposite end of that spectrum. Also, the majority of pop musicians were indeed engaged in creating works for entertainment rather than political critique. Those who expressed critique did so in subtle or allegorical ways that may not have been easily understood by large numbers of consumers, especially when the lyrics drew from the modernist works of *"she'r-e now"* (new poetry), which traded in "literary ambiguity [and] linguistic polysemy."[5] To top it off, following the collapse of the old regime and the Islamization of the revolution, pop became another word for promiscuity in the new leaders' eyes. Most of the well-known artists and producers involved in pop music fled the country, so that their side of the story was virtually nonexistent. In this vacuum, with no one left to defend pop music, musicians like Lotfi and others like him could advance their own narratives of pop music's total lack of political agency in pre-revolutionary Iran. This turn in the historical tide gave classical Persian music a small advantage in postrevolutionary Iran, though it seems petty to argue this point considering how disadvantaged all music was following the revolution.

The Chavosh group met in Lotfi's basement and at first recorded all their songs as a multi-vocal choir, to guard against identification and political persecution. Newly emerging technology—the audiocassette tape—really made a difference for Chavosh at the time, as it had done for the revolution itself. Like Khomeini's speeches, which were copied onto cassette tapes and disseminated across Iran, Chavosh music was widely distributed thanks to this new technology as well.[6] The only other means of mass broadcast at the time were television and radio—which were wholly controlled by the state—and the gramophone record, which was more expensive, laborious, and unwieldy to produce. In fact, without audiocassette technology, it is unlikely that Iranians inside Iran could have continued to benefit from new musical productions—whether created in Tehran or in the Iranian exile community in Los Angeles —after the revolution. Lotfi recalled that in the first few years after the revolution, he would personally stand in Imam Hossein Square selling cassette tapes of classical Persian music, due to the absence of locales for performing or selling music. This would not have been possible with records, as multiplication and stealth were important aspects of this endeavor.

Among Chavosh's first songs was "*Zhāleh khun shod*," (Dew Turned into Blood), a song that commemorated Black Friday. It is a marchlike song in the *chāhārgāh* mode of the Persian *radif* that rhymes on the somewhat abrupt sound of *od* and is sung in multiple voices that then crystallize into a youthful, nearly female voice with a resolute, but adolescent undertone:

> *Zhāleh* crashed on stone, what happened?
> Dew turned into blood
> What became of the blood? What became of the blood?
> The blood turned into madness

Using the word *zhāleh*, which means "dew" but is also the name of the site of the events of Black Friday, Zhaleh Square, the song creates a simile between the pure water droplets of dawn and the revolutionary movement, and its turning into blood with the act of madness (*jonun*), a point of no return, a word that in the Persian literary context signifies a drastically different state of being, hence the poem's extension of this state into the explicit overturning of the monarchy in the last lines:

> Dew crashed on stone, what happened?
> Dew turned into blood . . .
> Dew make blood! Blood make madness!
> Topple the monarchy with your madness!

Although at that point the voices of Chavosh were still anonymous, the explicitness and brazenness of the verses of this song radiated confidence that real changes were going to happen; that it was all just a matter of time. Unlike the depressing affect of the politically charged pop songs of the time, Chavosh songs sounded triumphal.

MARDOMI, NOT POLITICAL

Less than two months after the formation of Chavosh, Shajarian was no longer afraid to call for armed resistance in his own voice. In "*Shab ast-o chehreh-ye mihan siāh-e*" (It's Night and the Homeland's Visage Is Black), better known as "Shabnavard" (Night Traveler) or "*Tofangam-rā bedeh*" (Give Me My Gun), by most accounts written by Aslan Aslanian in remembrance of the Marxist Fedayeen activist Amir Parviz Puyan,[7] Shajarian passionately called on his compatriots to join in the struggle:

> It's night and the motherland's visage is dark
> Sitting in darkness is a sin[8]
> Give me my gun so I can get going
> Because every lover is underway
> The brother is agitated
> The brother is in flames
> The valley of the brother's chest is a field of tulips
>
> . . .
>
> The brother, he is an adolescent
> The brother, he is drowning in blood
> The brother, his forelock is all fireworks
> You who know the pain of lovers
> You who are our brother in arms and chains
> See the dear ones' blood on the walls
> Blow the horn of morning and illumination

Shajarian's teenage years coincided with some of Iran's most tumultuous political events, during the period of Mohammad Mosaddeq's oil nationalization in the early nineteen-fifties. Shajarian says that he remembers this time very well, as he accompanied his father to street demonstrations, but emphasizes that he was not political, with this surprising statement: "I never did political work and I never got myself involved in political issues though I was always aware of them; just like now, I don't engage in political issues but I'm fully aware of them."[9]

Despite his socially and politically engaged songs from fairly early on in his career, it turns out that Shajarian eschews the term "political" in regard to his work. When pressed in interviews, he calls what he does *mardomi* instead—

a word that translates as "popular" but has historically established connotations of democracy[10]—and adds that it is an artist's obligation to guide. This is an important distinction in the projection of his identity as an artist who is "with the people," as opposed to unjust governments or other political interests, though it does not mean that he has stayed away from expressing what many would consider "political" sentiments.

Similarly, Shajarian explained to me that the issues he raises are also to be understood on a humane level: "I don't enter politics. If at times my work has political meaning, then it's in defense of humane ideals and the homeland."[11] In the 2010 BBC Persian documentary about his life, Sadeq Saba prods him: "When the revolution happened, a new Shajarian appeared, a Shajarian who sang what back then were called revolutionary (enqelābi) or patriotic (mihani) songs." To this, Shajarian folds his arms and in a lower, more intimate voice responds:

> To tell you the truth, even then I wasn't very revolutionary. Why? Because I saw things among the politicals (siāsiyun) and various parties that I didn't like. But I was surrounded by people who had political views and leftist views, which I really didn't like at all but I had no option in the midst of those people, everyone around me talked politics. It's true that I was unhappy with a lot of aspects of the regime but, to be honest, I wasn't very optimistic about that situation in which no one knew where things were headed.

It is indeed hard to imagine how Shajarian could not have held revolutionary sentiments, considering that for many, he embodied the voice of the revolution in song. After all, he had sung, "Give me my gun so I can get going / Because every lover is underway." By framing his past this way, Shajarian creates distance from a revolution whose consequences have caused discontent for many if not most of his listeners. Furthermore, the term enqelābi (revolutionary), which Saba uses and Shajarian responds to, has by now taken on the near-exclusive connotation of sympathy with the Islamic Republic, because the state has used it so heavily in its own rhetoric. Other revolutionaries who wanted different outcomes were branded with a myriad of negative terms, including monāfeqin (hypocrites, usually reserved for members of the Mojahedin-e Khalq Organization), mofsed fel arz (corrupt on earth), kāfar (infidel), botparast (idol worshipper), mozdurān-e estebdād (lackeys or employees of tyranny), and hezb-e bād (literally, party of wind, i.e. opportunist). Hence, Shajarian's distancing of himself from the term enqelābi may be both substantive and semantic.

He seizes such questions as an opportunity to actively reproduce his position as one that has been independent throughout.

After Saba registers Shajarian's answer, which negates his implications that he was a revolutionary, he asks him to describe how he felt when he performed *"Iran, ey saráy-e omid"* (Iran, O House of Hope). It is no surprise that Saba points to the seminal performance of this song, often referred to as "Sepideh." In October 1979, Shajarian sang this anthem-like song at a concert at the National University. The song projects immense hope for a new Iran:

> Iran, o house of hope
> On your hilltops dawn broke
> Look how from this bloody path
> An auspicious sun arose
>
> . . .
>
> O Iran, may grief never be yours
> May splendor eternally be yours
> Our path is the path of justice and prosperity
> Unity, unity is the secret of victory

At the time of its performance, this song heralded the success of the revolution, though not necessarily in favor of any particular political party. When asked about it, Shajarian is keen to point out that the song conveyed a widespread sentiment in society that "people had risen"—"but then," he interjects, "they made a lot of mistakes"—and reiterates again that the song was about the condition of "dawn breaking" and "resurrection" in society, finally adding, "then you saw a few months later in their broadcasts that Mr. Khomeini is descending from the airplane and they are playing this song over that image. I didn't at all sing this song for him, I sang it for this condition that existed among people; it wasn't for a specific person, but I saw that it was being misused as such."[12]

Shajarian has long argued against politicizing music, all the while singing some of the most political songs of his time. He counters this seeming contradiction by suggesting a different vocabulary for what he does. One interviewer said incredulously, "I don't exactly understand your position. Shajarian is a political artist. For example your [song] in 1357 (1978), 'Brother Is Drowning in Blood,' or your other works such as 'Iran, O House of Hope,' they are political works."

To which Shajarian responded, "I don't go under any one particular political umbrella. . . . In order for my work to be more inclusive, I have resisted taking any sides, and that is why I now have friends in all sectors of society, from clerics to members of political parties, and individuals who have various ideologies. But I have always kept my art far away from political parties."[13]

This seemingly minute point that Shajarian makes is in fact quite subversive. In conditions where the word *siāsi* (political) can be a real liability for an artist, Shajarian claims that what he is doing is instead *mardomi*—in the interest of the people—precisely the term that the Islamic Republic claims for its decisions and policies. In effect, Shajarian is contesting the state's definition of *mardomi* and claiming it for his own views and positions. This became even more pronounced in his statements later on, following the election unrest of 2009.

Shajarian's aversion to allowing factional or ideological politics into his artistic life stems from his lack of respect for politics, based on what he witnessed growing up, as he says himself:

From childhood on, when I accompanied my father at political demonstrations, I always felt that political matters were rivalries where a certain group was advancing certain beliefs blindly against another group and no group was going the way I liked. The path I liked was not the path where they would offer certain slogans and then change them once they achieved power.... Because I saw hypocrisy in all of their works, I generally avoided all political activity and activists.[14]

In addition—and perhaps more importantly—Shajarian expresses a keen belief that music, as a vulnerable art with a volatile status, needs to be protected from the risky business of politics:

I believe that it is in the interest of music that we not politicize it. Music had no respect in our society. We have to regain respect for it. We have to first reinstate music in its rightful place. We shouldn't tie the destiny of music to the destinies of political views and groups. The world of politics is full of fluctuation.... Like the sun, music must shine equally on all. My aim was to dissolve the cloud of suspicion that was hanging over music. The biggest political act for Iran's artists is to garner respect for the arts.[15]

For Shajarian, garnering respect for music has meant different things at different times. Before the revolution, as he was becoming better known as a musician, it meant staying away from the light atmosphere of the "*kāfeh-kābāreh*" (the Tehran cabaret scene mentioned in chapter 2). During the revolution, it meant staying out of party politics but putting music at the service of what he calls *siāsat-e mardomi* (politics in the interest of the people). Since the revolution, it has meant "moving with the people." Shajarian calls all of these decisions "treading the right path."[16] This "right path" has often put Shajarian at odds with the governments of his time, and over the last thirty years this path has distanced him further and further from the government.

Islamic Republic officials do not deny the impact of the Chavosh movement. "Music had a great role in the victory of the revolution. The Chavosh songs reflected the people's feelings about the revolution," the then executive director of the Fajr International Music Festival, Babak Rezayi, remarked in early 2009.[17] Both in writing and in casual conversation, some observers allude to the fact that despite all the difficulties for music in general, in a perverse twist of luck, Persian classical music actually benefitted from the Islamic Republic. This is a point that Fariba Adelkhah gently makes in her informative article on music in Iran's first postrevolutionary decade, titled "Michael Jackson ne peut absolument rien faire" ("Michael Jackson Can't Do Nothing at All," mirroring Khomeini's revolutionary slogan "America can't do a damn thing"), pointing to sensitivities surrounding music at the time. In his equally informative "Third Millennium Tehran: Music!" Jean During, like Adelkhah, notes the inadvertent benefits of the revolution for classical music. These kinds of statements are often vehemently—and often quite angrily—rejected by musicians themselves. During writes:

> Even the revolution and Islamization have, in the end, worked out to the clear advantage of the great music, if only by eliminating certain rival forms like motrebi, the traditional entertainment genre deemed vulgar. In any case, music making was held in even worse regard in the past than under the current regime, and in retrospect, the repression of music in the Islamic Republic appears to have been more of a period of austerity consequential to the revolution and to the war than an implementation of religious law which is otherwise susceptible to opposite interpretations.[18]

While most other kinds of music were banned following the revolution, classical musicians like Shajarian and other members of the Chavosh movement were permitted to continue their artistic activity. But the conditions were by no means advantageous for music in any form, and professionally the classical musicians, too, suffered heavily. The founder of Chavosh, Lotfi, left Iran in 1984, only to return more than twenty years later; he died in 2014, at the age of 67. Another prominent member, Parviz Meshkatian, died of a heart attack in

September 2009, at the age of 54. At his public memorial service, his longtime friend, the music researcher and professor Mohammad Darvishi, blamed the country's cultural policy makers for his friend's death, grieving that "they do not value the country's artists." Shajarian, who was the most visible public face of Chavosh, chose to stay at home for three years following the revolution and discontinue all public musical activity.

(R)EVOLUTIONS IN STATE POLICY AND MEDIA TECHNOLOGY

Following the revolution, many musicians left Iran, and even well-known traditional groups such as Chavosh had difficulty continuing their work. "When the revolution happened, we emerged from the underground and started an official institute in Hoquqi Street, where we had private concerts every month and gave lessons," explained Majid Derakhshani, a former Chavosh member.

> But it just became too difficult to continue; the regime bothered us a lot, they attacked our building several times, *Monkerāt* (intelligence forces)[19] came and confiscated our production equipment; then they asked us to change two of the ten Chavosh tapes that were co-sung by women, Hengameh Akhavan and Sima Bina.[20]

In spite of this treatment by the government, a few traditional musicians such as Shajarian and Shahram Nazeri were able to continue creating their music, although it would be another decade before public concerts were allowed.

Toward the end of the nineteen-eighties, especially as the Iran-Iraq war was coming to an end, the suppression of music was no longer tenable. A look at the hyperactive black market for both foreign and Iranian *los anjelesi* music (the style of Persian music that came mostly out of Los Angeles) was enough to reveal that music could not be effectively eliminated or even ignored. For the first time since the war, a relaxation in policy occurred, as a result of Khomeini's response to an *esteftā'* (religious/juridical question) in 1988. The question was whether the sale of musical instruments was permitted, "given that they can have lawful uses, as in the playing of marches and hymns (*sorud*)." Khomeini's response, which subsequently raised the ire of some conservative clerics, was that the buying and selling of "ambivalent" (not per se haram) instruments for the purpose of permitted enjoyments was lawful. This signaled a change in the government's position towards music, and from then on musical instruments were no longer policed as illegal.[21] The more pragmatic leaders among the state officials had realized that concessions had to be made, and Khomeini's edict—which was taken as a fatwa by his adherents—served as the basis for policy changes.[22] Soon afterwards, Khomeini decreed another fatwa, which legitimized music on radio and television, with the words that such broadcasts were "on the whole unproblematic."[23] The new policy was justified as a form of *maslahat* (expediency), pointing to the government's own interests in allowing certain—albeit highly controlled—forms of music. In effect, Khomeini decreed that music is permissible within prescribed bounds, as long as it is policed by legitimate Islamic authorities. And so from 1988 onward, some Persian classical music was once again permitted to be performed in public.

This change in policy also appeared unavoidable due to advances in media technologies. Throughout the nineteen-eighties, videotapes had joined the audiocassette tape in the ranks of small, decentralized media enabling Iranians to consume culture outside of the strictures of the state. VHS players were widespread throughout Iran, and most willing families who could afford a VHS player possessed one and regularly watched tapes with a variety of content, including *los anjelesi* and foreign music, films, and children's cartoons, all of which were smuggled into Iran and multiplied and sold on the black market. I vividly remember, when I was growing up in Tehran in the nineteen-eighties, watching the music video of Pink Floyd's *"Another Brick in the Wall"* dozens of times and studying and performing Michael Jackson's "Thriller" dance with my cousins for the grown-ups. These were hot items for cultural consumption that cut across classes, and almost everyone in Tehran seemed to have seen these videos. Also on the horizon in the late nineteen-eighties was satellite television technology, which would break into the Iranian market in the nineteen-nineties. With the flood of media technologies that the Iranian state could not entirely control, the policy of *maslahat* (expediency) was in part a recognition of the inevitable.

TREADING CAUTIOUSLY

When Shajarian reappeared after his three-year postrevolution absence, he charted a careful course that allowed him to continue his work as a musician, but on his own terms, to the extent allowed by external conditions, both governmental and societal. Throughout those passionate years when many Iranians, including artists, took ideological positions and expressed political views, Shajarian, as we have seen, joined in with what he calls the "widespread people's goal,"[24] but abstained from taking any particular political positions. Finally, in 1985, his first post-upheaval album was released, titled "Bidād." "Its title *Bidad*," writes Houchang Chehabi in an encyclopedia article on Shajarian, "was widely perceived as a punning protest against the puritanical policies of the state: While *Bidad* is a piece in the *radif*, it also means 'injustice' and can be interpreted to signify 'without (bi) voice (dād).' This seemed to be a clear reference to the regime's efforts to silence musicians."[25] The lyrics to the song are drawn from a Hafez poem:

> I see no companions around, what happened to the companions?
> When did friendship end, what happened to lovers?
> Life's water has turned muddy, where is glorious Elias?
> The rose drips blood, what happened to the spring breeze?
>
> . . .
>
> This home was the land of companions and the kindhearted
> When did kindness end? What happened to the land of companions
>   (*shahr-e yārān*)?

"*Shahr-e yārān*," cited in the last line here, can have two different meanings depending on how it is pronounced; it can be read as two separate words, as above, to mean "land of companions," or it can be read as one word, namely "*shahriyārān*," in which case the meaning turns into "kings," leading to "what happened to the kings?" If one listens closely, Shajarian's pronunciation of the last verse is closer to the latter meaning. Shajarian confirmed to me in person that he did indeed sing the word in two different ways on the album: as *shahr-e yārān* the first time and as *shahriyārān* the second time where the word appears.[26] He told me that he did this in order to pose a question about the given circumstances.

Upon the song's release, Shajarian was attacked strongly in the press, and some members of parliament even lodged a complaint. Shajarian's detractors and critics often include those who have benefitted from jobs in government institutions, such Reza Mahdavi, the director of the music department of the Arts Domain (*Howzeh-ye honari*), who commented to me caustically: "'In the middle of the holy defense [the Iran-Iraq war], when people's children were dying on the front lines, he sang about what happened to the land of kings, instead of companions! The majles was up in arms, and Shajarian's sales doubled!'"[27] In the BBC Persian documentary, Saba asks Shajarian what he was trying to say with his choice of a fourteenth-century Hafez poem for his twentieth-century song. Shajarian responds:

> It was the protest that I expressed four years after the revolution of 1979. What happened to all the talk? What happened to the promises? What happened? What did we ask for and what did we get? Why didn't the people achieve what they wanted? [musical excerpt] I saw this protest within society and within myself and I expressed it.

Mahdavi was right. The album enjoyed record sales, presumably because people welcomed the sentiments and critique expressed within the song. Interestingly, however, *Ershād* (the Ministry of Culture and Islamic Guidance) did not punish Shajarian or prevent him from continuing his work.

Both Shajarian's choice of classical music and his reliance on the centuries-old words of revered giants of Persian poetry have in effect provided him with some immunity from direct persecution. In this particular case, his choice of poem "poignantly expresses deep disillusionment, hopelessness, loss, and resentment."[28] As a genre, Shajarian's music defies government condemnation on the usual bases of Westernization and moral corruption. Shajarian's work did not break openly with the "public transcript," but aligned itself with the hidden transcript (what people cannot voice publicly) just enough for that specific community of listeners to read the signals. He created ambiguity on the word *shahriyār* through a slight difference in pronunciation, allowing space for a subversive double entendre and, hence, the communal performativity of discontent, for which no other public space existed at the time.

During the war years, Shajarian held one performance at the Italian embassy in 1982 and a few private concerts in the houses of friends. The government, however, was becoming sensitized to concerts in foreign embassies and the cultural centers of Iranian minorities and pressured them to stop hosting such concerts, so that a few years later it had become practically impossible to perform anywhere even semipublic. In 1987 Shajarian finally went on his first postrevolution European concert tour, and in 1988 took to an Iranian stage for the first time in nearly a decade, for three nights of concerts in Tehran's Unity Hall in homage to the poet Hafez, performing his sonnets to the accompaniment of one or two instruments.[29] One observer writes about Shajarian's first public concert series in Iran after the revolution:

> Six evenings were planned, but after the third, the security services were completely overwhelmed by the crowd of fans, whose numbers were several

times larger than the capacity of the space. . . . During a concert the audience began calling for a piece entitled Bidad (lit. "injustice," "misfortune"), previously published on cassette; two thousand people chanted this word with an enthusiasm rarely seen before. The artists were covered with flowers to the neck and the cheering did not stop. One wouldn't anticipate that a singer, accompanied by two or three instrumentalists, could so mobilize the masses and provoke such a passionate reaction.[30]

Then in 1991, Shajarian gave a series of eight free concerts, with a full set of instruments, in the Bahman Cultural Center of less affluent South Tehran, where he performed "*Morgh-e sahar*" for the first time inside Iran. He explained his choice of this song to me in the following words:

> I tried to sing it in concerts where I felt there was that kind of socially conscious atmosphere, where the mood existed, and because this song reflects what is in people's hearts, people connected with it quickly and the *tasnif* found its rightful place and has become a national anthem.[31]

In 1995, Shajarian wrote a letter to Ali Larijani, then head of *Sedā-va-Simā-ye Jomhuri-ye Eslāmi* (Voice and Vision of the Islamic Republic, which I will refer to from here on by its English acronym, IRIB, for Islamic Republic of Iran Broadcasting), to condemn the IRIB's lack of respect for artists' rights, to protest against its use of his music without his permission, and to prohibit state radio and television from playing his songs.[32] In the letter, he also mentioned another incident that was quite revealing and probably representative of other power struggles between artists and state broadcasters over artists' use of meaning and the manipulations of those meanings by the IRIB for its own purposes. In this particular instance, Shajarian complained that many years earlier, during the Iran-Iraq war, he had sung a song that proffered "adoration and affection for the homeland," that it was banned for many years, and that when it was finally allowed to be broadcast, the IRIB took the liberty of eliminating parts of it. "I ask you, is love for one's country and homeland an unforgivable crime?" he wrote.

The song Shajarian was referring to was "*Mihan ey mihan*" (Homeland O Homeland), which is an intimate, nonpartisan declaration of love for one's country. Importantly, though, it is also secular and lacks the Islamic signifiers that would have aligned it with the official religious articulation of the nation at the time. State media only played it after the war, and when they did, eliminated the refrain, "*mihan ey mihan*." The song was very popular when it was released on the black market (with the refrain), and then later on state media (without the refrain), and is an example of how Shajarian very subtly inserted an all-embracing, secular notion of the homeland at a time when the state was still executing political adversaries in its prisons and tolerating nothing short of full allegiance to an *Islamic* republic. By removing the refrain, state media reduced the song's patriotic meaning and zeal, thereby denying it membership in the repertoire of patriotic songs of those years, which were either more Islamic, more revolutionary, or both, in their diction. Ruhollah Khaleqi's highly emotional patriotic hymn "*Ey Iran*," mentioned earlier, has in postrevolutionary times become a symbol of opposition to the clerical regime[33]; "*Mihan ey mihan*" is similar to the much more established hymn "*Ey Iran*" in that it is fervently patriotic but does not summon religion as a uniting social force.

OPEN PROTEST

Throughout the years, Shajarian has expressed his unease with the government and its policies in various forms, though he has done so even more vocally and openly since the 2009 unrest. On various albums, he has chosen poetry that expresses the sentiments of the time, making use of the language of sadness and desperation—though in a mystical and more sublime form than did prerevolutionary political pop music—as an idiom of protest.[34] Despite Shajarian's repeated insistence that his work is not political, his attempts at walking the tightrope that would allow him to function as an artist in the Islamic Republic and yet stay true to his views and values finally came to a head after the 2009 presidential elections. A few days after the elections, the newly elected (and contested) president, Mahmoud Ahmadinejad, vilified the protestors, calling them "riffraff" in his notorious inaugural speech:

> In a football match, fifty thousand, seventy thousand spectators gather and the ones whose team has lost get angry and create problems. In Iran, in the elections, forty million people were themselves the main players and main decision makers. Now if four *khas-o khāshāk* [literally "dirt and dust," "riffraff"] agitate in the corners, know that this clear river of the people will not leave any space for their ostentatiousness.[35]

Shajarian was one of only a few artists, and certainly the most prominent of them, to take a clear stance of protest against the government's handling of people's grievances. Following Ahmadinejad's speech, he forbade state television from playing his "patriotic" songs, as he explained to BBC Persian TV on 17 June 2009:

> In these conditions, where our people are subjected to astonishing pain, and the "riffraff" have been put in motion by the whirlwind that Mr. Ahmadinejad has created, there is no place for my voice on the radio and television of the Islamic Republic, which is why I have insisted that they do not use my voice, do not upset me, and do not violate my rights. This [i.e. "my voice"] is the voice of the riffraff and forever will be. . . . Every time I hear my own voice on these media, my body shakes and I feel shame. . . . These songs that I sang in the years 1979 and 1980 were for the uprising that people achieved then, it was for that movement, but now I see that they are making a mockery of these songs in my face and others like me and the face of the people for whom I sang these songs.[36]

There was a flurry of musical activity in direct response to the events that unfolded after the 2009 election. On YouTube, dozens of old, exuberantly optimistic revolutionary songs, like "Bahārān khojasteh bād" (Exalted Be the Spring) and "Beh lāleh-ye dar khun khofteh" (To the Blood-Immersed Tulip), were set to new pictures of street protests and state violence against demonstrators. At the same time, a raft of new songs was created to support the Green Movement or to mourn the killings of innocent protestors. One of the most popular of these was Shajarian's "Zabān-e ātash" (The Language of Fire), based on contemporary poet Fereydun Moshiri's verse by the same name, in which he directly addresses the perpetrators of violence and asks them to lay down their guns and seek a humane path:

Lay down your gun
As I am disgusted by the sight of this abnormal bloodshed
That gun in your hand means the language of fire and iron
But I, in front of that evil instrument of destruction
Have nothing but words of the heart, a heart brimming with love for you
For you, an enemy friend
The language of fire and metal
Is the language of anger and bloodshed
It's the language of Genghis-like wrath
Come, sit, talk, listen to words, maybe
The brightness of humanity opens a path in your heart

Whereas Shajarian had earlier claimed that his use of old poetry was due to a lack of new writing relevant to people's situation, he was now willing to cross that self-imposed boundary and use the more explicit verses of a contemporary like Moshiri. In the *tasnif* above, Shajarian addresses government agents and *basijis* (state vigilantes) as the perpetrators of violence, as they were the ones in possession of guns and had killed an undetermined number of people.[37] It would appear that Shajarian had undergone a transformation, from the young man of thirty years earlier who asked "Give me my gun" so he could seek revenge for his slain brother's blood to the Shajarian who is disgusted by bloodshed and invites the killer—whom he now even calls his "brother"—to sit down and talk. A blogger by the name of Ruhollah Shahsavar Rais comments on his weblog, titled *Shahryaran*:

> A society that is climbing the steps of democracy must transform itself as well. When resistance fighters were seeking guns for their victory they had to expect that one day someone else too would draw a gun on them. But yesterday's fighters have seen in the mirror of history the uselessness of this bloodshed and today are proclaiming "put down your gun."[38]

Shahsavar Rais reflects the nonviolent sentiments of a large part, if not a majority, of the young protestors who filled the streets in 2009. It may well be that the stark difference between the approaches of these two songs lies in the artist's personal or political maturity, but Shajarian himself insists that he has always held the same position: "I try to move in the right direction. I have always lived for integrity, for a humane integrity, for the integrity of the earth and arts and culture. The earth must have a good name, the arts must have a good name. Politics must move in a good and respectable path."[39] When I pressed him on whether his desire to walk the "right path" has not in fact meant walking quite a political path, he responded:

> Yes, exactly, but that's only because of my opposition to bad politics.... Bad politics is against all humane and cultural phenomena, and because we want to protect these phenomena, we get positioned right against it. When you're moving with the people your position is clear.... People know what they want but it is bad politics that positions itself against culture and against people for the benefit of power.[40]

FROM *OSTĀD* TO *MOTREB*, REVOLUTIONARY TO TRAITOR

Following Shajarian's appearances on foreign Persian-language television channels after the 2009 election unrest, and his open remarks about the event, state and pro-state media launched an unprecedented smear campaign against him. State media attempted to malign him in what appeared to be concerted action. In various outlets such as the archconservative *Kayhan* newspaper and the Fars News Agency, Shajarian was reminded that he owed his "fame, wealth and artistic position" to the Islamic Republic; accused of being a nonbeliever and a traitor, "a peddler singer" who in old age was selling himself to America; and addressed in insulting terms, such as *motreb* (a disparaging term for an entertainer) as opposed to *ostād* (maestro). *Kayhan* ran its most offensive article on 5 July 2009, claiming that other "prominent traditional musicians" were calling Shajarian a traitor, possibly the biggest insult within this highly patriotic discursive context. Needless to say, appearing on the television channels of "foreign conspirators" such as BBC Persian and the Voice of America (VOA) Persian was regarded as a clear sign of a breach with the government. *Kayhan* ran a cartoon that showed a balloon-nosed, clownish Shajarian in suspenders, playing a guitar made out of a BBC satellite dish, and singing into a VOA microphone, with the concert banner reading, "Authentic music concert of reforms," attacking Shajarian's patriotic credentials, the integrity of the reformers, and the reforms, all at once.[41]

The state continued its retaliation against Shajarian by suggesting that his recitation of the pre-*iftar Rabbanā* prayer should no longer be aired on state media. This piece had been broadcast since 1979 and had for fasting households become as much a part of Ramadan as *iftar* (the breaking of the fast after sunset during Ramadan) itself. In 2010, all state radio and television channels stopped broadcasting Shajarian's rendition.[42] This was a stark reversal, as previous to the 2009 upheavals the government had talked of registering this work as a national treasure. Throughout his protests and demands that the IRIB stop broadcasting his work, Shajarian had consistently excluded his *Rabbanā* from this demand, as he considered it to belong to the people since people had established "a spiritual relationship with it." For most Iranians, even secular ones, Shajarian's *Rabbanā* is a very powerful, nostalgic prayer that evokes associations with dusk and the breaking of the fast, as it was broadcast from many radio and television channels as well as mosques around Iran during the month of Ramadan.[43] Many articles appeared in newspapers and online protesting against this decision. The popular *Musiqi-ye mā* website was representative in its sentiment that "the moments of *iftar* this year don't have the same feeling thanks to the actions of radio and television officials" and also in posting an audio file of *Rabbanā* for download.[44] Indeed, when I was spending time in Iran during Ramadan in 2011, my own fasting family members played this piece from their personal audio devices (mostly mobile phones), as did many other fasters I spoke to. This act of taking charge and playing on personal devices a prayer that state media had eliminated from its official broadcasts was itself a tactic that allowed individuals to write themselves into the virtual public space, fracturing the state's hold on the "public transcript."[45]

In the meantime, radio and television have tried to find replacements, but none of the ones I have heard were in any way comparable to Shajarian's *Rabbanā*. The well-known music critic Seyed Hasan Mokhtabad echoed others when he wrote on his *Sarbāng* blog, "This work [*Rabbanā*] has many exposed and hidden perspectives that listeners for several generations have lived and grown with."[46] Shajarian himself was relatively equanimous about it when I saw him a couple of months after Ramadan, in October 2010. His company, Delavaz, is situated in one of the more traditional narrow streets of central Tehran, and on the day that I visited in 2010, I noticed graffiti for the first time on his wall, reading *Khosro-ye sedā-ye Irān*, Iran's king of voice. There were about ten of his students gathered in front of the building, waiting for others to arrive so that they could enter together, set up an elaborate table of fruits and dishes, and decorate the room on the third floor with flowers and cushions for a seventieth birthday party for the *ostād*. When I asked Shajarian that day about the ban on his *Rabbanā*, he said:

> They think they are doing me harm, but they're only doing themselves harm. They don't even have enough social awareness to understand that you can't take something away from people that they have connected with spiritually. Now they can't find anything to replace it with. Even if I myself sing it again and sing it better, people will still prefer this version because that's the piece they have connected with. Its broadcast brought me no benefits, material or immaterial. The ban even added to my popularity and made them look worse. People think, look, they have even pulled *Rabbanā* into politics.

The state's ban on *Rabbanā* was not just meant as punishment for Shajarian, but also as a demonstration of its power toward the people who supported him and still preferred his *Rabbanā*, ignoring or opposing the government's stance that his anti-Islamic Republic positions tainted his Islamic credentials. Eventually, by the time Ramadan came around again, in the high summer of 2012, state media had chosen a replacement *Rabbanā*, which was broadcast from all channels. The voice belonged to an audibly young boy by the name of Seyed Alireza Mousavi, a Qor'an reciter, or *qāri*, from Tabriz who long before the events of 2009 had been a guest at the Supreme Leader's annual meetings with the country's best *qāris* and the winner of the 2008 Qor'an recitation contest. Photographs showing Ayatollah Khamenei's approving hand stroking the boy's head, or kissing him on the head, attest to the importance of the political allegiance of voices broadcast from state media, especially for such important national occasions as Ramadan.[47]

PROJECTING AND CLAIMING A DIFFERENT IRAN

When I talked to Shajarian in Iran in the fall of 2010, no one among my family and friends could believe that he was still in Iran and had not fled for his life. Everyone assumed that following his statements on the BBC and the VOA, Shajarian would not return to Iran. But while the state media no longer broadcast his work, his immense popularity shields him from serious government retribution such as arrest or imprisonment. He continues to live in Tehran, and in the summer of 2011 even received a permit from *Ershād* for his new album *"Morgh-e khoshkhān"* (Songbird) after almost two years in which they had simply not responded to any of his permit requests. The permit was given to him by a new director at the music department of the Ministry of Culture, a certain Seyyed-Mohammad Mirzamani, himself a musician, which points to the relative influence that lone individuals within the bureaucracy can have on arts affairs. Shajarian told me that he had heard through the grapevine that Mirzamani had gotten into trouble for doing so, which was confirmed to me by a person who works in the music department.[48]

I last saw Shajarian on 17 October 2011, the night before his London concert, and he was very vocal about the unbearable economic and political situation in Iran, about how people felt suffocated and life had become quite miserable. It was shortly before this trip that he had received a permit for his new album, although he had first performed the album's track *"Yusof-e gom-gashteh"* (Lost

Yusof) in June 2008 in Tehran's *Tālār-e Vezārat-e Keshvar* (the hall at the Interior Ministry). However, the illicit recording of the song did not emerge until sometime in late 2009, at the height of a sort of national depression in Iran following the unrest, the deaths of dozens of young people, and a general sense of desperation and apathy; it instantly hit a nerve and became very popular. Once again, Shajarian's message was cunningly appropriate for Iran's political circumstances: even when there appeared to be no hope, the cyclical nature of all things would bring better days, he sang. The album's main *tasnif* is based on a Hafez poem and contains the following verses, with every distich ending in *"gham makhor"* (do not grieve):

> Lost Yusof will once again return to Canaan, do not grieve
> The house of grief will one day become the house of flowers, do not grieve
> This grieving heart's condition will improve, do not lose heart
> And this distraught head will find order, do not grieve
> If there is life for another spring on this bed of grass
> Under a parasol of flowers will you shield your head sweet-singing bird,
>   do not grieve

When I asked him whether it made a difference to him whether he was performing abroad or at home in Iran, he said it made a big difference:

> For Iranian audiences abroad, it is more the sense of nostalgia that is strong. But in Iran, it's like you're reminiscing and sharing secrets with people you've been imprisoned with and suffered with . . . we're all in the same boat and we know what the words mean. It's also a whole different feeling doing it in Iran because it matters more; everything you say carries so much more weight.[49]

The words Shajarian uses to describe his concerts in Iran are evocative of the words in which Ruhollah Khaleqi described Aref's 1923 concert (see chapter 2). More than a gathering for musical enjoyment, the concert constituted an alternative public sphere for the declaration of political sentiment.[50] As Shajarian has become more prominent with the years, and increasingly untouchable due to his immense popularity, he has become more outspoken in his critiques. In advance of the 2009 elections, the song *"Razm-e moshtarak"* (Common Battle), now better known as *"Hamrāh sho 'aziz"* (Join Our Path, Dear One), became a sort of campaign song of the reformists and, eventually, a more all-encompassing slogan song for change. Shajarian performed

"Common Battle" as part of the Chavosh group for the album *Chavosh #7*, which the group published in 1980 to commemorate the first anniversary of the revolution.

In his first concert tour abroad following the 2009 elections, Shajarian chose to revive this song at the end of his performances, singing it again for the first time in twenty-nine years. Due to his stature, as well as his public statements about the situation in Iran, Shajarian's concert tour was bound to be highly political and politicized. At his concerts across Europe, audience members bound green ribbons around their wrists and fingers and raised their arms defiantly in the air, flashing V for victory signs in support of the Green Movement. Now, Shajarian was no longer singing just "Bird of Dawn" at the end of his concerts, he was adding "Common Battle" as the finale, an explicit song calling for everyone to come together in the struggle:

> Join our path, dear one
> Join our path, dear one
> Don't remain alone with this pain
> Because this shared pain
> Never will be
> Separately cured

It was in the aftermath of the momentous 2009 elections that Shajarian openly came out to position himself in the "them" of Ahmadinejad's "us versus them" dialectic. In characterizing his own voice as the voice of the "riffraff" and prohibiting the IRIB from broadcasting his music, Shajarian broke free from the public transcript, empowered by the many years of credibility and popularity that he had accrued.

Throughout the decades and through the changing governments and ruling political cultures, Shajarian has had to rely on various sources of cultural capital to establish his authenticity with his fans. In prerevolutionary, "Westernized" Iran, where discourses of nativism were ubiquitous, Shajarian still practiced Qur'anic recitation. This, along with his pride at not having mingled in the cabaret scene, bestowed on him a cloak of respectability with state institutions in postrevolutionary Iran. But for the formulation of trust and intimacy between the artist and his audience, these associations no longer sufficed. Following the Islamic Republic's appropriation of religion for political expedience and repression, "Islam" as a source of authenticity had lost its revolutionary cachet. Increasingly, over the last decades, Shajarian has formulated new sources of authenticity, embodying the pained "Bird of Dawn" and agitating on behalf of the people for "*mardomi*" (popular) politics.

Both before and after the revolution, Shajarian found himself in an adversarial position with the government, though for different reasons in each time period. Under the Pahlavi regime, Shajarian resigned from state radio and television in order to protest the lack of respect that the government accorded the country's traditional arts, in contrast to its fullhearted support of Western-influenced music. Under the Islamic Republic, Shajarian has protested against the government's lack of attention to and support of music in general, but ironically, he has also protested against the IRIB's support and production of "trite" pop music. In his finely balanced quest to "tread the right path," Shajarian has mobilized the overarching discourse of "justice" and "freedom" embedded in the poetry of his music. Gradually, over the years in which he has performed the lamenting cries of the morning bird, he has also shed the bird's metaphorical cloak offstage and embodied the roles of the critic and guide. This, Shajarian stressed to me, is the artist's obligation:

> There is injustice in society, and we need to speak out about these things, because the artist is the voice of protest. We live among the people and from them we receive these messages and channel them. Like the clergy: their responsibility was to guide people, to deal with their immaterial needs and beliefs, not to get involved in political and executive work. Since they have entered that realm, they have lost their place in the people's hearts.
>
> "So, in a way, the work of the clergy and artists is the same?" I asked him.
>
> "Yes, their work is to guide people, but we do it more beautifully, accompanied by music."[51]

For their part, state bodies have taken note, and attempted to cut off the lines of communication between Shajarian and his vast audience. As this text was being finalized in 2016, Shajarian had not received any government permits to perform a public concert in Iran since his comments after the Green Uprising in 2009. In a speech at a 2015 conference on Hafez, he commented, "I don't have permission, I haven't for a few years, to sing in my own country for my own people."[52] In 2014, the spokesperson for *Ershād* said, in response to a question about Shajarian's ability to give concerts: "Shajarian must make good for his past behavior and come back into the fold of Iranian and Islamic music." When pressed further, he added, "It's not possible for someone to be extremely oppositional and critical, to not accept the ground rules and standards that pertain to the system, and still expect to work."[53] Indeed, the most powerful forum for Shajarian to enable the coming together of a counterpublic—however subtly—has been the live concert. For now, state bodies ban this aging musical guide from fulfilling what he sees as being the true essence of his work, in its most potent form.

CHAPTER FOUR

REVOLUTION AND RUPTURES

IN THE FIRST MONTHS after the revolution, on 21 July 1979, Imam Khomeini gave a speech to the staff of Radio Darya, in the Caspian holiday town of Chalus, that was initially understood as a fatwa against music. In it Khomeini claimed that the "machinery of the royal regime" had aimed to "corrupt the nation and deprave the young generation," and that it had used music as a principal tool toward this goal. He went on to say that music robs youth of seriousness and makes them useless, adding:

> If you want your country to be a righteous country, a free country, an independent country, take these issues seriously from now on, transform radio and television into educational radio and television, eliminate music, and ignore them if they tell you that you're old-fashioned (*kohneh-parast*). . . . Music is treachery to the country, it is the betrayal of our youth; eliminate music completely.[1]

However, about a year before Khomeini delivered this speech, the seminal event of Black Friday had caused a great wave of revolutionary song-making. The anthem-like *soruds*, as well as underground music produced by leftist groups and the Persian classical music produced by Chavosh, extolled themes of revolution, freedom, independence, and martyrdom. Recorded at night in makeshift studios, home studios, or even just using portable audiocassette tape recorders, these songs were then widely distributed to people on the streets and among friends.[2] In subsequent years, many have claimed that these songs helped the revolution succeed.[3]

One of the first state institutions that revolutionaries occupied following the collapse of the old regime was what had been state radio and television. After "cleansing" them of staff and programming that were deemed un-Islamic, the revolutionaries started broadcasting revolutionary songs from the airwaves. The first song to be broadcast on the radio was Fereydun Khoshnud's "Iran Iran."[4] The song begins with a slow, marchlike "God, there is no God but God" (*Allah allah, allah allah, Lā-elā-ha-ellal-lāh, lā-elā-ha-ellal-lāh*), then crescendos into a faster rhythm and a more urgent, staccato-tone "God, God is great" (*allah allah allah, allah allah allah, allaho-akbar, allaho-akbar*), inspired, according to its composer Khoshnud, by the rooftop cries of "*Allah-o Akbar*" during the revolution. Against this somber backdrop, the singer Reza Ruygari comes out with a burning voice, singing "Iran Iran Iran, bombarded with machine guns" (*Iran Iran Iran, rag-bāreh mosalsalhā*), "Iran Iran Iran, heralded on the rooftops" (*Iran Iran Iran, mozhdeh shodeh bar eyvān*). These *soruds* were considered to be outside of Khomeini's category of "music," so these and other revolutionary songs—including "*In bāng-e āzādi*" (This Cry of Freedom), "*Barkhizid*" (Rise Up!) and "*Khomeini ey emām*" (Khomeini, Oh Leader)— continued to be broadcast by radio and television even after Khomeini's statement forbidding music.[5]

Still, after the ayatollah's pronouncement, doubts arose among decision-makers in state radio and television about the permissibility of music in general, even march music. Arguably the most famous voice in revolutionary and war songs in the Islamic Republic, Mohammad Golriz,[6] recalled that the first song that was commissioned for broadcast by the new revolutionary state radio and television, in the fall of 1979, was the song "*Mo'allem*" (Teacher). Golriz had sung it in praise of Ayatollah Taleqani, who died under suspicious circumstances in September 1979. The song "*Mo'allem*" is a good indication of the anxieties regarding music at the time. An ode to "the teacher," it consists only of a male choir, without any instrumentals. It begins:

Oh teacher, you who give strength to our minds and spirits
You who sacrifice your own life in order to nurture our souls

It then goes on to pledge the students' eternal gratitude to the teacher, who is "the wise leader, honorable, the companion of the prophets."[7]

For several months, "music" on state media consisted only of these stern, marchlike revolutionary *soruds*, sung mostly by male choirs, although disagreements behind the scenes meant that there would occasionally be other music as well. But things took a real turn when one of Khomeini's dearest disciples, Ayatollah Morteza Motahhari, an important theoretician of the Islamic Republic, was assassinated and revolutionaries involved in state media produced a song in his honor (as I mentioned briefly in chapter 1). In contrast to the existing fare, this song, "*Shahid-e Motahhar*" (The Pure Martyr, a play on Motahhari's last name), was based on the classical Persian repertoire and even featured passages that echoed some of the heavier, prerevolutionary orchestral pop music of the widely respected diva Hayedeh. Between melodic passages, Golriz sang searing words about the lost martyr and the Imam's grief over his death:

> O warrior, you pure martyr
> The chosen one [a play on Motahhari's first name, Morteza], the
>   manifestation of faith
> I am in shock, what should I say lest grief break my straight reed?
> In the grief of your life-loss the chest burns like a star's fire
> May the hand break that ripped that corpulent tree from the grass
> . . .
> People's indignation boiled over mourning you
> In your absence the guide [Imam Khomeini] donned black robes
> . . .
> What should I say in grieving over you when the guide said the following:
> The harvest of my life has perished
> A part of my heart is torn
> You have gone but the pain of your absence remains
> You have gone but the thought of you remains

During this highly passionate period of revolutionary fervor, there were some *hezbollahis* who had a problem even with this song, this burning lamentation of grief over Motahhari's assassination. Within the postrevolutionary Iranian context, a *hezbollahi* is generally someone who zealously supports the Islamic Republic. The word *hezbollah* means "party of God" and its current connotations came about at the time of the 1979 revolution, when a loose-knit grassroots network of people, usually connected through mosques, identified themselves as *hezbollahis*, religious people committed to Imam Khomeini and the "Islamic" revolution—dedicated specifically to the religious rather than the republican aspects of the "Islamic Republic." One *hezbollahi*'s experience of seeing this song performed for the first time on state television highlights conservative society's heightened sensitivity toward any music in those early days. At a

2011 Fajr Festival panel discussion in Tehran, Dr. A'zam Ravadrad, a sociologist at Tehran University, reported that she and her equally revolutionary friends—whom she described as all tightly *chadori* (veiled) and *debsh* (hard-core)—were on a road trip in the fall of 1979 when they stopped somewhere for lunch. On state television there appeared, for the first time that anyone could remember, Golriz's "*Shahid-e Motahhar*." Everyone was surprised, and the woman next to her jumped up and switched off the TV set. According to Ravadrad, the woman was shocked by "*āhang*" (music) on TV and could not tolerate it, and she felt such social responsibility that she did not even ask for anyone's consent. Some friends protested, while others agreed with her. However, once the Imam had given his blessing to the song, there were no more disagreements about it.

Ravadrad here highlights the importance of Khomeini's approval.[8] The song's composer, Ahmad Ali Ragheb, recounts Khomeini's delight with the song, so much that he requested to see its creators. At the visit, the Imam told them, "I could not stop my tears upon hearing this song. I do not cry much, but I cried when I heard your song. This is the best and most beautiful music that I have heard and if you continue like this I will support you."[9] Golriz, who has gone on to sing about fifteen hundred *sorud*, *āhang* (a general term for songs, including the likes of "*Shahid-e Motahhar*"), and *marsiyeh* (songs of religious lamentation), has commented that "in reality one can say that Imam Khomeini's approval of this piece . . . and his consequent statements led to the freeing of the hands of musicians in the creation of enduring and exceptional songs so that we could witness the creation of everlasting pieces during the time of the Holy Defense [the Iran-Iraq war]."[10]

Had Khomeini had a drastic change of heart about music, on the basis of one song? According to Sadeq Tabatabai, one of Khomeini's closest advisers and an official in the early Islamic Republic who had direct access to the leader due to family connections,[11] Khomeini's views did not suddenly change but had previously been misinterpreted. In a lengthy interview with the monthly music magazine *Musiqi-ye Irāniān*, Tabatabai explains that even at the time when Khomeini made those strong statements against music, there were pieces on radio and television that one could categorize as "music," and he did not object to them. He then recounts an episode in 1979 when he showed Khomeini a tape from one of the greats of Iranian symphonic orchestra music, Morteza Hannaneh, in response to which Khomeini declared, "These works have no Islamic (*shar'i*) problem."[12] Khomeini and the Islamic Republic as a whole never found any fault with Western classical music either.

This is in accordance with Khomeini's earlier jurisprudential writings on music, as well as his later fatwas in response to questions regarding music. In his earlier writings he distinguishes between that which is *ghinā* and hence forbidden, and that which is not.[13] In Islamic law, *ghinā* refers to a kind of singing that comes from the throat and causes *tarab*, which in turn is defined as a state wherein one is "overly enraptured and excited due to immense ecstasy, or overly stressed and perturbed due to immense sadness."[14] *Ghinā* is usually the fare at gatherings of amusement and vanity. "Music," on the other hand, Khomeini defines as the sound that comes from musical instruments not meant for such gatherings. However, Khomeini also explains that certain kinds of *ghinā* (singing from the throat) are halal and excluded from the above definition, namely the kinds of singing that "remind the human being of righteousness, . . . such as songs of lamentation and Qur'an recitation and the songs of camel herders for camels and [songs] in weddings."[15]

In his last fatwas on music, in 1988, Khomeini is asked whether the music broadcast from radio and television is without Islamic problems and he responds (as noted in chapter 1) that "music that is *motreb* [causes *tarab*] is haram, and voices that are "open to doubt/question" (*mashkuk*) are not prohibited."[16] When he is asked who decides whether a piece of music is *motreb* or open to question, he gives two responses that are key to understanding the fate of music in Islamic Iran. First and foremost, Khomeini responds, "*'orfi ast*," meaning that it is up to convention or custom. But he also says that the nature of music's influence on a listener can be judged by the listener herself or himself. However (as I also pointed out in chapter 1), the lack of official freedom on these matters nullifies each of these two possibilities. Fully aware of the political power of cultural production in general and music in particular, the state keeps the official field of music under tight control and does not allow listeners to judge for themselves whether a piece of music has adverse effects on them. Nor, in the absence of a free public sphere or freely elected bodies, can any truly popular customs, conventions, or laws be established.

A conversation between the Imam and then-president Akbar Rafsanjani— reported by Khomeini's son Ahmad in a public speech—also offers clues to Khomeini's views. In this dialogue, Rafsanjani is said to have asked Khomeini: "Previously you declared that music was forbidden. Why do you no longer object to it?" The Imam's answer was: "Let us assume that the music in question was broadcast by the radio of Saudi Arabia. Then I would forbid it, because wherever *tāghut* [Satan, idol worship] is in power, opposition to what he

undertakes is allowed and such opposition conforms to *maslahat* [expediency].
But here where the Islamic state is in power, a different form of regulation is
valid" (Khomeini strongly opposed the Wahhabi regime of Saudi Arabia).[17]

Hence, it is not just the music and its effect on the listener that matter, but
also the context in which it is produced and consumed. Accordingly, it appears
that Khomeini's 1979 pronouncement on "eliminating music" from state radio
and television was directed at the specific kind of music that was prevalent on
Pahlavi-era media and in spaces of public entertainment. But the core of music's
precarious status is rooted in the ambiguities of the jurisprudential reasoning
that has been given on the subject, and even the revolution's mighty leader was
not categorical on music, reflecting these ambiguities in his statements and positions. For a long time, these uncertainties have left a lot of latitude for policy
makers to wield their own power over music. Which kind of music has adverse
effects on the listener? Which music is truly in the service of the revolution, and
which is not? This latitude has also led to a paradoxical atmosphere wherein
policy on music is highly regulated but is, at the same time, sometimes bent
to yield sudden surprises. As one might imagine, everyone involved in music
comments on this with great frustration, so that the phrase "music is in limbo,"
as already mentioned, has become a sort of sad mantra of music making in
postrevolutionary Iran.

Although these uncertainties still reign, the IRIB undertook and achieved
something unprecedented in early 2011. The organization published and distributed to all radio and television offices a ten-page document titled "Requisites for the Broadcast of Music in Media" (which I briefly mentioned in
chapter 1), consisting of the most important views on music expressed by Ayatollah Khamenei, an addendum of clarifications on Islamic terms regarding
music, and lists with dos and don'ts.[18] In my conversations with officials who
were intimately involved with processes of negotiating the permissible within
state radio and television, I came to understand how the publishing of this
document had finally come about. "The source of limitations within the media
has been the views of our *marāje' taqlid* [literally "sources of emulation," the
highest-ranking ayatollahs]," a senior official within the IRIB's vetting bodies,
Dr. Hassan Riahi, told me, adding, "as the highest sources of authority they are
very influential. However, they do not agree among one another. Some regard
music as completely haram; others have conditions under which it is halal."[19]

Eventually, it appears, managers within the IRIB itself got fed up with tiptoe-
ing around the many different sensibilities, never knowing which one of their

decisions might attract the ire of an ayatollah. "There was a lot of protest. People inside the IRIB were scared that broadcasting a given piece would get them into trouble. They would self-censor. Finally, we decided we had to do something about this," Dr. Mehdi Labibi, the general director of the IRIB's radio research team, told me.[20] (According to Labibi, from the point when it was resolved that matters had to be clarified until Ezatollah Zarghami, at that time the head of the IRIB, asked the Supreme Leader to issue written edicts, it took ten to fifteen years.) "This is now our foundation, and it makes sense. Why? Because the source who gives us direction [Ayatollah Khamenei] is both a high religious authority and the country's highest political official," Labibi explained. He continued, "Many ayatollahs have positions on religious principles, but Mr. Khamenei considers the political circumstances as well. Now no other sources can interfere, because we refer to the guidelines he has given us. After all, the expectation of our channels is that they make good programs and attract viewers and listeners, and one of our most important tools in this regard is music."

Placing Khamenei in the ultimate position of decision-making regarding these matters confirms, of course, that while Islamic foundations matter, it is also the case that due to the diverging interpretations of these foundations, and because the Islamic Republic is a political entity, decisions regarding music are necessarily based not only on religious but also on political considerations. And yet, Khamenei's guidelines have not eliminated all of the gray areas in musical policy making, nor even, for that matter, most of them. This is in part because the leader's guidelines still retain the same ambiguous language. Several of the items in the "Requisites" document, for example, involve forbidding the broadcast of music that is "trite" or "immoral," terms that are up for interpretation. But even for the more-or-less clear prohibitions, such as the ban on the solo female voice, the parameters can be flexible. That is because, as Labibi explained to me, IRIB officials can send individual requests to the Supreme Leader's Bureau of Response to Religious Questions (*esteftā'āt*). So, for example, they asked whether it was permissible to have a woman's solo voice in the title song of "*Mokhtārnāmeh*" (broadcast on IRIB TV1 in 2010–2011), an epic television series on the life of Mukhtar Thaqafi, an early Shia revolutionary who set up a rebellion in Kufa to avenge Imam Hossein's martyrdom. "Because the song was religious and for the elevation of man, Mr. Khamenei allowed it even though clerics from outside of IRIB protested," Labibi told me.

I should also note that the "Requisites" document, based on the Supreme Leader's guidance, was meant only for use within the strict confines of the IRIB.

Outside of this sphere, Khamenei's own jurisprudence can be more flexible, adding to the confusion. Toward the end of 2014 and early 2015, the issue of the female solo voice came to the fore in the media mostly because of two incidents, namely a concert in Tehran's Unity Hall, where the female *āvāz* singer Mahdiyeh Mohammadkhani sang certain segments solo, and a CD publication that featured only the female singer Nooshin Taafi on the cover, although she was accompanied on all tracks by a male singer, which is permitted. This led to misrepresentations in the media that led some *ulama* in turn to believe that *Ershād* (the Ministry of Culture and Islamic Guidance) had given a permit for solo female singing.[21] Three Sources of Emulation (the highest clerical rank) close to Khamenei issued statements attacking *Ershād*'s policies and reiterating that female singing was haram. In response, the director in charge of dissemination of Khamenei's edicts, Mohammad Hossein Fallahzadeh, was asked to clarify the Supreme Leader's jurisprudence on the permissibility of women singing solo in public. In a widely published piece, Fallahzadeh responded that Ayatollah Khamenei had decreed that "if the singing is not *ghinā* and the listener does not listen to it with the purpose of pleasure or without [sexual] innocence, and if it's free of other sources of corruption, it is halal."[22] On the one hand, this shows that Khamenei's religious views were on the whole more liberal than that of other conservative *ulama*, as Labibi insisted to me. On the other hand, there are so many qualifications inserted in that short edict that it eludes any clear deduction and only contributes to the general sense of confusion within the realm of music. In many ways, it is in the interest of leaders and state bodies not to have very clear policies on music, because then officials can make decisions based on the circumstances of the time. But this also means that some fairly absurd policies continue to remain in place. For example, musical instruments, ubiquitous everywhere else, are still banned on state television. As one official at the IRIB commented to me, "No one wants to make the powerful ayatollahs with more conservative views too angry. It's not worth it."

WAR AND THE LAMENTS OF KHOMEINI'S NIGHTINGALE

Less than two years after the revolution, on 22 September 1980, Iraq, under Saddam Hussein's leadership, attacked and invaded Iran's southern Khuzestan province with the goal of annexing this oil-rich region and denying Iran access to the important Shatt al-Arab waterway. Tens of thousands of Iranians and Iraqis died in the months that followed, until Iran recaptured the occupied territory in March 1982. Still, the war raged on for another six years, until it ended with a United Nations ceasefire on 20 August 1988; it had become the longest-lasting conventional war of the twentieth century. The combination of the revolution and the war that followed it led to the flourishing of certain genres of music in Iran and caused at least one prerevolutionary genre to more or less become extinct.[23] In this first austere decade of the Islamic Republic, during which hundreds of thousands of mostly young men died at the frontlines or were maimed or taken prisoners of war, only solemn music—though not necessarily music projecting grief—was broadcast on state media, including religious lamentation and eulogizing. Imam Khomeini is said to have objected —not unlike the shah before him— to excessively sad music and to have advised the officials responsible for radio and television to produce music that projected heroism.[24] Although, as I mentioned earlier, most of these revolutionary songs were not considered to be part of the category of "music," some of them did exhibit rhythmical qualities that made them closer to what was more generally considered "music."[25] A genre of singing that was similar to that offered by eulogists, one that promoted heroism, in a vocal art that easily slides from singing into *tabaki*, a simulation of crying at will, was promoted during this decade of loss. "Music," as it was known from the Shah's time, had to be emptied of its past meanings and associations.

The war decade was filled with the lamentations of *noheh-khāns* (religious eulogists) and *maddāhs* (panegyrists), beamed from state radio and television as well as neighborhood *hosseiniyehs*[26] and mosques. Among the voices, that of Sadeq Ahangaran—"Imam Khomeini's nightingale" as he was called—came to embody those years more than any other. Born in the southern town of Ahvaz, Ahangaran was barely into his twenties when the revolution gathered steam, during which he rallied crowds with slogans. Following the revolution, he joined the vigilante revolutionary neighborhood committees (known as the *komiteh*), and once the war broke out he joined soldiers at the warfront as a eulogist who sang prayers and songs to give heart to the soldiers in a deadly war. He was a little-known *maddāh* on the national stage when he first performed the piece "Oh Blood-Immersed Martyrs of Khuzestan" (*Ey shahidān-e beh khun ghaltān-e Khuzestan*) in the presence of Ayatollah Khomeini at the Imam's house in northern Tehran, Jamaran, in late 1980. This was one of the worst points in the early days of the war, and the Iraqi army had just captured Khorramshahr in the southern province of Khuzestan. (The city of Khorramshahr was only recaptured by the Iranian army in April 1982, long after it had been renamed *Khuninshahr*, the city of blood, in common parlance and acquired mythical sta-

tus among Iranians for the heroic war acts that freed it from the Iraqi army.)
Ahangaran, himself from Khuzestan, starts his *noheh* (lament) with:

> Oh blood-immersed martyrs of Khuzestan, hail to you
> Wilting red tulips of Iran, hail to you
> Endearing devotees and warriors of the nation
> Sacrificial fighters donning bloodied shrouds . . .
> Hail to Susangerd, Khuninshahr, and Abadan . . .
> Because of you, the plains of Khuzestan are now efflorescent with red
>   tulips

Ahangaran then goes on to name some of the most important martyrs of Ahvaz.
Throughout his performance, the thousands of men in the audience beat their
chests to the rhythm of Ahangaran's *noheh* and repeat the refrain back to him. In
a piece titled "War Musicians without Instruments," the music critic Hooshang
Samani comments:

> In this new and unique orchestra . . . [the singer's] audience were not only
> listeners, they also played two key roles. The first was accompanying the
> singer like a choir . . . and the second was "chest-beating," which on top of
> keeping the beat of the *noheh*, due to its own special sound, provided sonor-
> ity or a certain coloring to the whole sound . . . culminating in a grand and
> unique orchestra without any instruments.[27]

Ahangaran's Jamaran performance was broadcast many times on state television. He went on to become a household name after that. In what is perhaps his most memorable piece, "Army of the Savior of Times, Get Ready!"
(*Ey lashgar-e Sāheb-Zamān, āmādeh bāsh āmādeh bāsh!*), Ahangaran tells of
soldiers tying red martyrdom bands around their foreheads, readying their
firearms, tying shoelaces "fast like male lions," giving each other's cheeks "last
kisses," and heading toward Karbala, where Imam Hossein was martyred, evoking their readiness to die. In a video of the song that was repeatedly broadcast
on state television during the war, Ahangaran stands like the conductor of the
orchestra that Samani describes, in front of hundreds of men in khaki uniforms
seated on the dusty desert plain that is clearly a southern Iranian warfront. Lift-
ing one hand to motion to the crowd like an orator,[28] he sings:

> Army of the Savior of Times, get ready, get ready!
> For a combat without mercy, get ready, get ready!
> You fighters ready to die, the day of courage has come

Oh you army of the "soul of God" [a literal translation of *Ruhollah*,
  Khomeini's first name], the moment for martyrdom has come
This power of the Islamists has come for eternity
To thwart the enemy, get ready, get ready!
Army of the Savior of Times, get ready, get ready!

The men wear red and green bandannas invoking various Shia imams (as well
as Khomeini), hold pictures of Khomeini and other prominent ayatollahs,
beat their chests, and repeat the refrain. The camera pans over men of all ages
and halts briefly on a young boy who is no older than ten or eleven. Later,
young men are shown hugging each other good-bye and saying "*Inshallah*,
we will reach Karbala," many of them sobbing uncontrollably, eliciting heart-
wrenching sympathy from the viewer.[29] In an interview almost two decades
later, Ahangaran says:

> I was aware when I was singing this that some of these men would find mar-
> tyrdom, some would become hostages, some would be injured, and some
> would return. I was completely aware of this. These lyrics have roots in our
> beliefs. The idea is that you who are going into battle are continuing Imam
> Hossein's path. This path will take you to heaven.[30]

Ahangaran is widely revered by some and remembered with nostalgia by
others. But as Fariba Adelkhah points out, in some circles "Ahangaran is considered a traitor because he did not cease to encourage young people to go to their
deaths on the frontlines." Yet as she also points out, the biting remarks "never
go as far as denying him acknowledgment for the quality of his musical expression."[31] The seminal narrative of martyrdom has been a defining element of Iranian identity at least since the Safavid era (1501–1736), but the Islamic Republic
has employed it to a very great extent for a reaffirmation of its identity and for
postrevolutionary nation-building. And while the culture of religious lamentation or *noheh-khāni* has deep roots and popularity within Iranian culture, it has
gained immense governmental support and public visibility since 1979.

OFFICIAL STRUCTURES: REGULATING MUSIC PRODUCTION

Once the Iran-Iraq war ended, with the ceasefire agreement in August 1988, and
the period of reconstruction began, restrictions on the cultural sphere eased up
slightly. Slowly, the first music concerts were allowed, although certain restric-

tions remained: at first, faster rhythms, 6/8 time, and women's voices continued to be completely banned.[32] But the year 1989, when the new Supreme Leader, Ali Khamenei, took office, was a watershed moment for the world. The Soviet Union was slowly but surely falling apart and simultaneously, new forms of mass media, including VHS videos and (somewhat later) satellite television technology, were spreading the cultural products of a triumphant nineteen-eighties America to the rest of the world. After the end of Iran's decade of "holy defense" (the nineteen-eighties), Khamenei launched a campaign of defense against Western "cultural invasion" (tahājom-e farhangi-ye gharb), in 1992. This defense applied to everything, including music. Persian classical music and other folkloric forms had survived the revolutionary purges of the previous decade, but now, rather than just surviving, they even seemed to gain a sort of legitimacy because of the reinvigoration of this nativist discourse. Many of the bureaucratic structures that the new state established for the regulation of music had been determined in the first years following the revolution, but they were really put to full use in the greater cultural opening after the war.

The highest state body determining overall cultural and educational guidelines and policies in the Islamic Republic is the Supreme Council for Cultural Revolution. Established as the Headquarters for Cultural Revolution in 1980, this council was created to undertake a "fundamental revolution" in Iran's universities, purge them of "professors related to the East or West" (i.e. communism or capitalism), and turn them into "healthy atmospheres for the formulation of the supreme Islamic sciences."[33] Khomeini himself had launched this initiative less than a year after returning to Iran from exile, and in subsequent speeches and decrees, had reiterated its importance:

> Getting rid of the corrupt Western culture and replacing it with the benevolent Islamic, national, and revolutionary cultures in all areas throughout the country requires such a great endeavor that its attainment requires years of painstaking efforts and a long campaign to eradicate the deeply rooted Western culture.[34]

In 1984, the Headquarters for Cultural Revolution, as it was then still called, was further enhanced, upon the suggestion of then-president (and still) Hojjatoleslam (rather than the higher rank of Ayatollah) Khamenei (the current Supreme Leader), and renamed the Supreme Council for Cultural Revolution (SCCR). According to its constitution, the full cadre of the state's highest cultural decision-makers is to be represented at the meetings of the SCCR.

The nearly two dozen members include the president of the country, who is also nominally the head of the SCCR; the chief of the judiciary; the speaker of the majles; the heads of the IRIB and the Islamic Development Organization (also known as the Islamic Propagation Organization); the ministers of science, education, and Islamic guidance and culture; and several advisers to the Supreme Leader. In reality, some of these members often send representatives, and special advisers are invited to certain topical meetings.[35] In 1984, Khamenei asked Ayatollah Khomeini about the validity of SCCR statutes, upon which the leader declared, "Rules and regulations established by the respectful High Council of Cultural Revolution must be enacted."[36] In the stairway of the SCCR's brutalist concrete building on Felestin Street, where the country's most important decisions regarding cultural affairs are made, there is now a gold-framed edict by Khamenei, in his current role as Supreme Leader, echoing Khomeini's statement:

> Cultural politics is the politics of the Islamic Republic. An Islamic revolution means that Islamic culture has found truth, roots, and foundation in all individual and collective matters of the country. Hence, we must not forget that the Islamic Revolution was truly a cultural revolution and if not all might and resources, then certainly at least the most extensive measures should be taken for cultural development and empowerment in the personal as well as social spheres in the most efficient manner.[37]

The council has its own research arm but also commissions studies from other centers. As it is a revolutionary body with the primary objective of aiding the "spread and infiltration of Islamic culture in society,"[38] it gives fundamental direction in cultural matters to all government organs. This has included an early decision to eliminate music from university curricula (though music was later reestablished as a discipline in higher education), to disseminate a culture of religiosity and martyrdom in society through material artifacts, to build defenses against the West's "cultural invasion," to control and limit access to and the use of Internet in the country, and to fight against the "prevalent culture of promiscuity."[39] Although most government statutes are available to the public and to researchers, transcripts of the sessions held at the SCCR are not. And while—aside from the direct pronouncements and edicts of the Supreme Leader[40]—it is SCCR decisions that lay the foundations for cultural policy in the Islamic Republic, there are three main organizations that deal directly with the production and dissemination of music in Iran: the Office of Music and

Song (*Daftar-e musiqi va she'r*), or simply Music Office, at the Ministry of Culture and Islamic Guidance (*Ershād*); the Music Center (*Markaz-e musiqi*) at the IRIB; and the Music Center (*Markaz-e musiqi*) of the Arts Domain (*Howzeh-ye Honari*, henceforth referred to as the *Howzeh*), a subsidiary of the Islamic Development Organization. As a musician once put it, in the domain of music, these three organs mirror the three branches of Iran's armed forces. *Ershād* is like the more neutral military; the IRIB is like the Revolutionary Guard, highly ideological, well structured and funded; and the *Howzeh* is like the paramilitary *basij*, as it is under the direct command of the leader and can be more spontaneous and less beholden to official strictures.

It is probably fair to say that no building in Tehran has caused as much anxiety, disappointment, and desperation in musicians as the unremarkable building of the Music Office situated in Tehran's Rudaki music hall complex, renamed *Tālār-e Vahdat* (Unity Hall) after the revolution. Most musicians in Tehran make numerous pilgrimages to the offices on the fifth and seventh floors of the white marble building in order to request permits for their work.[41] Situated right behind one of Tehran's largest performance halls (*Tālār-e Vahdat*, whence the name of the complex comes), the location of these offices is a cruel tease, with vistas onto the halls and the possibility for public performance, for which the majority of these musical pilgrims never receive a permit. *Ershād*'s Music Office is in charge of issuing all necessary permits for the recording and publication of music, licenses for production studios and educational centers, as well as concerts and all other music-related matters. It defines its own duties as "determining the country's main policies in the field of music, as well as organizational (*setādi*), guiding (*hedāyati*), and supporting (*hemāyati*) responsibilities." More than halfway down its constitution, there is also a clause that for many musicians is *Ershād*'s most important task, namely "the execution of supervisory roles for live performances and music production toward the protection of the cultural identity of an Islamic Iran and the prevention of cultural decline."[42]

As countless nonestablished musicians have told me over the years, it is difficult for them to see clearly enough through *Ershād*'s bureaucratic fog to apply for permits, let alone actually make it through the long process and achieve any success.[43] Only in 2008 did *Ershād* publish a booklet to guide musicians through the process, but even this publication remains quite difficult to obtain.[44] Finally, in 2011, *Ershād* made some efforts to clarify the process by putting all guidelines and necessary documents on its website.[45] The Music Council (*Shorā-ye musiqi*) is in charge of approving or rejecting musical works.

According to the council charter, there are seven members of the council, made up of the general director of the Music Office,[46] the secretary of the council, and five "music experts," who between them must share expertise in classical, traditional, regional, world, and children's music. The council meets once a week, on Sundays, on the fifth floor, and sessions last a minimum of four hours. If disagreements occur in these meetings, outside expertise is invited to resolve differences.

This bureaucracy divides music into categories, giving each category a letter code: *dastgāhi* (S for *sonnati*, meaning traditional or classical Persian music), *navāhi* (N; regional), *jadid* (J; new), *kelāsik* (K; classical), *mardompasand* (T; popular), *pop-e Gheyr-e-Irāni* (P; non-Iranian pop), *mazhabi* (M; religious), and *āmuzeshi* (A; educational). The exact term for the T category has varied over the years, as the ministry has tried to find the right word for Iranian popular music. On newer forms, this category is called *musiqi-ye ruz-e Irāni* (literally "Iranian music of the day," i.e. "contemporary") and given the code (R).[47] Every work is examined in two domains, music and lyrics, usually by two separate councils, and graded on a scale from 1 to 5, from excellent to acceptable. The submitted work must conform to certain standards, including:

1. Should not elicit indecent behavior.

2. Should not promote secularism.

3. Should not insult the Islamic Government, high clerics, Islam itself, well-known figures, or distinguished historical personalities.

4. Must have musical as well as lyrical integrity.

5. Must encourage the spirit of national consensus, unity, and solidarity.

6. Lyrics with critical content must, in their essence and symbolically, strengthen social esteem as their main theme.

7. Must guide youth, ebullient forces, and, in general, all social classes towards an optimistic future invested with open vistas and hope.

The creator of the work is given two opportunities to correct his or her work as needed, based on the council's recommendations. If the artist still fails to receive a permit, he or she cannot submit any further work for another year, in the case of lyrics, or six months, in the case of music.[48]

The task of creating a music album in Iran, especially as a newcomer without a track record or professional relations, can be truly Herculean, as one can see in the following description of the procedure. First, in order to even begin the permit process, the musician must produce a full album and submit three copies of it, with all necessary forms, to the Music Office. It takes a minimum of six weeks—and can often take several months, as I have been told by many musicians—for the councils to judge the work on its music and lyrics. If the council should request any corrections, this part of the procedure can take much longer. Once the work receives approval, it is sent on to the director of the Music Office for his final approval, and subsequently, to the obscure *herāsat* (security) agency within *Ershād*, which is an arm of the intelligence ministry lodged in every governmental organization in Iran. *Herāsat* does a full background check on the artist, talking to former and current neighbors and employers, ascertaining whether the artist is religious and nonpolitical. Once *herāsat* gives the green light, the artist must then once again seek permission from the director of the Music Office, based on *herāsat's* evaluation. Following that, the artist must submit another formal application for the cover design, and wait for its approval. The artist must then introduce his or her chosen distribution company to *Ershād* for approval, and once the work is registered with Iran's National Library, *Ershād* finally issues the permit. There is yet a separate process for obtaining permits for concert performances, as well as for founding music companies (production and distribution, studios, and shops) and educational centers.

Aside from complaints about these arduous steps involved in simply getting a permit, musicians often also complain that the people evaluating their music on these councils are either not really musicians, too old to understand, or the gatekeepers of the regime and hence too cautious to sanction anything that lies even slightly outside their comfort zone.[49] Many even went as far as saying that these council members' sole purpose was to make it impossible for musicians to get their work out. The reality is that the core members of this council have changed little over the past decades and do happen to be professional musicians themselves. Among these members are Davud Ganje'i, a virtuoso *kamāncheh* (bowed string instrument) player who is active in the various musical institutions, including the semi-governmental House of Music (*Khāneh-ye musiqi*) and the Center for the Preservation and Propagation of Traditional Music (*Markaz-e hefz va eshā'eh-ye musiqi-ye asil*); Mohammad Sarir, an Iranian orchestral composer who has been active in various official positions, including at the House of Music and state radio and television, both before and since the revolution; Majid Kiani, a virtuoso *santur* (Persian dulcimer) player who has been active in Iran's music academies; Hassan Riahi, the composer of the national anthem of the Islamic Republic, who is active in various official posts, both within *Ershād* and in state radio and television and Iran's music academies; and Kambiz Roshanravan, a composer who has been active in official posts in Iran's music academies, writes for music magazines, and has composed the music for more than one hundred films. These are some of the more permanent figures on the vetting circuits of the various music and lyrics councils within *Ershād* and the IRIB, but as most musicians I have talked to confirm, there also always seem to be one or two people without a background in music who are assigned to these councils as minders of sorts.

The other important responsibility of *Ershād* is the organization of festivals, chief among them the annual Fajr International Music Festival. The Fajr Music Festival was launched in 1986 and was first called "The Festival of Hymns and Revolutionary Music." As the festival became more comprehensive over the years, it changed its name to Fajr (Dawn) in 1989. The designation "international" was added in 1999. From the outset, the festival emphasized the showcasing and promotion of Iran's regional music.[50] Starting in 1991, however, the festival also invited musicians from other Muslim countries to participate. Fajr has different sections every year, some more consistent from year to year than others. There is always a competitive section and a section for international music; often a section for Iranian traditional and/or regional music; sometimes a section for youth music; and as of 1997, there have been sections for music composition and a section just for women's music (performed for female audiences only).[51] Both the changing nature of the sections themselves and the level of musician participation in the festival function as political barometers, reflecting the government's thematic and political preoccupations at the time, as well as the willingness of musicians to participate. The 2010 Fajr Festival, for example, was lackluster because many musicians boycotted the festival due to the state's handling of the 2009 elections and the ensuing Green Uprising. At a news conference preceding the 2010 festival, Hossein Alizadeh, one of the country's most prominent musicians, responded to a reporter's question about his absence from the Fajr Music Festival by saying that it wasn't "an artistic festival but merely a political festival" and that "musicians' only means of protest against the current conditions was nonparticipation in the festival."[52]

All radio and television channels in Iran are entirely controlled by the state. They are independent from the elected government, however, as they are under the direct supervision of the Supreme Leader. The importance given to radio and television is evident in the fact that the head of the IRIB—along with those of the judiciary and the Revolutionary Guard—is appointed by the Supreme Leader. The importance of the IRIB is also physically visible. The IRIB grounds take up some of North Tehran's most prized lands, in Shemiran, and "the organization" (*sāzmān*, as it is casually referred to by its own employees) receives a hefty budget that is determined by the government every year.[53] At the IRIB's *Balal Masjed* entrance, there was at the time of my research a large billboard with images of Ayatollahs Khomeini and Khamenei, stating the latter's view about the IRIB: "The role of the IRIB in the entire country is more important than that of other organs" (*Naqsh-e sedā va simā dar sarāsar-e keshvar az hameh dastgāhhā bālātar ast*).

With its large budget and monopoly of the national airwaves, the IRIB is the greatest producer and consumer of music in Iran.[54] The seven television stations and dozens of countrywide radio stations "use music heavily in advertising, signature tunes, and as background music during and between programs,"[55] but also as the main program content. On joyous holidays, there are often TV programs celebrating the festivities with interludes of lip-synching performers, and in recent years, various channels have broadcast entire programs featuring sanctioned pop stars for Nowruz, the Persian New Year. The programs of some state radio channels, such as Radio Payam, consist of up to seventy or eighty percent music, and the newish twenty-four-hour station Radio Ava broadcasts only music.[56]

The IRIB has its own music operations, independent of *Ershād* or any other organization. It has its own college, with a music department that trains many of the musicians who feed into its system. It also runs its own lyrics and music councils, oftentimes represented by some of the same people that sit on the *Ershād* councils, and hence offers an alternative entryway for musicians to have their work published. However, as difficult as it can be to obtain permits from *Ershād*, it can be even more daunting to make it into a contract with the IRIB, let alone receive permits. Some musicians are wary of, or entirely resistant to, working for the IRIB anyway, as it is an ideological apparatus in the service of the Islamic Republic. Still, because the IRIB is one of the few employers in the field and pays well, musicians are often inclined to work for it, or even feel that for economic reasons, they have no choice. Then again, some musicians who willingly enter into a relationship with the IRIB have fewer ideological problems with the Islamic Republic, and hence fewer difficulties with its particular restrictions on artistic freedoms. However, the IRIB has been criticized on a host of issues regarding music, and many musicians, especially the more prominent ones, refuse to collaborate with it in any form, whether for music production or interview appearances. Probably at the top of the list of the criticisms against the IRIB is its ban on exhibiting instruments on television, along with what is perceived to be its disinclination to promote higher-quality music. Considering that even Imam Khomeini declared the sale of instruments for halal purposes to be unproblematic, many are puzzled by this policy and regard it as an expression of the state's essential hostility toward music. And although it is possible for artists to enter the IRIB through preproduced work (which still has to attain the necessary permits from the organization itself), IRIB produces a lot of its work internally. This can be a very mechanical process, whereby contract poets write lyrics that are then stored in a database, which can in turn be accessed by musicians, who pick a poem, and then often choose the appropriate voice from a preestablished list of singers signed to the IRIB.[57] In a Fajr panel talk in 2011, Mehdi Labibi, director of research at IRIB Radio, said that around five hundred pieces of music were broadcast on Iran's radio stations in a single day, and that the IRIB had to work very hard to produce and meet this demand.[58]

Whereas the IRIB is a mammoth, nationwide organization controlled by the state, the Arts Domain Music Center of the Islamic Development Organization (the *Howzeh* I have referred to above) has more independence and freedom but operates with a much smaller budget. It was instituted early in 1981 and was conceived from the beginning as an ideological body with the aim of creating "committed" art for the revolution. Artists who belonged to this collective subscribed to Imam Khomeini's motto that the Islamic revolution was nothing if not a cultural revolution, and had "gathered around the current Supreme Leader in order to create and revive a cultural movement for Islam," according to the organization's own website.[59] Due to his involvement in its beginnings and his rumored love for the arts, especially poetry and traditional music, the current Supreme Leader, Khamenei, has remained "highly supportive of the *Howzeh* despite tremendous pressures from *ulama* in Qom," according to Reza Mahdavi, who was the director of the *Howzeh* at the time that I spoke to him, in 2011.[60] The head of the Islamic Development Organization is designated directly by the Supreme Leader. Since 2001, that head has been Hojjatoleslam Seyed Mehdi Khamushi, whom Mahdavi praises as a powerful facilitator. The *Howzeh*, as Khamushi described it in 2010, is "the custodian of committed art (*honar-e mote'ahhed*) and the cradle of *hezbollahi* artists, and must move in the direction of the revolutionary art that is to the satisfaction of the departed

Imam and the Supreme Leader."[61] It has its own publishing houses, colleges, music and film production, distribution arms, and festivals, and aims to "nurture and support artists, youth, enthusiasts, and talented individuals."[62] While remaining committed to the Leader and the revolution, the *Howzeh* also aims to stay "up-to-date and move with the times," Mahdavi told me.

The *Howzeh*'s declared goals are reflected in the atmosphere emanated by its centrally located campus. Its beautiful building is large and airy, centering on an open, hexagonal atrium, and while the women and men working inside all sport impeccable attire and hijab, the palpably formal religious committedness of the place still allows for a certain dynamism and artsy flair. Precisely because of its undoubted allegiance to the Supreme Leader, and because it is viewed as an educational and research center that promotes and discovers talent, the *Howzeh* allows itself to undertake projects that other institutions would not dare to undertake. So, for example, its *Andisheh* concert hall, in its various series such as "The Free Tribune," has over the years provided a platform for artists who otherwise had few if any possibilities for public performance. Most prominently, the irreverent Mohsen Namjoo performed his work there, including his "*Daheh-ye shast*" (The Nineteen-Eighties), which at one point refers to Tehran as "Ali-Ābād" (which could be interpreted as a mocking reference to Tehran as the town of Ali and belittling the Supreme Leader by calling him by his first name; I discuss this piece in chapter 7).

The *Howzeh* has its own recording studio, Studio Pezhvak, as well as its own production and distribution company, *Sherkat-e Sorush*, and together they have released hundreds of albums. It has a fair amount of independence in terms of publishing work, and has ordinarily not been required to obtain permits from *Ershād* because it has its own supervisory councils. The *Howzeh*'s then-director Reza Mahdavi personally supported the publication of Namjoo's album *Toranj*, just as he had personally supported Namjoo's appearances on the "Free Tribune" over a period of five years, despite many protests.[63] He believed Namjoo to be a real innovator, pointing out that "because of Namjoo, those young rappers and hip-hoppers knew what the *setār* and *santur* were, which they would not otherwise, because our national television does not show instruments," and added that he found Namjoo's lyrics to be unproblematic "because they were all poems by Hafez and Sa'di."[64] Mahdavi was very passionate about emphasizing that it was not the government that created problems for music in Iran, but classical musicians, who "were frightened that newer works like these might impinge on their popularity." Hence, the *Howzeh*—especially under the man-

agement of Mahdavi, who was young and had a special penchant for the "currents of the day" and the "needs of the market"[65]—straddled a fine line between
unconditional support for the Leader and the state's *hezbollahi* ethos, on the
one hand, and an openness to innovation on the other. Thus, the *Howzeh* heavily supports the production of religious music, but its subsidiary, Sorush, and
other associated companies, such as Barbad, have produced artists as various as
Namjoo, the pop star Alireza Assar, and the avant-garde modernist composer
Alireza Mashayekhi.

CHAPTER FIVE

OPENING THE FLOODGATES TO POP MUSIC

ALIREZA ASSAR

THOUSANDS ARE GATHERED in neat rows of seats to witness what is, in 2001, one of postrevolutionary Iran's most exciting and technically elaborate pop concerts of its time. They are among some sixty thousand Iranians who have managed to get tickets to this series of sold-out Alireza Assar shows at Tehran's Milad Auditorium. After several spurts of audience applause eagerly requesting the concert to begin, musicians finally start filing onto the stage, among them five men and one woman holding the frame drum, *daf*. They join a large orchestra of about twenty violins; another two dozen instruments including a bass, keyboard, guitars, and percussion; and twenty male and female choir members. The *daf* ensemble is seated prominently, high up at stage left. The pregnant pause is broken by the sound of two drumsticks dictating the beat. As soon as the orchestra starts playing the first notes, the audience breaks out in applause and cheers in recognition of the song "*Qodsiyān-e āsemān*" (Heaven's Celestials). The opening consists of the guitars, percussions, and *daf*s sounding a marchlike row of anticipatory notes, followed by an overwhelming upbeat play of violins, and the audience cheers again as the star—Alireza Assar—enters the stage and positions himself center stage in front of the microphone. The whole choir then sings in a measured, rhythmic tone:

> Oh caravan, oh caravan, I am not a night thief
> I am the champion of the world, I cross swords face to face

Assar, a stark vision of a large man dressed all in black, with long hair and a thick black beard, intones the same lines in a declamatory fashion in his deep and commandeering voice, and then continues:

> To the sky's angels every night I call *yāhu* [a Sufi's greeting to God]
> As soon as the Sufi intones "no" I intone "no God but God"
> I am not the sky's falcon to be taking the lives of partridges
> I am the phoenix of the nearby Qāf [a mythological mountain]
> When would I ever yell at a partridge?[1]

The turn of the millennium was the golden age of (state-approved) pop music in postrevolutionary Iran, when Iranians were thirsty for upbeat, home-made musical creations to lift the nation out of the somber mood of the preceding two decades. At one point, Assar performed twenty-four concerts, two each night on twelve consecutive nights, every one of them to a full house, with a total of approximately sixty thousand audience members, a record for concert attendance in postrevolutionary Iran that is unbroken to this day. He belonged to what today is popularly called "the first generation of pop singers," along with Mohammad Esfehani, Shadmehr Aghili, Qasem Afshar, and arguably the creator of the very first pop song in Islamic Iran, Khashayar Etemadi.

In a 1999 video of the performance of "Heaven's Celestials," broadcast on Iran's foreign satellite channel, Sahar, which is intended for Kurdish speakers and has laxer guidelines (allowing the exhibition of musical instruments), a younger Assar with shorter hair is joined by Esfehani and Aghili, two other giants of Iran's first post-1979 pop music scene. The Elvis lookalike Aghili plays the violin, while Esfehani sings the following stanza melodically, in contrast to Assar's declamatory style:

> Should the army-commanding emperor not submit and become my
>   confederate
> As the rightful king of the world, I shall assault all army and confederacy
> Get up in my presence, oh powerful man, and kneel in respect
> I am the king of the land; when would I ever kneel in front of you?[2]

Aghili was probably the most popular singer of this generation, a heartthrob and a talented musician. But although both his work and his persona created a lot of excitement at the time, he encountered problems with permits, was banned from state media early on, and emigrated to Canada in 2002, moving on to join the large community of expatriate musicians in Los Angeles soon thereafter.

All the other artists belonging to this first group remained in Iran, however, and Assar was arguably the most popular among these, with the highest record sales and concert attendance.[3] His debut album *"Kuch-e 'āsheqāneh"* (Amorous Migration), released in 1999, was ubiquitous in households and cars for years. To this day, Assar says, "Heaven's Celestials" is his most popular song, the song that the entire concert hall sings along with.[4] Assar himself reckons that Iranians like this song because "there is a strength in its discourse, it gives you a sense of power" (*gardan-kolofti*, literally, "having a thick neck"). The *pahlevān* (champion) is of course a recurring character of honor and valor in Persian literary culture, and the concept of this most noble and powerful figure pervades Iranian stories—most prominent among them the *Shahnameh*, the Book of Kings—and is an ideal that men aspire to both in character and physique and have cultivated for centuries in *zurkhānehs* (traditional gymnasiums or "houses of strength" in the Persianate world).[5] The song depicts a mighty being, the "King of the Land" and the phoenix of the skies. The reception among Iranians of this projection of strength was a reflection of the mood of the late nineteen-nineties, when for the first time since the revolution Iranians were sensing an improvement in their economic and political lives and were optimistic about a better future.

The song shot to popularity in part because it was played frequently on national media at the time of Eid-e Ghadir, the holiday honoring the birth of Imam Ali, leading to the perception that it had been written to commemorate him.[6] Imam Ali is considered the epitome of the spiritual and ethical chivalry cultivated in the *zurkhāneh*, where men will repeatedly chant his name and summon his blessing. He is also the Sufis' most highly revered saint, and they invoke his name in their *zikrs* (devotional prayers). This all coincided well with Assar's own spiritual leanings and (out)looks. He had developed an interest in Islamic mysticism at an early age, when his father gave him a book of Rumi's poetry for his fifteenth birthday, and eventually dressed only in black, growing his hair long and his beard thick. Part of Assar's appeal at the time was that he was a homegrown original, different from the *los anjelesi* pop singers in both personal and musical style but also different from most of the trendy new pop singers inside Iran. He represented an authentic alternative path that connected with Iran's culture of mysticism, claiming spirituality outside of the strict bounds of the Islam formally propagated by the state while also distancing himself from imitations of the Western or *los anjelesi* style.

At the turn of the millennium, a sort of Iranian New Age lifestyle had become a perceptible trend among mostly middle-class Tehranis. This lifestyle often involved engaging with the Sufi poetry of Rumi and Hafez, sometimes in private gatherings; pursuing self-improvement (*khod-sāzi*) activities, such as therapy and yoga; and adopting a more natural look by wearing Iranian fabrics and designs and taking a more liberal attitude toward hair growth. Assar adopted this lifestyle, which has been variously called "Sufi cool" or "Sufi chic."[7] It was reflected in his performances by the prominent role given to the *daf*, an instrument used in Sufi gatherings. Assar's style was also unique in musical terms. He sang in a self-assured and somber voice that did not sound anything like the sometimes gaudy "Tehrangeles" productions, and his album *Kuch* was at the time considered by critics to be Iran's most original pop recording.[8] Emanating mystical spirituality and a radiant confidence, the star and his work seemed the perfect combination of a sort of connection with the spiritually testing life-and-death years of the war and, at the same time, a clean, strong break from them.

THE CREATION OF STATE-APPROVED POP MUSIC

The revival of Persian pop music in the late nineteen-nineties, in the form of Iran-based pop creations broadcast by the Islamic Republic's official state media after fifteen years of prohibition, was one of the most momentous events in postrevolutionary Iranian music.[9] The very first attempts at pop music were mostly spontaneous productions by the first generation of young music academy graduates and their friends. These young musicians succeeded because they were supported in their efforts by music officials who were motivated by a variety of factors, chief among them to create "music for the youth" and to stop the tide of "cultural invasion," a term that referred equally to Western and expatriate Iranian creations.

There is still a lot of speculation about the reasons behind the government's decision to permit pop music. Many believe that the government decided to end its ban and partake in this lucrative entertainment sector simply because it was powerless to control the flow of expatriate pop music through the black market and newly emerging technologies such as satellite TV and the Internet. The prominent and basically accepted narrative about the launch of state-approved pop music is that the policy makers, in a calculated move, launched young singers—often with voices and styles similar to those of popular *los anjelesi* stars—in order to draw the attention of Iranians away from what the authorities considered to be depraved expatriate content invading the country and inward instead, toward a state-controlled, conforming discourse. While there is debate about the reasons behind this move, the outcome was clear: the government blunted the subversive potential of *los anjelesi* and other forms of pop music by legalizing certain types of it, and it did so by employing as its weapon of counter-subversion the very form of cultural resistance people had used against it in the nineteen-eighties.[10]

Throughout, suspicions about government intentionality have been fueled not just by the common perception that anything that happens in state media must necessarily be orchestrated and directed from above, but also by what many perceived as uncanny similarities (referred to as *shabih-sāzi* or *shabih-khāni*, imitation) between the new voices and those of prerevolutionary pop stars. In an interview conducted with one of the main facilitators of the revival of this genre, Fereydun Shahbazian, the journalists press him on the similarities between the voices, asserting that "it seems that a special policy wants this imitation to take place. The idea that this happened totally by coincidence is hard to believe. Even if we assume that this was the case, it is unexpected of the IRIB to simply concur with [it] and for this music to be able to continue without any problems."[11]

However, my research points to an inevitable confluence of several factors that facilitated the rebirth of pop music in the late nineteen-nineties, rather than to some government-orchestrated effort. For one thing, nearly a decade had passed since the grief-stricken years of the Iran-Iraq war, and the somber atmosphere had eased. Crucially, it was also around this time that the generation called "children of the revolution," namely those born around 1979, was coming of age. Although the country had been broken, this generation was young and was now yearning for bigger, brighter horizons. Many of these youths listened mostly to *los anjelesi* and Western music, even though neither the expatriate Iranian music, often set against the backdrop of Los Angeles beaches, nor the music of Madonna or Michael Jackson aptly reflected their lived realities as young people coming of age in an austere Islamic Iran. Meanwhile, the first generation of graduates from the state's music academy were looking to make their living as musicians, not so much for ideological but for careerist reasons.

The rebirth of pop was also helped in no small measure by important facilitators. These processes were happening toward the end of President Akbar Hashemi Rafsanjani's reconstruction period, when a new wave of expatriate Iranians with various kinds of cultural and/or material capital had started to return to Iran, either permanently or periodically, contributing their skills and knowledge. Significant among these for the creation of pop music was the prominent composer and producer Babak Bayat,[12] who had produced many albums in shah-era Iran, went on to produce many more in Los Angeles, and then returned to Iran again to produce the "first" pop album in nineteen-nineties Iran. Also key was the fact that the official in charge of music at state television, Mohammad Ali Mo'allem Damghani (known as Ali Mo'allem), had both an artistic background as a poet and a great deal of revolutionary capital due to his close ties to the Supreme Leader Ayatollah Khamenei. This meant that Mo'allem could enable the process of pop's rebirth from deep within the system—namely in the state's conservative propaganda machinery, the IRIB—and bypass the bureaucratic hurdles that would have stopped many others.

In the interim between the end of the nineteen-eighties, when the airwaves were filled with religious, war-related, and traditional music or national hymns, and about 1997, when the new pop really emerged, there existed what is now variously referred to as traditional pop (*pāp-e sonnati*) or classical pop (*pāp-e kelāsik*), depending on the music. Most of this music could not be classified within the registers of the war decade; it represented something new. Bijan Bijani, for example, sang mostly classical or folkloric lyrics over Iranian music arranged to Western instrumentals.[13] Hassan Homayunfal's work was often a combination of Iran's regional music, more accessible lyrics, and vocals that retained a quality of the sorrowful wartime intonations.[14] Bijan Khavari's music was often pop instrumentation with *sorud* or anthem-like stretches and also simpler lyrics.[15] Similarly, Mehrdad Kazemi's music was based on pop rhythms but contained folkloric and spiritual lyrics.[16] Mohammad Esfehani, a medical doctor who had recited the Qur'an as a member of the welcome committee for Imam Khomeini's landing in Iran in February 1979, sang verses by the classical poets Hafez and Sa'di to pop instrumentation, and even covered songs of the prerevolutionary alto diva Delkash.[17] The music these men sang was aired on state media. When it was broadcast on television, scenes of nature often provided the backdrop, or middle-aged singers, stiff as trees in tan suits, lip-synched into wireless microphones on sets decorated with colorful geometric forms and flowers. Almost all of these songs drew on classical poetry, folkloric verses, nature, or spiritual themes for content and had an overall familiar and wholesome quality to them. Homayunfal's "*Nasim-e Sahari*" (Dawn's Breeze), frequently aired on television and radio in the mid-nineteen-nineties, is representative of this genre. It's a sentimental song about nature, seeking escape from the dusty streets by riding the morning breeze, heavy on Iranian percussion instruments, flute, and violin.

For a long time, even this traditional pop music was still called *sorud* (the march-hymn genre). As Ali Moʻallem, the poet mentioned above who was the director of the IRIB's Music Center for about a decade, starting in 1995, explained to me in an interview:

> Music had to be emptied of its past meanings, and in pursuit of that goal we had to name it differently and interpret those names differently. In the first years, *tasnif* [rhythmic song], *tarāneh* [usually a "light" song], *ghazal* [love song or lyric], and all variety of vocals were withdrawn in favor of the term *sorud*. We called every kind of music that we produced *sorud*, because this term was more acceptable, referring as it did to a kind of music that had the qualities of a march, musical connections with the movement and beat of the soldier's march. In addition, the *sorud*'s theme and content was heroism or epic and encouragement to manliness, bravery, and combat. This was acceptable.[18]

Moʻallem explained that what music was called was crucial because music was one of those issues that some *fuqaha* (Islamic jurisprudents) could get very upset about. And so all music was categorized as some version of *sorud*: *sorud* for the youth, *sorud* for the elders, *sorud* for promoting the Persian language, *sorud* for children, and so on. While traditional pop music, or an approximation of what was called "pop" within the Iranian context, still existed, almost all of the lyrics distanced themselves from direct earthly matters and often had a spiritual or mystical quality to them.

What made the new pop that came after this genre wholly new and different was not just the music, which sounded decidedly more upbeat, but also the youthfulness of the new stars and even what the music was allowed to be called. The first attempts at the kind of pop music that was reminiscent of Iran's prerevolutionary pop heritage, with pop instrumental arrangements and faster beats, were made by Khashayar Etemadi, a music enthusiast in his early twenties. Etemadi had studied music from an early age and had come into contact, through his family, with prominent musicians, among them Babak Bayat, mentioned earlier, one of the great composers and producers of Iranian pop music both before and after the revolution. Etemadi was in a group of friends along with Shadmehr Aghili, Alireza Assar,[19] and Fouad Hejazi (who composed for Assar and other musicians), all of whom would later go on to make remarkable contributions to postrevolutionary pop music. They sometimes played together at weddings and other occasions, mainly performing covers of prerevolutionary pop songs.

Etemadi's voice had (and still has) a notable resemblance to the voice of one of Iran's most beloved and respected prerevolutionary pop singers, Dariush Eqbali (simply referred to by his artist name, Dariush). Dariush was the foremost political singer of shah-era Iran, and he has continued to sing politically and socially critical songs in exile since 1979. He was only twenty when he shot to popularity in 1971, and was jailed several times by the shah's regime for political songs, including "*Jangal*" (Forest), about a crushed uprising in the Siahkal forest; "*Buy-e khub-e gandom*" (The Good Smell of Wheat), about poverty and disparity; and "*Ali Konkuri*" (*Konkur* is the university entry exam), in which he sings about prison as a university. With his distinctive melancholic voice and his equally distinctive style and themes, Dariush is an unusual musical icon. He has retained many fans from his young days and accrued new fans with the years, so that young and old will sing along with his popular songs word for word at his concerts abroad. He is also unusual because he does not fit the Islamic Republic's characterization of *los anjelesi* musicians as purveyors of a depraved Westernized culture. It is conceivable that Dariush could have stayed in Iran after the revolution and remained unscathed, though his voice would likely have been silenced, like those of the pop musicians who stayed behind (the most famous of those being Googoosh and Farhad). Dariush told me that he saw no choice but to leave because of the "killings and absence of any kind of tolerance that befell Iran after the revolution."[20] He enjoys immense popularity both inside and outside of Iran to this day and is still respected among some Islamic Republic devotees, as I have learned in my conversations over the years.[21]

In the early nineteen-nineties, the Dariush soundalike Etemadi had submitted several songs to the IRIB, all of which had been rejected. It was still a few years before Mo'allem's tenure as director of music at the IRIB, and Etemadi was dealing with a music council whose members he described as showing goodwill but ultimately unwilling to green-light his work.[22] As he explained to me in a private recording studio lodged in a dark apartment, high in a residential tower in West Tehran's Sa'adatabad:

> Because of my voice's similarity to Dariush, they constantly rejected my work. They would hang the label of *shabih-khāni* [imitation] on me and write me verdicts in green ink that read, "dismissed due to resemblance to one of the overseas singers." I kept arguing with them and saying that it was

not my fault that my voice was the way it was, especially since it resembled one of the good singers who was never considered to be *mobtazal* [trite[23]].[24]

Finally, in March 1995, Etemadi received a permit for one song, titled "*Rāz-e Penhān*" (Hidden Secret) and based on a Hafez poem that starts "*Del miravad ze dastam, sāheb-delān khodā-rā*" [My heart is rent, oh, you men of heart advise!]; the song was broadcast on radio and television for Nowruz of 1995.

But Etemadi's success was short-lived at that point. In the following two years, he approached the IRIB with several more tracks and was rejected on all counts. Throughout this time, he was contemplating emigrating to Los Angeles and promoting his work there. But, as he told me:

> I believed that a current had to sweep in and eliminate this problem. Pop music had to start again. I saw the music that entered Iran from overseas, and most of it was no longer relevant to people's lives inside Iran, and still it met with a great public reception. People would play it in their houses and their cars, and this at a time when those tapes were considered a sin and one could be severely punished for having them. I was certain that we needed to talk to the country's officials and convince them that this ban on pop was a mistake.[25]

During this time, Etemadi's association with the pop music veteran Bayat motivated him to conceive of creating what he and others describe as Iran's first pop album after the revolution. The bureaucratic process for producing any music in those days was even more elaborate and time-consuming than it is today. The artist had to take a voice test at *Ershād* just to receive a permit for a test recording, which had to take place in a government-approved studio. Once recorded, the work could not be taken out of the studio until *Ershād* issued yet another permit, for the sole purpose of allowing the work to be transported from the studio straight to *Ershād*. *Ershād*'s strict protocol in that pre-satellite and pre-Internet era, when state media were the only means of widely disseminating works of cultural production, shows how highly sensitive the state considered these works to be.

By 1996, Etemadi had managed to sell an apartment and invest the money in recording the album, which he says cost him about seven million toman, equivalent to about forty thousand dollars at the time.[26] Etemadi said that the news that someone was investing that much money in an album had become the talk of the town. Under Bayat's direction, they employed about fifty musicians, and the studio costs ran high as they felt their way forward through numerous trials and errors. Quite appropriately, Etemadi called the album "*Delshureh*"—Anxiety. In my interview with him in 2011, he still spoke with immense excitement about the project:

> I really insisted that it had to be a great album to stand the test, as it was the first of its kind. Everyone was so enthusiastic. For the first time in fifteen years, the sound engineers were once again recording pop music; the capable players of the symphony orchestra who for a long time had only played anthems or film music suddenly had to play these really fast rhythms. . . . We were all experiencing this kind of work again either for the first time or for the first time in a very long time. Even the graphic designers had to make substantial adjustments for the album cover and the posters: after all, the work was very different from what they had done for traditional or classical music.

Upon completion of the album, Etemadi submitted it to *Ershād*, which took nearly two years to approve it and allow for its release. In 1997, however, even before the official release of the album, state radio and television took the liberty of broadcasting the tracks individually.

The first song to be broadcast was "*Monji*" (Messiah, Savior) also referred to as "*Mardi miāyad ze khorshid*" (A Man Will Come from the Sun). It was broadcast frequently on state radio starting in December 1997, coinciding with the birthday of Shia Islam's twelfth and hidden imam during the *Nimeh-sha'bān* celebrations, and got a lot of attention. The song begins melancholically, with fragile violin sounds, and builds up into a more up-tempo rhythm as a male choir hums, a female voice weaves in, and Etemadi's clear, strong voice begins to sing words that herald the coming of the Messiah:

> A man shall come from the sun
> A man shall come searing all injustice
> . . .
>
> A man from the generation of Mohammad
> Wearing a storm cloud as a shroud
> Of blood his horse's armor
> Humanity's last savior
> A man from a better world
> Clearer than a mirror his soul
> The dirge of Karbala his word
> Flying the highest trajectory of a dove

Aside from the resemblance to Dariush's voice, Etemadi's singing is also reminiscent of the mode of singing of the prerevolutionary era. At the same time, there are interludes that represent a stylistic continuation of the march-like songs prevalent on television in the Islamic Republic. The lyricist of this particular song, Akbar Azad, had also written for Dariush in the past, which may contribute to the similarity in style. It is not hard to imagine that many who heard this song for the first time on the radio thought that they were witnessing the return of a shah-era pop giant to Islamic Iran. Etemadi recalled the first time he himself heard the song on state radio; he was in a taxi, and "the driver just froze and stepped on the brakes. He said he couldn't believe that Dariush had returned to Iran! Surely, things were about to change in a big way." This song, however, in contrast to Dariush's subversive political songs, is well-aligned with the postrevolutionary state's promotion of religious ideology. The Mahdi, "man's last savior," occupies an important place in the Shia belief system and strikes a chord with most Iranians regardless of their political tendencies.

Etemadi's subsequent songs continued to be about spiritual or religious themes,[27] but the transition to a full-fledged kind of pop music with light lyrics and faster rhythms was slowly underway. In 1999, state television broadcast a pop song by Etemadi that was unprecedented. It made a big bang in Iran, not only because of its light musical style and content but also because of its higher visibility: literally, because it was aired on TV. Titled "*Man o to, derakht-o bārun*" (Me and You, Tree and Rain), the song is considerably different from the traditional or classical pop music discussed previously, as well as from Etemadi's own first songs, in that it had lost all religious or spiritual overtones, both in the music as well as the lyrics. Musically, it is reminiscent of the more sentimental, romantic prerevolutionary songs of Googoosh and Dariush, and the words are an ode to a nurturing love, drawing on earthly allegories and references to nature. Oftentimes, when people in Iran talk about the "first postrevolutionary pop song," they are really referring to this one, rather than "*Monji*." Despite the more risqué feel of the song (compared to the pop precedents of the time), it was perfect for state television, as its lyrics of trees and spring matched the IRIB's (much-ridiculed) practice of backing songs with footage of nature scenes, rather than with musicians and instruments:

I am the spring, you the earth
I am the earth, you the tree
I am the tree, you the spring

The caress of your rain-like fingers makes me a verdant garden
Vaulted in the midst of forests

Moreover, the lyrics are based on a poem by the dissident poet Ahmad Shamlu (1925–2000), whose work many perceived, quite rightly, to go beyond the state's unwritten red lines. Shamlu is one of modern Iran's most influential and popular poets, possibly even *the* most influential and popular, but his Marxist background and sociopolitically critical poetry meant that both the pre- and postrevolutionary governments were and are apprehensive of his work. The fact that Shamlu's words—even words of a nonpolitical, romantic nature—were broadcast on the IRIB created more curiosity still and lent itself to optimistic views in the Iran of the late nineteen-nineties that real changes, greater social and artistic freedoms, were soon to come about.

The first time that Etemadi himself appeared on television, he even sang live at a piano, with a large choir and orchestra (on Channel 5's "*Shab bekheyr Tehran*" [Goodnight, Tehran] program in 1999). This shows a great level of flexibility on the part of state television at the time, considering its unofficial ban on showing musical instruments on domestic channels. Etemadi sang his track titled "*Az Pārs tā Khazar, Irān neshasteh ast*" (From the Persian Gulf to the Caspian, Iran Is Steadfast), which praises Iran, this "lion that has broken the claws of demons." It is not only a highly nationalistic song, but also very militaristic, with prominent passages of march music and self-aggrandizing, chest-thumping lyrics. (The military nature of the song may in part explain this exception to the ban on exhibiting musical instruments, since these are also visible on television at the annual Defense Week parades and marches, although they never include a piano.) The song's overly optimistic and proud tones about Iran are an indication of the general national mood at the time:

Oh you pride of the East
On the rooftops of this world
Your name echoes
A promise of hope

As I have already mentioned, my conversations with those involved in the process of reviving pop music in postrevolutionary Iran show that, contrary to common perception, official agents within state television were rather disinclined to promote singers with voices and styles similar to prerevolutionary stars. It appears that in cases where the similarity was evident, the process that led to it was in fact an organic one, possibly explainable by the fact that the young people behind Iran's first wave of Islamic Republic pop music were simply heavily influenced by the style of prerevolutionary stars, who were the only role models they had. With time, and more flexibility on behalf of certain officials, these young people were finally permitted to showcase their music. As the homegrown Etemadi told me, upon meeting the expatriate Dariush—whom he himself and others consider "a much better singer"—he told him, "I became a singer because of my love for your voice."

However, it is also possible that after they had seen Etemadi's successful example, there was a reckoning on the part of state officials that this kind of imitation was desirable, because "voice nostalgia" could really attract Iranian listeners away from *los anjelesi* productions, so the officials stopped opposing it. Whatever the subsequent official motivations, in that first phase of pop music in the Islamic Republic, nearly every singer seemed to be filling the vacuum left by a specific exiled singer.

On the official side, the two men most engaged in facilitating this revival at state TV both deny that a conscious effort to simulate prerevolutionary pop music was at work. In the interview with Fereydun Shahbazian mentioned earlier, the interviewers remain skeptical that this pop revival could have happened without the systematic planning and approval of the highest bodies within state television. They keep pushing Shahbazian, saying "until that day, no one believed that if pop happened someday, it would start at the IRIB," insisting that this music would have never come from within conservative state television had it not been for a conscious policy decision on the part of officials. In response, a baffled Shahbazian simply says, "I just believed that the youth could produce good music, and needed it. I don't know why, but no one stopped me." When I pushed his hierarchical superior Mo'allem, on the other hand, he had an intriguing response to this question of imitation:

> Similarities in voice are accidental.. . . . This here is the mother country. Rivers flow into the ocean and not the other way around. There is no problem if the singers here are imitating their own past. This has nothing to do with Dariush or Khashayar. They had a past that they liked, and they are imitating that past.[28]

Mo'allem in effect breaks down the dichotomy between the pre- and postrevolutionary periods to reclaim the tainted past that had been fully rejected by the state that he serves. In doing so, he claims agency and authenticity for the artists that he has promoted from within state television, at the cost of legitimizing at least parts of that past. Indeed, without the reclamation of parts of that past, the creation of state-approved pop music from within the IRIB might never have happened.[29] One could even argue that only Dariush's voice could have offered that first transitional space, that first "imitation," as he was viewed as a political singer in the shah's time and hence had retained his revolutionary capital. It is telling that in recounting the first days of pop music, Mo'allem completely confused Dariush and Etemadi. Reminiscing about this phase, he told me, "the first youth who came to us . . . by the name of Dariush, yes I think his name was Dariush, brought a very epic (*hemāsi*) and committed (*mote'ahhedeh*) pop song and we gave him a permit for the song to be broadcast by state radio." Mo'allem then paused for a few moments because he was unsure about the singer's name, although in trying to get my help in remembering the correct name he kept mentioning Dariush songs. Eventually I offered the name Khashayar Etemadi, upon which Mo'allem continued, "Yes, yes, Etemadi, after him, others slowly came into the field and pop music of all kinds was produced, from pop that was sad to mystical or epic, all varieties of pop based on what Iran's music could offer."[30]

Most first-generation pop musicians ascribe the opening of official airwaves to pop music to the efforts of Mo'allem. Etemadi has said about him: "If it was not for him, I and others like me would never have gotten anywhere. He is the only person to whom Iranian pop music will forever be indebted."[31] According to Mo'allem's deputy Fereydun Shahbazian, who was in charge of music at the IRIB in the nineteen-nineties, Shahbazian had long been interested in opening the gates to *musiqi-ye pop-e fākher* (high-quality pop music),[32] but it appears from most accounts that it was Mo'allem's revolutionary capital and his approval of permits that finally launched this process.

After Etemadi's first releases, and a few concurrent semi-pop tunes by the singer Mohammad Esfehani, mostly laid over the title sequences of television serials, the works of other first-generation pop musicians also began to receive permits and be aired. Not surprisingly, most musicians' first works were of a religious or spiritual nature. An album titled *"Fasl-e āshenāyi"* (Season of Acquaintance) released in 1998 by Sorush, the IRIB's publishing arm, showcases all the singers of this very first generation except for Esfehani. The featured singers are Khashayar Etemadi, Qasem Afshar, Hossein Zaman, Alireza Assar, and Shadmehr Aghili. The most popular among these singers, as mentioned earlier, was the heartthrob Aghili. This young man with the trendy haircut and mischievous look came from a *khānevādeh-ye shohadā* (martyrs' family) background,

having lost two brothers to the Iran-Iraq war, and therefore had the right po-
litico-cultural credentials. Although his first album, *"Mosāfer"* (Traveler), contained love songs as well, the two best-promoted and most popular songs on
the album were of a sad, spiritual nature, one about a lost and eternal traveler
and another about a beautiful jasmine flower (*"gol-e yās"*). Both of these songs
allude to beings that are no longer present in the tangible world, recalling lost
loved ones in a mournful voice over melancholic music. More importantly, the
latter song's symbolism of the jasmine flower alludes to Fatemeh, the Prophet
Mohammad's daughter, aligning the song with the state's Shia ideology of promoting the *ahl-e beyt*, the house (or descendants) of the prophet.

But even on this first, sanctioned album, there are hints of the direction that
Aghili would strike in his later albums. Several other songs on this album are
about love and heartache and are sung over faster, lighter rhythms. In addition,
Aghili's undeniably youthful, visual charm contrasted with that of the other,
more serious singers in this first set. Before he was stopped in his tracks and
his voice declared *mamnu'ol-pakhsh* (banned from broadcast) on state media
after the release of his second album, *Dehāti* (Villager, read "bumpkin"), in
1999, Aghili was permitted to perform several of his songs on the IRIB's foreign satellite channel, Sahar. In one video, Aghili performs his song *"Bitābi"*
(Restlessness) with a full cast of young musicians moving ever so slightly but
visibly rhythmically behind their guitars, percussions, and keyboard.[33] Part of
the song's lyrics are:

> Thinking of you, I have no other thoughts
> Night till dawn, I like crying and waiting for you
> I know that you will come one day, a lifetime I've been waiting
> Waiting for you and this restlessness, I like very much

Although the song could very well be interpreted as being about the culture of *entezār* (anticipation) for the Mahdi, the playfulness of the music and
Aghili's gaze and smile leave no doubt that this is *entezār* for a lover and not
the Messiah.[34] Aghili's entire countenance communicates an affect that Iranians love, namely a benign mischievousness called *sheytanat* in Persian, literally "devilishness." After the surprising official release of his much-anticipated
album *"Dehāti,"* Aghili decided to leave Iran for Los Angeles, where he joined
prerevolutionary singers in spirit and style. The restrictions that motivated him
to leave eased with time; had he appeared on Iran's music scene five years later,
he may not have had to emigrate to make his music.

Like Aghili, Alireza Assar was also allowed to appear on the IRIB's foreign satellite channel, Sahar TV. But as one can see in the recording of the performance mentioned early in this chapter, Assar's performance is in stark contrast to Aghili's in terms of all the subtle visual clues. For one thing, Assar's song is unambiguously about "Heaven's celestials," leaving no possibility for human *sheytanat*. For another, it is performed with an orchestra comprised of violins and a choir, instantly giving a more "serious" cast to the music. But more importantly, Assar's own demeanor is somber, and there is no rhythmical swaying perceptible in him or in any of the other band members. Although Assar too had been planning to leave Iran in order to pursue his musical career abroad, he told me that "six or seven months after my work was published, I no longer thought about it." Assar and Esfehani are the only members of that first generation of pop stars to have maintained their star power and popularity in Iran. Over the last fifteen years, Assar has trodden a fine line in his music by producing a range of works, from mystical and spiritual pieces to lighter, more up-tempo tracks in line with the trendy dance pop of the time, as well as a few socially critical songs,[35] one album dedicated entirely to Imam Hossein and his martyrdom at Karbala (*"Mowlā-ye 'eshq,"* Master of Love), and another to Iran-Iraq war veterans (*"Bāzi 'avaz shodeh,"* The Game Has Changed).

"THIS LOVE IS DIVINE"

Alireza Assar was born in 1970 to a family of four in ancient Shahr-e Rey to the south of Tehran. While there were many music enthusiasts in his mother's family, Assar ascribes his musical career to the presence of a piano in their house that his father had purchased at some point. He started playing the piano at an early age, and at age eleven was referred to Iran's most famous piano virtuoso of that time, Javad Ma'rufi, and continued studying with him. He also took lessons in music theory from the Iranian composer and music theory professor Mostafa Kamal Purtorab. Purtorab arranged a concert for all of his students in 1984, in the Abu-Reyhan Hall of Tehran University. A public musical performance at this very austere and ideological time was extremely rare, and Assar believes that this was the very first public display of music since the ban. He says the event was only permitted because it was held inside a state university and was semi-private, as the occasion was the graduation ceremony for the medical school and no tickets could be purchased. It was at this event that Assar presented one of his compositions publicly for the first time, a piece in the *Chāhār-Mezrāb Shushtari dastgāh*. Pieces in this mode are fast and rhythmic and hence difficult to perform. Assar says he was the only performer to have composed a Persian piece for that event, and as such drew considerable attention. Several prominent musicians and music officials were present at the performance, including Shahbazian, who many years later, when the young musician got in touch to present his first work to the IRIB, remembered Assar.

In addition to the effect on his life of the accidental presence of a piano, Assar also counts his father's gift of a volume of Rumi poetry for his fourteenth birthday as life-changing. He told me he was "completely enthralled" by Rumi's *Divān-e Shams*, and in effect started leading a double life whereby he was the fun, mischievous Alireza with his friends, and an adolescent drawn to mystical poetry and literature in his time alone. Reading Rumi helped Assar grapple with all the existential questions that teenagers coming of age face, but it also helped him gain distance and stand above the confines that define human experience in general and especially that of a youth within the Islamic Republic.

Although Assar had enrolled at Tehran University to study law after high school, he was pulled away by his interest in music, never really worked toward his degree, and eventually dropped out. Throughout his twenties (the nineteen-nineties), Assar earned a living by teaching piano. He also performed privately and, very rarely, publicly, including in the 1991 theater performance of "*Piruzi dar Shikāgo*" (Victory in Chicago), one of the first musicals composed and performed in postrevolutionary Iran. Since the play happened to be about Chicago in the nineteen-thirties, the music was all jazz and blues, written by the pop music composer Babak Bayat.

This early cultural opening had been facilitated by Mohammad Khatami, minister of culture at the time, who resigned from his post not long thereafter due to accusations that he had facilitated Western "cultural invasion." During the three-month run of the play, Assar became acquainted with graduates of Iran's then recently reopened Music Academy and became close friends with Fouad Hejazi, who would later compose or arrange most of Assar's albums. Assar says of this fruitful period: "All of us who were young and doing music knew each other. It was mainly the first generation of Music Academy students and others like me, who had not studied music academically but were tied in through our friends or teachers. My *ostād* Purtorab, for example, was highly active at the academy."

Not much else is known about Assar before he became famous, in the year 2000, at which point he was already thirty years of age. In order to maintain his image as a serious and devout youth, Assar (like all other artists in the Islamic Republic who become public personalities due to the popularity of their work) had to be cautious about divulging certain parts of his private life because conservative detractors were always on the lookout, waiting to pounce on those they found to be inadequately "Islamic." At that sensitive moment for pop's revival, the de-legitimization of a performer like Assar could have hurt the entire current.

None of the first generation of pop singers came from Tehran's upper middle class, which is often called "Westernized." They all came, instead, from more traditional backgrounds, often from the central and southern parts of Tehran, and some even had revolutionary credentials such as the loss of one or more family members as martyrs. Still, given the pervasiveness of prerevolutionary pop music in families of all backgrounds, and the prevalence of music in all but the most religious and conservative households, these youths had necessarily grown up to the songs of those stars. As Assar said to me, "It is the music of our childhoods; how can you not like Ebi, or Googoosh, or Dariush?"

Assar gained some of his "formative experiences of success," as he calls it, by performing at weddings and private functions, singing songs by these banned and exiled performers in settings that could have cost him his future career had they been raided by the morality police. In addition to the necessary experience that they gained in these private spheres, Assar and his cohorts spent many nights in unoccupied studios playing music together. These were often private or makeshift studios in people's homes; sometimes, however, they were IRIB studios that one of the friends had somehow managed to arrange through connections to the organization. Needing to burn the midnight oil for their passion seems to have left a permanent mark on Assar and most other musicians I have met in Iran, who function on a night-owl schedule—although this is of course not unique to musicians in Iran. Later on, studios in garages and basements mushroomed across Tehran, but this was still in the early to mid-nineteen-nineties, when circumstances were much stricter. And finally, in addition to his performances at private functions, Assar was also able to gain singing experience in another public setting, namely on the "free zone" island of Kish in the Persian Gulf. Due to its status as a free-trade zone as well as a place of vacation and transit,[36] Kish has always allowed for a more relaxed social atmosphere. When I visited in 2002, one could hear prerevolutionary pop music blaring from the loudspeakers of outdoor cafés and restaurants.[37]

About a year before Assar's first track was aired on IRIB radio in 1999, he was invited by a friend to sing at the Hotel Kish Elite, where he performed several nights a week for a period of six months. In comparison to the weddings he performed at, where dance songs were requested, at the hotel he was freer to sing songs that pleased him. He says that while at most other venues perform-ers were singing prerevolutionary pop hits, he sang a great deal of Farhad—a serious, melancholic prerevolutionary pop star whose songs often had socially or politically critical content. But this was also where Assar tried out his first compositions based on Rumi poetry, many of which were later released on his first album. According to Assar, he created a devoted clientele of mostly elderly ladies "who consumed nothing but tea until two in the morning and sank in their nostalgia," so that after six months the owner said, "enough, you have driven me bankrupt." And yet the hotel owner, while judging him unprofitable on Kish, where Iranians went to experience a measure of freedom and joy away from the stricter settings of the mainland, nevertheless encouraged Assar to continue his work, saying he had the potential to become famous because he was unique.

This experience was instrumental to Assar's later success, as he was able to gain considerable public performance experience despite the well-known stric-tures on music at the time. Assar remained unscathed by conservative detrac-tors not just because little is known about his life before fame but also because there is little to fault: even on the "free" island of Kish, he offered a serious music program that relied mostly on a repertoire of Farhad songs and origi-nal creations inspired by Farhad's lyrical and musical gravitas. Still, singing the songs of Farhad—a singer whom the Islamic Republic effectively silenced—was not perfectly in line with the state's public transcript.[38] And so in printed mate-rial, the official story about the beginning of Assar's career is very short. In the interviews that Assar has given over the years, the only information is that his career took off quite suddenly after his friend Fouad Hejazi visited him and convinced him to audition, reasoning, "Now that the atmosphere is favorable to pop music, why don't you sing?"[39]

The same sensibilities that curtailed his willingness to openly share his musical trajectory may have led Assar to cautiously cultivate his visual image, though in the interview with me he attributed his look to happenstance rather than planning, which is of course equally possible. The way he tells it, Assar grew his beard one day and kept it because people liked it, and he just felt more comfortable wearing loose black clothing due to his Pavarotti-like figure. Cloaked in black, with his hair tied back and a long beard, Assar projected the image of a devout mystic. On his first album, *"Kuch-e 'asheqāneh"* (Amorous

Migration), Assar is captured with an intense, soulful gaze; the liner notes high-light his lineage as a *seyyed*—a descendent of the Prophet Mohammad—and a quote by the artist asks God to help him "not to leave the honest path." In other interviews he has said, "in truth my calling as an artist is to deal with people honestly, and in order to achieve this goal we have to get closer to them,"[40] and "I am a *seyyed* and without intending to show off, I believe that this success has been given to me for a higher reason, not just singing."[41] In his interviews, Assar also casually mentions that he does not socialize much, since he works throughout the night, and that he avoids "parties where men and women min-gle or alcohol is served."[42] Assar's popularity has rested in good part on his ability to embody the nuanced cultural capital of spirituality—in contrast to the more rigid piety promoted by the regime—by plugging into the differentia-tion that many Iranians make between their "honest Islam" versus the corrupt "official" Islam. This judicious act has also, at the same time, allowed him to stay under the radars of government censors, because as far as they can see, he projects many of their cultural signifiers: the color black, the beard, solemnity, and God.

Assar's first track was called *"Eydāneh"* (Eid Gift) and was based on well-known verses from Rumi's *Ghazaliāt*, in the *Divān-e Shams*, beginning with:

The beloved materialized
May it always be so
All doubts turned to faith
May it always be so

It is an upbeat song that celebrates Eid and the turning of all things to the good, with strong vocals that are closer in style to the prerevolutionary singing of Ebi, for example, than to those of the post-Iran-Iraq war and pre-pop-revival era. The song was a hit. It was broadcast on state media throughout Nowruz 1377 (March 1998). After the holidays, Shahbazian called Assar personally to tell him that his song was so popular that people kept calling the radio to request it, and invited him to sign a contract for his second song for the IRIB. Assar's second work, titled *"Omidvārān"* (The Hopeful), was again based on a Rumi *ghazal*; it starts out with a marchlike crescendo and then mellows into a softer song that spreads the message of hope, beginning with:

Do not despair dear, hope has appeared
The hope of all souls arrived from the unseen

Assar's third track was again based on classical poetry, this time a piece from Hafez's *Ghazaliāt*. Assar and his IRIB pop cohorts were not the only young musicians experimenting with classical verse in combination with nontraditional Persian music at the turn of the millennium. Classical verse had until then been the purview of Iran's classical musicians, who had diverged little in the ways in which they coordinated the poem's weight and meter with the music's rhythm. But the novelty of setting Hafez and Rumi to nontraditional music attracted many fans to Assar, who has continued to use this poetry for his work over the past fifteen years.

After the release of his first songs, Assar's work had begun to gain some recognition, but it was not until the release of his hit song "*Qodsiyān-e āsemān*" (Heaven's Celestials) that he became a household name. He attributes this to the fact that he was not "imitating" anyone, stressing in the interview with me that he has "no role models," claiming pure originality as a distinguishing mark of his being a "real artist." The debate over the imitation of voices has been fraught from the beginning, as all artists and officials involved have vehemently rejected its intentionality, while most Iranians that I spoke to in those early years didn't view it negatively, and even welcomed it.[43] Assar confirmed this perception of mine, adding:

> The similarity of voices was a prominent phenomenon and singers tried to mobilize people's nostalgia by singing like others: Dariush, Ebi, Ghomeyshi . . . and that also became a way for people to identify the new singers. Someone would say "have you heard the newest from so and so?" And if the person did not recognize the name, you'd say, "You know, the guy who sounds like Ebi." But I didn't have that advantage because my voice was not like anyone's. "Do you know Assar?" If the answer was "no," there was nothing more to say.

But even Assar's voice was being compared to that of the prerevolutionary, now *los anjelesi* Ebi, though not to the same extent as was done with other voices. While fans believed that this "resemblance" was at times willfully projected, and they often welcomed the resemblance, critics and journalists began to cast it in a negative light after a while, accusing pop singers of imitation. In a 2002 interview, Farhang Fatemi asks Assar how he responds to those who accuse him of imitating another's voice. Assar says, "You could claim that my voice has similarities to some old singer, but if someone claimed that I am an imitator of that voice, I'd disagree. In my opinion 'similarity' and 'imitation' are two different and separate issues."[44] These accusations ceased after a while, as with time the new stars gained ground and occupied their own place in the public's imagination, and were finally regarded and judged independently of the only pop precedents the country had known.

The relationship between the officials engaged in the creation of this pop music and its young makers varied. For the most part, these musicians were acting independently, choosing their own projects, and only saw Shahbazian, Mo'allem, or other IRIB officials who worked in this field occasionally, to discuss their music or other related matters. Every now and then, the officials would either directly commission work or suggest ideas. So, for example, Mo'allem asked Assar to his office in the winter of 1999 and told him that he had read a Rumi poem the previous night, cited only the first verse, and told him to look it up, as he thought it would be a suitable song for him. The story of the song's making has since accrued a legendary quality. According to Assar, he and Hejazi composed the song in a single night and took it to the *Howzeh*'s Studio Pezhvak at 5:30 in the morning. By the time others were arriving for work at the *Howzeh* office, the studio was crowded, as word had spread that something special was being recorded there. The ensemble included a large orchestra and a choir, as well as a *daf* player, who according to Assar got so carried away that he let down his long straight hair and thrashed it in circular motions as they do in Sufi gatherings. In the midst of it all, the singer Mohammad Esfehani entered the studio and was intrigued, and started humming some lines that Assar and Hejazi found so beautiful that they asked him right there to put down his briefcase and collaborate. When Assar took the track to Mo'allem at the IRIB, Mo'allem and Shahbazian listened to it and were so impressed that Mo'allem got up and kissed Assar and said, "We will broadcast this."

From what was relayed to me by the artists as well as the officials I interviewed, it appears that for a long time Shahbazian and Mo'allem had full power to accept or reject a piece personally, without actually going through the approval process of the IRIB's music and lyrics councils. When I asked Assar why Mo'allem cared so much about this poem, Assar reacted defensively, as if I had insinuated that his work had been dictated to him by a state official. "No, no, no, it's not like that, from the start if they said do this, sing that, I wouldn't do it, and they knew me. He just liked the poem and when I looked it up I liked it too . . . but I never thought it would become the most popular song in my concerts, even after twelve years," he added. As an artist, Assar is respected and has the kind of stature that would not seem to be vulnerable to accusations that he is a creation of the state propaganda apparatus. And yet, like many other artists whose sense and projection of authenticity is of paramount importance, he still seemed to feel the need to emphasize his artistic independence at this point in our interview.

"*Qodsiyān-e āsemān*" (Heaven's Celestials) was broadcast for Persian New Year in March 1999, played repeatedly on several television and radio channels, and became an instant sensation. Assar was invited to interviews with the IRIB and had soon become a recognizable star. Through 2003, Assar released one album per year and gave dozens of concerts every year all over Iran. Among his albums, the most successful was "*Eshq-e elāhi*" (Divine Love), released in 2001, with the hit singles "*Eshq-e elāhi*" and "*Khiāl nakon*" (Don't Dare Think) filling the airwaves for months on end. On this album, as on others, Assar showcases a variety of songs and themes. Its title song is an upbeat track about divine passion, with loud Sufi overtones. The main stanza is:

> I whirl and dance and drink from this chalice
> I abandon myself to the passing of days without malice
> This is agape
> God is infinite
> This is agape
> This passion is divine

"*Khiāl nakon*," the other hit single on the album, portrays a self-confident rebellion against a self-righteous lover. The track is a bossa-nova-esque tune with a lot of percussion and saxophones, and a nonchalant lover singing:

> Don't dare think that without you I'll die
> I did say that I was in love and, well, I take it back
> Don't dare think that if you leave, that will be the end of me
> Leili is only in the fairy tales; which love-induced madness?
> Who says that without you the stars won't shine?
> Let everyone know that love is a lie

Finally, the third really popular song on the album, vastly different from the two mentioned above, is "*Khiābān-khābhā*" (Street Sleepers, i.e. the homeless). It is based on a poem of the same name by the young poet Khalil Javadi, whose work is often politically and socially critical and, in recent years, increasingly satirical. Javadi, whose poetry has in the past been approved by *Ershād* and published within Iran, became famous with this piece. The musical characteristics of Assar's song are what is called *hemāsi*, epic or heroic, often performed with a full orchestra; in this case the song uses heavy drums that announce the spirit of battle, some flute, and Assar's declamatory singing of the verses, including:

Only words of steel remain
Public trust has been shattered
[Instrumental interlude]
Oh! Street-rambling children, on cold nights
Again must you warm your hands with your breaths
Oh! Homeless men and women you must bear
Crumbs from tables shall be your night's share
Standing in rows of prayer
Thugs yet again abound
Caring for nothing but your own benefit
Going where the wind blows
One day, though, the money you usurp
Shall choke you in your throat
I said it to the door
But the walls take note, word for word

In 2001, the year this album was published, analysts and the public at large were directing a lot of criticism against the government and the state, in the media and in more informal public forums, over the state of the economy. In the late nineteen-nineties and the early years of this century, state revenues from oil were rising in Iran, but inequality and corruption were also growing, as business contracts were often distributed through personal relations and systematic nepotism. Hence, the poverty of street children is presented as a direct result of the actions of those traitors at the top who have filled their pockets unjustly, who are *māl-e mardom khār*, a contemptuous phrase that condemns those who unjustly usurp that which is not theirs, and whom the song equates with Ibn Moljam (the quintessential enemy of Shias, Imam Ali's assassin). Assar says that Mo'allem personally issued the permit for this song, but only after a long discussion. He had argued with Assar that it was not in the singer's own interest to release this track. According to Assar, they then decided, however, after weighing up every consideration, that it was better that the song should be published. When I asked him whether there was a particular point in the conversation that had won Mo'allem over, Assar said, "I think the turning point came when I offered to take out any line that was not true. 'Is any of it a lie?' I asked. 'Do we not have Ibn Moljam? Do we not have hypocrites?'" Agreeing that the song was a reflection of certain phenomena in society, Mo'allem finally withdrew his objections to the song's production. This anecdote shows that Assar was not simply content with producing music "committed" to Islam and sometimes pushed for music that—at least from a state careerist perspective— did not seem to be in his own interest as a singer. Assar has openly said in his interviews that he performs a wide range of music in order to attract larger audiences: "I do 'Khiāl nakon' (Don't Dare Think) so that those who buy the album will also hear 'Khiābān-khābhā' (Street Sleepers)."[45] But perhaps the more surprising insight that this anecdote reveals is the frankness and purity of intent that underlay some of the conversations with a state official about the publication of certain musical pieces on national media.

A look at Assar's work gives one the sense that he has played a calculated balancing act throughout his career between producing IRIB-commissioned work, which some would call propaganda for the Islamic Republic (usually single tracks that are not found on his albums), work that is both close to his heart and in line with the ideology promoted by the state (such as his albums on Karbala and parts of his album on war veterans), and work that is critical of certain elements or cultures within the country's official power structures as well as the status quo.

In addition, he has kept a highly guarded profile, revealing close to nothing about his private life, and in recent years has often allowed publications only to publish interviews with him conducted by his own website. He has also re-frained from certain activities that would mark his position too clearly. While other singers of his and later generations have often accepted invitations by the IRIB to lip-synch on their programs because of the viewership that such an ap-pearance creates, Assar says he has told them that he would only sing on state television if it was live and his instrument was shown, adding, "As musicians, it is us who must protect the dignity of music. And guard our own dignity, too." From early on, he chose to appear on state television only once a year, on Eid-e Ghadir-e Kham, the night on which according to Shia lore the Prophet Mo-hammad ordained Imam Ali to be his successor. This was a strategic decision that allowed him to bolster his projection of Sufi identity while not appearing to be a puppet of the regime. And even since before the 2009 election unrest, he told me, he has refrained from appearing on IRIB television, explaining that he doesn't agree with their politics and with the way they treat musicians.

For several years, it seemed that Assar had managed to create enough ambiguity about his positions that he was both green-lighted by the government and able to retain a large fan base that interpreted his person and his works variably, according to their own stances. Those among his fans who were most interested in his oppositional stance were quick to superimpose his "Street Sleepers" on video clips featuring corrupt Iranian politicians. After the 2009 election unrest, at least two other old Assar songs were retroactively claimed for political purposes, namely "Khāk-e khunin" (Bloody Soil) and "Mowlā-ye 'eshq" (Master of Love). On the other hand, those who identify with his devout, mystical side post his songs on sites that provide collections for religious holidays, such as birthdays of imams, and post comments such as "Yā 'Ali!" or "'Ali hamrāhet bāsheh!" (May Ali Be Your Companion!) under his videos on YouTube.

In recent years, however, Assar has projected the image of an artist who is having difficulty with the state. Whereas in a 2006 interview he said, "From the first day that I've worked there has been no sign of any restrictions and I have worked in peace" and "I have never felt suffocation (khafeqān),"[46] in 2010 he cited the lack of a permit for one of the songs he had submitted as the reason why he had not published an album since 2006.[47] In his interview with me, Assar said, "I have fallen into this track where it's hard for me to just sing about gol-o bolbol [the rose and the nightingale, referring to lyric poetry]; I have to sing what appears right to me." He went on to complain that "we all secretly self-censor before we even hand in any work, so when even that work gets censored, you just don't know where else to get a song from." When I asked him what the cost was of staying on the "honest path," as he described his trajectory in the liner notes to his first CD, he responded, "It means that I haven't been able to work for five years, a high price to pay when there is the Internet, satellite TV, and dozens of new singers every day." Assar claimed that over the previous five years, he had been playing musical ping-pong with Ershād, submitting twelve tracks, being asked to replace seven of those, sending a few new ones back, being asked again to alter some, and so on. In an interview with the culture magazine 40Cheragh, he said that the specific problem was the song "Mast-o mohtaseb" (Drunkard and Officer), based on a poem by Parvin E'tesami. To what degree it was Ershād that hindered Assar all those years, as opposed to his own productivity, however, is still an open question, as both a source at Ershād and Assar's own manager told me at different times that the problem was not Ershād, but rather the fact that Assar had been dragging his feet and had not submitted a full album for assessment.

Whether Assar chose to delay the process of releasing an album because of the post-2009 atmosphere, in which many artists were "on strike," or was indeed hindered by *Ershād*'s supervisory councils, the result has been the continuing reproduction of the ambiguity of his position. Especially since 2009, but even before, it was essential to an artist's projection of authenticity for him or her to be seen to have difficulties with state monitoring. The fact that some of Assar's fans are inclined to interpret his songs in a political light was evident at a 2010 concert at which he sang "Street Sleepers" to a thirty-five-hundred-strong audience. When Assar intoned the verses about corruption and betrayal by the authorities, the crowd cheered, flashed V for victory signs, and shouted the name of the opposition candidate Mousavi. Late in 2011, after a five-year hiatus, Assar released two albums: "*Mohtaseb*," which includes the E'tesami poem, and another album, about the plight of Iran's war veterans. Aside from its title track, "*Mohtaseb*" is uneventful, with songs that are thematically dispersed and musically a mélange of various genres. His album about war veterans, on the other hand, is a perfect example of Assar on a tightrope. As it is about the war and war veterans, it is likely to please ideological music officials, at least on the surface. On the other hand, several of the songs are highly critical of the negligence of war veterans by state and society and are likely to send the right signals to those among his audience who conceive of him as a dissident artist. Criticism of the conditions of war veterans has grown stronger in society over the last years and, as a discourse, functions to highlight the hypocrisy of a state and society that in speech elevates martyrdom and sacrifice but in practice does little for its war veterans.[48]

POP GENERATION 2.0

Since the days of Etamadi's first shows, pop concerts have multiplied manifold and in any given week, unless it is a period of religious mourning, one can choose between various concerts to attend, especially ahead of joyous holidays such as *Nimeh-sha'bān* (the birth of the Mahdi) or Nowruz (Persian New Year). Alone in the Iranian calendar year 1388 (2009/2010), *Ershād* issued permits for nearly three hundred pop concerts, and that in a year of highly decreased concert activity due to the election upheavals, the Green Uprising, and the social discontent associated with that.[49] Oftentimes, the most popular stars will perform many nights in a row. In November 2012, for example, Maziar Fallahi performed eighteen consecutive concerts, two per night, to more than twenty-five thousand fans in total.[50] The fact that artists can give this many concerts is a testament to remarkable audience interest. However, as Mohammad Hossein Tutunchian, owner and manager of Qoqnus, probably the most prominent concert production and ticket sales company, told me, the need to bunch so many concerts together—what he calls *hojum-e lahzeh-i* (moment's rush)—arises from the limited periods during the year when there are no religious mourning days (and hence concerts are allowed), as well as the fact that the largest concert hall in Tehran holds only thirty-two hundred seats.[51]

And yet, multitude does not necessarily mean variety. In recent years, the top artists have remained more or less the same few, with their images ubiquitous on the pages of pop culture and music magazines: Reza Sadeghi, Mohsen Yeganeh, Hamid Askari, Ehsan Khajeh-Amiri, Benyamin Bahadori, Mohsen Chavoshi, Farzad Farzin, Alireza Assar, and a little more recently Maziar Fallahi (just mentioned above), Behnam Safavi, Sirvan Khosravi, Sina Hejazi, and 7Band. For the most part, the top artists have managed to present something original—whether in voice, persona, or music—that differentiates them somewhat from the many other acts on offer. But especially among the less successful acts, unless one listens very closely, many of the pop acts sound quite similar, and the concerts are sound-and-light extravaganzas of little originality and mediocre-to-low quality, where one can often hear variations of famous Western pop tunes integrated into the songs. It appears that now, more than a decade after the difficult rebirth of pop, the state is comfortable allowing any form of pop music as long as it does not present explicit sexual lyrics or threaten the legitimacy of the values propagated by the state.

When the first generation of pop singers started, earthly love seemed to be a taboo subject, and most singers offered lyrics that were either about other subjects altogether or about the more spiritual aspects of love. There was then a period of transition, when singers dared to sing words that weren't easily pinned down to either the earthly or the heavenly realm. Teen idol Benyamin Bahadori best embodied this period of equivocation. By 2005, his albums were being sold legally in stores, and he was promoted on state radio and television because his music was loyal to the state-imposed public transcript, among other reasons. Benyamin's most famous song was in fact picked up by the scandalous *hezbollahi* panegyrist Abdol Reza Helali (a leaked video of Helali smoking opium with a woman had made him a persona non grata among Hezbollahis for a couple of years around 2010),[52] who sang words of praise for Imam Hossein's most courageous warrior companion, his half-brother Abbas ibn-Ali, to the melody of Benyamin's song.[53] Benyamin himself, however, sings the song in a manner that suggests it is being sung for a lover, although nothing in the lyrics per se necessarily points to an earthly love reflected in the figure of a woman. Still, the song is titled "*Khāterehhā*" (Memories) and starts out with "I close my eyes and envision you," in a way that seems to denote a personal, intimate experience with a real person.[54] But Benyamin also sings religious pop songs that are unambiguously about religious figures or places. His song "*Āqām*" (My Lord), besides being a feast of longing for the hidden imam, is a tribute to the most important Shia shrines.[55] In the song, Benyamin wonders where Imam Mahdi is: whether he is a guest of Fatemeh, the daughter of the Prophet Mohammad, in Medina; or perhaps visiting Imam Hossein in Karbala; or whether he has gone to Damascus to visit Zeinab, Imam Hossein's sister, "the lady of love"; or is spending the night at the shrine of Imam Ali in Najaf; or maybe in Samarra, where Imam Mahdi's own shrine is situated. The lyrics draw on a purely Arabic and Islamic heritage, though of course that heritage has for centuries now been integrated into and appropriated for an Islamic Iranian identity.

At the time, Benyamin was a novel phenomenon of hybridity, in that he complied with the public transcript but didn't conform to it all the way, facilitating his popularity with Iranians of various religious and ideological walks of life. For example, when he sang about religious themes, he couched them in modern techno and pop beats, or he took religious melodies and secularized them into songs of romance. Similarly, while his Myspace homepage carried a Qur'anic plaque confessing "*Lā Illāh-al-il-allāh, Muhammad Rasul-allāh*" (There is no God but God and Mohammad is his Prophet), it also had slick photos of him as an urbanite with a fashionable haircut, trendy clothes, and sunglasses, not to mention the fact that he had scantily dressed girls as his friends on Myspace.[56]

By now, stars like Benyamin no longer need to pretend they are singing about God or his prophets and imams. Benyamin sings "*Āsheq shodam*," saying "I hope she won't find out . . . if she knows I know she won't stay," about a girl who is interested in a relationship without commitment, to raging fans at sold-out concerts. Most pop songs in Iran right now, in fact, also have themes either of romance, with titles like "*Bi to mimiram*" (I'll Die Without You)[57] and "*Beh 'eshq-e to*" (For Your Love)[58]; of heartache, with titles like "*Khiyānat*" (Betrayal)[59]; or even of anti-love, like "*Injā jā-ye to nist*" (This Is No Place for You),[60] a popular genre in which resentment and near-hatred is expressed toward former lovers. Judging by the shallow uniformity of these themes, it appears that the authorities have made an unwritten decision that love songs are in fact unproblematic and should be facilitated. After all, *Ershād* must sign off on every song, and the prevalence of these songs suggests that they are—at the very least—easily passed.

The relations between Iranians inside and outside of the country, and their mutual impact on one another, have been instrumental to creative endeavors in this field. As late as two decades into the Islamic Republic, Iranians inside Iran were for the most part still listening to expatriate productions streaming in from Los Angeles, and the flow of music was largely unidirectional. By about 2005, the flow had nearly entirely reversed, as music made in Iran had achieved such sophistication that not only were expatriates listening to music by the likes of Benyamin—who now, in fact, like others such as Ehsan Khajeh-Amiri, even goes on annual concert tours to Europe, Canada, and the United States—but expatriate artists were also collaborating on various levels with artists in Iran. Famous musicians in Los Angeles started commissioning their lyrics from poets like Maryam Heydarzadeh in Tehran, one of the most sought-after providers of song lyrics to musicians inside and outside of Iran, to cite one example, and working with prolific songwriters like Roozbeh Bemani, also in Tehran. As of this writing, the flow has now reversed again to some degree, as some of the most popular underground Iranian acts, including Sasy and Hossein Tohi, have now migrated to Los Angeles and are broadcasting their work back into Iran via satellite.

Nor do the authorities now seem to find much fault with fast beats or dance-inducing rhythms. This is also evident from the fare that is offered at concerts. In fact, fast pop songs have become so unproblematic, desirable, and profitable that even artists like the classical singer Alireza Eftekhari and the conservative singer Mohammad Esfehani have strayed over to the genre. When I attended Esfehani's concert in July 2011 in Tehran, the star looked very much like an official or bureaucrat of the Islamic Republic, with a loose-fitting gray suit, yellow shirt, and tinted glasses. The person next to me commented in the middle of a song, "If there wasn't music you'd think he was a *noheh-khun* [religious elegist] at a funeral." Yet Esfehani's music was what in Iran is called "disco" music: sometimes techno, sometimes reggae, almost always fast, with thrilling passages offered by a guitar player with a huge Afro.

Not all Iranian pop songs, of course, are love songs, or shallow. One of the most popular singers in Iran is Reza Sadeghi, whose biggest hit for a long time was *"Vāysā donyā!"* (Stop, World!), in which he reprimands a world that is full of sadness and conflict and asks the world to stop so he can get off. Heavyset like Assar, and also like Assar always dressed in black and sporting a beard, Sadeghi is a messenger of love and kindness. Besides promoting love in his songs, at his concerts he also calls out dozens of times to his fans: "*Man 'āsheqetam*" (I love you), which is often reciprocated by spontaneous calls of "*'Āsheqetam*" (I love you) from audience members, to which he replies back "*Gholāmetam*" (I'm your servant).[61]

The joyous nature of the songs and atmosphere offered at the hundreds of pop concerts in Iran every year makes it tempting to read the immense audience attendance as a willful act on the part of consumers, who function as secondary producers, to endorse this culture of joy against the generally depressed and somber mood that otherwise prevails in the public sphere in Iran.[62] And this is no doubt in fact partly what is happening, though the restricted nature of music production and performance in Iran complicates any interpretation of audience support. Still, just like the heavy sadness of the lyrics in some prerevolutionary pop songs functioned as an oppositional idiom, I believe that the generous promulgation of love in some postrevolutionary pop songs and at some concerts similarly functions as an idiom that opposes the officially promoted culture of grief.[63] Hence, even when the music itself is often unremarkable and the lyrics completely innocuous, musicians' use of the idiom of love and Iranians' enthusiastic support of concerts may very well be where producers and audiences alike are inscribing their messages into the public transcript.

Iran's first generation of postrevolutionary pop stars did groundbreaking work in opening the gates to pop music nearly two decades after the revolution. However, as my interviews show, there was also a will within government circles to facilitate the creation of sanitized music for the country's youth. Hence, although these musicians faced bureaucratic obstacles at first, the bureaucracy eventually came to the aid of their endeavors. This was not, however, the case for rock musicians or alternative musicians, whose work was not palatable to Islamic Republic officials.

This is said to be Aref Qazvini's first concert, held in honor of constitutionalists in 1909 in Zahir o-Dowleh's garden in Tehran. The poet and musician Aref, as he's commonly referred to (center of front row, in the white cap), is credited with being the first to turn music into a political medium. [Source & credit: Nashr-e Sokhan, Tehran]

Pop diva Googoosh (Faʿeqeh Atashin), crowned as a beauty queen in 1974, on the cover of *Javānān-e Emruz* magazine. Googoosh remained in Iran after the revolution but was silenced for twenty years by the ban on the solo female voice. In 2000, she left Iran and relaunched her career, meeting with a spectacular reception. [Source & credit: *Javānān-e Emruz* magazine]

"Composing Music Secretly," by Iman Maleki: a painting depicting the Chavosh music group producing revolutionary songs in Mohammad Reza Lotfi's basement in the lead-up to the 1979 revolution. Vocalist Mohammad Reza Shajarian is shown illuminated under the lamp. [Source & credit: Iman Maleki]

"Khomeini's nightingale," Sadeq Ahangaran, chanting to inspire and hearten soldiers at the Iran-Iraq war front, ca. 1981. [Source & credit: Nashr-e Zahra, Tehran]

Tehran University sociologist A'zam Ravadrad at a research panel at the 2011 Fajr Music Festival in Tehran. Ravadrad told a story about the shock she and her equally *hezbollahi* friends felt when they heard music on state television in the summer after the 1979 revolution. One of them jumped up and turned the TV off. Soon, they found out that Imam Khomeini himself had greenlighted "committed" music. [Source & credit: author]

Iran's preeminent vocalist of Persian classical music, Mohammad Reza Shajarian, on a 2010 cover of the popular youth culture magazine *Chelcheraq* illustrating a piece titled "The Voice of Love," one year after the state violence against demonstrators in the 2009 Green Uprising. [Source: author; credit: *Chelcheraq* magazine]

Ali Mo'allem Damghani, confidant of Supreme Leader Ayatollah Ali Khamenei and the former state media music council director who opened the gates to pop music in the late nineteen-nineties after a nearly-twenty-year prohibition. Here he is pictured in his office as director of the Iranian Academy of Arts, 2011, Tehran. [Source & credit: author]

روی الف

بهونه شعر: بامداد جویبار

نوای غریب : شعر: اکبر آزاد

سفری شعر: اکبر آزاد

روی ب

بنستر شعر: اکبر آزاد

دیباچه شعر: دکتر شفیعی کدکنی

دلشوره شعر: اکبر آزاد

دلشوره

DELSHOOREH

خواننده: خشایار اعتمادی

آهنگساز: بابک بیات

تنظیم : فؤاد حجازی

Cover of the cassette tape of Khashayar Etemadi's 1997 album *Delshureh*, recognized as the first pop music album in postrevolutionary Iran. Etemadi's voice has similarities to the voice of prerevolutionary star Dariush Eqbali (who emigrated to Los Angeles in 1979), which added to Etemadi's popularity. [Source: author; credit: Sherkat-e Payghām-e Sahar]

Pop star Alireza Assar on set, singing with the TV Philharmonic Orchestra, conducted by Nader Mortezapur, in 2001. This performance, broadcast once on state television, showing a long shot of the instruments, was one of very few occasions where instruments were shown on Islamic Republic television. Assar was one of the most popular of the first generation of pop stars and still holds the record in postrevolutionary Iran for the number of consecutive concerts given: he gave twenty-four concerts on twelve consecutive nights (two per night) in 2003 in Tehran, with a total of sixty thousand tickets sold. [Source & credit: Alireza Assar]

The "first" underground rock concert in Tehran, by the band O-Hum, in the Russian Orthodox Church in 2001. O-Hum finally managed to get a permit and stage an authorized concert in 2014 in Tehran. It had been long enough since the band's beginnings that some fans brought their children to the show. [Source & credit: Ali Shahbazyar]

O-Hum concert ticket, 2001. The band was able to stage a semipublic concert at this church because in Iran the religious and cultural centers of minorities, like foreign embassies, are sovereign spaces. [Source & credit: Ali Shahbazyar]

Two administrators in one of the offices on the seventh floor of the Music Office of the Ministry of Culture and Islamic Guidance in Tehran, 2011. This is where musicians must submit their paperwork to start the daunting task of obtaining permission to publish their music or give concerts. [Source & credit: author]

Mohsen Namjoo on a 2007 cover of the magazine *Maqām-e Musiqāyi*, which was published by the conservative governmental arts organization, the *Howzeh*. The *Howzeh* also gave Namjoo a permit for his album *Toranj*, which infuriated officials in other organizations. This issue of the magazine was confiscated from newsstands after its publication because it featured Namjoo. [Source: author; credit: *Maqām-e Musiqāyi*]

Iran's "Godfather of *rap-e farsi*," Soroush Lashkary, aka Hichkas (left), leaving a studio
in Tehran with his collaborator Mahdyar Aghajani in 2007. They both left Iran for good
following the 2009 Green Uprising; Hichkas's "*Yeh Ruz-e Khub Miyād*" (A Good Day
Will Come) was a criticism of the bloodshed. Hichkas is flashing the Tehran rapper
hand signal (021, Tehran's telephone area code). [Credit: Ehsan Maleki]

Reza Sadeghi, the pop musician nicknamed "Sultan of the Realm of Love," shouting "I love you" to his fans at a fairly typical pop concert in Tehran's Milad Auditorium, 2011. [Source & credit: author]

CHAPTER SIX

THE REBIRTH OF INDEPENDENT MUSIC

THE BEETHOVEN AUDITORIUM in the nongovernmental House of Artists in central Tehran was filled way beyond its three-hundred-person capacity on a Sunday afternoon in early March 2008, with at least forty people crowding its entrance and spilling over into the adjacent hallway. Inside, the heat was on—both literally and figuratively. A visibly excited audience of mostly twenty-something men and women was there for a discussion with and about Mohsen Namjoo, the new sensation whose work combined classical and folk Persian music and poetry with Western influences like rock and blues, in an arguably unprecedented way. Namjoo's unconventional fusion of music had stirred a lot of debate and controversy from the beginning, and everyone seemed to have an opinion about it. Some hailed it as a breakthrough in Iranian music, others discounted it as nonsense, and still others regarded it with amused bafflement. Indeed, the scene at the cultural center was more like that of a courthouse, with Namjoo on trial.

The only person sitting still seemed to be the artist himself, positioned center stage, with a slightly hunched back, a thick fountain of shoulder-length gray hair, and a distinctive aquiline nose, looking many years older than his actual thirty-two. The moderator of the event started the session diplomatically, pointing out that "whether we like his music or not, we can't deny that it has produced a strong reaction." At first there was a discussion of the number of copies that Namjoo's first legally published album—*"Toranj"* (Citron)—had sold since its release six months earlier; the moderator said he believed that the official number of eighteen thousand seemed to be correct, basing his estimation on the sale of "*Toranj*" at Beethoven, one of the most popular music stores in Tehran. He added that he believed the rumors to be incorrect that said eighty thousand copies had been sold in the first few weeks alone. Namjoo, who all the while looked detached, even annoyed at having to take part in his own trial, responded that he had no idea about the number of records sold, since he had not received any remuneration from those sales, but pointed out that many more people had downloaded his work from the Internet even before it came out as an album.

Once the gratuitous and unresolved exercise of confirming the work's popularity in terms of official sales numbers had been carried out, the first critic began to explain the criteria by which he would judge the singer's work, among them "expertise in music." But a few minutes into his explanations, there were already protests from the restless audience, with one voice heard over the others shouting, "His work is different. You can't judge it with your usual criteria." Then an official sitting in the first row got up and implored, "Could you please all just be quiet so that the critique can continue?" The critic then continued in a monotone voice to list his categories of judgment, "Three, power and artistic potential of the music, and four, the degree of sincerity in the music and its philanthropy [*mardom-dusti*]." But before long, he was interrupted again: "Let Namjoo speak for himself," people in the audience cried again, and at this point, the other critic, who had not even spoken yet, got up and complained about the audience's "intolerable impatience." While quitting the stage, he added, "Mr. Namjoo's work is much ado about nothing, and musically there is nothing new in it. But from the view of studying its audience and the reception it has received, it is worth reflection and research." With that barely disguised insult, he left the stage. An audience member then got up and said that the Persian poets Hafez and Rumi, both of whose lyrics Namjoo uses, had no place in blues and rock, but he too was shot down by a girl who shouted, "If we wanted to listen to Hafez set to classical music we'd be listening to Shajarian, thank you very much!" Not long afterwards, the critic who had spoken first left the stage as well, reiterating the other's comment that this session itself was more deserving of sociological study than Namjoo's music.

Aside from the moderator, the stage was now left entirely to Namjoo, and although several people rose from the audience to criticize his music for all its faults or apparent banality, many more rose up to shut down those critics. One official from the city council, Abbas Sajjadi, who had initiated the "Song Critique" series (*Barnāmeh-ye naqd-e she'r*) of which this session was a part, spoke in a calming voice, referring to the Constitutional Revolution and the flowering of a new genre of protest songs and saying about Namjoo: "It is society that in effect urges artists to break with structures and traditions and produce new forms. For three decades, the only thing we have had to say about music is that it should be *fākher* [fine/ high-quality]. If music doesn't progress with society, there will be a vacuum and that vacuum will be filled." Sajjadi expressed this sentiment with the finesse of ambiguous speech that an open-minded official in the Islamic Republic must learn to master if he is to succeed within the system, which meant that it was not clear whether he supported this particular "filling" of this vacuum or not.

Finally, two songs from the *Toranj* album were played for communal listening. This prompted a youngish composer of classical Persian music with long black hair and a beard to get up in the third row and complain: "In this album, the fusion of song and music isn't done correctly, and the *setār* is out of tune and *fālsh*[1] eighty percent of the time." He was interrupted by outcries of dismay from the audience but struggled to continue, "If someone wants to say 'I love you,' he doesn't shout and whinny[2] 'I love you,' he says it in a quiet manner, but unfortunately in all of his work Namjoo has tried to scream out[3] meanings that should have been expressed quietly."[4] Namjoo responded indifferently that he had intentionally set his *setār* to be out of tune and that in about thirty other unpublished songs that he had produced, the *setār* was equally out of tune. Then the soft-spoken Pari Maleki—a vocalist in her fifties who has persevered and continued in her profession under the forbidding circumstances prevailing for women singers in the Islamic Republic—got up and said in a passionate voice, "Every kind of music must be allowed to exist so that every music finds its listeners. Every kind of music must be allowed," she said again for emphasis, which elicited roaring applause from the rest of the audience.

Maleki seemed to be pointing to the core of the problem in this critique session. The restrictions that *Ershād* imposed on music did not allow for "every kind of music to be heard." In fact, Namjoo's album had failed to receive the necessary permits from the ministry by conventional means and was finally published by the Islamic Development Organization's Arts Domain, the *Howzeh*. This brought the *Howzeh* enough criticism from conservative centers that in retribution, the *Howzeh*'s official publishing power was dissolved for at least two years. Since the early years of the new millennium, dozens of concerts had been staged in Tehran every year, but aside from a few rock or alternative music concerts granted exceptional permission and held in unusual venues such as hospitals or university halls, almost all had been concerts of either Persian or Western classical music, Persian regional or folk music, or the approved form of pop music already discussed.

Namjoo's music surfaced more widely in Tehran toward the end of 2006 and was noticed as different and talked about in those terms.[5] His music pushed the envelope both in its transgressions against classical Persian music and in its subversive lyrics, and so the official release of his first album took many by surprise, not least because one of his most popular early songs was set to a video clip featuring a television actress who at the time was embroiled in a sex tape scandal.

Namjoo's "trial" at the House of Artists, as well as the audience's impatience with it, was emblematic of the two conflicting political currents that ultimately culminated in the election unrest a year later, in the summer of 2009. On the one hand were the reformist policies of Mohammad Khatami's government, which along with greater and more widespread access to the Internet had created an opening to the world and a swell of intellectual and artistic creativity. On the other hand were the overpowering forces of conservative political and cultural factions—supported by the Supreme Leader Ayatollah Khamenei—who viewed this opening as a threat to their beliefs and positions and had played both fair and foul to counter reformist developments. By early 2008, Namjoo's sudden and immense popularity had prompted the Tehran City Council to include him in its thirteen-part "Song Critique" series, where his music was to be formally analyzed. But frustrated first at the slow pace and then the reversal of reforms, the youth at the House of Artists no longer had any patience for critique. They cared little for what the critics had to say. They had come to hear the artist speak.

MOHSEN NAMJOO

Mohsen Namjoo was born in 1976, the youngest of seven children, in Torbat-e Jam, about two hours north of Mashhad. His father was a Qur'an reciter who had been relatively strict in the supervision of his older children's religious practice, but by the time Namjoo, the youngest child, came along, his father's strictness had worn off. He was then well into his sixties and was "not so dogmatic in his religion, although [Namjoo's] mother was and still is."[6] Namjoo grew up and finished high school in Mashhad, where his family had moved.

Twenty-one years younger than his eldest sibling and six years younger than the next-to-youngest in the family, Namjoo grew up surrounded by two sets of parents, as it were. Situated between his parents' religiosity and the more flexible attitudes of his siblings, Namjoo remembers growing up with "ideological contradictions that were inscribed at the heart of not just the bigger society but also the smaller society of the family" that he belonged to. This "ideological contradiction"—the conflict between tradition and modernity—would later become the biggest thematic preoccupation of his early work. At school and in family gatherings, little Namjoo showed vocal talent, but his earliest memory of receiving professional affirmation was rooted in Tehran, where he was sent on vacation with family as a twelve-year-old.

It was late spring 1988, when the Iran-Iraq war was still raging and music and other expressions of joy were severely punished. By chance, a family friend took Namjoo along with him to a private singing class taught by Ostād Nasrollah Nassehpour, who, as Namjoo would later learn, was "the greatest teacher of *āvāz*" at the time. Namjoo remembers being shocked, as a child, to find that "a singing class like that even existed in Iran under those circumstances." It was an intimate class and Namjoo was encouraged to sing something. "I remembered a Shajarian song and sang it, and he encouraged me a lot and said he was supposed to give some private classes in Mashhad and that I should join." Namjoo's return to Mashhad coincided with Ayatollah Khomeini's fatwa on music in late 1988, which indirectly led to the public legitimization of certain kinds of music and music education. The adolescent Namjoo eventually took classes with Nassehpour for nearly two years, during which he studied about four of the twelve principal *dastgāhs* (modes), beginning with *shur*, considered to be the "mother *dastgāh*."

At this point, Namjoo was about fifteen years old and felt that he had gained the capacity to continue his musical education on his own. Following the new fatwa, the provincial branch of *Ershād* had started some music classes, and Namjoo attended a few classes in music theory and solfège. But the most important educational tools for him were tapes of the *dastgāhs*, *āvāzes* (art songs) and *tasnifs* (shorter, melodic songs), by Abdollah Davami, whose work is generally considered to be the most comprehensive oral treasure of Iranian *tasnifs*. The historian of music Ruhollah Khaleqi wrote about him in 1954: "In reality, he is the secured source for old rhythmic songs. Whenever masters of music and those interested in old songs with a beat (*zarbi*) face a problem in the performance of any of these tunes, they turn to him and accept his opinion as competent and final."[7] These tapes were later published commercially, but at the time, Namjoo received them through an informal insider channel. In his own narrative of his life, it was at around this time—namely during his early high school years—that Namjoo fell away from the more socially respectable path of education oriented toward the achievement of middle-class goals such as "professional success and domestic bliss." This was the beginning of his conscious construction of himself as a rebel, as someone who follows his heart and goes against the mainstream. He dropped out of the highly competitive and prestigious school run by the National Organization for the Development of Exceptional Talents (NODET)[8] because, as he says, "music and film had filled my life and I had little time for homework." At the time, he knew that the expectation for him and his cohorts was for them to become doctors and engineers and "join NASA," but in his own words, he became "playful and decided that until the end of my life music would be my work."

Already then, he perceived his choice to be equivalent to "waging a war on a battlefield," because of the psychological and social pressures that he felt were imposed on him by society and his family. To this day, most parents in Iran are disinclined to support their children in pursuing the arts professionally, not just because of the presumed "lightness" or lack of seriousness of the arts but also because, like elsewhere, the arts are associated with potential poverty. Parents in Iran, as elsewhere, are famous for encouraging their children to take up professions in the esteemed fields of medicine, law, or engineering. This is reflected in contemporary honorific titles. Whereas older forms of honorific address included titles such as *khān* (Sir/sovereign) or *hāji* (someone who had made the pilgrimage to Mecca), more modern forms include *āqā-ye doktor* (Mr. Doctor) or *khānum-e mohandes* (Mrs. Engineer).

When I asked him what gave him the strength to continue, Namjoo said, "If you'll allow me to give a clichéd response," and cackled before continuing, "it's love, love for music," but then took on a more serious demeanor and added, "to frame it intellectually rather than romantically, it was also a kind of *sheytanat* (mischief) to go forward and see if you can laugh at all these things that everyone else takes so seriously: life, money, house, wife . . . ." When he chose to take his national university entry exam, the *konkur*—the horrifying, all-determining test—in the arts, Namjoo officially declared his path. He remembers his mother coming to him on the morning of the exam and saying to him softly, "my dear, when you get there go change your exam subject so you can study mathematics," unaware that the choice had already been made and there was no going back.

Namjoo still remembers that morning vividly, as a tragicomic memory that he says nurtured in him the desire to practice adopting "a bemused smile, not a stupidly happy smile nor a bitter smile, just the smile of a silent witness," what one might perhaps even call a cynical smile, a role that Namjoo, as auteur, takes on in his later work. As trivial a step as it might seem within other contexts, for the young Namjoo, who came from a modest background with little cultural or artistic capital, choosing the arts at a young age was the first step in taking up an oppositional stance toward societal values and inserting his own will.

In 1994, Namjoo moved to Tehran to attend Tehran University's College of Performing Arts and Music, but his course was delayed by a year due to a shortage of students, so he took theater classes for a year. The next year, when he finally started the course in music, he began with units in harmony, counterpoint, composition, form, and analysis, and chose the *tār* and *setār* as his instruments. Pumped up with youthful self-confidence, he found it hard to accept the traditional Iranian educational model of master-apprentice knowledge transmission (*morid-morādi*) and soon lost heart. He was eventually expelled from the university. In Saman Salour's documentary film *Ārāmesh bā Diāzpām-e 10* (Calmness with Diazpam 10, henceforth referred to as *Diazpam 10*), filmed in 2003, Namjoo's disappointment with the university is still fresh as he speaks about it, and one senses the stubborn pain in his voice: "That really hurt me. I was in my first term and I had so much motivation. Never again before or after that term did I write as many scores as I did in that term, with all that excitement. I felt like it was the period of blossoming and taking flight." Namjoo walks outside the university campus in a symbolic show of his exile and points to the building where the notice of his expulsion from the university was signed, after only five terms.

> I was eighteen or nineteen years old and realized "oh! This guy [the professor] won't even let me think." Sure, when I was thirteen I would sit on my knees for two hours and be completely at the service of Ostād Nassehpour, listen and not say a word, but by the time of university I knew some things; but they paid no attention to you and your work, they showed no pedagogy. When I tried to compose a piece, Professor Dariush Talayee admonished me, saying, "You're not even at the level of composing, what are you talking about?" He killed some things inside of me right from the start. Now imagine, I had such high hopes for this, the best music university in Iran, and there I was and I knew I wasn't in the right place.[9]

One of his friends explains in the film that unlike others in his course, "Mohsen wasn't interested in learning the *radif* of Mirza Abdollah . . . and being examined on it and being judged and graded as to whether he was doing it well or not." Sasan Fatemi, a professor of musicology at Tehran University who did not teach Namjoo but was privy to the conversations of the faculty at the time, said that most believed that Namjoo had himself to blame, because "the remit of a university is to teach the foundations; nowhere in the world does higher education have the responsibility of producing a deconstructivist or taboo-breaking artist. He should never have come here if he had a bubbling spring of inspiration inside him, he should have gone and done it by himself from the start."[10] For his part, Namjoo was projecting authenticity by rejecting conventional music education, however unintentionally. After all, our romanticized notion of the artist dictates that he be original and self-made, not a product of the automated machinery of the university.

For a couple of years after his dismissal from Tehran University's College of Performing Arts and Music in early 1998, Namjoo did all sorts of odd jobs. He worked as a sound engineer's assistant on a few films, and even as an actor, in a feature film called "A Few Kilos of Dates." He wrote poetry; later, he dedicated himself only to song. He performed some of his work in the *Howzeh*. In the documentary film *Diazpam 10* mentioned above, Namjoo elaborates on his disagreement with traditional music education in Iran and even goes on to criticize the entire musical establishment. He demonstrates on the *tār* a few examples of how traditional music has been bound to the rhythm of Persian poetry itself, and criticizes traditional musicians for their lack of innovation and their inability to set a classical poem of a certain meter to a counterintuitive rhythm or, put simply, to "do something different." He even imitates, in a derogatory manner, two of the most respected names in Persian music, Houshang Kamkar and Shahram Nazeri, referring to a recent recording for which they engaged a large choir, presumably in order to do something unique, but were fundamentally still enslaved to the meter of the song's poem and other structural precedents.

The problematic to which Namjoo was referring was of course nothing new. Iranian intellectuals, especially modernist poets of the nineteen-sixties and nineteen-seventies, have long produced piercing criticisms of Persian classical music. This came to a head in 1990, in a debate between the poet Ahmad Shamlu and the *tār* virtuoso Mohammad Reza Lotfi, after Shamlu casually remarked, "Iran's traditional music has made no progress." Shamlu had argued that the pride of Persian music belonged to the past, and asked, "What have you done for today's music and for this generation?" Namjoo referred to this debate in an interview in *E'temad* newspaper in 2008, saying that it had a strong impact on him, so much so that in his musical endeavors, he kept asking himself, "What kind of music do I make so that Shamlu would like it, too?"[11]

As Namjoo constructs the narrative of his alternative music education, several elements become prominent. Intellectually, he draws inspiration from modernist poets like Nima Yushij, Reza Baraheni, and Ahmad Shamlu, who created a body of work in the twentieth century that is arguably as important and prominent within Iran's cultural life as that created by the revered poets of centuries ago, such as Hafez and Rumi. Structurally, Namjoo demonstrably sought his education outside of traditional institutions. In order to free himself from the obligations of respect to elders that are part and parcel of a continuation of traditional arts within Iranian culture—the master-apprentice relationship that he so objected to in his university education—Namjoo adopted an iconoclastic attitude that expressed itself in various forms of disrespect. This ranged from his derogatory remarks about traditional musicians, to barking like a dog after traditional vocals, to singing traditional vocals in the shower. This happens in the documentary film *Diazpam 10*, where he talks about traditional music's lack of progress and sings examples while washing his hair in the shower. In conversations, I have often heard this scene referred to as the identifier of this film: "the film where he sings in the shower." Traditional Persian music, considered one of the greatest treasures of the culture, ordinarily sung in beautiful clothes in quiet, respectable settings that demand attention and respect, is here "desecrated" by a skinny, nappy-haired guy with a provincial accent, imitating traditional vocalists in the shower.[12]

THE REFORM GOVERNMENT AND ITS MUSIC POLICY

Namjoo's expulsion and musical "training" outside the university walls in the late nineteen-nineties coincided with the beginning of Iran's reform period. The turn of the millennium presented an important juncture for politics and music in postrevolutionary Iran. In 1997, a former culture minister by the name of Mohammad Khatami ran for the presidency against the man favored by the Supreme Leader, speaker of parliament Ali Akbar Nateq Nuri. Khatami ran on a reformist agenda that reflected and invigorated the hopes and aspirations of a people looking for greater social and political freedoms and economic openings and opportunities. This period was in many ways the awakening of Iran's electorate to politics in the Islamic Republic. With a turn-out of eighty percent, almost seventy percent of the voters chose Khatami as their new president. President Khatami's friendly demeanor and light-colored robes signaled a break with the severe face of officialdom that Iranians had known to that date. Khatami's foreign policy motto was "dialogue among civi-lizations," which he promoted in response to Samuel Huntington's theory of a "clash of civilizations." Nearly two decades after the revolution, Khatami's conciliatory slogan—which the United Nations also adopted as its slogan for the year 2001, upon Khatami's suggestion—had replaced the previous dis-course of "cultural invasion" (*tahājom-e farhangi*). Interest in and exchange with foreign—read "Western"—cultures no longer seemed forbidden in the government's official language.

In his position as Minister of Culture and Islamic Guidance, which he held for a total of nine years between 1982 and 1992, Khatami's easing of restric-tions on film, music, art, and literature had earned him a national reputa-tion as a "moderate"[13] but also finally cost him his post, because conservative members of parliament consistently accused his ministry of enabling "cultural invasion." Following the death of Imam Khomeini in 1989, which coincided with the fall of the Soviet Union and the opening of former Soviet states to the West, Iran's leaders found themselves in a particularly vulnerable position. The Iran-Iraq war had ended, complicating the state's self-righteous justifica-tions for the repressive and securitized policies that spilled over into people's private lives. Soon, the state's new Supreme Leader, Ali Khamenei, started warning his followers of the "two-pronged strategy" of a cultural invasion, which he claimed aimed to "replace local culture with foreign culture, con-tinuing the policies of the Pahlavis," and to "attack the Islamic Republic, its values, and the values of the people, by cultural means."[14]

The chorus against this "cultural invasion" reached such heights that it was referred to the Supreme Council for National Security, where several leaders of various state organs gathered to discuss the issue, among them the hard-liners Ayatollah Ahmad Jannati and *Kayhan* editor Hossein Shariatmadari. Accord-ing to Said Hajjarian, an associate of Khatami's, the majority of the criticisms at this meeting (on 22 May 1992) were directed at the Ministry of Culture and Islamic Guidance (*Ershād*), leading Khatami to declare angrily, "So according to you, I am to blame for this cultural invasion, and if I leave *Ershād* the cul-tural invasion will no longer exist!" The next day, he submitted his letter of resignation to the parliament,[15] and in it he "severely criticized within a Khomeinist framework the conservative restrictions on freedom of speech and the press and the punishments imposed on those who don't support them."[16] In the letter, Khatami also drew a damning picture of the country's cultural conditions, under which all sorts of tactics for the attainment of "particular goals" had been counted as permissible, including:

> the breaking of all legal, Islamic, moral, and conventional boundaries, . . . so that an unhealthy and distressed atmosphere has been created, the most immediate effect of which will be the disillusionment and insecurity of intellectuals and artists who are sound and deserving of respect, and who are even pious and committed to the revolution and Islam.

He further warned that in this "chaos even the accepted foundations of the state, including the opinions and fatwas of his highness the Imam, are implicitly and even explicitly contradicted and opposed," and later added that the opposition to the Imam's views "begins at music but does not end there."[17]

Five years later, Khatami was elected president on a platform that emphasized the importance of civilian participation in political life, and in his speeches, he popularized the term "civil society." Khatami's "principles of cultural policy" (osul-e siāsat-e farhangi) even called for government institutions to abstain from constantly promoting Islam and imposing severe religious views upon the public, for fear of adverse reactions to religion in society. During his first term as president, religious enforcement and government intrusion into private lives eased up, student activism in universities increased, the press flourished, and spontaneous street celebrations following soccer victories took place for the first time. These celebrations came to be known as the "soccer revolution" and presented a cultural turning point, since such "non-Islamic" emotions of jubilation had not been expressed in public since the revolution.[18] After almost twenty years of austerity, Khatami's presidency ushered in a period of liberalism which included profound changes in cultural policy, with far-reaching implications for music in particular. Khatami's choice of culture minister upon his election in 1997 signaled the shift in the new leadership's ideology.[19] Ata'ollah Mohajerani, the former parliament member and previous president Akbar Rafsanjani's deputy, was known for his liberal views. Once Mohajerani took office, it was his men who facilitated the rebirth of pop music in the Islamic Republic by allowing for the release of fifty-odd Persian pop albums in the first two years of Khatami's presidency.[20]

Then as now, cultural policy in the Islamic Republic was made in a hierarchically diffused manner that left room for the personal agency of individual officials. Hence, it was the personal and political perspectives of reformists like Khatami and Mohajerani—rather than a systematic transformation of cultural laws and regulations—that allowed for a greater sense of freedom in the public sphere. More liberally predisposed, these actors were using the social and ideological capital that they had garnered over the years to nudge the republic to allow for both more liberties in the public sphere and less interference in the private sphere. More often than not, Khatami's government allowed greater freedoms because of its actors' more reformist reading of already existing laws, though sometimes their predispositions also led them to change existing laws, with even longer-lasting consequences.

One incident that perfectly illustrates how a permanent change in regulations arose from openness on Khatami's part (and enterprise on the petitioner's) is the story of the legalization of piano importation more than two decades after the revolution. In their airy, all-glass Yamaha piano gallery in the elegant *Jām-e Jam* shopping center in northern Tehran, Bozorg Lashgari and his daughter Maria told me—with a lot of relived excitement—how father and daughter hatched an ad hoc scheme to ambush Khatami during his visit to their tent at Tehran's 2002 International Exhibition in order to gain his permission to import pianos to Iran.

Lashgari had been a prominent name in the Iranian music scene of a bygone era, which had seen the creation of what was called "national music" (*musiqi-ye melli*) by the greats showcased on the *Golhā* radio program (discussed at length in chapter 2). Lashgari, now an octogenarian, had studied violin with Abolhasan Saba, one of Iran's foundational twentieth-century musicians;[21] joined Morteza Mahjubi's orchestra (the best of the ensembles performing Persian music using mostly Western instruments); and ultimately became the conductor for the orchestra of the state radio and television. A few years before the revolution, the political instability had led him to leave temporarily for England,[22] but he soon moved his family back to Iran. "Especially because I had religious views, I believed that heavenly angels would descend on this land and great transformations would take place in everything, and there would be real progress," Lashgari explained. Upon his return to Iran in 1979, however, he realized that the situation had changed: "Music had been completely cut off, and from that point on my only care was that our national music would not be lost and forgotten." He dedicated himself to teaching music; then, during Akbar Rafsanjani's presidential term in 1990, he received a one-off license to import 110 pianos, as Yamaha's representative in Iran. Over a period of more than a decade following that first license, however, he received only a few more such licenses, until the encounter with President Khatami changed the import situation for good.

At the exhibition, Lashgari's daughter Maria was representing Yamaha at a stand in the Japanese national tent when they were told that the president would visit the Toyota stand and were warned severely not to interrupt his flow through the tent. Maria initially objected that they had a petition, knowing full well that for many years her father had sought to eliminate the restrictions on piano imports, but the severity of the security detail's response silenced her. Her father would be unable to make it to the exhibition in time for the president's visit, but told her, "See what you can do." Soon thereafter, Khatami's delegation entered the tent and walked along the red carpet laid out for him; it was "a very official-looking delegation, including many clerics like himself as well as his extremely conservative commerce minister, Mohammad Shariatmadari, whom father had petitioned at least ten times for piano import permissions without getting anywhere," explained Maria, who had now taken over telling the story:

> As Mr. Khatami approached, I threw an imploring look at his security de-
> tail, who threw me back a "no way!" I realized that within a moment he was
> going to pass and the opportunity would be lost. Suddenly I took a jump
> start, made a beeline straight through, and came to a standstill right in front
> of Mr. Khatami and his delegation.

Here Maria chortled to relay her surprise at her own action. She went on: "This was still at a time when things hadn't opened up; women weren't considered human beings yet and women's *manteaux* [coats] had just made it from here to here" (she motioned from her mid-shin to just below the knee).

> He looked at me and then looked over his shoulder to his entourage with a
> look of "Who is this?" There was complete silence, and then I greeted him
> and introduced myself, as the daughter of Mr. Bozorg Lashgari, one of the
> country's masters of music. Khatami's face contracted; he thought hard and
> then asked his assistant whether this was the same musician whose work
> Iran's orchestra had performed in China, with Khatami in attendance. After
> establishing that my father was still alive, he changed his route and made a
> turn toward our music stand. The whole scene was flooded with the flash-
> lights of all the cameras around us. Imagine! A cleric turning his attention
> to music; you have no idea what a splash this made in the media.

Khatami went on to observe the young students who were playing Persian compositions at the pianos, and then made the gesture for holding a *tār* and asked, "But who plays this?" alluding to the regime's anxieties about the foreign nature of the piano. This unusual moment, in which the president of the Islamic Republic—and a cleric at that—mimed playing the *tār*, was captured on film and made the pages of newspapers the next day. When Khatami finally asked Maria what Lashgari was requesting, she explained:

> "Father says too few pianos get imported into Iran, and they are very expensive and don't reach the appropriate consumers. The country's music schools and conservatories have pianos from before the revolution, which are no longer any good. His request is that import restrictions on pianos be eased so that more able musicians can be trained." I made sure to say what father had told me to emphasize, namely that the piano is a "mother instrument" and can be tuned to Iranian scales and should not be viewed as Western.

Khatami was particularly interested in this last point. He then turned to the cameras and microphones and raised his arms in his characteristic way, as if to receive a friend, saying, "I am at the service of this generation, it is these young people that I work for," and asked his assistant to give Lashgari an appointment at eight o'clock the next morning.

The next morning, when Lashgari arrived at the president's office and repeated the request, Khatami responded, "As you know, everyone is against it; they say our youth will become *motreb* [the derogatory term for entertainers]." Himself a traditional man of faith, Lashgari did not deny the concept of *motreb* or the possibility of an instrument's use leading to such a state, but argued, "The piano is a classical instrument; no one will become a *motreb* with this instrument. It's a foundational instrument that is necessary for music education. They teach it in our schools, but there aren't enough of them." Khatami told Lashgari that he agreed with him, and a few weeks later the general ban on piano imports was lifted. It should be noted that more than any other instrument, the piano is a marker of class, and does not really play an important role in the kind of music to which the clergy objects. But the piano served to pave the way for the import of other instruments, which slowly followed.

Khatami's and by extension Mohajerani's more tolerant views toward the arts in general and music in particular also meant that the government became more liberal in issuing permits for records and concerts. This atmosphere of openness encouraged the creation of new bands and new forms of music. And concurrently with the Khatami government's policies of greater freedom, there were two other important developments that affected the life conditions that contributed to the makings of the generation coming of age in those years.[23] The first is that these young people belonged to the upper age bracket of what is often referred to as the "burnt generation" in Persian, *nasl-e sukhteh.* They had experienced some of the most repressive policies of the state in their late childhood and adolescence, during the nineteen-eighties and nineteen-nineties. And the second is that now they were not just witnessing an increase in openness at home but also, more generally, an unprecedented kind of interconnectedness and exchange with the world due to the gradual spread of the Internet and what we now call globalization.

EARLY ROCK AND FUSION

All around Iran, young people were getting together and creating music. Many Iranians will comment that it was the subversive nature of music—in the given political circumstances—that made it such a popular pastime not just for young people but in the wider social fabric. In 1998, Hossein Alizadeh, one of Iran's most prominent living musicians, credited the spread of music in society to the state's repression of it in the state's first decades, explaining that "the performance and education of music itself had become a sort of resistance and preservation of identity."[24] Until this period, the late nineteen-nineties, Iranians inside Iran had continued listening either to prerevolutionary-style Iranian pop music produced by "Tehrangeles" stars or to Western music that made its way to Iran (usually the giants of the Billboard Awards). But now, during this period of opening, a grassroots music scene emerged within Iran itself, so that Iranians started to listen to homegrown creations, both state-approved and underground, for the first time in nearly twenty years.

Heavy metal and death metal were perhaps some of the first kinds of rock music to find a devout following in postwar Iran. In his *Heavy Metal Islam,* Mark LeVine relays in the words of his protagonists the "metal fever" that hit Iran after the Iran-Iraq war at the end of the nineteen-eighties, "when death was everywhere" and when, paradoxically, metalheads, through their grueling representations of death, "offered a 'community of life' . . . against the community of death and martyrdom propagated by the Iranian government."[25] Throughout the late nineteen-eighties and nineteen-nineties, young people around Iran were taking risks to acquire and play various kinds of rock music, whether it involved buying foreign music from black market "smugglers," transporting music instruments concealed in layers of blankets, or practicing in egg-carton-insulated basement spaces.

One insider, Sohrab Mahdavi (who ran a webzine I discuss below), told me that by 2002, there were around fifty rock bands in Tehran alone.[26] Several of the members of this first rock scene knew each other. Arash Mitooie, the son of well-known folk musician Sima Bina, for example, gave a first private concert in a house belonging to a friend of his mother's as early as 1989, which other members of this scene also attended. Mitooie was classically trained on the *santur* (Persian dulcimer), but had grown up listening to Western rock and pop bands like Pink Floyd and Dire Straits. In 1991, Mitooie's band Chert o pert (Nonsense) released an underground album that merged the poems of Hafez with rock music and even experimented with playing *navā* (a *dastgāh* of the Persian *radif* repertoire) and the Persian quarter tone on an electric guitar, probably planting the first seeds of fusion music, known as *talfiq*, in postrevolutionary Iran.[27] Ramin Behna, the composer and pianist who is well-known as a pioneer of fusion music in postrevolutionary Iran, described to me how already during the unforgiving years of the Iran-Iraq war, he was getting together with fellow music enthusiasts to perform covers of Pink Floyd and Deep Purple. With the help of the IRIB manager Dr. Hassan Riahi, his band Avizheh gained access to a recording studio within the organization and published several albums between 1998 and 2001 that fused pop, rock, and elements of Persian classical music. These songs were repeatedly broadcast on state radio and television (though without giving any credit to the band), and Avizheh gave a series of sold-out concerts during those years. This was all music without words or vocals, and Behna emphasized that considering the sensitivity around new music, and especially lyrics, at the time, he and his bandmates understood that their best chance for getting a permit lay in making instrumental music.[28]

The core of this initial group went on to produce some of the first rock music creations that were given permits for concerts. Behna's next band, Raz-e Shab, with the charismatic vocalist Hooman Javid and the guitarist Arash Sobhani (later of the famous band Kiosk), for example, is often credited with giving the first officially permitted fusion or rock concert in Islamic Iran, in 2002. Pedram Derakhshani of Avizheh soon formed his own band called Rumi, a fusion of rock, Persian classical, and other world music sounds, that has since

2003 given dozens of concerts in official settings. The rock band Meera was also one of the early ones—along with bands like Pejvak, DNA, and Piccolo—and gave its first officially permitted concert in 2002. And Babak Riahipour, an accomplished guitarist, gave his first concert in 2003 and has since been engaged in music production of various kinds in the Islamic Republic. These are musicians with real rock-star appeal whose music falls within the "alternative" category, because of its creative qualities, but who have chosen to work within the given governmental frameworks. However, many musicians also felt constricted by the limitations on their work and left Iran, splitting many of these early bands apart.

One of the best-known heavy metal bands, early on, was probably Ahoora, which formed in 2001 and according to its own account gave the first officially permitted metal gig with vocals in 2005.[29] However, the second night of the concert was cancelled, perhaps not surprisingly considering the band's musical influences, Iron Maiden and Black Sabbath. Another well-known metal band at the time was Kahtmayan, whose album *Exir* was officially released in 2005, though it was purely instrumental music without lyrics. With Mahmoud Ahmadinejad's election as president in 2005, the cultural sphere tightened significantly. The rock and metal scene continued to flourish, but to a greater extent underground. Some of the "generation 1.5" rockers (such as the band 127, Hypernova, Font, and The Yellow Dogs), whose work really came to the fore starting around 2003,[30] never received permits for publication from *Ershād*, not least because their lyrics were in English. And by 2007, various state arms attempted to create a "moral shock" around the underground music scene by painting it as satanic, making it even less conceivable that rock groups would ever gain official acceptance.[31]

But there has existed and still exists some "official" space within educational institutions, such as Farabi Hall at Tehran University of the Arts, or much smaller rooms and halls in the music academies, as well as within nonconventional performance contexts such as hospitals and senior homes, where underground bands can occasionally receive permission to perform. These concerts are sometimes categorized as "experimental" or "research" shows. Because *Ershād* won't give permits to such groups, educational institutions will sometimes issue letters confirming that these bands consist of art students, taking advantage of a loophole that allows new groups to try out their music in a public setting. I witnessed one such concert, by the heavy metal band Prana7, in a small room of Tehran's Conservatory of Music. The green curtains were drawn shut to obstruct views from outside. The band consisted of three electric guitar-ists and a drummer. Several audience members were headbanging (while seated on velvet foldout chairs), while others held up the "sign of the horns" gesture popular in metal music. The vocalist Adrijan Mirbagheri was singing words in a made-up nonsense language. When I asked him about it, he commented that it was not the "words that were important but the context."[32] Staying clear of the contentious issue of lyrics by using nonsense language seems a clever move for any band, an act whose absurdity highlights the lack of complete freedom in this sphere. But perhaps more importantly, as Mirbagheri seemed to imply, a band's belonging to the community of metalheads that viscerally rejects the anodyne norms valorized by state monitoring bodies is enough to mark posi-tion and authenticity. Words are not necessary.

Quite frustratingly for all participants involved, even officially authorized shows are sometimes finally not allowed to go on. In the summer of 2014, the raid of a concert by the metal band Dawn of Rage was reported in the media. Although the band had staged legal concerts since 2010, and had received a permit for this "experimental" concert in 2014, all two hundred attendees were briefly arrested and only released upon posting bail.[33] Still, rockers are thriv-ing in Iran, and the Persian Rock and Metal Festival, which has been staged in countries like Turkey, Armenia, and Georgia since 2012, attests to that. Several of the bands that have attended this festival in the past have even had female vocalists. Nevertheless, as the 2015 arrest of the metal band Confess shows, metalheads can face prison sentences and even execution if found guilty of blasphemy, especially if they have a song titled "I Am Your God," as that band did. Two of the band members were kept in solitary confinement for several months before they were released on bail and are now, as of February 2016, to face trial.[34]

Among those "alternative" musicians whose work mostly failed to gain official permission, only a few managed to reach critical success by other means and leave a mark on this period. One of the very first bands to release an "underground" rock album was O-Hum (though the term "underground" itself is problematic; see the discussion below). In 1999, they created a stir with *Nahāl-e heyrat* (Sapling of Wonderment), an album of ten tracks that the band's official website described as "Western rock music melted with Persian music, scales, and instruments."[35] The lyrics were all drawn from the classi-cal Persian poetry of Hafez and Rumi, but they were contemporized against the backdrop of O-Hum's edgy rock music. At the time of its appearance on

Tehran's music scene, this music was a real novelty. In some ways, the revolution's nativist aspirations seemed to have borne fruit: here were young Iranians who partook in the nationally treasured poetic discourse of Hafez but reconfigured it to reflect their sense of being young and cosmopolitan in an increasingly interconnected world.

Ultimately, despite O-Hum's persistent efforts, even Mohajerani's reformist ministry refused them a publication permit. Then as now—as we will see again in the more detailed description in chapter 7 of Namjoo's attempts to receive a permit—artists applying for permits were often confused and unclear about the real reasons behind official refusals, in part because those denying the permits themselves had no clear guidelines on what should and should not be permissible. When O-Hum was asked in a 2001 interview about the "exact reason" why it was denied a permit, the band members began responding with the actual reasons they were given, but then went into a sarcastic and comical crescendo that is equally revealing:

Shahram: The latest problem is two lyrics that have been rejected by them. See? Though these are Hafez poems, they still don't accept them!
Shahrokh: I think the poems and the way Shahram sang them are their main problem but there are some tiny (!) [exclamation mark in original text] problems too, including the fuzzy guitars, the punchy drums, and restless bass!
Babak: Yeah, the reason is the whole album itself: the music as well as the lyrics we've chosen.
Shahrokh: As a matter of fact they want the music to be freed of poison for people's ears . . . this defanged music must have slow and jazzy drums, . . . some flamenco-like guitar . . .
Shahram: . . . add a very low pitch and sad vocal to this list too![36]

In effect, the O-Hum band members were suggesting that regardless of the existing ambiguous regulations on music, they believed that the reason their music was rejected was that it was simply too wild for a state that wants music to be either slow or sad.[37] As we saw earlier, Ayatollah Khomeini had broken the long silence on the legitimacy of music, shortly after the end of the Iran-Iraq war, by issuing a fatwa in response to a question about the sale of musical instruments. Khomeini's statement was, "The purchase and sale of common (*moshtarekeh*) instruments with the intention of furthering halal interests is without fault."[38] The Supreme Leader who succeeded him, Ayatollah

Khamenei, further expanded upon this position in various speeches and meetings, though in fact his words barely provide any clarification: "Definitely haram is that kind of music which drives one away from one's self (*az khod bi khod mikonad*), away from the truths, away from God, and draws one toward lust (*shahavvat*)."[39]

O-Hum half-jokingly interpreted these regulations to mean that only slow, and preferably sad, songs were allowed, but still kept trying to get a permit for years because they were never told that their music was categorically haram. However, although—or maybe even precisely because—O-Hum uses the poetry of Hafez and Rumi for its lyrics, the discourse it creates is fundamentally antithetical to that of Ayatollah Khamenei. Although Hafez and Rumi are regarded as learned Muslims and national treasures, they are also Sufi masters whose mystical variety of Islam did not aspire to govern the polity. Hence, while Khamenei deems that music to be haram which makes one lose one's self or *khod*, O-Hum's most famous song, "*Darvish*"—based on Hafez—tells of a dervish who seeks to be freed from himself by the lover, often an allegory for the Creator. The music video weaves images of a dervish headbanging himself into ecstasy with excerpts from a cartoon of a dervish coming face to face with his beloved, only to realize moments later that she is an illusion.

In a review of O-Hum's first—unofficial—concert in the Russian Orthodox Church in Tehran on 1 March 1999, the writer reports that when the band opened the set with "*Darvish*," the crowd went crazy after the first beat, and all one could see in front of the stage was "slam dancing, raging, diving."[40] It is as if Khamenei, as the highest official mouthpiece of the Islamic Republic, and O-Hum, as young musical innovators, existed on wholly different planes of perception and expression. While Khamenei has been engaged over the last two decades in making regular pronouncements on music by delineating a morally stratified world where there is a definite haram (*harām-e qatʿi*), a definite halal (*halāl-e qatʿi*), and a range of ambiguities (*moshtabeheh*) in between, O-Hum's band members talk about music in a different linguistic register altogether. Shahram, the vocalist, talks of an "extraordinary good vibe and feel from the audience," and Babak, the bassist, says "groove is something you have to feel inside, it's a kind of vibration, an energy which moves you from within, which makes you feel great and happy, and sometimes even crazy."[41]

Unable to get a permit after four years of running back and forth to the ministry, O-Hum finally decided to establish its own website and put all its music online in 2001, after which its members believe their music "really took off."[42] Indeed, both the Internet and satellite television were increasingly uti-lized as spaces serving as an alternative to the closely guarded and regulated official space.

TEHRANAVENUE

Sometime around the turn of the millennium, a young man who had left Iran for France during the Iran-Iraq war raised the idea of an online city magazine with his cousin, Sohrab Mahdavi, who had just returned to Iran after a long stay in the United States. The young Mahdavi, a writer, translator, and art aficionado, took the idea and turned it into Iran's first city webzine, called *TehranAvenue*. The site both revealed and energized the budding arts and culture scene among young, culturally engaged Tehranis who appreciated this forum for announc-ing and offering reviews and critiques of cultural events. Young people in their late teens and twenties were part of a big youth bulge coming of age at the turn of the millennium, often referred to in mainstream media as the children of the revolution. Many of these young people belonged to the capital's cultural and educational (though not necessarily socioeconomic) elite, who knew each other through school and university, cultural activities, or mutual friends. They met over cappuccinos at hip cafés—which were springing into existence all over Tehran—and filled up ashtrays as they discussed arts and politics. I met Mahdavi in the fall of 2002 on the top floor of an open-air shopping enclave on Gandhi Boulevard, at one such café in a row of equally bustling competi-tors. One of his colleagues, the musician Hesam Garshasbi, had sparked the imagination of Mahdavi and of the *TehranAvenue* collective by suggesting that they host an online music contest, and when we talked, Mahdavi—dressed as he often is in coarse Iranian linen and espadrilles—could not quite hide the excitement he harbored for the project underneath his soft-spoken calm, say-ing: "It is really important that we use this opportunity to allow young musi-cians to come out into the public with their work." Indeed, although it was only communicated through word of mouth, the idea caught on like wildfire. "We brought in people in the music business, like the Beethoven Music Cen-ter and several recording studios, including Bamahang and Patu, and a few top musicians such as Ramin Behna," Mahdavi explained.[43] The objectives of the contest were to bring out music that had been "played in seclusion" and, in the process, to introduce musicians to each other and to the music world around them, crediting "unrecognized talent" in an effort to "prevent [them] from going unnoticed" and to "open the debate on the state of alternative music in Iran."[44] *TehranAvenue* organized Iran's first online music contest that fall, the Underground Music Contest (UMC), and it brought out into the light of day the many bands that had formed in previous years and been busy practicing, hidden away in soundproofed garages and basements. "Until the festival, we thought that there were perhaps two or three other bands like us in Tehran," Payman Mazaheri of the now-dissolved band Fara, whose song "*Pasheh*" (Mosquito) won first place among twenty-one chosen works, told me some years after the contest.[45] Other bands felt the same way. Ali Azimi, lead singer of the current rock band Radio Tehran, told me, "We were perplexed to see that so many bands were out there."[46]

Equally intrigued were the online listeners, fifty thousand of whom voted on the songs. There were five hundred thousand successful downloads of songs altogether, which as Mahdavi rightly points out "is remarkable anyway, but especially for that era, when the Internet was super slow; it was the time of dial-up."[47] The four winners of the contest were supposed to give a concert each, on four consecutive nights, preceded by lectures on music by governmental music officials, including Hassan Riahi, the composer of the national anthem of the Islamic Republic, and other music experts, including the pianist and composer Payman Yazdanian. All four concerts were sold out and there was a great deal of excitement for what would effectively be the first series of legitimately staged "above-ground" concerts given by these officially unapproved "underground" bands. "None of these bands knew how to appear in front of a public; it's not like any of them had done it before," Mahdavi explained, "so Ramin Behna was coaching them on that."

It was just one day before the first concert, and in the middle of a practice session at the Bamahang studio, as Mojtaba Mirtahmasb's insightful documentary *Off Beat* recounts, that the director of *Ershād*'s music office called in to cancel the entire series of concerts. "For most band members, it was not such a big deal, because they were used to disappointment," says Mahdavi, looking back, but then adds, "But there were a few consolation concerts given in private homes afterwards to counter the depression."

Those involved in the events of those days may never know exactly why the government decided to pull the plug on these concerts, but through the opaque glass that obscures most government communication one clue did emerge. Soon after receiving the devastating news of the cancellation order, Mahdavi learned from Babak Chamanara—the manager of the Beethoven

Music Center—that the ministry had objected to the term "underground."[48] It is uncertain how the term "underground" had become the dominant term used to describe non-state-sanctioned, often Western-tinged music, but Mahdavi says he regrets that *TehranAvenue* is in good part to blame. He says that the term "underground" was something the crew came up with for the first contest "because it was playful and we liked it," and as far as he remembers, "it was not being used yet and is a *TehranAvenue* coinage."[49] The reason Mahdavi regrets the term in retrospect—besides the fact that it may have contributed to *Ershād*'s decision to ban the contest—is that he does not believe it actually applied to these groups: "None of these bands were political; they had nothing rebellious to say, they were just a bunch of young guys wanting to play music." Mahdavi went on to say that he believed the term "underground" caught on, to a large extent, because of the Western media, "whose viewers could relate to Woodstock and all those spirits of the nineteen-sixties, rebelliousness and non-conformity, and also the appeal of seeing Western cultural power inseminate young people behind the veil."[50] He argues that the rock bands of those days did not push the government, and that they were making fairly inoffensive music whose only claim to rebellion was that it was not rooted in Persian music, strictly speaking. (Due to the absence of any authentic, non-state-sponsored musical vocabulary, outside of art music, young Iranians drew mostly on rock music and other Western popular genres to create a localized form of Iranian rock, though they fused those with Iranian musical and lyrical elements. As Laudan Nooshin points out in a 2005 article, the lyrics of Iranian rock music are usually rather innocuous, which is partly to be explained by the fact that "rock's strong associations with both the West and a broadly 'anti-establishment' ethos mean that its musical 'language' is sufficiently challenging in itself [and therefore the lyrics don't necessarily need to be]."[51])

Still, as Mahdavi has remarked elsewhere, the perceived liability of the term "underground"—not only crystallized in the title of the UMC, but also crystallizing its own problematic nature once the contest was banned—eventually led to the term "alternative" increasingly taking its place in public fora. Musicians were wary of being seen as *zirzamini* (underground), as many of the bands I spoke to tried for many months and sometimes years to gain permits and they assumed that if they were seen as *zirzamini* it would be even harder. More and more musicians rejected the term, for various reasons and to varying degrees. The lead singer of Radio Tehran, Ali Azimi, echoed others in arguing that without the existence of a truly free mainstream (i.e. unrestricted by the government), the term "underground" was misleading, since what was described as "underground music" was oftentimes quite "aboveground" in that it was listened to as widely as authorized music, if not more widely.[52]

In other ways, however, the Persian word for "underground," *zirzamin*, which is also the word used for "basement," seems more apt for describing non-authorized music than the translation "underground," with its Western connotations, would suggest. Since the revolution, the *zirzamin* has been not just symbolically but also physically a liminal space in which boundaries between the private and the public domains become blurred. Following the government's imposition of Islamic strictures on public spaces, the basement took on increasing architectural importance in the urban residential space. First functioning as a place of refuge during the aerial bombardments of the Iran-Iraq war, the large basements of Tehran's apartment complexes were later gradually transformed into spaces where mixed-gender wedding parties and, even later, fashion shows, music concerts, and parties were and still are held. In the absence of dedicated spaces for the practice and exhibition of officially unapproved music, the *zirzamin* came to be where most "underground" music was practiced and performed. Therefore, while "underground" may not perfectly apply due to the restricted nature of music production in the Islamic Republic, its semantic range, denoting music that is somewhere on the illegal spectrum, and its connotation of brave people expressing themselves at some risk, are quite apt.[53]

However, most musicians seem to have an uneasy relationship with this term, not just because of its Western contextual liability and the government's sensitivity toward the notion that unauthorized activity is thriving in spaces that are out of its control, but also because of the inconclusive debates about the term. In an interview with the *Zirzamin* webzine (based in Sweden), one of the first online music magazines to cover the Iranian "underground" music scene, one of the organizers of the festival comments on this point: "We live in a country where an explicit duality of inside and outside exists. To talk about this duality, in a sense, is to question the ruling order, both politically and socially—it's taboo." The organizer then explains that *TehranAvenue* was later told by those in the "cultural establishment (officials and decision-makers)" that they should avoid calling bands "underground" because that could put them "in harm's way."[54]

The following year, *TehranAvenue* changed the name of its contest to *TehranAvenue* Music Open (TAMO) and also changed the format. Whereas all bands participating in the Underground Music Contest had heard about it through word of mouth, TAMO was publicly announced on *TehranAvenue*'s website, and bands were only allowed to participate if their lyrics complied with "the propriety conditions of the day."[55] Mahdavi and his colleagues were surprised at the time that out of forty-four works that were submitted, "there was none that was subversive or political." Most songs were categorized as "rock of various hues," but there were also two rap songs, one reggae song, and one that was "a fusion of traditional and progressive."[56] This song that stood in its own category was *Begu Begu*" (Tell, Tell) by Mohsen Namjoo, whose unique style was to draw much attention over the course of the next years.

CHAPTER SEVEN

PURPOSELY *FĀLSH*

MOHSEN NAMJOO

IN THE YEARS AFTER his expulsion from university, Namjoo dabbled in some work with state institutions. In addition to his performances at the *Howzeh*, he created a few pieces that were used as title songs on state television series, such as his title song "Ali" for the series by the same name, and another title song that was pulled from a Ramadan series following a scandal surrounding another one of his songs. When Namjoo was twenty-four, he and a friend with connections to state television managed to receive a commission for eighteen songs. With a lot of enthusiasm at the prospect of paid work, Namjoo and his friend dug in and wrote and submitted the eighteen songs, seventeen of which were based on classical poems by Naser Khosrow, Hafez, Saʿdi, Jami, and the like, and one of which was based on a poem by Imam Khomeini, "thrown into the mix by my friend to fortify our revolutionary credentials," Namjoo said sarcastically. All but the song based on Khomeini's poem were rejected, and even for that song, state television made its approval conditional on a green light from the Institute for the Compilation and Publication of the Works of Imam Khomeini. Namjoo recounts with a mix of lingering bewilderment and bemused disdain:

> I mean in that moment, this irony just threw us into hysterical laughter rather than depressing us over our tragic situation. It had been a long time since we had learned to laugh in the face of these situations. Look, you gave them eighteen songs, and they weren't even from Nima Yushij or Shamlu, don't even think about it, and not even from Malek al-Shoʿara Bahar, they

were from Hafez and Saʻdi directly. In such moments, you wonder if there are any principles or foundations at all, does the guy even know poetry? Or is he just some bureaucrat who is really good at being suspicious and doubtful of everything?[1]

Eventually, Namjoo's dealings with state institutions like state television infused in him a sense of absurdity and anger that made it impossible for him to collaborate with them in any form. While he recounted this story with a sense of retrospective humor, at the time the young Namjoo and his friend had worked for months on writing these songs for state television, so the total rejection of all the songs meant not only the dashing of their hopes and ambitions but also months of work that went unpaid.

A year later, unable to make a living in music and uncertain of his future, Namjoo decided to put an end to his state of limbo—as he puts it—and fulfill his military service requirement. Both in the documentary *Diazpam 10* and in various interviews, including his interviews with me, Namjoo stressed the importance of his two years of military service for his musical education. While stationed near Mashhad, he met other musicians, prominent among them Abdi Behravanfar, a guitarist who had just formed a band named Mād. "Abdi," Namjoo recounts, "had a very good collection of music that I could listen to in a concentrated way." Namjoo was already familiar with a wide range of Iranian music; the collection he refers to here was of Western music, at a time when the Internet had not yet caught on in Iran, making that collection all the more valuable. Although Namjoo was familiar with some Western music—such as Pink Floyd and Chris de Burgh, the two highest-selling artists on the black market, next to Michael Jackson, in nineteen-eighties and nineteen-nineties Iran—it was through Behravanfar that Namjoo discovered his love for blues and became familiar with artists like Leonard Cohen and Nirvana. Around the same time that Namjoo was exploring alternative connections between Persian poetry and music, and digging in Behravanfar's music collection, he was also visiting the famous Khorasani bard Haj Qorban Soleymani in Quchan most Fridays and learning *maqāms* from him.

COMING OUT: ABSURDIST NIHILISM

Namjoo's rejectionist attitude eventually culminated in an absurdist nihilism that was easy to grasp for audience members of a similar age who had grown up in the same repressive and dogmatic circumstances. Namjoo presented an early taste of his artistic manifesto, so to speak, in his first concert appearances with Behravanfar's band Mād. Their experiences were a combination of exhilaration caused by the overwhelmingly positive audience reception and disillusionment caused by the paramilitary *basij*'s violent interruptions of their concerts. In December 2002—about two years after O-Hum had given the first concert of its kind in postrevolutionary Iran (described in chapter 6), at the Russian Orthodox Church in Tehran—Mād and Mohsen Namjoo performed their first concert, in provincial Mashhad. Mashhad, which hosts the shrine of Imam Reza, Iran's most important Shia site, ranks as Iran's holiest city, and so the authorities are usually even stricter about cultural events there than in other towns. To stress the extraordinary nature of their concert, Namjoo says, "No one had seen any such thing at the time, the term 'underground music' didn't even exist as a category of music, and our concert just exploded onto the scene in Mashhad."

Mād gave three nights of consecutive concerts in a rented cinema, to a sold-out audience of about three hundred and fifty every night. Behravanfar was the lead singer for most songs; about his own role, Namjoo says: "For the first time on stage, when acting as Abdi's backup singer, I was standing there and howling on and on . . . something like that had no precedent at all, howling like that, in an Islamic country in its holiest city." There are a few videos on YouTube that show the practice sessions for these concerts, as well as one of the concerts itself. Behravanfar is playing a classical guitar, and every now and then plays the harmonica; two other musicians play electric guitars, with one of them occasionally playing the flute; and a drummer bangs away on a full drum kit. A skinny Namjoo, with his hair just growing out of the military shave required for service, plays the *setār* and, true to his own description of his vocals, glides from Persian *āvāz* to more folk-rock singing and onto animal sounds, such as barking and wailing, even in one song barking out the words *vāq-vāq-e sag*, literally, the "dog's woof woof."[2]

All three concerts were a great success, and the band members gained a lot of confidence from the experience. It also led to sources of income for most of them, as audience members approached band members for music lessons, and other connections were made. Namjoo, who had been planning to return to Tehran, decided to stay on in Mashhad for a while, leaving for Tehran later in order to record a studio album (which was never released, it appears, due to disagreements with his collaborators). The following summer, Namjoo returned to Mashhad for a second series of concerts with Mād. Buoyed by the experience of their first concerts, the band members had put a lot of hard work into the concert program, created posters, paid for a billboard advertisement in one of Mashhad's main squares, and generally planned to take their performance to a higher level. Namjoo says it was "one of those situations" where they weren't sure until the last moment whether they would receive a permit, and once *Ershād* did issue a permit, it made it conditional upon the approval of the "Office of Enjoining the Good and Forbidding Evil," an Islamically sanctioned body that polices people's behavior. When the band went to the office to get that approval, they were questioned and lectured by a cleric, who warned them not to move rhythmically on stage and told them to seat women and men separately.

Throughout, Namjoo says, he and the others were trying to charm the cleric, saying things like, "*Hāj Āqā*, by God, it's done, right? We've already printed flyers and even put up a billboard," and so on. "We were a bunch of young kids and had invested all our money in this concert," Namjoo remembers. The posters for the concert had an abstract skeleton head on them, and Namjoo says that from the start the authorities had a problem with the skeleton head, asking them, "What is this skeleton you've spread throughout the town?!" In the end, they gave the band the permit and the concert went ahead. Once again, the hall was jam-packed and the concert was proceeding well. As soon as the first set finished and the band announced the intermission, however, more than half a dozen *basijis* stormed the stage and shot several unfriendly questions at them. They demanded that Namjoo hand over his lyrics, which were on pieces of crumpled paper that he was holding in sweaty hands. Then they said, "Gather your stuff and shut down the concert." Namjoo's recollection of the event is that throughout the encounter, he and the band responded with cheeky humor, maintaining their dignity by not getting into an argument with the *basij*. The *basij* had no official authority in that situation to force the band into any particular action, but having grown up in the Islamic Republic with an understanding of the power relations at hand, the band knew that it had to shut down the concert. Namjoo has no idea whether the *basijis* had been sent by a security organ, such as the Revolutionary Guard's Intelligence Unit or even the Intelligence Ministry itself, or whether they had shown up of their own accord. When I pushed him to explain what, precisely, led the band to obey the *basij* and shut down the concert, he said, after a long pause:

> We're musicians, after all. We are not like them. How do you know the guy is not hiding a pistol under that baggy shirt of his, and if you get into an ar-

gument with him, he won't empty a bullet somewhere and kill your friend, create a tragedy? In the back of your mind, these kinds of thoughts are always in your file [he uses the English word], and you know that you have to act responsibly.

The consequences, Namjoo says, "were devastating." The *basij* had pulled the rug from under their feet. Even if they tried their best, the band could not rely on achieving success. It was not in their hands. This anecdote presents in a nutshell the source of the desperation that many Iranian young people feel about their lives and the (im)possibilities within them. It is where aspirations come up against a reality of constant uncertainty, the details of which can be determined by radical fragments of a state that ultimately gives them impunity. Although the band members knew that their concert was pushing the boundaries of political and even social norms, they had still retained a youthful sense of optimism, of possibility, that Namjoo is amazed by in retrospect.

After that experience, Namjoo remembers, "the band as a whole fell into a deep depression." A few months later, they were supposed to give two concerts in Birjand, and while they went ahead with it because they had already received the permits, Namjoo says that the experience as a whole was not very successful, in part because a loss of motivation had caused rifts among band members. Still, the first night's concert passed without interruption. But the second night, Namjoo recounts, "the same people, their copy in Birjand, with the same clothes and looks" showed up, pulled Namjoo, as the singer, aside and told him that they had seen a videotape of the band's performance on the previous night. In a song called "*Āh, keh intor*," (Oh, and So, in this case an expletive sigh of resigned acknowledgment), Namjoo had sung the line, "*Bāzgasht-e hameh beh su-ye u nist*" (All do not return to him [meaning God]), twisting the common Persian expression "*Bāzgasht-e hameh beh su-ye ust*" (All return to him), which is used in common parlance in the context of someone's death (on flyers and announcements, for example), or as an everyday proverb that calls forth humility and piety to the one God, essentially pointing to the equal status of all human beings in front of the ultimate arbiter. His interrogators stopped the tape at this song and demanded to know what Namjoo meant. "That's where my comic act set in," Namjoo says, explaining that in effect, he used humor to cope with this situation: "*Beh su-ye u nist?!?! Mageh misheh?!*" (Do *not* return to him?!?! Impossible!!). Namjoo became very serious, acting as though he were insulted by the notion that they would even suggest that he might sing something so sacrilegious: "*Beh su-ye u hast*" (*Do* return to him). At first, they were incredulous, citing the video, but Namjoo insisted that the bad audio quality had distorted his words: "Does it make sense to you that I would say that?! Of course we all return to him." (*Khob ma'lumeh keh beh su-ye u hast.*)

Namjoo took advantage of the *basij* members' own performativity of their identity—namely their overt commitment to Islam—to shame them into accepting that Namjoo could not possibly have uttered such a blasphemous thing. In Namjoo's words, "*taraf tu rudarbāyesti gir kard*" (the guy got caught up in *rudarbāyesti*, a cultural concept that is linked to notions of honor in Iranian culture, whereby a person will say, do, or accept something in order not to embarrass—or in order to accommodate—the other person). With Namjoo insisting on his innocence, and the poor quality of the tape, the *basij* would have had to accuse Namjoo of the greatest sin—namely blasphemy—without being able to be absolutely certain. It is precisely because blasphemy is such a grave sin for the *basij* that Namjoo's ploy worked. They allowed the concert to go on, but the band members were nervous and the concert as a whole was not a positive experience. It appears that Namjoo's lyrics and style were putting a band that was already in a precarious position directly in harm's way, and the band quit their collaborative concerts with Namjoo after that, although they continued working with him on his records.

The *basij* eventually accepted Namjoo's assertions that he could not have possibly sung what they thought he had because at that time, in 2002, it was truly unthinkable that a musician would publicly hint at a rejection of God anywhere, let alone in a provincial town of fewer than two hundred thousand inhabitants, where people tend to be more culturally conservative. The song "*Āh, keh intor*" (Oh, and So) was astounding in both its music and its words. It starts with an ominous rhythm interspersed with hits on a cymbal, and a male choir that repeats the refrain *Āh, keh intor* in a deep, dark, and dispassionate manner four times, at which point the beat picks up and Namjoo sings:

> The journal is a notebook written in the morning not night
> Love is an unceasing nocturnal longing, and the libertine is in pursuit
> The soul does not submit to the creator
> All do not return to Him[3]

Namjoo describes a world that is upside-down, a world where things are no longer as we know and expect them, where absurdity reigns: as he says in another stanza, "Day does not end in night" (*Ruz beh shab nemineshinad*), and "Mating does not happen before birth" (*Shab-e vasl qabl az tavalod nist*). Needless to say, the lyrics are unusual. To put this into perspective, remember that the pioneering rock band O-Hum, as we have seen, used classical Persian poetry for its music at the time, without meddling with the words.

Namjoo, by contrast, has appropriated segments of poetry from the works of three very different poets from different eras and combined them into verse that sounds vaguely familiar, contributing further to the song's strangeness. The song moves forward with a fast rhythm and Namjoo produces an unexpected string of sounds, such as that of a pistol shooting, a dog barking, deranged laughter and howls, torturous screeches, a donkey wailing, and perhaps most surprisingly, the recitation of a fragment of the *adhān*, the Muslim call to prayer. Having broken with his strict musical education in the classical Persian repertoire, Namjoo now considers all sounds in his soundscape to be legitimate for use as music or in music. Having been raised with the paradox of an ideological regime's propagation of a clear right and wrong in the face of widespread moral corruption within government and society, Namjoo creates a world of relativity and absurdity in his music, a world in which nothing is clear or certain. Namjoo's nihilistic discourse is at odds with the Islamic Republic's highly moralistic ideology, and as his later popularity would show, his discourse resonated with an Iranian youth clamoring for greater freedom at the turn of the millennium but finding its political, social, and cultural aspirations repressed by that same ideology.

GEOGRAPHICAL DETERMINISM

The years after Namjoo finished his military service, around the turn of the millennium, looked bleak for him. He was musically creative, but his efforts failed to reach fruition. "Oh, and So" is the first song on Namjoo's second album, called *Jabr-e joghrāfiyā-yi* (Geographical Determinism) and produced in 2004. The album consists of eight songs; Namjoo wrote the lyrics to all of them, although some are combinations of fragments of various poems, like the song discussed above. Like his first album, which never made it out of the studio because the financial investor failed to pay, his second album was never released, though some of its songs later found their way onto the Internet.

The state's control over music production meant that artists who were unable to attain permits for their work were unable to make a living, unless they shifted to teaching or to other professions within music. Namjoo wrote several articles about music during these years, made some recordings, and won second place in the *TehranAvenue* contest with his song *"Begu Begu"* (Tell, Tell), but his work was not taking off. In many countries, a musician can at least perform publicly to earn a meager living, even if it is on the sidewalk or in the subway, in cafés, or in bars, but in Iran it is nearly impossible to make money from performing music in public without government permission.[4] Unable to create a productive life with his music, it appears that Namjoo slowly drifted into depression. When I asked him what had caused his lack of motivation at the time, he said that the reasons were too complex to name, but then added:

> Iran's environment, that whole way of life, everything was destroying me, my person, my positive energies. . . . You see, it just doesn't work, in a country with a huge youth population with so much energy, when a regime beats you on the head and says, you as a journalist don't have the right to write, you as a musician don't have the right to sing, you don't have the right to act and so on . . . and you think to yourself, all right, I'm just going to go at least enjoy myself at home, have a drink, and they invade your home too and say, you don't have the right to drink alcohol either, and give you lashings. It's pressure on all aspects of your life; eventually, something gives.

I was working as a journalist in Iran during those years and vividly remember the sense of desperation and hopelessness about the future among many young people. Not only was unemployment very high, even among the well-educated, the state's restrictions on the public sphere also meant that there were very few possibilities for leisure or entertainment that appealed to the large youth bulge that was coming of age in those years of Iran's opening to the world and the world's opening onto itself, thanks to the Internet and processes of globalization. In the absence of unregulated concerts, cafés, bars, or public spaces where young people could feel at ease, they often met in each other's homes instead. The downside of this privatization of social activity was that drug consumption could and would happen more easily. Eventually, around 2007, there was greater public interest in Namjoo's music, when he felt that he was "becoming public," and this induced in him a "sense of responsibility" and a sense that his music mattered.

Around the same time, a film by the name of *Santuri*, about a drug-addicted musician, was screened at Iran's 2008 Fajr Film Festival, where it received the Audience Award. It was a clichéd portrayal of the real-life predicament of young Iranians who, out of a general sense of desperation, lack of opportunities, and the easy availability of drugs, succumb to drug abuse. The film was subsequently banned and never made it onto Iranian cinema screens, but it is fair to say that almost anyone interested in film—and that's most people in Iran—saw a bootleg copy of the film, as it was the much-talked-about cultural "it" item of that season.[5] The film, made by one of Iran's most celebrated directors, Dariush Mehrjui, personified for many the sad state of music in Iran in the tragic life story of the young and charming Ali Santuri, played by Iran's blue-eyed heartthrob movie star Bahram Radan. The story line is worth mentioning briefly within this context. Ali Santuri, a highly talented *santur* player, is unable to make a living with his music through legitimate means. At one point, his wife—played by star actress Golshifteh Farahani—mentions that he has failed to get permits for his records, forcing him to seek work as an entertainer at private parties and weddings, where he is often paid in drugs and alcohol instead of cash. As Santuri drifts into drugs, his life comes crashing down on him; people do not offer him work anymore, his wife leaves him, his parents disown him, and he ends up on the streets. Many were puzzled that the film's screening permit had been pulled. Wasn't this the kind of alarmist cautionary tale that state censors liked, linking music with drugs and abjection? Still, the story's ending is happy, with Santuri kicking his habit and teaching music to drug addicts, though even the happy ending, paradoxically, seemed forced and designed to please censors rather than reflect reality.

Regardless, the film resonated strongly not just because of its portrayal of the hopelessness that pervaded a musician's life—which was symbolic of life in general—but also because many Iranians are afflicted by drug addiction in their families. Still, what turned it into a sensation at the time was that the film's central tracks were sung by one of Iran's most popular young musicians, Mohsen Chavoshi, who like the film's protagonist Santuri had never managed to receive permits for his music until that time, despite attempts over seven years. (Chavoshi has received permission and released several albums since then.) There were also many rumors that *Santuri* was based on Chavoshi's life, which Chavoshi denied, stating that he had never been addicted to drugs. In an ironic reflection of life imitating art imitating life, Chavoshi was not even mentioned in the film's credits—possibly due to his "illegal" status—was not invited to the film's screening at Fajr, and received minimal compensation for his work.[6]

Soon after I saw Namjoo at the critique session at the House of Artists in March 2008 (described in chapter 6), he left Iran for Europe, never to return again. In Vienna, where he had intended to join the conservatory, a sunny afternoon at a café brought him a simple yet quite powerful insight. He ordered a cold beer and took it to a table outside. After the first few gulps, surrounded by peace, he realized, in his own words, "Oh boy, all your life you were deprived of this simple thing, of this moment of peace, not just me, that entire society, a moment of peace to think about your song, your painting, anything productive."

BECOMING PUBLIC

Those in the know had generally heard of Namjoo's work by 2005 or 2006, if not sooner. I got a CD of his work from a friend who had been involved in the recording of what would be called the *Damavand* album. My friend was a friend of Said Ganji, a sound engineer with a home studio near Mount Damavand, to the northeast of Tehran, and had offered to record a set of Namjoo's still-unrecorded songs, concerned, as my friend told me, "that the opportunity might forever be lost due to Namjoo's condition." The people present at the recording in 2005 were stunned that Namjoo was able to get all the instrumentals and vocals perfectly right on the very first take. Songs from this album and from other, previous work of Namjoo's floated around on the Internet and were traded on CDs, but it was in 2007 that a series of events caused Namjoo's music to really break out into the view of the wider public. First, for Nowruz, in March, *TehranAvenue* released a music video clip of Namjoo's song *"Zolf bar bād"* (Hair to the Wind), a Hafez poem that Namjoo sings in a searing, powerful voice that combines classical Persian *āvāz* and folk song intonations with a modern twist, set to a simple but atmospheric guitar sound. The video went viral and had thousands of hits in its first few weeks on YouTube.[7] It became a sensation in part because the video featured the young TV soap star Zahra Amir-Ebrahimi, who had recently been the subject of a sex tape scandal.[8] The lyrics, seemingly in tune with the actress's predicament, consist of a lover's desperate warnings:

Don't let your hair flow in the wind or else I will perish
Don't disseminate your charms or else my foundation will dissolve

In the same year, to everyone's surprise, Namjoo's album *Toranj* was released officially. Many of the lyrics are excerpts from classical Persian poetry, and Mād band members perform most of the instrumentals. The producer of the work had tried for more than a year to acquire a permit, but failed after repeated attempts. Namjoo himself recalls sitting outside the room in which the *Ershād* Music Office's Supervisory Unit, composed of five or six music experts, was considering his work. "They kept playing the first forty seconds or so of *Toranj* over and over again, and never made it beyond that," he told me. When I later asked one of those supervisory members, Mohammad Sarir (the composer on the council mentioned in chapter 4), what had kept them from issuing a permit, he strongly denied that they had rejected the work. He insisted that they did not have any problem with Namjoo's work, and that it was higher up that the permit was rejected, mainly because the work had already been released on the Internet. (Although artists do not have full control over whether their work is leaked to the Internet, they are often punished by *Ershād* when it is.) At least two other insiders I spoke to suggested that Namjoo's work was rejected at first because of strong opposition from a group of well-known traditional musicians, who considered his work to be damaging to Iran's music. One insider said that three prominent musicians wrote an official letter to *Ershād* gravely portraying the terrible consequences that Namjoo's music would have for Iran's musical heritage. Whatever the veracity of these claims, they do point to anxieties over Namjoo's work.

In the end, it was a record company associated with the Arts Domain, the *Howzeh-ye Honari*, of the Islamic Development Organization that published Namjoo's work. Namjoo's relationship with the *Howzeh* started after he was expelled from the university. According to Reza Mahdavi, the *Howzeh*'s director at the time, Namjoo had given a comedy performance at the *Andisheh* Hall of the *Howzeh* about once a month for more than five years. Mahdavi was impressed by Namjoo's work and tried to help him by various means, such as using his official position to enable his performances at *Andisheh*, find him work with state television, or arrange for him to appear on a live show on state radio. The *Howzeh* has the unofficial authority to publish music without the permission of *Ershād*, as it is under the direct authority of the Supreme Leader's Office. Mahdavi made use of this prerogative to publish Namjoo's *Toranj* album through its subsidiary, the Barbad record company. The album was announced with fanfare even by the conservative *Fars News Agency*, which reprinted the biography of Namjoo verbatim from the CD sleeve. The text declared:

> Although Namjoo's works in this album at times cross beyond innovation and form-breaking into near-transgression, it is clear that the essence of innovation and fusion in music and art does not have the opportunity to blossom and grow amidst intolerance and backward thinking [*khoshk-andishi*]. This opportunity would not have been possible without the responsible leadership of the *Howzeh-ye Honari* for the publication of the album *Toranj*.[9]

This led to *Ershād*'s public airing of its dismay with the *Howzeh*. Soon after the record's publication, *Ershād* warned in a statement:

> Recently, a number of music records which had been awaiting permits from the Ministry of Culture and Islamic Guidance were published commercially without undergoing the legal processes required by this ministry, based merely on permission documents issued by other cultural centers. Since the publication of any kind of album is only permissible through the permit of the Office of Music in *Ershād*, the issuance of permits by other cultural centers is forbidden and those opposing the specified laws will be dealt with.[10]

A few weeks later, the *Howzeh* published a special Mohsen Namjoo cover issue of its monthly magazine *Maqām-e Musiqā-yi* (Musical Mode), but *Ershād* ordered it to be confiscated from newsstands. Soon after, Mahdavi, an insider in the conservative establishment within the Islamic Republic, was relieved of his duties as director of the music department at the Islamic Development Organization, though he was reinstated about a year later. Clearly, Mahdavi had crossed a line in promoting an artist who could not be approved by the larger system, and an unequivocal measure had to be taken against him at the time.

BREAKING WITH THE ISLAMIC REPUBLIC

It was hardly possible to bring up Namjoo's name among Iranians, starting around 2007, without getting reactions of either extreme approval or extreme disapproval if not disgust. In my many conversations about Namjoo over those years, I heard everything from "Namjoo is a genius who has changed Iran's music forever" to "Namjoo is a con artist who doesn't understand the first thing about music." No other artist within the Iranian context caused so much controversy. Still, although his previous works were highly contested among music makers and consumers alike, it was not until the song referred to as Namjoo's "*Qur'an*" song appeared on the Internet that he became persona non grata within Islamic Republic establishment circles. In this 2003 piece, titled "*Shams*" after the *Surah al-Shams* (a Surah about the might of God and his act of elevating the Prophet Mohammad from an orphan to the messenger of God), Namjoo merges a core part of his upbringing and culture—namely Qur'an recitation—with the rock music that he was immersing himself in at the time.[11] In essence, this track is similar to a lot of Namjoo's early work, in which he is engaged with the idea of creating fusion music, as he explains:

> I knew Arabic *maqām* and I knew Arabic recitation. Due to my own inter-
> ests and the connections that developed later, such as my friendship with
> Abdi and others during military service, I had a chance to practice singing
> in different rock styles. I would try, for example, to sing like Roger Waters.
> We have three parameters, you see, in any musical piece: we have the style of
> singing, the music itself, and the text. So in rock music, you'd have the singing
> in "rock style" [Namjoo uses the English words here]; the scales are usually in
> blues; and the text is in English. In Qur'an recitation, we have the Arabic scale
> *maqām*, the singing style of Qur'an recitation, and the Arabic text from the
> Qur'an. . . . So we have six parameters that we can intertwine. This all led me
> to think of this fusion, where you have one part that's performed like Qur'an
> recitation—which I have taken from 'Abd al-Basit[12]—one part that is sung in
> rock style but in Arabic scales and with an Arabic text, and so on.[13]

As is evident from the above quote, Namjoo disregards the philosophical traditions and conventions of Qur'an recitation and simply equates *qirā'at* (recitation) with a form of singing. The result is a song that sounds very much like an
absurdist experiment: a fusion of Qur'anic recitation at times à la 'Abd al-Basit
and other times à la Namjoo, via rock tunes on a *setār*, underlined by the "Rico-
chet" melody of the Krautrock band Tangerine Dream. Namjoo seems to take
a cue from Tangerine Dream founder Edgar Froese, whose motto is said to be,
"In the absurd often lies what is artistically possible."[14]

In Iran, as in all Muslim societies, the Qur'an is a sacred text, with long
traditions about its recitation, which is why one never encounters such a completely unconventional reading of the holy text, let alone one set to rock music,
not to mention the female vocals that accompany sections of it. But that is not
all that Namjoo does. He takes the Qur'anic text and plays with it as he pleases,
singing it, declaiming it, interspersing it with sighs and strange animal-like
sounds, doing away with centuries of tradition and taking authority over the
text, and, more important perhaps, treating the Qur'an as just another text.[15]
Namjoo said he never intended for the song to be publicized, an explanation
he also gave to intelligence ministry officials who interrogated him about the
song in late 2007. "I told them: you know what, the Internet is completely out of
my and your control," before laying out his concept for this fusion. At its core,
Namjoo explained to an official, was a sense of curiosity and a sense of humor

and comedy: "Can you combine 'Abd al-Basit who recites the Qur'an with Roger Waters," who hails, culturally, from another planet? Namjoo says that the official seemed genuinely intrigued by the question and listened closely.

TALFIQ

It was during Namjoo's time in military service that he formed his understanding of fusion, which became the key signature of his music. He explained how he and Behravanfar would sit for hours while Namjoo "tested the *setār* within this framework of non-Iranian music," and how after hours of playing the *setār* and guitar together, Namjoo would play blues chords on the *setār* and Behravanfar would play Iranian scales on the guitar. Namjoo told me that that period for him "was as beneficial as the classes at university."

In the documentary *Diazpam 10*, Namjoo relates his astonishment at the similarities between some chords and melodies in Western and Iranian music:

> You are just stunned, right? For example, the *gusheh* "*Salmak-e Shur*," which my Ostād Nasrollah Nassehpour learned from Mirza Abdollah, which Mirza Abdollah learned from Mirza X, and Mirza X learned from Mirza Y Khan, these are the very quintessence of tradition; they wouldn't even conceive of music existing outside of Iran, let alone know any other music. But look, this is the fragment we have, in the *gusheh* "*Salmak-e Shur*," in the fourth interval of Shur. . . . [Here Namjoo demonstrates this particular note in the *gusheh* with his *setār*]. Now, we have the same in the blues key. [Here Namjoo demonstrates a similar chord in blues.][16]

Namjoo's new familiarity with blues as well as his keen interest in creating a fusion between the different musical traditions led him to discover similarities that furthered his evocations of artistic authenticity. This is reflected in Namjoo's definition of fusion: "*Talfiq* is not only in the form, putting a *daf* [a frame drum] next to a guitar. You've got to listen. *Talfiq* is in the discovery of the minute details of the scale. . . . This is no longer forcibly constructed, this is in essence finding the same in the other." It appears that Namjoo approached the creation of fusion in his music quite systematically, as a research question, while taking innovation in Persian poetry as a source of inspiration. In an interview with an Iranian newspaper while he was still living in Iran, he explained that he had three specific issues that he was investigating: one concerned finding new ways out of the "limitations and dead ends" in the relationships between poetry and music, another involved exploring the relations between Iranian and non-Iranian scales, as described above, and the third was about decoupling poetry from its meaning "and seeing it as a formal medium for voice as opposed to a medium for meaning."[17] He explains elsewhere that what he is following here is the "externalized" poetry school best associated with the poet Reza Baraheni, whereby the expressive sounds of vowels and words in a language are used to convey a sentiment or meaning rather than the lexical meanings of the words themselves.[18]

Namjoo's urge to constantly reach out beyond his national and cultural borders and to seek encounters and fusions with other forms and contents is in part a predicament of his generation. In Iran, as I mentioned in chapter 6, people refer to this approximate age cohort as the "burnt generation," because its members were burnt by the outcomes of a revolution to which they barely contributed. War veterans, for the most part, belong to this generation. They are now mostly in their late forties, and although Namjoo is about a decade younger, his life was marked by many of the same consequences of revolution and war. Another prominent condition that marked this age cohort, especially in its formative years, was international isolation. Unlike the generation that followed, the burnt generation, although it was too young to have fully participated in the revolution, was heavily sacrificed in the war, and by the time new media began to reduce Iran's international isolation, this generation was beyond its formative years. Hence, growing up, the burnt generation did not have much access to the Internet or satellite television—both of which have become more widely available in Iran since 2002 or 2003—and was raised in a closed atmosphere of social and political repression and anti-Western propaganda. For many, the result has been a sort of longing for the Western way of life. Namjoo expresses a sense of doom over having been born in Iran and in some ways engages in the discourse of a "colonized mind," one that is still trying to establish itself in relation to a better "other"—the West—going against everything the Islamic Republic has been preaching for close to three decades, namely a sort of nativism and independence from a "blood-sucking West."[19] This is clearest in Namjoo's earlier songs, such as "Geographical Determinism." At his 2016 New York concert, the one passage that Namjoo really got nearly the whole concert hall to sing along with was the refrain to this song:

> One day you wake up and you realize you've wasted away
> You're all alone, you've forgotten everyone
> A few more of your hairs have turned white, you unprincipled man!

Your birthday is another funeral
You're totally finished
. . .
[Refrain]
The fact that you're born in Asia, it's called "geographical determinism"
The fact that your life is suspended, your breakfast made of cigarettes and
    tea
. . .
You heavenly throne, what do you have in mind for us?
When are you going to do something for us, for your mother's sake?
. . .
That they make a clown of you
That they totally ignore you
That they don't let you in on their game
That they constantly tease you
[Refrain]
The fact that you're born in Asia, it's called "geographical determinism"
The fact that your life is suspended, your breakfast made of cigarettes and
    tea[20]

Imam Khomeini's vision of a new Iran establishing its own independent
path and identity, neither East nor West, is rejected here. Namjoo places Iran
squarely on the wrong side of the tracks in a binary world, where being born in
Asia, i.e. the East, already puts you at a disadvantage in a world where the West
rules. His song "Neo-Kantian Beliefs" ('*Aqāyed-e Nokānti*) similarly positions
a losing national identity against an "other" to whom the good things belong.
The song recounts the many depressing conditions of an Iranian life, easily recognizable to Namjoo's audience, and repeatedly contrasts those conditions with
the three seemingly positive values that the imagined "other" possesses. Hence
while the Iranian is preoccupied with philosophy and his or her metaphysical
condition, the other possesses "flowers from Normandy," "fifteen-centimeter-
long love" and "whatever you wish," symbols representing beauty, love/sex, and
freedom/possibility:

Neo-Kantian beliefs, my share
Flowers from Normandy, your share
Sweetness and impatience, my share
Fifteen-centimeter-long love, your share

. . .

Neo-Kantian beliefs, my share
Flowers from Normandy yours
. . .

Two-day-old *kuku* [a kind of quiche], our share
A copy of *The Godfather*, our share
Unbidden offspring, our share
A copy of *The Godfather*, our share
A sorry government, our share
Thickness of bureaucratic files, our share
A losing national player, our share
A sorry government, our share
Constructive criticism, our share
Maybe the future, our share
Maaaybe the future, our share
Neo-Kantian beliefs, my share
Flowers from Normandy, your share
Sweetness and impatience, my share
Whatever you wish for, your share

Each verse in this song refers to another aspect of the failure or desperation of the Iranian condition. The "copy of *The Godfather*" is a reference to
the nepotism and mafia-like relations within the Iranian government and institutions, where there is more of a runaround, and hence a greater "thickness
of bureaucratic files," the fewer relations one has, and where bribes are com-
monplace. But the thickness of files is also a reference to the prohibitive and
dysfunctional government, under which one easily accumulates complaints.
The phrases "constructive criticism" and a "sorry government" refer to the defeat of Khatami's reformist government, and the "losing national player" is a
reference to Iran's failing national teams, especially its soccer team in the 2006
World Cup, where Iran's low morale and poor performance led to an abysmal
loss. "Unbidden offspring" probably points to the number of illicit sexual relations and ensuing pregnancies, which have reportedly increased over the years,
leading to many illegal abortions. And finally, Namjoo sings *"shāyad"* (maybe)
with an intonation of "don't even think about it" when he mentions the future.
By the time Namjoo reaches this verse, toward the end of his song, it is clear
that the conditions it alludes to will not add up to much of a future; the future,
Namjoo implies, does not belong to "us," the Iranians.

AN IMAGINED COMMUNITY
OF POST-IDEOLOGICAL CYNICS

When Namjoo took positions that went against officially acclaimed ideas such as revolution, martyrdom, and God, he was aware that he was engaging with a large community of people who traded in this alternative public, usually by means of jokes and anecdotes. Drawing on these elements, he tapped into an existing community of memory that shared an intimacy based on past, often legendary, experiences suffered under a draconian state. Although many Iranians were on the receiving end of these harsh policies, postrevolutionary society was divided enough that it might be more appropriate to modify Michael Herzfeld's concept of "cultural intimacy" and call this shared intimacy "subcultural," as not everyone shares equally in this collective memory and language.[21]

Namjoo points up some of the cornerstones of this shared intimacy in his song now called *"Daheh-ye shast"* ("The Sixties" [this is referring to the Iranian calendar; it roughly corresponds to the nineteen-eighties]), which, to his own surprise, he was allowed to perform at the *Howzeh* at the beginning of the millennium. In the song, he draws out nostalgic but painful moments that were part of living through the nineteen-eighties in Iran. A YouTube video still exists of the *Howzeh* performance, where a visibly insecure and gaunt Namjoo first introduces his song by explaining that the title, "Burn the opium on your breath," means "your breath is so hot, light the opium on your breath, no need for fire."[22] The song as performed that day is nearly identical to the later renditions that he performed mostly outside of the country, with two important changes: in his later performances, Namjoo eliminates the verse about opium, and he emphasizes the refrain in which he refers to Tehran as *"Ali-Ābād"* (Town of Ali), alluding presumably to the Supreme Leader, Ali Khamenei. At his performance in Tehran, he only declaims this sensitive refrain once, and subsequently says, "The same refrain comes here again."

The other popular performance of this song on YouTube is from Namjoo's first concert in the United States, in San Francisco in the summer of 2008.[23] Here a vibrant and self-confident Namjoo gives his musical poem a lively performance, accompanying himself on the *setār*. There is not just a stark difference between the two performances, but also a stunning contrast in the audience's reactions. In Iran, there is muted reaction, even to some of the funnier parts, which speaks to the closed political atmosphere and public self-censorship on the part of audience members. In the free concert setting abroad, of course, the audience is much more responsive and clearly appreciates the nostalgic vignettes that Namjoo conjures up. Both in Iran and the United States, a large part of the audience is likely to have belonged to Namjoo's generation, and hence to have been fully versed in the poem's references. The text below is from his later version of the song abroad:

> The day when mother bought a schoolbag, red, like a suitcase, for first
>   grade, with a key
> The day when the essence of geometry was hard to solve, the teacher from
>   Hamedan, a hundred caravans of martyrs
> The day when death wanted children's lives
>
>   . . .
>
> [Refrain]
>
> The day that was lost to the wind, the day that gave into the wind
> The huge city that one day would be *Ali-Ābād*
> The day that was forgotten, the day that remained in memory
> And so it has been, oh dear, and so it shall be
>
>   . . .
>
> The day when the neighbor's girl shat on you
> The day when the neighboring country butchered your father
> The day when death entered through the locked door, the window
> The day when there were two TV channels: One went to war, from Two
>   came Wattoo Wattoo
>
> [Refrain]
>
> The day when a tank-crushed adolescent was our leader
> The day when short sleeves guaranteed a kick in the groin
> The day when beard
> The day of shirts torn under the armpits
> The day when the shirt collar was filthy from deep faith
> The day when Douglas was not Michael yet, he was Kirk
>
> [Refrain]
>
>   . . .

The day when the shah left, the republic became one-way
The day when the only way to freedom was through revolution
The day when there was moonshine, a mirage, a unique mirage
That soda that I drank next to her eminency Ma'sumeh when I was eight,
    mother had bought, green it was, 7Up it was

[Refrain]

The day that was cold
Haram were the chess and backgammon board
The only halal was carrying this yellow complexion
The only halal were opium and dust

. . .

It wasn't Tehran, the street was the plain of the bravehearted
It wasn't Iran, it was the cradle of the thirsty

. . .

So much have we suffered in these thirty years
So much have we suffered in these thirty years
That we have done nothing but suffer, thank you . . . thank you . . . thank
    you!

In this song, Namjoo gives at once a very personal and very communal "counter-memory" account of the nineteen-eighties, claiming the authority to articulate a description of that decade that differs from and challenges the state-sanctioned discourse.[24] These revelations of the "hidden transcript" have been a sort of social pastime since the revolution, but they have more often taken the form of jokes, gossip, and heart-to-hearts in informal settings within Iran, or more formal settings among expatriate Iranians abroad such as concerts and TV shows; they were rarely, if ever, revealed in this form in public fora inside Iran at the beginning of the millennium. While Foucault calls this practice "counter-memory," in that it diverges from the dominant constructions of memory, Namjoo's text is quite in tune with the collective memory of his generation and target audience, which is why this song has found such resonance and popularity. The song weaves itself into this collective memory thanks to associations with a poem which, at the time of its publication, likewise revealed the unspoken transcript, albeit in a much more powerful way for its times, coming as it did from one of Iran's most acclaimed poets, Ahmad

Shamlu. Shamlu's "In This Dead End" was banned upon publication in 1979, but soon became an anthem for the early nineteen-eighties:

> They smell your mouth
> lest you might have said: I love . . .
> they smell your heart.
>   Strange times, my dear!
> And love
> they flog
> by the roadblock.
>   We should hide love in the larder.
>
> In this crooked blind alley, at the turn of the chill
> they feed the fire
> with logs of songs and poetry.
> Hazard not a thought.
>   Strange times, my dear!
> He who knocks at your door in the noon of the night
> has come to kill the light.
>   We should hide light in the larder.
>
> There, butchers
> posted in passageways
> with bloody chopping blocks and cleavers.
>   Strange times, my dear!
> And they chop smiles off lips
> songs off the mouth.
>   We should hide joy in the larder.
>
> Canaries barbecued
> on a fire of lilies and jasmines
>   Strange times, my dear!
> Satan, drunk with victory
> squats at the feast of our undoing.
>   We should hide God in the larder.[25]

Namjoo echoes Shamlu's refrain "strange times, my dear" (the word Shamlu uses for "times" (*ruzgār*) contains the word "day" (*ruz*) that appears in Namjoo's recurring phrase "the day that"), thereby tracing a line to Shamlu's poem, positioning himself within Shamlu's legacy, and drawing on Shamlu's stellar credentials as a dissident writer. However, because he wrote the song many years after the actual sufferings described within it, Namjoo exhibits a characteristic cynicism but also nostalgia about his childhood. Namjoo's song is effective in great part because it contains cultural and historical references that are symbolic expressions of larger issues. For example, the line "The day when there was moonshine, a mirage, a unique mirage" refers to a period in 1978 when a rumor swept the country that Khomeini's face could be seen in the full moon.[26] Later on, those who resented the blind cult of the leader mocked the superstition of those who had climbed on rooftops to see Khomeini's face in the sky, characterizing the supporters of the Islamic Republic as ignorant religious fanatics. In a different stanza, Namjoo portrays a child's memory of the war, which is anything but heroic, unlike the regime's idealized "tank-crushed adolescent leader," a reference to war hero martyr Mohammed Hossein Fahmideh, a 13 year old who in 1980 threw himself under an Iraqi tank and detonated his grenade belt, stopping the Iraqi advance in that part of Khorramshahr, and garnering Khomeini's idolization as "our leader." It is a time when the child's father is "butchered" in Iraq, death is everywhere, and there are only two channels to connect the child to the world outside: one that was constantly covering the war, and another that showed children's cartoons, like "Wattoo Wattoo."[27] Namjoo's poem is full of symbolic markers, so much so that one line just goes, "The day when beard." Namjoo correctly assumes that his audience will know exactly what he is talking about, namely the fanatic decade in which the beard ruled. Not sporting a full beard or, worse, being clean-shaven, was interpreted by the *hezbollahis* as a clear marker of anti-regime sentiment and could get one into trouble, even into jail.

Namjoo questions the hypocrisy of a world in which a lack of sartorial care and cleanliness, including "shirts torn under the armpits" and collars "filthy from deep faith," were proof of allegiance to the revolution. He describes an Iran that is the "cradle of the thirsty" and finishes the song by saying that the reign of the Islamic Republic has been nothing but suffering, but he does it lightly, picking up a melody and ending with a sarcastic *"merci!"* (thank you!). The most remarkable thing about Namjoo's song and performance in Tehran was that he publicly revealed a very well-known hidden transcript, at a time when the beard still ruled and in a conservative setting—the *Howzeh*—that was and is under the direct supervision of the Supreme Leader's office.

"THE PRETTY JURIST"

Namjoo had barely surfaced from the scandal around his *Toranj* album when, in the fall of 2007, another one of his works—a leaked track titled "Shams"—caused a religious uproar. The song contained strangely sung verses of the Qur'an. Although, as we have seen, Namjoo eventually used this irreverence toward religion as a form of cultural capital that gained him many fans, it was not clear at the outset that he would take this step. Before his first album was finally published, it appears that he was still weighing whether he might be able to play within the legal and structural confines of the Islamic Republic. However, once Namjoo realized that his path to musical success in Iran was permanently blocked, he became more outspoken and irreverent regarding religion and the Islamic Republic. As he slowly departed from Iran's field of music production and entered the field of music as an "exiled dissident" abroad, he assumed the role that this cultural capital afforded him. At various concerts and venues in Western capitals, he highlighted his persecution as an artist and called for freedom and democracy in Iran. In turn, his welcoming reception by international organizations and by the Iranian diaspora in the West facilitated Namjoo's construction as an authentic dissident artist in need of support. This is not to say that Namjoo misrepresented any part of his trajectory or work, only that when he saw himself forced to continue his life and work outside of Iran, he ceased the prevarications that had been intended to keep the door open to a return home to Iran.

In 2008, shortly before Namjoo was scheduled to give his first series of concerts in the United States, starting in San Francisco, a well-known Qur'an reciter, Abbas Salimi, filed a legal complaint against him with the much-feared General and Revolutionary Prosecutor of Tehran, Sa'id Mortazavi. Salimi claimed that Namjoo's crime was a clear case of offense against religion and the Qur'an, and requested punishment for the singer.[28] Namjoo's brother acted as his lawyer and issued letters in which he argued, in profuse terms, Namjoo's religiosity.[29] The plaintiff then issued an enraged response in which he dismissed Namjoo's brother's letter, questioned Namjoo's piety, and asked how the culture of faith and religiosity would allow anyone to "howl in a ridiculing manner one of the heavenly titles of the honorable prophet [Peace Be Upon Him; *yā ayuhā al-muzzamil*] with the height of repugnance and using sounds that have no place even in so-called traditional, pop, jazz, rock, etc. . . . music."[30] Several other prominent figures from the Qur'an recitation community issued statements of condemnation in the following days; then, a day before his performance in San Francisco, Namjoo himself released a letter, which the *International Qur'an News Agency* titled "Mohsen Namjoo's Letter of Remorse and Apology to the People of Iran."

In this letter, Namjoo apologized first to the "blessed and sacred presence" of his mother, who "was my first Qur'an teacher in my childhood days and fortunately has never heard the piece under discussion in order to lose hope in me forever"; second, he apologized to "all honorable authorities and religious dignitaries of my country"; and third, he submitted his "most official apology" to "all Muslim people, especially those in my dear country Iran."[31] He told me that he had apologized first to his mother "to shame those people," adding, "it was to make the point that if I were to apologize to anyone it would be my mother, who raised me and taught me this religion and tradition." Not so subtly, Namjoo rejected others' authority to demand an apology for his perceived Islamic "misdoings." But quite subtly yet powerfully, he challenged his persecutors' definitions of what it meant to be an abiding Muslim. In the rest of his letter, Namjoo continued to challenge Salimi's dogmatism on what is Islamically permissible by positioning himself as a viable Muslim, someone born of Muslims, who had produced several "Islamic" tracks and always wore the Islamic protection prayer necklace that his mother had given him.[32] He also asserted his allegiance and claim to his country, Iran, by stating that such complaints could provide him with grounds to gain permanent residency in a foreign country, but that "God is witness that being far from Iran is like certain death" for him and that if he were to disown Islamic Iran, it would be equal to "negating himself and all his roots."

But Namjoo also equivocated somewhat in justifying himself, listing his religious credentials, and apologizing to the religious authorities and the people of Iran, using religious markers in his own interest. Ultimately, parts of Namjoo's letter turned out to be prophetic about his future. After the concerts in San Francisco, he remained in the United States; after about a year, he received a fellowship from Benetton's "applied creativity laboratory," Fabrica, in Treviso, Italy, aided in part by the publicity of the lawsuit against him in Iran. In June 2009, the court found Namjoo guilty of "insults against sanctities, the derisive performance of verses of the noble Qur'an, and disrespect toward the holy book of the world's Muslims," and sentenced him to a five-year prison term in absentia.[33] Convinced now that his bridges home had been burned, Namjoo used his safe position in exile to become much more politically outspoken. Due to the Green Uprising, there was a sudden explosion of Western fixation with Iran.

At his first concert after the 2009 election unrest, at an Iranian event in Berlin, Namjoo sat against a backdrop of one of the iconic photographs of the Green Uprising, a photograph of a girl shouting with apparent revolutionary fervor, with her green-ribboned fist in the air, in front of the Azadi monument, where the largest post-election protest took place. He started by announcing, "Considering the events that have happened, I have decided to stop censoring myself." He then explained that he was about to present a song he had composed eight years earlier, which he had decided to "pull out of the drawer these past days." He then added in a calm demeanor, "It's a letter of adulation or praise, like one that a poet would write for a king, it's for the religious leader of Iran, and it's called 'Faqih khoshgele' [Pretty Jurist]," in response to which there was immediate laughter from the audience.[34] The song begins with "Amān az dastet ey maqām-e moʿazzam-e bartari" (Cry for help against you, Honorable Office of Superiority!),[35] and continues, in line with the title, to further emasculate Khamenei:

> They say he has had enough and has given up on everyone, has divorced
>   his one hundred and twenty-four thousand wives for you and that
>   Jir-e Pamārān[36] [Khomeini], the loves of his old age
> . . .
> You are the most senior wife of God
> So much so that he even divorced Mohammad for you
> And the children who are born from your belly are all female, females
>   like me
> Our share and inheritance is half and like you, we must become
>   housewives
> In the hope that one night, God shall visit each one of us in our beds
> . . .
> I don't know which demon worked its influence on me that your husband,
>   or his illusion, never visited my bed
> . . .
> In the end your husband left me a virgin—Can you believe it?

After drawing this haremlike imagery of God and his prophets, Namjoo then ridicules Khamenei's exaggerated religiosity by portraying him as God's favorite wife. He then further accelerates his declamation, switching to imagery of a sinister Khamenei who orders his "gladiators"—thuggish *basijis*—to wreak havoc on town and people by all means, using Islam as legitimization when necessary:

Hey gladiators, throw yourselves on women
Hey gladiators, cover the hair of women
. . .
Hey gladiators, thunder on top of each other
Hey gladiators, twist in front of each other

Hey gladiators, it's a side-street runaway
Hey gladiators, it's approved by religion, pull it out
Hey gladiators, it's poisonous, distribute it
Hey gladiators, it's heroin, circulate it

Namjoo portrays Khamenei as the evil head of a dark empire that distributes
heroin and poison to destroy the young, and his so-called gladiators as automa-
tons who will do anything they are ordered, including "pulling it out," whether
this refers to pulling out weapons for killing or their members for rape. The song
is unprecedented in many ways. Whereas his previous songs were also irreverent, depicting a world bereft of values and meaning, this song not only ridicules
Khamenei, it also denigrates the idea of God and the prophets in the most offensive terms, a radically postreligious stance that only a minority of Iranians would
find palatable, let alone sympathize with. And yet, this minority still represents
a reasonably large fan base for Namjoo, even within Iran, and among expatriates
all the more so. After publicly ending his self-censorship, Namjoo employed an
extreme discourse to call together a cross-border public of like-minded cynics,
to whom nothing is sacred. In the years since his emigration from Iran in 2008,
however, his work has become less explicitly political, perhaps because he is no
longer living within a repressive social and political context. He has even said to
me that art should be free of politics.

The discourse that Namjoo created in the works discussed above is squarely
rooted in his generation's experiences of living within an isolationist context
and having to deal with a state that meted out symbolic and physical violence
in equal measure. This becomes especially evident when we turn our attention to artists who are more popular with the generation following Namjoo's,
younger by about five to fifteen years. The generation to which these artists
belong came of age during a general time of opening—both politically, under
Khatami, as well as technologically, thanks to the Internet and satellite television—and had its attention turned elsewhere.

CHAPTER EIGHT

GOING UNDERGROUND

IT WAS THE SUMMER OF 2006 in Tehran and *Rap-e Farsi* (Persian rap) was starting to come out in a big way. Fifteen year-old skinny and skinny-jeaned Farid with his spiked hair was standing on a sidewalk outside of his school and raging about a song by the rapper Hichkas that he was about to *blutus* (send by Bluetooth) to his friend Parsa. He said it was called *"Khodā pāsho"* (God, Wake Up!), referring to the rapper's song *"Ekhtelāf"* (Disparity), which begins with *Injā Tehrān-e* (This here is Tehran) and would make Hichkas into a household name years later. Farid said that he either got his files from friends or downloaded them from the Internet, including from sites like 021-music.com (021 being Tehran's area code). The website had made it possible for young—mostly teenage—rappers in Tehran to converge and find a community online to parallel their freestyle rap sessions in parks and homes.

Another friend joined Farid and Parsa and asked Farid if he had brought him the flash drive with the rap files. Farid reached into the front pocket of his jeans and pulled out a USB drive with what he said were hundreds of files, including photos, interviews, and songs, all rap. There were several files of Hichkas "freestyling" here and there. One showed Hichkas and three other rappers—Hossein Tohi, Amir Tataloo, and Arash AP—on the road to the ski resort of Shemshak, each performing a verse or two. Another captured Hichkas in the rapper's uniform of dark hooded sweater pulled over a rimmed cap, surrounded by young teenagers in what seems to be a parking lot, rapping his segment of *"To masti"* (You're Drunk), a collaboration track with the rapper Eblis, which includes the lines:

> I was about to sit down and get drunk but then you came and put your
> arm around me
>
> . . .
>
> I like cars and girls with a high chassis

Like other macho talk around the world, this is a song that puts women and cars in the same category of desire. But even in this party song, Hichkas inserts his social awareness and critique in the last lines:

> Tonight we're together but tomorrow not so
> Because in social standing we're different from head to toe

There were also more than three hundred JPG files of Hichkas and at least a dozen other rappers on the drive, posing on their own or with their posses and fans. Another video on the drive seemed to be an official recording for a possible music video clip. Hichkas is sitting behind a desk, dressed formally in a dark suit and shirt, rapping his patriotic ode to Iran, *"Man vāysādam"* (I'm Standing). As a large camera on rails closes in on Hichkas, two young men on the left record the scene on their mobile phones and then film each other, possibly creating material for other USB drives. Toward the end of the clip, most of the young crew present—including some young women in dark official veils (*maqna'eh*) and protruding blond hairdos—raise their arms and start tapping their palms forward from the wrist, imitating a concert-crowd gesture they have probably picked up from watching Western music clips on satellite TV or online.

Not long before the recording of this particular clip, Hichkas had met the man who would become his longtime collaborator, the UK-based rapper Mehrak Golestan aka Reveal Poison, on the social networking site Orkut. Together they produced what was perhaps the first *Rap-e Farsi* music video clip, to the track *"Tiripe mā"* (Our Way). Grainy and low-budget, it turned out to be the first of many collaborations. Another Hichkas collaborator who joined the team later, Mahdyar Aghajani (then just a teenager), emigrated to France in 2009 but still works closely with Hichkas. Hichkas's second music video, *"Yeh mosht sarbāz"* (A Bunch of Soldiers), went viral on YouTube and hip-hop websites in 2008, and though it was made by the same young director, it bore little resemblance to "Our Way." The director and producer was Farbod Khoshtinat (known as Fred), who was still just nineteen years old but already a little older than when he directed the first video, and this second video clip is infinitely smoother and more professional in its presentation.

Thanks to the Internet, Hichkas, Reveal, and Mahdyar were able to collaborate many times over the years, even before the rapper finally left Iran in 2010, following the 2009 Green Uprising and the ensuing repressive political conditions. While he was still in Tehran, Hichkas would go to a studio and record his section, Reveal would do the same in London, and the two of them would send their pieces to Mahdyar in Paris, who would put it all together and email the track back to them to check. When Hichkas was invited to give a concert with Reveal in London but could not get a visa, they recorded Hichkas's section and set things up, including shills planted in the audience, to make it seem as though Hichkas was joining Reveal via a live link.

Despite his inability to operate legally in Iran, Hichkas's online presence on sites such as RapFa and Facebook enabled him to attract an ever-increasing fan base inside and outside of Iran. Once he had decided to leave Iran for the foreseeable future, in early 2010, he gave instructions to friends to post his *"Yeh ruz-e khub miyād"* (A Good Day Will Come) online as soon as his plane took off from Tehran for Kuala Lumpur (see chapter 9). Utilizing new media, Hichkas was able to transform himself from a little-known rapper in Tehran to a rap musician with a large online presence and following who resides in London, sells his work on iTunes, and travels to give concerts to expatriate Iranians around the world.

A CHANGE IN POLITICS:
FROM KHATAMI TO AHMADINEJAD

By the time this new generation of underground rappers came of age, a few years into the new millennium, the world was a whole different place from the one in which Iran's first postrevolutionary generation of alternative and underground musicians (mostly rock and fusion artists) had grown up. Many of the rappers who had acquired visibility and a reputation by the middle of that decade were in their teens or early twenties then, part of postrevolutionary Iran's Third Generation (*nasl-e sevvom*). These youths came of age entirely during the Islamic Republic, with no memories of the revolution and little or no memory of the war. For most of them, the worst years of repression were over by the time they hit their later teens. Politically, this generation's consciousness was born with the election of reformist president Mohammad Khatami in 1997, whose policies allowed for greater cultural and intellectual freedom and tolerance. Despite the serious pushback by hard-liners soon after Khatami's election—in the form of renegade groups within the Intelligence Ministry, carrying out the "Chain Murders" of intellectuals and journalists, for example, or *basijis* meting out violence to students in the 1999 Tehran University protests— Khatami's policies continued to allow for greater openness in the public and cultural spheres. Concurrent with the Khatami government's policies of greater freedoms, two important factors affected the lives and worldviews of this particular generation.

The first of these was the terrorist attacks of 9/11, a few months into Khatami's second term, and the ensuing Manichaean proclamation by George W. Bush to the world, "either you are with us, or you are with the terrorists," putting Iran in a vulnerable position. Over the following years, as the United States invaded Afghanistan and Iraq, anti-Islamic and anti-Iranian rhetoric was prevalent in Western politics and media, and no Iranian could be oblivious to it. With images of death and destruction pouring in from neighboring countries, and their own country under the threat of an attack by the United States, Iranian youths were forced to define their positions vis-à-vis this new world order. As reflected in its cultural productions, this younger generation was less reactionary against the state than Namjoo's generation, and patriotic themes pervaded its rap songs.

The other crucial development during the early years of the new millennium was the increase in access to the Internet. Young Iranians were populating cybercafés across the country and connecting to the outside world, viewing themselves as part of the new global information technology generation. Even in the pre-Facebook era, Internet users from Iran made up one of the largest groups on the social networking site Orkut, along with users from the United States, Brazil, France, and India.[1] Hence, the Third Generation came of age in an atmosphere of both defiance and openness: defiant against the West's attacks on their culture and at the same time open and enthusiastic about being part of this new globalized generation. Within this transnational system, music played and still plays an important role. Music, especially hip-hop and rap, became a "vehicle for global youth affiliations and a tool for reworking local identities all over the world."[2]

Khatami's period of cultural liberalization, however, came to an end long before his second term was over, leading to frustration among his constituents—

many among them young people and women. Young people's disappointment with Khatami's failure to institutionalize fundamental reforms was made clear in his last face-to-face meeting with students—commemorating National Students' Day at Tehran University in December 2004—where a rowdy assemblage of fifteen hundred students severely criticized Khatami, heckled and harangued the visibly shaken president, and shouted slogans such as "Khatami, shame on you!" and "Khatami, our votes were wasted on you."[3]

In 2003, the newly regrouped *Osulgarāyān* (literally, "Fundamentalists"), who decried the direction that the state had taken and wanted to return it to the promises and principles of the revolution, won Tehran's city council elections. A year later, their political companions, the equally conservative *Ābādgarān* (Developers) won an overwhelming majority in the majles (the parliament), culminating in Mahmoud Ahmadinejad's rise to the presidency in 2005. Iran scholars have interpreted Ahmadinejad's ascendency as the result of the neglect of millions of financially humble and culturally conservative Iranian families who had sacrificed their sons for the revolution but were "left behind during Rafsanjani's reconstruction and could care less about Khatami's 'dialogue of civilizations'"[4] and, in a throwback to the early days of the revolution, signed up for Ahmadinejad's rhetoric of "populism, social justice, and unflinching loyalty to the martyrs of the revolution and war."[5]

Part of Ahmadinejad's campaign platform was the promise of a renewed phase of Islamic piety. Both the majles and the conservative Tehran city council pushed for faster action on this front, and by the spring of 2006, the morality police were once again ubiquitous on Tehran's streets. By 2007, the state had designed a campaign called the "Public Safety Program," which assigned regular police forces to crack down viciously on what were declared to be "Western mannequins" and *arāzel va obāsh*, an insulting all-inclusive umbrella term meaning thugs, thieves, and addicts. In the first four months alone, nearly one million people were publicly humiliated, or "disciplined," in the streets; forty thousand people were arrested, eighty-five percent of whom were youths aged sixteen to twenty-six.[6] Due to the prevalence of the Internet as a means of communication and the omnipresence of mobile phones at these scenes, images of these encounters were distributed widely and soon there was a strong backlash, even from within Ahmadinejad's own government.[7]

With the coming of the new government, the reformist culture minister Ahmad Masjed-Jame'i was replaced by Mohammad-Hossein Saffar-Harandi, a former deputy commander in the Islamic Revolutionary Guard Corps, who brought back the pre-Khatami rhetoric that considered "cultural invasion" as one of the nation's main challenges. In his introductory speech to the majles, he clarified his views on culture by saying that "if freedom is not guarded, freedom will become the enemy of freedom," thus justifying censorship.[8] Upon assuming his post, he stated that "one of the first issues that he would combat would be the types of music that are against the values of the Islamic Republic, including rock and rap."[9] He vowed to support "authentic" and "constructive" music as well as regional music with themes of the Islamic Revolution and the Holy Defense (the Iran-Iraq war). In a later meeting with the members of the House of Music, he expressed hopes that government censorship could be reduced to a minimum by nurturing in artists a mechanism of self-censorship.[10]

Along with the enforcement of "piety" in the public sphere, the state also cracked down on the cultural sphere. Several cultural institutes that had flourished during Khatami's term were closed and "others were severely restricted, the budgets of cultural centers in Tehran were cut by half, while more funding was provided to religious institutions."[11] Halls within existing cultural centers that had in the past served as concert venues remained closed for long periods, their managers reluctant to open their doors for fear of repercussions from hard-line pressure groups. During these years, several music production companies, among them the well-known Barbad record company (which has appeared in earlier chapters), were also fined and suspended for "violations of law."

Even before Ahmadinejad took office, Ali Moradkhani, who had generally been viewed very positively, left office after thirteen years as *Ershād*'s music director. Although bands like O-Hum had failed to get permits even under his management, he had been a relatively lenient director who facilitated the spread of pop music, at times even acting against the IRIB to allow permits for records such as Shadmehr Aghili's *"Dehāti"* (Villager), which contained the formerly banned 6/8 rhythm, and popular melodies reminiscent of prerevolutionary pop songs. During his long term in office, record releases and concert performances had gradually multiplied.

As public venues for musical performance became more limited in number and artists' hopes for permits diminished, the Internet became an ever more important venue for music, and many varieties of underground music mushroomed online. At the same time, while placing greater restrictions on the official sphere under its purview, the government also started going after the more popular underground musicians—mostly rappers[12]—and widely publicized their arrests as a warning to others. Throughout the years 2007 and 2008, there were frequent reports of arrests of members of music and music video production groups that were usually described as dressed in "unusual" ways (*gheyr-e-mote'āref*), engaging in unhealthy girl-boy relationships, and/or producing works that were "indecent" (*mobtazal*) and "obscene" (*mostahjan*).

VISTAS VIA TECHNOLOGY

Prior to the advent of the Internet in Iran, Iranians had found various informal means of communicating political and social sentiments in their shared "semi-secret" public sphere. These means encompassed everything from small media like pamphlets and cassette tapes to informal communications such as gossip, jokes, and conversations with strangers in shared public spaces (including taxis, shops, cinemas, and bus stops).[13] However, the Internet provided an entirely new level of connectivity and networking that revolutionized the concept of the public sphere within Iranian society. Over the last decade, scholars and journalists have observed and studied the groundbreaking impact of the Internet on the various realms of Iranian life, increasingly moving from utopian notions of the capabilities of new media to more critical assessments of its role in facilitating social and political change.

Iran was the second country in the Middle East, after Israel, to gain access to the Internet; it was launched there in 1992, at the Institute for Studies in Theoretical Physics and Mathematics, and then spread within Iran's university system.[14] By 1995, *Newsweek* was already reporting that "If the computer geeks are right, Iran is facing the biggest potential revolution since the Ayatollah Khomeini."[15] From the beginning, the state encouraged the development and expansion of the Internet, and even conservative authorities saw its potential for the promotion of revolutionary ideology and state propaganda.[16] Indeed, seminaries in Qom and Mashhad embraced the medium early on for educational purposes, Shi'ite ulama used the Internet to offer spiritual guidance, and even Iran's Supreme Leader, Ayatollah Khamenei, launched his own official website in 2004. Today, many of the Islamic Republic's highest-ranking officials have Twitter accounts.

Equally enthusiastic about the web, if not even more so, were reformists, who created online versions of their serially banned newspapers, as well as young people and women, who embraced cyberspace for the freer expression of their own views and the creation and positioning of their subjectivities within this space. Early on, weblogs became the most significant area of Inter-

net growth in Iran, and by 2009 blogging was a national pastime, with estimates
that Persian blogs numbered four hundred thousand, or even seven hundred
thousand, and with Persian being one of the most-used languages of the blogosphere.[17] The so-called godfather of Persian blogging, Hossein Derakhshan,
who first wrote Persian instructions on how to write a weblog in 2001, perfectly
encapsulated the spirit of blogging in his own blog title, "Editor: Myself."

In the early years of the millennium, Internet access was still too expensive
to permit large numbers of Iranians to get online. A 2001 survey showed that
even among residents of affluent North Tehran, only 6.1 percent had access to
the Internet.[18] However, Internet cafés, called *kāfinet*, were mushrooming at the
rate of one new Internet café per day in Tehran; there were fifteen hundred of
them in 2001 and within a few years, there were seven or eight thousand of them
in Tehran alone.[19] By mid-decade, the proliferation of Internet service providers
and the improved infrastructure meant that at about twenty dollars per month,
many more people could afford an Internet connection in their own home. The
number of Internet users in Iran has been growing steadily, from a quarter of a
million in the year 2000 to forty-two million in 2012, more than half the population.[20] Bloggers have enjoyed this free virtual space: as one of them explained
to me, "all of a sudden, we were all addicted. There were no restrictions in we-
blogistan, whether we wrote about politics or personal matters."[21] Although the
government was slow in curbing freedoms within the new space, however, by
2003 it had a systematic strategy to block Internet websites[22] and had imprisoned Iran's first weblog casualty, a young journalist named Sina Motalebi.

While the government has become increasingly sophisticated in block-
ing sites, and even disabling virtual private networks (VPNs), users have likewise become more adept at circumventing these filters, so that cyberspace still
remains a significant public forum for the display and exchange of political
dissent, cultural and artistic content, and intimate personal revelations, all of
which have contributed to the blurring of the traditionally rigid lines between
Iranians' private and public lives. Hence, where there used to be informal (and
usually oral) channels of communication, the Internet has provided a more
tangible space where much larger networks of Iranians can coalesce, exchange
views, and mobilize toward certain cultural and political goals.[23] The political power of these networks became most evident in Iran's 2009 presidential
elections and its aftermath, where new communications technologies—the Internet, cellular phones, and satellite TV—enabled "interactive networks . . . to
mobilize protests and stage identity formation."[24]

Since 2009, the government has viewed these new media as a threat to the very foundations of the state and further tightened its grip on this sphere. In September 2009, the Mobin Trust Company, a front for the Revolutionary Guard, bought fifty-one percent of the shares of the Iran Telecommunication Company, and soon thereafter the police launched a unit called the "Internet police" to monitor online activities.[25] Whereas before the elections it had been possible to bypass filters quite easily, using VPN connections, following the unrest the government found ways of disabling all VPN networks and, at times of heightened turmoil, either shut down the Internet completely or brought it down to such snail speed as to render it useless. In addition, it has devised ways of manipulating new media for its own purposes, by constructing fronts and infiltrating anti-government networks for information gathering as well as spreading messages to its own advantage. Iran is today believed to have one of the world's toughest Internet control and filtering systems, after China, thanks to a combination of its own scientific inventions and purchases from giants such as Nokia Siemens (later renamed Nokia Networks).[26]

Although Iranians have still found ways of circumventing some of these controls, the state's narrowing of this space has led to a preponderance of voices that view the Internet's potential in Iran critically, arguing that rather than furthering democratic aims, the Internet helps authoritarian regimes tighten their grips on their populations.[27] Others argue that rather than reshaping social structures in the actual world, new media simply reflect already existing social and political conditions, so that the digital divide, for example, "limits who takes part in the dialogue in this emerging public sphere."[28]

THE IMPACT OF NEW MEDIA ON MUSIC

Around the turn of the millennium, globally, new communications technology slowly overturned and revolutionized the sphere of music creation, consumption, and exchange. This happened most of all in the West, where four or five multinational corporations had previously dominated the music industry, while about the same number of radio conglomerates controlled the selection of music that was disseminated to the public.[29] Even then, however, the "cultural imperialism hypothesis" that saw a linear domination by Anglo-American music of global markets and musical tastes was fraught, since this music itself was often influenced by music streaming in from the rest of the world, such as Algerian rai or West African Afrobeat.[30] And until the advent of the Internet and satellite TV, this gatekeeper role played by Western conglomerates was less evident in Iran than elsewhere. In Iran, the government was the purveyor of all "legal" music, and the proliferation of other kinds of "illicit" music was quite random, although pop giants like Michael Jackson and Madonna seeped into Iran just as they did elsewhere.

Throughout the nineteen-eighties and early nineteen-nineties, certain bands and musicians, such as Pink Floyd, Chris de Burgh, Modern Talking, and Dire Straits, left a particularly deep mark on popular tastes. Although in the Iran of those years one could often find the works of the megastars on the black market, variety was very limited unless one looked diligently or had relations who smuggled in tapes from visits abroad. Another explanation for why tastes often converged around the same few bands or musicians is that most people received their music from friends who had obtained theirs in turn from other friends, and this happened to be music that these friends had access to and liked. If one were to trace the source one would ultimately arrive at a music dealer (or a friend returning from abroad), but inevitably, this underground friend-to-friend network of repeatedly copied cassette tapes meant that some artists were huge in Iran and others were barely known, even if they were famous in the West. And yet, this still only partially explains the immense reach and popularity of certain bands, with Pink Floyd, in particular, being arguably the single most worshipped Western band in postrevolutionary Iran. After all, Pink Floyd had songs like "Another Brick in the Wall"—the music video of which went viral on VHS in Iran in the mid-nineteen-eighties—and other songs that highlighted the surrealism of human existence; rebelled against authority, constrictions, and homogeneity; and hence resonated with Iranian youth.[31]

As more Iranians gained access to new media technologies, two processes occurred. On the one hand, Iranians became more susceptible to the commodification and commercialization of globally marketed stars such as Céline Dion, Mariah Carey, Yanni, Jennifer Lopez, and Ricky Martin. More importantly however, musicians who were coming of age during the period of Khatami's "dialogue of civilizations," with greater openness and access to global cultural currents, used this new realm as an alternative space for the creation, production, and exchange of their own musical ingenuity. At this time and even through to the first few years of the new millennium, most musicians were still following a dual track of pursuing permits with *Ershād* while at the same time promoting their unlicensed work online. Even squarely "underground" rappers like Hichkas and Yas were trying to gain permits at the time.[32]

In those early days of Iran's online music community, the rapper Hichkas says he was the first to start a rap website—021-music.com, which I have already referred to briefly—and invite other rappers to join in and post their work there.[33] By 2005, there were several such sites where people posted music and their opinions about music. As these sites were and are usually set up by young rap enthusiasts, financed either personally or through small ads, they tend to have relatively short lifespans, of at most several years. Furthermore, over the years, the Iranian government has not only blocked but at times closed down sites by directly confronting the people who run them and often fining them or extracting pledges from them not to continue running the sites. As a result, there has been no one website running continuously since the early days, but there have usually been several popular ones concurrently at any given time, and often variant versions of a single website coexisting in order to evade government censorship. So, for example, one of the most popular sites throughout—RapFa.com—has had various other addresses at different times, such as RapFa3.com, Rap-Fa4.com, 63rapfa.com, and so on.

Besides promoting music, these sites also sometimes post interviews with the artists, and there is an online community of ratings, comments, and gossip that accords popularity to artists and songs. Starting in 2007, when the state began to systematically persecute stars of the underground music scene, rap sites sometimes offered the only credible source of news on arrests and ensuing events. Within this sphere, motivated entrepreneurs made it their business to produce a sort of citizen journalism of the rap scene. A young man named "Yashar Rapfa" conducted many short but insightful interviews with rappers and posted them on rap websites, foremost the RapFa website, which he managed. Looking only at state media and other approved media outlets, one would be forgiven for thinking that hip-hop and rap were either nonexistent or a very niche music scene, but surfing the web and the myriad of heavily frequented sites and weblogs makes it clear that this music has a lot of fans, especially among young people.[34]

Aside from such websites, the Internet has also facilitated the expansion of this particular musical sphere in other ways. The Tehran-based webzine *Tehran-Avenue* (discussed in detail in chapter 6) played an important role in this regard starting in 2002. The Internet, and new media more generally, have also "paved the way for the emergence of a global public sphere for Iranians,"[35] enabling the flow into Iran of works by financially and technologically better-endowed and governmentally unrestricted producers abroad. So, for example, in 2003 the *Zirzamin* ("underground") online zine (also mentioned in chapter 6) launched in Sweden—subtitled the "Iranian Alternative Music Magazine"—and became an indispensable free forum for the wide range of underground music, not just hip-hop. A few years later, in 2006, the Dutch government funded the launch of the Internet radio channel Radio Zamaneh, which in the same year staged the first live Iranian underground music festival in Zaandam, Holland, inviting about a dozen of the hottest acts—many directly from Iran—to put their music on stage.

Beginning with Orkut and continuing with MySpace, Facebook, and Twitter, social networking sites have also been popular platforms for the promotion of the Persian hip-hop scene. BBC Persian Service's *Ruz-e Haftom*,[36] presented by Behzad Bolour, offered some of the first professionally recorded programs on the Iranian rap scene, released via podcasts. The program only ran from 2006 to 2007 and was discontinued as the BBC launched BBC Persian TV in 2009, where Bolour showed less interest in Iran's underground music scene and tended to feature expatriate Iranian stars. In 2011, the new Persian-language satellite television channel *Manoto* (Me and You) also launched a music program called *Sakkou* (Platform), the first weekly TV show to feature Iran's alternative music scene.

Tightly intertwined with the Internet as an alternative public sphere for the circulation of music are the dozens of expatriate Persian television channels that are received in Iran via satellite. There are no precise figures for the number of Iranians who watch satellite TV programs, but most sources estimate it to be about half the population.[37] In the nineteen-nineties and into the early years of this millennium, these were mostly Los-Angeles-based TV channels that beamed exile productions into Iranian households. However, with the proliferation of both approved and "underground" music in Iran, these and other newer channels—foremost among them PMC (the Persian Media Corporation, based in Dubai)[38]—as well as radio stations such as Radio Farda and online music channels such as Radio Javan, have become sites for the broadcast of Iran-based musicians and Iran-made productions. The Iran-based music broadcast on these channels is produced either inside Iran or, if outside of Iran, by recently emigrated Iranian musicians, such as Shadmehr Aghili since 2002 or Sasy (known previously as Sasy Mankan) since 2012. These channels offer venues absent in Iran's state broadcasting system. However, "legal" Iran-based musicians and even some musicians who have not yet received permits but are still pursuing the official track do not consent to their work being broadcast by these channels due to possible punitive repercussions. "Underground" acts like

Barobax and Sasy Mankan, on the other hand, have achieved fame by allowing channels like PMC to broadcast their songs. Expatriate television channels, in particular, have greatly facilitated the further expansion of this music scene into the daily lives of Iranian families, since television is a more inclusive and cross-generational medium than the Internet.

In an unprecedented new development, the state has allowed a group sponsored by beeptunes (a sort of Iranian Apple iTunes) and PersianPars (car dealer) to produce a music show titled "ChaarGoosh" (Rectangle) starting in March 2016, where even acts that would be regarded as "underground," such as the rapper Reza Pishro and the band Barobax, are interviewed and featured. The majority of guests tend to be newer bands whose music presents a fresh form of fusion, music that distinguishes itself in originality from the pop music fare, such as Dang Show, Bomrani and Pallett, but also rock acts such as Comment and Reza Yazdani. Beeptunes is an online site that advertises itself as the "biggest source for the legal download of music in Iran." The program, which only airs online, presents content that would not pass hurdles for broadcast on state television, but keeps within official regulations with a moderator, for example, who wears a headscarf, and conversations that are within the realm of the public transcript. This, it seems, is the government's way of carving a space where it can control content that is catered to the needs of its young population, without raising the ire of more conservative elements within society, or ceding the space completely to expatriate or underground channels.[39]

Another vastly influential new medium for the proliferation of this music has been the mobile phone and, in particular, Bluetooth technology. Since about 2005, Iranians have circumvented slow speed and government filters on the Internet by making greater use of Bluetooth technology. Mobile phones have been abundantly used to spread both live-recorded events (such as rap battles in parks or home freestyle sessions) and music audio and video clips downloaded onto phones and then spread via Bluetooth. This practice is so common in Iran that most mobile phone owners add extra memory to their devices and often have dozens, if not hundreds, of clips to share (like Farid, with whom I began this chapter).[40]

"UNDERGROUND"—THE NEW GENERATION

Since 2007, the strength and spread of the underground music scene has become hard to ignore, and the government, research centers, and the media have been organizing events and grappling with the issue. The topic has usually been framed as a generational phenomenon: a curiosity that needs to be dissected, examined, and understood. In an article published by the Institute for Anthropology and Culture, for example, the authors use Bourdieu's theory of distinction—the use of symbolic goods and cultural capital by a socioeconomic class to distinguish itself from lower classes—to argue that underground music in Iran is used by the younger generation to make not so much a socioeconomic as a generational distinction: "With this kind of music, this new generation has distinguished itself from previous ones," they write.[41] Hence, the Third Generation has found itself under a magnifying glass, not only because it constitutes a large proportion of Iran's population, but also because its underground cultural productions have entered homes and families.

Among the discourse produced about this generation, there has been mostly overlap and consensus about its characteristics, but also some disagreement. A report commissioned by the conservative Islamic Revolution Document Center titled "The Islamic Revolution and the Confrontation with the Third Generation" first quotes the most revered Shi'a Imam Ali on young people, saying: "Don't constrict your children to your ways and customs; they have been created for a time different from yours."[42] It then goes on to give thirteen characteristics of this generation, among them that it possesses a more established and independent identity than earlier generations; cares more about the essence than the appearance of religion; prefers to be seen as it is rather than to hide; thinks positively about relations with the world and its different cultures; wishes for a modification of the relationship between politics and religion but not a separation between the two; is disinclined toward politicization and rather than feeling aligned with political personalities and parties, will spontaneously take steps toward the continuation of the Islamic revolution; is more likely to be inclined toward aesthetics and art; is dynamic and has a critical soul; and is committed to Iranian culture and traditions, as well as to religion and morality.

After this assessment, the text goes on to affirm this generation's commitment to the revolution, quoting from the Supreme Leader's speech to students at Tehran's Amir Kabir University on 27 February 2001. Khamenei begins this section of his speech by pointing to a comment that he calls "the enemy's psychological war," namely the claim that "the revolution's Third Generation is no longer committed to the ideas of the revolution," and then digresses into a discussion of revolutions before returning to the crux of his conclusion:

If the ideas of a revolution can convince the second, third, and tenth generation due to its authenticity and veracity, that revolution will have an eternal life. Seeking justice will never become old; seeking freedom and independence will never become old; fighting foreign interference will never become old; these are values that will always appeal to the generations.

The author of the report concludes by referring to the three main categories of needs of this generation, namely "cultural, socioeconomic, and political," and continues to define the attainment of these needs within a state-approved framework. Thereby, "true freedom" is defined as "emancipation from factors of external and internal pressure," in the words of disappeared Shia scholar Ayatollah Musa al-Sadr, and the "renunciation of the flesh," in the words of Imam Ali. The author's ultimate and lucid conclusion, quoting revolutionary ideologue Ayatollah Morteza Motahhari, is that "if our third generation senses incongruity between the discourse and the actions of our religious leaders, it will not be able to trust their ideas and follow them."

In speeches at music roundtables in Iran, in my conversations with people in the field of music, and in journalistic and academic texts, I have frequently encountered the attribution of similar characteristics to this Third Generation. At a daylong event organized by the cultural and social research arm of the Center for Strategic Studies on "underground" music, one of Iran's most prominent academics on the subject made what is a commonly accepted observation, namely that "this generation . . . has no inhibitions (*rudarbāyesti*) toward the revolution and the country's cultural officials; hence they are much more comfortable expressing their criticisms."[43] The well-known guitarist Babak Riahipour, who started out with the rock band O-Hum but has since performed with both legal and underground bands, has expressed the same sentiment from a different angle, saying that rap was popular because in current Iranian culture, where a lot of two-faced or hypocritical behavior reigned, rap offered a clear, straightforward language that facilitated criticism, which young people appreciated.[44] Babak Chamanara, the owner of Tehran's oldest continuously operating record store, expressed a similar sentiment to me, saying, "The generation of the nineteen-eighties is not still struggling with the revolution like us. For them Khomeini is not a person they knew as a revolutionary leader; it's not about the revolution for them, they're beyond that."[45] Before the 2009 election unrest, this generation was often described as being too apathetic to be political. As one observer put it: "The Third Generation has almost renounced all politics and has, instead, embraced an epicurean or absurdist view of life."[46]

However, following the elections and the overwhelming participation and leadership of young people in the subsequent protests, this generation has now been reconsidered as more of a political force, and one that retains an element of surprise and unpredictability. As a friend of Chamanara's put it, "This generation will take a taxi from Vali Asr to Enqelab [a short distance] but it will walk all the way from Imam Hossain to Azadi [the path of the largest postelection protest, approximately seven kilometers]."[47]

DEFINING *MUSIQI-YE ZIRZAMINI*

It appears that the mere existence of the label "underground music" gave rise early on to a great deal of rumination in writing and discourse in Iran about the nature of this kind of music and its position vis-à-vis "underground" music as it is understood in the West. By now, however, this kind of rumination is no longer a necessary prelude to every discussion of Iran's "underground" music, as certain points of consensus appear to have emerged on what constitutes "underground" music: namely either music for which someone has tried and failed to receive official permission for its production and distribution or else music whose makers are not even attempting and do not desire to be government-licensed. In the second case, that could be because they know that their music stands no chance of receiving a permit or because they prefer the symbolic capital of being "underground" to the possible economic capital that being "aboveground" could generate. Nonetheless, the term continues to mean a number of things. It often refers to music that crosses the boundaries of the publicly permitted as far as content, language, and musical form are concerned; it can also allude to a wide range of musical genres, depending on government restrictions. So, even certain kinds of pop can be "underground" music, depending on their other characteristics. And the music it refers to can have a tenuous position between the "underground" and "aboveground," depending on circumstances.

Prior to the legalization of pop music in the late nineteen-nineties, *los anjelesi* pop music—despite its mostly innocuous lyrics—represented the realm of the "underground" for Persian music. But once new, homegrown Iranian pop music was legalized, its expatriate relative half a world away lost some of the subversive cachet that it had accrued since its banishment in 1979. This newly created official space, along with its underground counterpart, represented the emergence of postrevolutionary Iran's first grassroots pop music scene. Within both spaces (official and underground), bands created compelling music. As pop lost its subversive character, rock music (which had been equally subversive but much less listened to), became for a while the new battle-ground between musicians and censors. Iran's early underground music scene consisted nearly entirely of rock or some form of rock fusion music, but over the years all sorts of music have taken up residence in the *zirzamin* (basement/underground), with the most vibrant currently being hip-hop.

As the newest generation of musicians came on the scene, and rap songs overtook rock songs in both novelty and sheer quantity, "rap" became increasingly synonymous with the unauthorized sphere of music in Iran. Like rock previously, "rap" referred to a musical style but also served as a discursive category denoting this music's "alternative" and "uncontrolled" nature. But the semantic range of the term also extended to the kinds of youth who listened to this music. Hence, when someone said so and so "is really rap," the image that was usually conjured was one of a young person with outrageously styled "*mu-ye fashén*" (fashion hair)—normally in the *sikh-sikhi* style (hair spiked with enormous amounts of gel)—and clothing that, for boys, often entailed sneakers, drop-crotch jeans, and tight shirts with English words or Western logos on them. For girls, being "rap" often meant wearing tight, very short *manteaux* (coats), sneakers, and the latest, rapidly changing, headscarf fashion: with both ears sticking out at the beginning of the millennium; a large quantity of *sikh-sikhi* hair sticking out in front by 2008 or so; and in 2011 a very large pile of hair, up to a foot high, on top of the head, under the scarf.

However, as "underground" music has become more and more widespread, and people have acquired a greater understanding of and familiarity with the different genres, the term *musiqi-ye zirzamini* has taken over what pop, rock, and rap used to stand for. For a time, there was a backlash against the term "underground," as many argued that the Western connotations of the term did not apply to the Iranian context and that this music was indeed so widespread that it was quite "aboveground"; many therefore preferred to refer to unauthorized music as "alternative."[48] But despite all criticisms of the shortcomings of the label *musiqi-ye zirzamini*, it has had the most traction in public discourse and is the term that most people, including journalistic and academic observers, now generally use.

Several documentary films have tried to capture this "underground music" scene. Mojtaba Mirtahmasb's pioneering 2003 films *Off Beat* and *Back Vocal* tell the stories, respectively, of Iran's "underground" rock groups as they participated in the first *TehranAvenue* Underground Music Contest in 2002, and of the struggles of Iran's female musicians to be heard and make a living despite government restrictions. Amir Hamz and Mark Lamarz's 2006 film *Sound of Silence* paints a picture of the large variety of musical genres in this scene, capturing the desire of many musicians to infuse their Iranian heritage into their respective kinds of music. Bahman Ghobadi's 2009 film *No One Knows about Persian Cats*, meanwhile, exploits the rising international interest in this music scene to present an overly simplified image of oppressed musicians, all desperate to emigrate so that they can pursue their passion.

Broadly speaking, most kinds of contemporary music are represented in this "underground" scene. While most of these bands are known only to the smaller community of Iran's rock aficionados, some of them, such as Kiosk, have made real breakthroughs and are known as well to more mainstream listeners in Iran. There are also varieties of fusion and rock music, such as the innovative *khāl punk* of the band 127 that fuses rock and jazz with sounds and diction associated with Iran's traditional *kucheh-bāzāri* music, usually in the 6/8 rhythm. In addition to variations on rock, electronic music categorized as electro-rock, dance, or trance has also found both makers and followers in Iran, among them performers and groups like the female electro-rock singer Maral; Ashkan & Kooshan; various DJs who sample songs and create new tracks; and the dance-pop stars Xaniar Khosravi and Sina Hejazi, underground until recently but now officially approved.

Pop music has been a particularly instructive genre as far as the thin line between underground and aboveground music is concerned. Many of today's most famous pop stars started their work as underground musicians and only managed to receive permits and surface officially after several years of music making. Observers of Iran's music scene often comment that "these are all games," suggesting that powerful producers of the highly lucrative pop music scene strategically collaborate with censors to raise the subversive cachet of certain artists by branding them as "underground" before green-lighting them, and then share the spoils together. It is difficult to ascertain the veracity of these claims, but one thing I learned in my research is that there are so many players in the music scene juggling for advantages, and so many multiple factors constantly affecting outcomes across the illicit-to-legal spectrum, that it would be fairly difficult to strategically plan and achieve specific results in the way that these simplistic insinuations suggest.

In addition to the binary categories of underground and aboveground, it might be fruitful to think of a third category of "hyperground music" in the Iranian context. I have already mentioned Sasy Mankan and Barobax as two underground groups that were able to achieve great success because their Iran-made music videos were broadcast into Iran by highly watched expatriate satellite TV stations. Conceptually, this music constitutes a category beyond underground or government-approved, because it has skillfully navigated the available media technologies and governmental constraints to become truly popular and, until recently, to allow its makers to continue to operate and make a living inside Iran itself. Groups like these have real mainstream appeal because they offer entertainment not just for the young but for the whole family, as their music is often played at family parties and weddings. Their music is also more accessible to a larger demographic than are rock and rap. This music is best described as "hip-pop," as it often combines melodious pop-dance music with the lyrical elements of rap and hip-hop. Popular groups like these are exceptional: they are hardly underground, since they enjoy more fame than do most approved artists, and yet they are not aboveground, either, since they operate outside of the state's legal structures.

Groups like Barobax and Sasy Mankan managed to remain in Iran in defiance of the state's structural and moralistic impositions, making a living as musicians mostly through private performances. Unlike other underground groups that never sought approval from official bodies, these bands kept their music within a socially acceptable framework while at the same time pushing creative boundaries. In Barobax's most famous video, for example, titled "*Susan khānum*" (Miss Susan) and shot and produced entirely in Iran, the camera's point of view is that of Miss Susan, so that we never see anything of this woman except an Islamically acceptable hand clad in a black satin glove. At the same time, the track is musically unique and incorporates a female voice. Similarly, in Sasy Mankan's not-quite-so-wholesome song "*Nināsh Nāsh*" (baby talk for "dance"), also produced entirely inside Iran, the only girl we see is a parody, a boy in grotesque make-up covered by a headscarf. However, while cheekily acquiescing to traditional norms by presenting a boy as a girl, the video also ridicules this necessity through the vulgarity of its portrayal of the "girl" and undermines it with explicit lyrics such as "Only wear the clothes for tango night for me"[49] and "if she doesn't give me her lips my heart will churn," as well as idealizing the kind of girl who represents the opposite of the Islamic Republic's image of female piety, namely a girl with platinum-blond hair, "fake nails that are for real," and a super-short miniskirt.

As Khashayar, one of the three front men of Barobax, told me,

As far as the law is concerned, what we do is not right, but there is the important issue of convention ('*orf*), meaning what the people themselves don't have a problem with in their homes. Our music is about topics like marriage and it respects conventions, there are no girls without hijab in our videos, and it is meant for the whole family.[50]

Khashayar's statement and his specific mention of '*orf* accord with Khomeini's and even Khamenei's jurisprudential positions on music, the permissibility of which depends to a great extent on social acceptability and convention. However, as I discussed earlier, Iran's authoritarian political structure has not made room for the free determination of convention in the cultural sphere. This also explains why Barobax was left to function fairly freely for several years, as long as they posed no threat to the government's legitimacy.

But following the 2009 Green Uprising and the state's ensuing sense of insecurity, censors cracked down on cultural activity and Barobax, Sasy Mankan, and other bands like them were actively pursued and banned. Some, like Sasy Mankan, left the country. The members of Barobax, on the other hand, stayed in Iran, stopped their musical activity for several years, and opened a burger chain in Tehran called Burger Land. As of 2013, they started pursuing a permit with *Ershād* and planned to take their music aboveground. However, by 2016, although they still had not obtained an official permit, they had made a new music video called "'Eyn-e māmān-e man-e" (She's Like My Mommy), which debuted on the government approved online show ChaarGoosh.

THE GOVERNMENT'S RECKONING
WITH THE UNDERGROUND

With the government's increased assault on liberties in the public domain under its "Social Security Project" in 2007 also came a concerted and often vicious campaign against the underground music scene. As of early summer there were reports of arrests of rockers and rappers both in the national media and in blogs and online communities. In June the authorities made the first large-scale attempt to identify and interrogate rappers, although many discounted these reports as rumors created by the rappers themselves in order to achieve greater fame.[51]

In a BBC *Ruz-e Haftom* podcast in 2007, the rapper Shahin Felakat relates that he was arrested and repeatedly interrogated at the Judiciary's Committee for Social Corruption, a well-known government building on Vozara Street where mostly youth arrested by the morality police are taken to be charged.[52]

Along with Reza Pishro and Diaco, he had rapped the somewhat nefarious tracks *"Asar-e manfi"* (Negative Effect) and *"Man kheng shodam"* (I'm Dopey), one drawing on the worst Persian swearwords to depict an adversary's mother and sister as whores, and the other extolling getting high on drugs. Felakat says that he saw a piece of paper on his interrogator's desk titled "Project for the Elimination of Underground Music" (*Tarh-e Jam'āvari-ye Musiqi-ye Zirzamini*). The officials accused him of *fohsh* (swearing, obscenity) for one song and "incitement to drug use" for the other, and extracted a written pledge from him that he would no longer produce such work. In the program, Felakat says that the officials had the details and addresses of other popular rappers, including Hichkas. For his part, Hichkas had heard from various other rappers that the interrogators had inquired about him, so he chose to take the initiative and introduce himself to the authorities. Another rapper, Amir Tataloo, left Iran for Dubai for fear of possible consequences. Ehsan, the owner of a studio where many rappers recorded their songs, says on the program that the authorities visited his studio with a list of rappers that they were curious about and questioned him as to whether they had produced their works in his studio. Although Ehsan answered in the affirmative, they took no action, since at the time no directive existed that held the recording of rap songs to be a criminal offense. Clearly, however, the authorities had become sensitized to "underground" rap music and were taking concerted action.

In August of that year, the media reported large-scale arrests at an "underground" music concert in Karaj, a town outside of Tehran, using headlines such as "The Arrest of Satanists at a Karaj Concert."[53] The concert had been organized through the initiative of the rock band Dativ, with performances by another rock band, named Font; it also featured the female electro-rock act Maral and included two DJs who spun in between the sessions. The police later falsely reported that the concert had included both rock and rap groups, even mentioning several acts by name, attempting to demonize both of these genres together. It was initially supposed to be a smallish private affair in a garden in Karaj's Mohammadshahr, but as participants have reported, more than the intended number of people had heard about the event and flocked to the party, so that there were possibly as many as six hundred attendees.[54] By the time the police had surrounded the premises, the party was at its height, with hundreds of young men and women dancing to the music, drinking alcoholic beverages, and cheering on a female fire acrobat. All attendees that I have spoken to expressed bafflement at the police's conjecture that it was a concert for

Satan-worshippers.[55] Ashkan Koosha, Font's lead singer at the time, described the situation best, saying that "it was so inconceivable for them that a group of young people could get together and enjoy music and party" that when a high-level official entered to inspect the grounds —where Koosha and dozens of others had been rounded up—and saw the stage banner depicting an alien face with flaming hair, he said to his escort, "These are Satanists; write down that they are Satan-worshippers."[56] Dozens of reports—in newspapers and online—carried the same "information," handed to them by the authorities, depicting the concert as a matter of organized crime with phrases such as "fully organized operations" (*'amaliāt-e kāmelan sāzmān-yāfteh*) (i.e. organized crime) and reporting an abundance of alcohol and drugs as well as obscene CDs and semi-nakedness among the participants.[57]

About two weeks later, a large Persian rap concert took place in Dubai, and about a dozen of Iran's most popular rappers were invited to perform. According to several of the performing rappers, they were promised that this concert would not create any problems for them, as it was in celebration of Imam Mahdi's birthday and the proceeds would go to charities in earthquake-struck Bam. When the rappers returned to Iran, however, the authorities interrogated all of them, confiscated their passports, and made them sign pledges to abstain from their musical activities until they had received official permits, which they seem to have been promised for good behavior. In interviews with the young rap journalist Yashar, from the website RapFa.com, several of the rappers seemed truly perturbed by the incident and expressed extreme regret. Ardalan Tome told Yashar, in tones similar to those of a reformed criminal and echoing the words of some of the other rappers, "Our problem was not just taking part in an illegal concert, but also producing illegal music. Also there is illegal music and vulgar (*mobtazal*) music and our music was both. I will try from now on not to produce this kind of music and not to have image and sound broadcast from satellite television. From now on, I will try to do everything only with government permits." It is of course hard to take these words at face value. These rappers were either concerned about getting their passports back and were willing to dissimulate and please the authorities, or they were genuinely fooled by promises that their work would be approved should they cooperate with the government and renounce all of their illegal activity.

Considering the state's ensuing actions, and the arrests of underground musicians and closures of recording studios in the years since, it appears unlikely that there was ever a plan to allow these musicians to operate within a legal framework. In 2008, state television heavily advertised what it called a "documentary program," titled "Shock." Indeed, the program shocked a lot of viewers, especially the wide range of young people who, because of their associations with banalities like hairstyles, clothing brands, and jewelry, or certain kinds of music like rap and rock, were portrayed as Satan-worshippers. "Shock" drew a direct link between young people's engagement with rock and rap music and Satan worship, drugs, illicit sexual relations, and ultimately, ruin. It consisted of a collage of seemingly normal but trendy-looking young people, criminalized for the purposes of the program through jarring sounds and disguised identities (using pixilation and out-of-focus effects); excerpts of rap sessions, including a cut of Hichkas's music video to "A Bunch of Soldiers"; some Iranian rock footage; Western images of horridly painted faces of what appeared to be actual Satan-worshippers; "confession" interviews with former Satanists whose lives had been destroyed, including girls who said they were tricked into joining the cult and implied that they had lost their virginity as a result; all interspersed with scenes of youth shooting up drugs in ruined buildings and so-called psychological and security experts commenting on this purportedly widespread and highly alarming phenomenon. In one segment, the reporter asks a young man, "Do you know anything about devil-worshippers?" to which the man responds, "they sing rap and play heavy metal music," and his friend joins in, "they don't believe in God. They believe in Satan. They slit their arteries and let their blood intermingle." Another pixilated "satanic cult member" says, "at their parties they drink blood, and if they go a step further, eat each other's excrement." There are also scenes of the Karaj concert, including interviews with what are portrayed as clueless girls lured to the event to be abused. The director general of the police's social research unit, a Dr. Bayat, then sums up the message of the program, saying: "Music is a tool for these groups to spread their message of Satan worship. These are not musical groups; they just exploit music."[58]

The criminalization of this "underground" music scene has continued in the years since 2007, and is evident in the language that the state's various organs, especially its security apparatuses, have used in this regard. Since that documentary, there have been numerous articles and interviews in the media, often with so-called experts such as sociologists, criminologists, and clerics, that have addressed Satanism at length and portrayed it as a real danger to society. The director of Islamic Studies and Research at Tehran's prestigious Sharif University of Technology, for example, has tied the supposed trend of Satanism in Iran to a Zionist-capitalist world conspiracy that aims to rob Iranian youth of their identity. He even refers to the *TehranAvenue* music contests (though he doesn't mention the contest by name) as a means of discovering talents to facilitate this mode of world domination and concludes, in a most alarming manner, that Satanism is the "most important spiritual and religious current of our time and if the plans of the arrogant superculture [i.e. the United States] reach fruition, will become the religion of many of the world's people in the near future."[59]

Tehran's police chief enumerated the following threats posed to youth by these "deviant groups": the propagation of cursing, the usage of foul language, the normalization of ignominious Western behaviors, the normalization of wrong behaviors for young people, the facilitation of paths of influence toward abnormal and base behavior, the distancing of youth from Islamic culture, the perturbation of young people's minds, the undermining of the sanctity of elevated (*fākher*) music, the normalization of unhealthy relationships between boys and girls, painting society's conditions as grim, agitating young people against others, and promoting indifference toward family, religion and, nation as a virtue.[60]

Other media echoed this language, criminalizing musicians in reports with ostensibly precise numbers such as "Eighty-seven 'underground' music groups with 133 singers have been identified, who have produced and published 376 music clips in the virtual arena since last June;"[61] "At least two makers of vulgar video clips who produce works for illegal groups inside and outside of the country have been arrested;"[62] and "Fifteen persons associated with the 'underground' group Barobax have been arrested at a house of corruption in the south of Tehran."[63] In arresting musicians and video directors who operated both inside and outside of Iran, the authorities attempted to send the message that even expatriate Iranians working in the music industry inside Iran, or Iranian musicians performing outside of Iran, would be punished.

While the state's security apparatuses were demonizing these "underground" music groups and the media was reflecting and multiplying that view, academics, journalists, policy makers, and musicians convened in seminars and press events to discuss the phenomenon of "underground" music in Iran. At least once each, on separate occasions, musicians like Namjoo and Hichkas were even invited to contribute their own views on their work. In what may have been the first such series, "The Research Seminar on Underground Music" organized by the governmental *Mehr News Agency* in July 2007, music experts expressed opinions that ranged from dismay at "underground" music as a Western import to the inevitability of "underground" music due to new media technologies, but also included other views, such as that of Namjoo, who made the point that the main characteristic of "underground" music is that it "contains protest," or of the music policy veteran Mohammad Sarir, who equivocated in typical fashion that "any music that does not create tension in society must be legal."

FACTS ON THE GROUND

Whereas early on, most debates circled around mostly existential questions about "underground" music—namely whether it was legitimate and whether it should exist, how the government should deal with it, whether it was any different from approved music, and whether or not it was a music of protest—in recent years the debates have evolved toward a recognition of this music and greater attempts at classifying it and its creators.[64] Similarly, statements about the unsustainability and unsuitability of this music within Iran have disappeared as the music itself has gained an increased presence in everyday life. In 2007, however, at *Mehr News Agency*'s second seminar series, several music experts argued that "underground" music does not suit Iranian tastes and will not last,[65] and an official at *Ershād*'s music office admonished "underground" musicians:

> It's not like you imagine, that you've gone underground and will remain an artist. Rather, your first work will be your last. Second, you won't be able to prove your artistic personality. Third, you won't have any financial returns. Fourth, even if you reach fame, our society has shown that underground currents have defamed identities.[66]

It would be ludicrous for anyone to attempt to make those points today, as "underground" musicians have proven all of them wrong.

In the more recent atmosphere, with its greater recognition of "underground" music, various academics and musicians have stepped forward to define the genre and to condemn the state's demonization of it as satanic. The music scholar Masoud Kowsari has said that "underground" music fills a vacuum of critique in traditional and pop music, and that the young are attracted to it precisely because of its critical nature as well as its ease of production. Rappers themselves have alluded to the genre's capacity for critique. In an interview on *Ruz-e Haftom*, for example, Yas admits that he became attracted to the rap form because he understood that it was a language of protest. He says,

"At first I really liked how they rapped to the beat, but then I realized that this music is about screaming out loud in protest, screaming out from the bottom of the heart, that these people are really protesting their conditions, they're really upset. I chose rap because of its critical dimension."[67]

Others, such as the musicologist Arvin Sedaqatkish, have argued that it is not necessarily the music's critical nature that has attracted the young. Rather, the government's censure of the genre is what made it attractive to young people, by turning it into appealing cultural capital. The guitarist Babak Riahipour confirmed this view in an opinion piece in 2008 by arguing that television programs like "Shock" were counterproductive, in that they only drew more young people to this illicit music. He decried the authorities' portrayal of rock and rap as satanic and urged the government to greater tolerance, especially toward rap music, which he believes is extremely popular because "people understand its language and stories . . . since its base is among the common people with common language."[68]

Regardless, whether in spite of or because of the government's smear campaign against underground music more generally and rap music more specifically, rap has grown strong roots in Iran and has found a committed following, especially among younger men. Today, some of the early protagonists of Iran's rap scene, such as the collective Zedbazi, Shahin Najafi, and the rappers Yas and Hichkas, are household names, especially among families with younger members and Internet and satellite connections. Some rappers, like the Zedbazi group, often use foul language, and others, like Najafi, sometimes choose taboo themes that make their music less appealing in family contexts. But other rappers, including Yas, Hichkas, Tataloo, and Hossein Tohi, mostly use lyrics that stay within socially accepted conventions. As it turns out, Iranian culture, with its strong poetic heritage, has accommodated this new word-centric musical genre rather well, and rap has been embraced and Iranianized in a way that rock music still has not. The genre, as we have seen, is now commonly referred to as *Rap-e Farsi*, and perhaps its best representative is Hichkas, whose sobriquet among fans is "the godfather of Persian rap."

CHAPTER NINE

RAP-E FARSI

HICHKAS

ALTHOUGH AUTHORITIES and official media have portrayed rap music as wholly foreign to Iranian culture, even linking it to Satanism (as we just saw at the end of chapter 8), in seminars and talks that I have attended in Iran over the years, several speakers have alluded to what they have called the *kalām-mehvar* (word-centric) quality of this genre: this allows it to be at home within Iranian culture, with its illustrious poetic heritage and people's quotidian use of that heritage. Indeed, stories based on the *Shahnameh* (Book of Kings), as well as religious panegyrics and elegiacs such as those commemorating 'Āshurā (the martyrdom of Imam Hossein), are usually recited rather than sung. Moreover, Iran's traditional *ruhowzi* songs, briefly discussed in chapter 2, have a strong conversational, dialogic, and biographical quality to them, as exemplified by the many folkloric songs, such as "*'Amu sabziforush*" (Uncle Grocer), "*Māshin-e Mashdi Mamdali*" (Mashdi Mamdali's Car) and "*Ābji Sanam goft*" (Sister Sanam Said), that the popular actor and singer Morteza Ahmadi has written into history with his book "Evergreen Oldies."[1] In addition to these works, I have also encountered mention of the nineteen-forties song "*Yek yāri dāram*" (My Lover), by the influential singer Javad Badi'zadeh, as one of the first Persian "rap" songs, with the song's poetic format of *bahr-e tavil* (literally long meter or composition) being equated with present-day rap. *Bahr-e tavil* is a nonmetrical form composed in sections rather than regular verses and stanzas, with each section rhyming on irregular repetitions of a particular word ending.

In postrevolutionary times, the group Sandy, based in Germany and later Los

Angeles, was the first to release Persian songs that were a form of hip-hop, as they rapped to a background of percussive *bandari* music from southern Iran (this was in the late nineteen-eighties; the group became famous in the early nineteen-nineties). Later on, Shahkar Binesh-Pajouh, dubbed the "Dapper Rapper" for his smart suits and ties, was the first to officially release a rap album in Iran, titled *"Eskenās"* (Banknote). While Sandy occasionally criticized the government and religious hypocrisy in its songs, Binesh-Pajouh took on what he described as the tastelessness of the nouveau riche. These artists based their works on topical issues, whereas the new generation of rappers often use their tracks to break taboos.

Bahram, one of the most successful of Persian hip-hop's politically and socially critical rappers, explains in an interview why tracks by Sandy and Binesh-Pajouh do not count as part of the legacy of *Rap-e Farsi*:

> Underground art is revolutionary, grassroots, and unorthodox. Underground art breaks taboos; it distances itself from clichés and taboos, and the underground artist has something more than societal conventions to offer, and that is why undergrounders are able to infuse new artistic and cultural currents into society. . . . People like . . . Sandy produced works but because they didn't have the underground mentality, they couldn't introduce a different culture with their works.[2]

Bahram continues, recounting that at first everyone ridiculed rap music, saying that it was as if the singers were reading the newspaper, but that eventually, by 2008, *Rap-e Farsi* had become so popular that it had become "the music of our generation."[3]

The first track that was recognized as a true Persian rap song in online forums was *"Dastā bālā"* (Hands Up) in 2003 by the group Deev, from the United States, calling for the ouster of the mullahs and using a simple 2/2 beat, with lines such as:

> Put your hands up, gentlemen, ladies, everyone hands up
> Fuck the clerics, middle fingers up
> How much more of the mullahs? Enough already!
> . . .
> It's enough, it's time for revenge
> It's time for your ouster with an uprising
> It's time for your execution in public
> Know that this is not a slogan, just a message

Although inside Iran, rappers like Hichkas and Yas were already at work experimenting with their own productions, it was not until a few years later that they made a name for themselves outside what was then the small circle of mostly young male rap insiders, many of whom knew each other or at least knew of each other. By 2008, however, rap had become widespread. There is by now some academic writing on rap music in Iran, most of which agrees on the reasons for its popularity. These works concur in highlighting rap's capacity to meld with Iranian culture, due in part to the centuries-old tradition of poetry in Iran, allowing for a musical style that Iranian youth can claim as their own.[4]

In Persian, there is more writing on *Rap-e Farsi*, with a number of academics taking part in seminars and publishing papers on the subject of "underground" music.[5] In speeches and writing about rap music across the board, observers overlap in their view that rap's most pertinent quality within the Iranian sphere is its capacity for divulging "the truth" or criticism. One writes that "Persian rap is a form of social commentary and empowerment through self-expression . . . an act of retaliation against authority and prejudice," and another agrees that sentiments expressed by rappers suggest that "hip-hop as a means of expression is the single most important factor in its wide appeal."[6] Similarly, these observers inside Iran attribute rap's popularity with Iranian youth to its inherent "directness and openness" and consider the genre's capacity to allow for biographical storytelling as a means of protest and critique to be an important factor in its appeal.[7]

When questioned about their choice of genre, most rappers echo these readings. Yas, a musician who is mostly concerned with social issues in his tracks, says, "with this music style I can tell a whole story, which is impossible in other styles. I have a lot to say. . . . It is only this genre that can direct the attention of the audience to what you want to say."[8] Similarly, Hichkas says, "with this music the singer has great power of speech, so the lyrics must be very strong. Words are very important, so you must pay hairsplitting attention to them."[9] Bahram, for his part, says, "the words in hip-hop music are simple and deep. It speaks of the realities around people directly and without pleasantries," and adds that the genre itself is a form of protest, "regardless of the content of the song."[10] Hichkas also highlights what he calls the "realness" of rap, "meaning the rapper must be himself in his songs, and not be acting," referring in effect to the importance of authenticity.[11] Other factors that rappers and observers alike cite for rap's popularity are the low cost and the ease of production. And finally, unlike musicians performing other kinds of music, a rapper does not need formal vocal training.

Another important aspect of hip-hop in Iran is that it allows the young, Internet-and-satellite-TV-connected, generation to articulate itself in the context of the global hip-hop scene, expressing its belonging to an increasingly interconnected world while also highlighting its Iranian identity through the use of Persian poetry, subjects, instruments, and sounds. As Hichkas's collaborator Reveal put it to me in an interview, "A lot of kids didn't think their own culture was cool, but now they've found a way to make it cool, through Persian hip-hop."[12] Bahram reckons that hip-hop answers a need because it "gave us the audacity to . . . scream out our differences" from the previous generations.[13] In other words, hip-hop is different and familiar in equal measure, lending itself to be adapted or indigenized while allowing a break with more traditional values that were not conducive to the blunt expression of taboo subjects.

Rappers have treated topics such as prostitution, drug use, and domestic violence in their songs, but even rappers who simply spit out obscenities and rhyme and grunt about sex are breaking Iranian social norms and partaking in hip-hop's countercultural dimension. Moreover, by unabashedly rapping in unprecedented ways, especially on such taboo topics as sexuality—as in Zedbazi's early song "*Ājili*" or the teenage female rapper Sahra's graphic description of a sexual encounter and vocalization of an orgasm in the song "*Darajeh-ye seks*" (Sex Degrees)—these musicians are pushing conversational boundaries and perhaps contributing to national emancipation. Other authors have brought to light the fact that the topic of sexuality has been absent from debates on modernity in Iran and argued that without the open discussion of sexuality in the public realm, the full emancipation of a state's subject from the state is not possible.[14] Iran's moralistic Islamic government and its conservative society have both contributed to the traditional stigmatization of topics around sexuality, so that both state and society are able to use transgressions as a reason for punishment, in effect disowning Iranian individuals' power over their own bodies. These rap songs, though discounted by many as simply offensive and inconsequential, could be a step toward opening up the seal on the public conversation about sexuality and hence breaking down its moralistic and disciplinary instrumentalization by the state and traditional society.

CATEGORIZATIONS OF *RAP-E FARSI*

Various recent texts on rap, relying on unofficial sources, estimate that there are somewhere between one and two thousand amateur and professional rap-

pers in Iran and that the number is growing by the day.[15] Among producers
of rap, there is of course a wide spectrum of styles, mostly grouped into a few
defined categories. "Street rappers" are one prominent set. These rappers are
described as having "adopted the aggressive features of the Gangsta Rap style"
and "dig[ging] into street slang to find a voice through which to speak of social
taboos and expose the stark reality of modern urban life."[16] Another category
is made up of the socially aware or conscientious rappers, whose style is more
conservative than that of street rappers and who express their rhymes in ways
that are in line with social morals. And then there are the rappers who mostly
produce songs about romantic or sexual relations, or about partying. The two
final categories that are often mentioned are "commercial hip-hop influenced
rappers," whose work is purely for entertainment, and "diaspora rappers," who
live exclusively outside of Iran but often rap about Iran.[17] Within the aforementioned categories there are also prominent themes, some of which span
multiple categories, such an emphasis on Persian (as opposed to Arab) identity,
sagas and condemnations of social and political corruption, and boasting or
"dissing" other rappers.

Hichkas is best described as a representative of the "street rap" category. At
least while he was still living in Iran, Hichkas's work best reflected the pulse
of the street and addressed pertinent subjects such as Tehran's socioeconomic
disparities, corruption, and drug use. (Other popular rappers often assigned
to this category are Zedbazi, Felakat, Pishro, Bahram, and Shahin Najafi in his
later, more aggressive songs.) Hichkas gives voice to the street, highlighting the
injustices and corruption of a society in which the constitution means nothing and even God may be susceptible to bribes. In his song *"Qānun"* (Law),
he makes a mockery of the eponymous concept by showing society's lawlessness. This is how he describes a world of total moral depravity in which
even the highest sanctity, the arbiter of ultimate justice, may be susceptible to
corruption:

> Here the pit-bottom is asphalt
> It's a post where even the constitution can be trampled upon
> . . .
> The child's soul isn't black when it's born
> I'm the same child but the child within has perished
> I'm innocent and God's my witness
> Or do you think it's possible someone will bribe God too?

Social critique has been a prominent feature of *Rap-e Farsi* from the early days. The most popular rappers in this category are Bahram, Yas, the female rapper Salome, and, in his less explicit songs, Shahin Najafi. Najafi, who emigrated to Germany in 2005, has produced some of Persian rap's most political and antireligious songs. He became famous with his *"Mā mard nistim"* (We're Not Much of a Man[18]) in 2008, which describes men's abuse and exploitation of women and urges women to take the lead, with the refrain:

> We died of our own manliness, at least you be a woman
> And sprinkle a bit of your honorable scent on us

As for Yas, his critiques often evoke familiar accusations against a hypocritical and corrupt government that breeds its mirror image in society. This is evident in his song *"Yek nafas begim"* (Let's Speak a Breath):

> Raise your head and see what's going on around you
> See that everyone's got a Colt on his belt ["gun" in Persian is *haft-tir,* or
>   "seven bullets"]
> Seven bad vices around the belt and ready to shoot
> Deceit, lies, intrigues, backstabbing, accusations, slander, and
>   brownnosing for power
> . . .
> Let's speak a breath . . . open our hearts
> Let's leave the cage, go fly together
> I'm really in disbelief over these evil people
> They who kill the living and worship the dead[19]

Talking about "worshipping the dead" is not just a criticism of the people but also a barely veiled stab at a state that glorifies martyrs but offers little hope for the living. Many of Yas's works also highlight Persian pride. Here his work dissents from the official discourse mostly by omission. Iran's Islamic identity simply plays no part in his songs, whereas Iran's pre-Islamic past and Persian identity are prominently on display. In one of his songs, titled *"Hoviyat-e man"* (My Identity), written in response to the Hollywood blockbuster *300,* Yas evokes nationalistic feelings by glorifying the Persian empire. While the ministry seldom gives explanations for why specific songs are denied permits, Yas pulls his Ahura Mazda (the Zoroastrian God) necklace from underneath his shirt to show why he thinks "My Identity" was rejected: "I say in the song, 'For us Iranians our foundation is Ahura Mazda' . . . well, they disagree with that. Our foundation is *Islam,*" he says with emphasis.[20]

While congratulating Yas on having finally, after two years, received a permit for one of his songs in 2007,[21] the BBC reporter Behzad Bolour says: "This Bam earthquake song is very emotional, but certainly pasteurized [Bolour uses this to mean inoffensive] enough to be sure of receiving a permit from the ministry." To this Yas protests:

> For God's sake, don't think that way. Rap's beat is seen as illicit and criminal by the authorities. They think that those who listen to rap can be aroused to do certain things. This style is forbidden. It has nothing to do with the content, or the lyrics. But I guess because I'm rapping about runaway girls, street children, the Bam earthquake . . . the authorities ultimately acquiesced.

Asked why he thinks that he's unable to get more permits, he says:

> They keep sending me on a wild goose chase, keeping me hanging. They just don't want a rap album to be published. They're bothered by the beat.[22]

It is clear from Yas's comments that although he has a strong hunch that rap as a style is problematic for the government, he is not sure exactly why he is being censored. At times he cites certain lyrics or words from his songs, at others he becomes altogether hopeless that any rap album could ever be published.

Younger rappers have been even more forthright in their critique of power, or of the government directly. The rapper Bahram's "A letter to the President" in 2008 established him as one of the strongest voices of *Rap-e Farsi*, with his work spanning the "gangsta rap" and "socially aware" categories. In this track, he puts his finger on the pulse of the sentiments of the time about what many perceived to be President Ahmadinejad's intentional deception of the electorate in one of his televised appearances before his first election in 2005. Bahram's track starts with the president's statement (in Ahmadinejad's own voice):

> Seriously, the problem of our people right now is the look of our children's hair? Well, our children want to wear their hair however they want; what business of yours and mine is that?
>
> Government must provide for stability in the economy, must provide for peace in the country's atmosphere, provide for psychological security, support the people.

In response to Ahmadinejad's claim that he seeks to bring peace and welfare to society, Bahram raps:

> I never imagined things would turn into this
> That we'd have millions of youth who run away from religion
> . . .
> People still go to the mosque, but in order to steal shoes
> By God, this much pretense deserves mockery
> Iran exports eighteen-year-old girls
> You sit on the floor and think you're the pinnacle
> . . .
> By God, the Qur'an on your shelf needs dusting
> It's only empty slogans that you spout

In the "party/love" category, some of the more popular rappers are Hossein Tohi, Amir Tataloo (who in recent years has delved into social and political topics, too), Rezaya, Armin 2afm, and Ardalan Tome. Unless they are fast dance songs, their tracks often have elements of rhythm and blues or soul, and either deal with romantic and sexual relations or boast about the rappers' lifestyles and the parties they attend. These musicians often collaborate, such as in the song "*Gheyr-e mostaghim*" (Indirectly), one of their more popular songs.

By now, this pioneering group of rappers has been joined by a new generation, including artists like Ali Sorena, Behzad Leito, Dariush (not to be confused with Dariush Eqbali, mentioned earlier), Khalse, Safir, and Tik Taak. This newer generation sometimes collaborates with members of the pioneering group; Khalse and Behzad Leito, for example, have collaborated with Zedbazi's Sijal and Alireza JJ. Much more often than the first group, the newer generation also incorporates vocals by female rappers (like Sogand, Nassim, and Cornellaa) in their tracks. Among the first generation of rappers there were very few women, with the most widely known being Salome MC; aside from her, there were maybe only two others, Sogand (just mentioned) and Farinaz, who made a name for themselves in that generation, but now their numbers are growing.[23]

The rapper Justina has been a strong presence on the scene since 2011, when she won an underground music contest staged by the Tanbe10 hip-hop group and then collaborated with the group on a track titled "*Artesh-e Tanbe10*" (The Tanbe10 Army). She says that she first heard *Rap-e Farsi* on tracks by Zedbazi and Hichkas in 2006, when she was sixteen, and since she had written poetry for years, she then slowly tried her pen at writing rhymes for rap. "Everyone around me was listening to rap, underground studios were mushrooming around Tehran, and the prices were not expensive either, so it was relatively easy to record a song," she told me.[24] Justina takes a positively feminist stance in her lyrics. A number of her songs, including *"Beh in Āzādi Bekhand"* (Laugh at This Freedom), *"Kāsh Donyā Behem Yeh Dokhtar Bedeh"* (I Wish for the World to Give Me a Daughter), and *"Dokhtar-e Rap"* (Rap Girl), have been endorsed by the prestigious Avang Music record label and broadcast on satellite TV channels, though without any remuneration for Justina from either Avang or the stations. Justina told me that rappers and younger musicians still seek endorsements like this because of the prestige associated with it, hoping that the exposure will lead to successful and financially viable careers in the long run.

While Justina has been very prolific, there are still few female musicians in Iran's underground scene, whether within rap, rock, or other genres. Justina says that she thinks the third generation of rap in Iran will bring forth many more female musicians, adding, "I think we'll even be ahead of the United States in terms of the representation of women in rap." There is, for example, the remarkable Afghan rapper Sonita Alizadeh, who grew up in Iran and was inspired by the work of Eminem and the Iranian rapper Yas. In 2015, when she was only eighteen, Sonita released a music video titled *"Dokhtar Forushi"* (Brides for Sale), which starts in a whispering voice:

> Let me whisper these words to you
> So no one hears me talk about the selling of girls
> So no one hears my voice—it's against the Sharia
> They say women must be silent—that's the tradition in this town

And then goes on loud and clear:

> I scream to make up for a woman's lifetime of silence
> I scream for the depth of wounds on my body
> I scream for a body exhausted in its cage
> A body that broke under the price tags you put on it[25]

As for the dearth of female artists in Iran's underground music scene, Justina believes that the problem is related to the stigma that women still face in the field:

> Even now in Iran, if a woman enters music as a singer, especially the underground scene, her life changes. People start looking at her differently; it's still not socially palatable. She can't go the conventional path of marriage and children anymore. She will be perceived as someone who has no shame,

a quality that our culture cares about very much in women. Society views her as a woman who wants to draw attention to herself. And then there are also the risks of the underground itself. Men will make inappropriate requests in exchange for helping a girl with her music. I was lucky to find the Tanbe10 group, which is a group of educated young men who really helped me. But still, my life has changed. Because of my tracks people have accused me of being bisexual or homosexual. But I no longer care what others think of me.[26]

Justina believes that this attitude is increasingly shared by younger female musicians, for whom self-realization and a sense of authenticity overshadow the negative societal stigmas attached to women singers. As more women enter the field, there will also be more role models to encourage others to join. It is important to remember that nearly all of the pioneers of *Rap-e Farsi* were male.

"THERE WASN'T NO ONE BEFORE US"

Soroush Lashkary (the rapper known as Hichkas) was still a young teenager when he first encountered rap music. Born in 1985 into a fairly traditional, middle-class family, as the only son, Lashkary grew up around Vanak Square, a busy Tehran neighborhood just at the edge of what today is called North Tehran. He says he received a tape in the late nineteen-nineties, when "the young were into break dance," that contained a pop song with "bits that we later realized were called rap."[27] He liked rap because "you can say more in it than in other genres," and because "it's a serious genre, it's more for listening than dancing, and because I'm not into dancing and generally don't like that kind of sissy business."[28] He had always liked poetry and had composed Persian verses in school and shared them with friends. Inspired by the rap that he had heard, he started recording his own verses on a cassette tape recorder, and later laid them over instrumental tracks that he found online. "My English isn't so bad, so at first I recorded a few songs in English, but then I realized I'd be much more capable and my work more potent in my mother tongue, so I switched over to Persian," he said about the very beginnings of his work.[29]

Eventually, toward the end of high school, in 2001 to 2002, Lashkary started the rap website www.021-music.com because, as he told me, he thought it was "rotten to be the only one in a field."[30] As he described the birth of rap in Iran, Lashkary continued, "Besides me there were only two other guys, Yashar and Shayan. So I started to bring various people into it, I wrote songs for them and told them how to rap, and with time there were more talented students who became professional rivals. In general, whoever raps in Persian has in some way been affected by me, meaning everyone who raps in Persian is inevitably, directly or indirectly, my student. There wasn't no one before us."[31] He recorded his first proper track in a studio near Vali-Asr Square in the center of town, but does not remember the studio or the song: "In general, we were completely out of it, but would just go ahead and do things. This was the stage when we were all still learning."[32]

Still, Lashkary says, he was never interested in commercial American hip-hop or the bling culture that celebrates money and denigrates women: "My friends and I were teenagers making music that described our own culture, the society we grew up in, and challenging the clichés associated with it."[33] For his rhymes, Lashkary uses the colloquial language of the streets, in what one could describe as an updated (though much rougher and more critical) version of the *kucheh-bāzāri* (literally, "of the street and bazaar," as discussed in chapter 2) style, but in the rap register. When asked at a talk in 2011 what music he listens to, Hichkas affirmed his affinity for this style with his response that he liked to listen to "Āmaneh," a song by the quintessential 1970s *kucheh-bāzāri* singer, Ne'matollah Aghasi.[34] And yet, while using rough street language, Lashkary still refrains from using foul words and has said that he believes in keeping within certain boundaries because his music is often listened to in familial contexts, and he does not want to have "a negative effect on the young."[35] Unlike many other Iranian rappers, Lashkary does not usually don the international rapper's outfit of baggy drop-crotch pants, oversized shirts, statement sneakers, caps, and big necklaces, though he does sometimes wear a cap. More often, he looks like a trader from the bazaar and sports an unclean beard, which might have contributed to early rumors, which he quickly put down as lies, that he was a reformed *basiji* vigilante turned rapper.[36]

His "Iranianness" was what drew one of Lashkary's early collaborators—the Iranian-born, UK-based rapper Mehrak Golestan, aka Reveal Poison—to him. In the early years of the new millennium, Golestan became interested in Persian hip-hop after hearing the US-based Iranian rapper Deev's "*Dastā Bālā*." He contacted Deev, who introduced him to Orkut and the small online Persian hip-hop community there, and there Golestan stumbled on Lashkary's work. In 2004, Golestan travelled to Iran and met Lashkary at the Kargadan recording studio. "I thought the first thing he was going to ask me was 'what's the latest 50 Cent song?' but he was so different from the other young Iranians you would meet, so Iranian, the way he was dressed and talked," Golestan reminisced. When I asked him about the traditional Iranian values that Lashkary highlights in his work, like "God, family, and the Iranian flag" (which he rhymes in his song "A Bunch of Soldiers"), Golestan said, "Yeah, we have a very similar value system," and added that he thinks the work of some Iranian rap groups is "devilish" and "misleads youth," echoing Lashkary's comment.

Soon after this encounter, in 2004, Lashkary wrote the first track that was musically entirely independently composed and produced (as opposed to borrowing beats from existing rap songs online), namely *"Tirip-e Mā"* (Our Way), featuring Reveal. The song begins with notes played on the Persian *santur* (dulcimer) and, despite a pounding hip-hop beat, sounds Iranian throughout. The video, made by a very young filmmaker named Fred (mentioned earlier), also emphasizes Iranian elements, showing young men smoking hookahs and handling daggers, imitating street fights. In 2006, Hichkas released his first full album, titled *Jangal-e Āsfālt* (Asphalt Jungle), composed and arranged by then-seventeen-year old Mahdyar Aghajani, who has also composed nearly all of Hichkas's work since then. This first album contained the track *"Ekhtelāf"* (Disparity), which made Hichkas into a near-overnight sensation. But recording *Asphalt Jungle* was not easy, as the government bodies had become aware of the widespread popularity of the newly emerging hip-hop music. "At the time, security services would go to studios and check the computers to see what was being recorded. We recorded all of *Asphalt Jungle* in a studio well past midnight," says Golestan. In order to avoid being caught, he explained, "the studio technician would first lay down an entire hour of classical music and then put down ten lines of rap vocal recording, all in one line, so that it was basically a jumble when the minder scanned it: the guy just wouldn't hear it when he streamed through it."

After the release of *Asphalt Jungle*, Hichkas drew the attention of the authorities; he was arrested for selling physical copies of the album on the streets and was also called in for questioning a few times. It had become harder for him to find studios that would record his work. "In general, whatever studio we recorded in would be shut down after two months," Lashkary commented.[37] In 2008, he released the single *"Yeh mosht sarbāz"* (A Bunch of Soldiers), which was a sensation because of both the music and the accompanying video. After the summer of 2009 and the Green Uprising, it became nearly impossible for Hichkas to find a studio that was safe and would record his work. The last track that Hichkas recorded in Iran was his 2009 post-Uprising commentary *"Yeh*

Ruz-e Khub Miyād" (A Good Day Will Come). Around that time, the authorities confiscated his passport and called him in several times again for questioning. According to Golestan, they called Lashkary one day in late 2009 and told him to go collect his passport, and "kind of told him, you should go, look, you have a chance to leave, you should use it." Soon after that, in early 2010, Lashkary left Iran, not sure when he would return.

THE NEO-*LUTI*

Lashkary's artist name, Hichkas, means "no one" in Persian. In earlier interviews, he said that he chose the name to "create a contrast between the name and the effect that I want to have with my words."[38] In later interviews, once he was well-known, he said that he chose the name because it signifies the humility of the *luti* (a neighborhood enforcer or warden; see below) and the importance of remaining down-to-earth, though Lashkary modernizes the understanding of the *luti* based on the codes of his newly adopted field, the global art form of rap.[39] Indeed, the enduring historical ethic of which the *luti* is a part has deep roots in Iranian culture but is also constantly in the process of adaptation and has taken on varied forms, depending on the social contexts and necessities of the actors who have employed it.[40] Lashkary views himself as the main founder of *Rap-e Farsi* (and many others concur), and he has gained the epithet of *pedar-e rap-e Farsi* (the father of Persian rap), which in English-language texts has become "the godfather of Persian rap." In his song *"Pedarkhāndeh"* (Godfather), Lashkary declares:

> To Iranian rap I am like a father
> So to me you are all like my sons

This self-description as father or godfather is both in line with and in opposition to Lashkary's self-projection as a *luti* (or what in the old days people would have called a *javānmard*). Prior to the population explosion of Tehran in the nineteen-sixties and nineteen-seventies and the disintegration of the previously tight-knit neighborhoods, there existed a sort of public sphere within each neighborhood or district, where people knew each other and the neighborhood *lutis* were prominent. In its best modern embodiment, the *luti* is an exemplary chivalrous man of neighborhood or regional repute who agitates for justice, often in a gang with other such *lutis*, whose "social ethic is centered on selflessness" and "who possesses fully the quality of a man, referring to his courage, honor, modesty, humility, and rectitude."[41] A *luti*'s social capital and power is of course entirely dependent on his recognition by others, especially other *lutis*, as bearing those qualities and on their subservience to him. In the context of this structure, Lashkary portrays himself as the top *luti* within *Rap-e Farsi*, reaching back into Iranian tradition and drawing on an old ethic based on notions of honor for the construction of his public persona. On the other hand, the *luti* code prescribes humility, which Lashkary has to violate in order to mark his position as the founder of Persian rap and to align himself with the competing code, within rap culture, of stating one's supremacy, which has given birth to a whole branch of "diss genre."

Hichkas has achieved wide popularity with his music in good part because his work is a modern interpretation of various aspects of this traditional Iranian ethic. First, like the *lutis* of earlier times, Hichkas claims the streets for himself and his gang, whom he variously refers to as *bachchehhā* or *bax* (an Internet-age abbreviation of the word *bachchehhā*, "children," which has the connotation of "guys" in English) or "a bunch of soldiers." This claiming of the streets gains even more meaning within the context of the Islamic Republic, wherein the government aims to control the public sphere. Second, Hichkas follows the code's great emphasis on a quest for justice.[42] Hichkas presents this preoccupation both in his songs—often in protesting unjust conditions—and in his barely veiled political comments in interviews and public appearances, where he says, "We are against oppression in general, wherever it appears; whether it comes from my mother or anywhere else, opposing oppression is a priority."[43] Third, as contained in the etymology of the word itself, the *javānmardi* value system is based on ideas of *mardānegi* (manliness), which in turn are ultimately built on notions of honor. This aspect of this old value system or ethic expresses itself in Hichkas's work through his emphasis on the pride he finds in his Iranianness, i.e. modern-day nationalism. That same idea of honor (*nāmus*) or pride in one's country also extends to other entities that are under a man's protection, such as his wife, family, and reputation. Hichkas confirmed this in the response he gave when I asked him why he cared so much about Iran's honor. He responded, "I don't know. It's kind of like *gheyrat* [a term that connotes a combination of zeal and honor-based jealousy]. For example, why is someone mad if his wife goes and sleeps with someone else? There is no logic to it, it's just the way it is; it's *gheyrat*."[44] As the gender studies scholar Afsaneh Najmabadi has explained, historically, in Iran, *nāmus* was closely linked to the maleness of nation and the femaleness of homeland and "was constituted as subject to male possession and protection in both domains; gender honor and national honor intimately informed each other."⁴⁵ Hence, Hichkas's discourse of protecting the nation's *nāmus*, or honor, allows for the performativity of masculinity among a wide segment of disenfranchised young men who form an entity—a "bunch of soldiers"—to rival the state's might. In effect, they claim for themselves the role of protecting the honor of the nation and its women. The heteronormativity that Hichkas promotes in his songs and interviews is part and parcel of this constellation.

CLAIMING THE STREETS

In raps about his gang and its "special affection for the street,"⁴⁶ many Hichkas songs offer a reconfiguration of traditional neighborhood associations of men as well as an alternative to existing groups, mostly either ideologically or materially state-sponsored. As the rapper Bahram describes in his manifesto on the subject, the hip-hop subculture "reflects the street culture of an urban society in various forms."⁴⁷ At the same time, the advent of hip-hop culture in Iran happened alongside the expansion of Internet use among the youth, so that many more of them were able to participate in this alternative public sphere. In many ways, rap music and the discourses expressed within it have allowed for the creation of a "sense of community against the grain of the regime's wished-for Shi'a utopia, very often without arousing the suspicion that it's doing just that."⁴⁸

Hichkas set the tone for this pose with the video for his "*Tirip-e mā*." This grainy, black-and white-production features Hichkas's gang. The song starts with melancholic Persian tunes on a *tār* as Hichkas, still teenage-skinny, leans against a street wall. As the camera zooms in on him, he turns his intense gaze to the viewer in slow motion; in the next frame, he blows shisha (hookah) smoke into the air with a friend. We then see drive-by images of a Tehran street with characteristic sycamore trees, and a group of adolescent men from behind as they walk down the street in a posse. As the camera sways down to the street asphalt and one of the guy's marching sneakers, a broken hip-hop beat kicks in and in a series of frontal images of the gang framing "the father of Persian rap," Hichkas starts his rap in a coarse voice:

> In the name of God, the life-giver
> He who created speech for the tongue
> The streets are familiar with us, our footsteps on them are eternal
> . . .
> We'll tell you how we roll with our bros

Sabers on our belts we whisper this phrase
God let us survive in this asphalt jungle
Our gang still has principles
They accord me the ways of friendship and loyalty
. . .
Aryan blood runs through my veins
As long as this thing called life continues
I'll live an Iranian and I'll die an Iranian
Come war I will take up arms
. . .
This is our way
In the streets

Borrowing the relatively recent form of rap diction yet integrating Persian instruments, Hichkas blends macho elements of the Iranian *javānmardi* ethic with those integral to American rap culture, creating a unique sound that resonates with his mainly young, male, Internet-savvy, and globally aware listeners from mostly traditional family backgrounds. With sabers on their belts, Hichkas's gang is proud to live and die Iranian and is prepared to take up arms should there be war. Again, Hichkas offers an alternative gang to the other prominent organized groups within Iranian society: one based on religion, namely the *tekkiyehs* (spaces, often private, that are "clubs" for religious commemoration), and the other based on the might of the state, namely the Revolutionary Guard or its associates, the *basij*.

In other songs, Hichkas establishes his gang by boasting about the characteristics of its members. In *"Bax-e Soroush"* (Soroush's Guys/Gang), he describes his group's "badass" qualities to establish its street cred. He says that in parties "all eyes are on my gang" and "in your shorty's diary is a picture of me." Soroush's gang "gets your girls" and breaks its adversary's horns. He goes on to rap about his troop's capacity to drink its enemies under the table and describes some of his friends by name, extolling their loyalty and toughness. In sum, he describes a group of young men who are *lāt* (ruffians/hoodlums) and rule the streets as well as the party scene. The discourse about parties, alcohol, and girls of course has no place in the aforementioned traditional groupings such as the *tekkiyehs*, though it would have had a place in the *luti* culture. Many a Persian movie depicts a *luti* in a Pahlavi-era Lalehzar cabaret, drinking and ogling scantily dressed singers and dancers. But this correlation with *luti* culture is barely even necessary, as it is a common pastime in postrevolutionary Iran among younger people, especially men, to gather with friends for a session of *araq-khori* (where a cheap moonshine distilled from raisins called *araq sagi,* "dog's liquor," is often consumed). A YouTube video depicts one such *araq-khori* session where Lashkary and another well-known rapper, named Quf, sit topless, noticeably inebriated, and rap together. The rapper's name is an anglicized spelling of the Persian letter qāf, which is the first letter of the word *qāfiyeh* (rhyme). Quf's piece is a shot at Persianizing rap, as the opening lyrics show:

> They say G has become Quf
> Was something wrong with it?
> Quf is better
> What was the problem with G?
> . . .
> Let G become Quf so my name becomes Persian

"G" is of course used often in English rap and stands for "gangsta," and here Quf is supplanting "G" through his very presence as a *Rap-e Farsi* rapper and his choice of name. In a newer song, *"Mā az unāshim"* (We're of That Sort), on the album *Anjām vazifeh* (Tour of Duty), Hichkas once again lays claim to the streets and draws distinctions between his sort of people, who have to hustle for a living, and those who have money, thereby aligning himself with the majority of Iranians. He raps:

> We're of the sort that somehow has a special affection
> For the street and in addition for the *pāssi* [joint/spliff]
> From evening onward we're in the neighborhood park
> And keep hearing: pass it on, my turn
> . . .
>
> We're of the sort that covers the streets' every inch of asphalt
> Always caught in dreams and thoughts
> . . .
> [Refrain:]
> We're a bunch of soldiers . . . more real than documents . . . our words
>   and actions are one . . . we're in the streets, come visit, you piece of
>   garbage
>
> Hold on a minute
> I have a seen a lot of people who when with me

Are like me but in reality are of a different kind
I'm never home because more money
I have to make, they say your dad is filthy rich and you've managed
To get yourself a good place in your mom's heart
The result of your brownnosing is another super car
We're of this sort, you're of that sort, life is different
We're not like each other and the reason is money, what else?
When you decide to get a wife they quickly buy you a house
What's your whining all about? What are you missing?
To be honest I feel relieved when I yell a little
And by the way, I dig your foreign clothes
We're of the sort that for example
Just this past year
In a few dangerous incidents
Got our clothes ripped into pieces
So why waste money? Fuck Versace

[Refrain]

. . .

We're of the sort that is wholesale badass
My old man never gave in to force and neither did my ancestors
We're of the sort that doesn't fear anything
By the ghosts of the graves . . . I swear

In the last stanza, Hichkas makes reference to another quality that resonates not only with the *javānmardi* code but also more generally with the current national psyche, namely the readiness to fight against unjust force. His posture of fearlessness is compelling in an environment where Iranians are subject to an authoritarian government as well as Western sanctions and threats of war.

PROTECTING HONOR

In Hichkas's work, the projection of honor within the traditional Iranian *javānmardi* ethic expresses itself in postures of modern nationalism. The track "*Tirip-e mā*" (Our Way) was released in 2004, when Internet access was spreading in Iran and, at the same time, rap was beginning to attract a larger audience. This was also the time of the important post-9/11 global dynamic in which the United States had pitted itself against the so-called Axis of Evil, polarizing politics into a West-versus-Islam binary. Under these post-9/11 conditions, with Iranians for several years concerned over a potential American military attack on their soil, the gaze of some in the younger generation of musicians had turned outward, away from an internal battle with an authoritarian regime and toward a greater patriotism and an insertion of the Iranian identity. There is of course more than just a hint of posturing and nationalism in "Our Way," themes that Hichkas picks up again four years later in the track "*Yeh mosht sarbāz*" (A Bunch of Soldiers), his most watched video clip on YouTube.

The "Bunch of Soldiers" music track and video clip are infinitely more polished than the music and video of "Our Way." The clip starts with ominous beeping sounds, interlaced with flashes of broken white lines on street asphalt and a backlit gang of boys standing in the dark. Along with shots of urban Tehran, a whisper accompanies the sharp beeping: "Mā yeh mosht sarbāzim jun-be-kaf" (We're a bunch of soldiers, ready to give life), before a high-energy rap beat backed by the sounds of a *santur* suddenly kicks in with the "bunch of soldiers" throwing their arms up in the air and Hichkas's thick voice proclaiming: "I want your arms to go higher and higher, 021 forever" (021 being, as mentioned earlier, Tehran's area code). He says that he'll begin this song, like "Our Way," in the name of God:

> God is with us because we
> Are ever thankful to him in good times
> But also in times when you can curse the world

After establishing their faith in God, Hichkas says that his bunch of soldiers, who have master's degrees from Iran's biggest university, namely the streets, are willing to give their lives for four things: God, homeland, family, and friends. The flag is flying at high mast, says Hichkas, so "take my rap seriously, I'm not in a joking mood," before continuing to pay homage to the country's martyrs to whose "pure blood we owe our existence." He says to all the *lutis* that "if you're a man, we're on your side," effectively announcing himself as the chief *luti* of Tehran, keeping the flame of chivalry alive.

In the past, *lutis* commanded respect in their neighborhoods and were often used by both religious and secular leaders as proxies in their power games. But as the government has gained more administrative and disciplinary control over its citizens, the *lutis* have lost their role in Tehran's neighborhoods. Some people have even suggested that many of those who in the past would have been neighborhood *lutis* "have now become agents of the government in the guise of members of the *basij* [the paramilitary revolutionary forces]."[49] While this may be technically correct, semantically, the term *luti* can carry connotations of a fairly permissive lifestyle, qualities that few Iranians would ascribe to the *basij*. Hichkas here is calling for a force independent of government—one that is only beholden to values of honor—to band together and protect the nation and its flag, saying, "tell them we're ready for war if they force us." In calling for this nationwide brotherhood of manliness, Hichkas creates agency for himself and his "soldiers" as well as for all the other *lutis* out there.

It is more appropriate, I believe, to look for the modern-day *luti* in the kinds of young men that Hichkas addresses, namely men of lower (though not the lowest) socioeconomic status, often but not always lacking a university degree, who engage in various kinds of paid work and socialize with others like them. They are not a marginalized group, not only because they make up a comparatively large segment of the male population but also because their stance, reflected here in Hichkas's discourse, is self-empowering. It is difficult to generalize about any specific group of men in Iran, but the "street" that Hichkas addresses is often dressed in Western markers such as denim clothing, a good amount of hair gel, the latest trend in sneakers, sunglasses, and a watch, the more expensive the better, but often cheaply acquired thanks to Chinese imports. These young men care about the latest phone and computer technology, even if they can't always afford them. They are highly status-conscious and know, for example, how much a certain brand of car or sunglasses costs. And like Hichkas, they know when someone is not like them. Important among these young men are certain ways of greeting, kinds of personal conduct, and an implicit code of honor that often expresses itself in their relationships and through language. These men may not care about intellectual debates on civil society and democracy, but like the classic *luti*, they care about opposing injustice, and they were particularly visible during the 2009 unrest. While a very wide cross section of Iranian society took part in the protests, with women prominently involved, it was often young men like these who set up neighborhood fronts to fight government forces, in part taking advantage of the situation in order to inscribe their presence into the streets. They were also reasserting their subjectivity and defending their honor vis-à-vis a state that directly and indirectly humiliates and punishes them through its adverse economic and socially restrictive policies.[50]

Military themes run through several Hichkas songs. "*Vatanparast*" (Patriot) starts with an army drumbeat reminiscent of revolution and war-era *soruds* and then begins:

> Oath, oath, to Siavash's pure blood
> To the name of Iran and its soil
> That I would give my life for this earth, come on!

In themes that he repeats in other nationalistic songs such as "*Man vāysādam*" (I'm Standing) and "*Bā ham*" (Together), Hichkas recalls Iran's former glory by drawing on the animal kingdom:

> Now it's a cat but once it was a tiger
> With such majesty this tiger stretched from west to east
> The cradle of civilization was right here
> You want a patriot, I am right here

In a staccato manner that imitates the drumbeat, Hichkas then draws on Iran's history to prove Iran's steadfastness and Iranians' patriotism:

> Here seventy million
> Men, women, and children
> Are on watch that they don't steal Iran's honor and that its flag
> Isn't lowered
> We are paying
> Full attention here
> So we conclude that
> Iran's enemy
> Must be foolish because this soil has willing devotees everywhere
> These are truths, the *Shahnameh* is a myth
> The proof is
> The eight-year war
> The red in our flag is the color of our blood
> For this soil our lives are sacrifice

Hichkas then turns to current affairs and Iran's predicament in world affairs, aligning his stance on nuclear energy with that of the majority of Iranians at the time, as well as the government:

> If I lie alone with a dog tag under the earth
> It's better than hiding in fear under my shell

Now their pretext is nuclear energy
Tell me why do you yourself have nuclear weapons?
Invading Iran is not a joke my boy
There is no doubt anymore in your fear [of Iran]

Interlaced with Hichkas's verses are two long stanzas by Reveal, who reiterates similar points in English, including:

Persian blood in my veins I live and die for Iran
If it's war blood I take up arms and fight for Iran
For centuries we went in peace but they won't let us be
Now they're telling me we ain't allowed to have nuclear energy
. . .
They'd rather see us rest in pieces than see us progress in peace
They must be sniffing on an ounce of powder
Label us as terrorists when everybody knows that Bush knocked down
    the towers!

As the verses above show, the flag and the army, two of the most pronounced features of modern nationalism, play a prominent role in Hichkas songs. His collaboration with Reveal allows Hichkas to tie into the global discourse of rap by drawing on a popular rap song by the band Immortal Technique, titled "Bin Laden," which includes the phrase "Bush knocked down the towers."

In "A Bunch of Soldiers," as mentioned above, Hichkas names "God, homeland, family, and friends" as the four things that he and his "cool soldiers" are willing to give their lives for. When asked by an audience member at a Hichkas event which of these items was the most important, Lashkary replied that they are important in that order, but that he was not necessarily using "soldiers" in a military sense. Rather, "everyone will have a stage in their life when he or she has to serve his country, people, and humankind, not necessarily in a military sense, but fighting for pride and love."[51] In his "*Bā ham*" (Together), the refrain of the song goes:

Everyone hand in hand, raise the flag
Hand in hand, raise the flag

[Background chorus:]
Hand in hand, let's plant the flag up there
Now it's a cat, once it was a tiger

The song basically calls on Iranians to join hand in hand to march toward reconstruction because it's "shameful when Iran's name is at the bottom." So he pleads:

Let's all work together
The experience of the past plus the science of now
Let's all together form a mountain
Give some soul to this tricolor flag of ours
Let's take this flag to the summit, hand in hand
We must break all obstacles by hand

In effect, when Hichkas calls for the flag to be raised, he cares above all about elevating Iran's name and honor. At his first concert in London, on 28 May 2011, as he stepped onto the stage he repeatedly called *"bālāst chi?"* (what's up?) in response to which the mostly young audience shouted *"parcham"* (the flag). Now, working abroad, Lashkary sees himself as a sort of cultural ambassador, raising Iran's name high and protecting its honor.

SEEKING JUSTICE

An important aspect of the *javānmardi* ethic is the Robin-Hoodesque drive to seek justice and remedy inequalities; the *luti* acts as an arbiter within the public realm where other instances and institutions, such as the family or the state, fail. The real or perceived increase in inequality and disparity among the people is a much-discussed subject in daily conversations in Iran, and is often pointed to as the most potent sign of the failure of the Islamic revolution.[52] To decry disparity within the Islamic Republic is to be inherently critical of the state, which has claimed since its beginnings to be based on a revolution that "belonged to the disinherited (*mostaz'afin*) and the barefooted (*pāh-berehnegān*), and promised large-scale redistribution of income and wealth."[53] In his piece *"Ekhtelāf"* (Disparity), Hichkas highlights the discrepancy between the "extremely wealthy" and the poor guy who sells salt from his cart, whose entire existence is worth one ride in the wealthy man's Mercedes Benz. The ubiquity of this "screaming class disparity" and the fact that not "gravity" but "money makes the world go round," "wounds people's souls and makes them sick." Hichkas again puts himself on the side of the dispossessed and asks God to wake up and talk to "this piece of garbage"—meaning himself. His description of an existence where "money comes before God" and where even God may not rise to talk to this human garbage if it has no profit for him flies in the face of what the self-described socialist theocratic state claims to stand for. The track starts with:

> This is Tehran, a city where
> Everything that you see in it causes provocation
> Provoking the soul all the way to the garbage bin
> Until you finally get it that you too are garbage, not a human being
> Here all are wolves; you want to be like a lamb?
> Let me open your eyes and ears a bit
> This here is Tehran you damn fool, it's no joke
> Forget about flowers and popsicles
> This here is the jungle, dog eat dog
> Here half the people have hang-ups, the other half are savages
> Here class disparity is out of control
> It wounds the people's souls and makes them sick

The refrain calls on God to wake up and answer for this state:

> God wake up! I've got several years' worth of stuff to talk to you about
> God wake up, wake up! Don't be mad at me
> . . .
> God wake up! I'm a piece of garbage that needs to talk to you

"Disparity" struck a cord with Tehranis, and Hichkas became so widely known after the release of this song in 2006 that *Injā Tehrān-e* (This here is Tehran) was picked up and became a sort of signal phrase that encapsulated all that the song states about the city. In the internationally screened documentary *No One Knows About Persian Cats*, Hichkas performs the song to a backdrop of homeless people and poverty-stricken workers and children. At a public celebration of Imam Mahdi's birthday put on by state television in the Bustan-e Azadegan park in southeastern Tehran, in July 2011, I witnessed a contest where men from the audience had to sing a segment of a song, and the spectators were supposed to choose a winner. One of the men had barely finished saying "*Injā Tehrān-e*" when his microphone was cut off and he was sent offstage. In its way, this episode shows the sensitivity that surrounds this song, which is not even directly or explicitly critical of the government. However, neither its rap format nor its content is tolerated by the state. In addition, Hichkas's casual address to a God who is asleep and needs to be called to his senses, as well as his insinuation that even God may be considering financial profit before heeding the rapper's call, put the song outside the officially tolerated boundaries:

> You must be blind not to see destitution everywhere
> Not to see poverty and prostitution on the streets
> Wake up God, a piece of garbage wants to talk to you
> Or do you, too, only consider what's profitable for you?

In other songs, such as "*Qānun*" (Law) and "*Zendān*" (Prison), Hichkas takes the position of the street thug who is a victim of the lawlessness of the streets. In "Law" he clarifies that in reality he is a *lāt-e bi-khatar* (harmless hoodlum) whose words are nothing but posture, necessary for survival on the street. He also elaborates that the reason he may end up in prison is that he would oppose oppression:

> So many harmless hoodlums are in prison because they were against all
>   oppression from anyone
> What am I guilty of?
> If I'm a defendant, I have a ton of things to say if this mouth lets me

He pleads in the song's chorus:

> Wait, wait don't put handcuffs on me
> When you do that you're telling me to shut up
> Let me tell you I'm a victim of the jungle
> Me, me, I'm a victim of the jungle

In these songs, Hichkas presents a world in which the police and the constitution mean nothing and the protagonist must fend for himself, giving agency to the individual *lāt*, not unlike the traditional neighborhood *javānmard* who would take matters of justice into his own hands.

Until his departure from Iran in early 2010, Hichkas's work never contained direct criticism of the government, critiquing social ills and injustice instead. Then, following the post-2009 election unrest, the government cracked down on social and artistic spaces, detaining dozens of journalists, activists, artists, and prominent persons who had expressed sympathies for the Green Uprising. Hichkas says that he was "deeply affected" by the events of that summer and fall, but waited with his artistic response until he had planned his departure. In his track titled "A Good Day Will Come," which he waited to release until he had left the country, Hichkas still does not directly criticize the state's handling of internal affairs, but points to its failings by elaborating on the blood that has been shed and the dire circumstances within the country. Nevertheless, he ends his images of bloodshed on a hopeful note and in traditional phrases familiar to Iranians, seeking God's help and a mother's prayers:

> After all this rain of blood
> Finally, a rainbow will emerge
> The sky won't appear cloudy from all the stones
> The water in the aqueducts won't turn red like tulips
> Muezzin, call to prayer
> God is great, harm be far
> Mom, tonight, pray for us

He then aligns himself with the protests by evoking the name of Neda Agha-Soltan, the young woman who became a symbol of the violence against peaceful protesters and whose first name means "message" or "revelation":

> For as long as I remember, this land has always given revelations [*neda*, in Persian]
> A good day will come

In the next two segments of the song, Hichkas hints at conditions during the protests and continues to draw images of the good day that shall come:

> Blood stays in the veins and does not become familiar
> With the sky and asphalt
> It doesn't splash and clot
> No mother goes to her child's grave
> Home isn't a shelter and outside war

Hichkas finishes with tones of nationalism and patriarchy, drawing promises from the song's addressee that when that good day comes, the addressee will give a flower to every soldier that he/she sees; ending with hopes that no "free woman" will be left a widow; and finally, transferring his voice to the mother in her role as a homemaker who tells her daughter:

> My daughter, your father is coming home
> Yes, go set the table for dinner

The track conjures intimacy in the way that it addresses a singular listener, and Hichkas's use of the religious, nationalistic, and patriarchal signifiers mentioned above are only likely to heighten this sense of intimacy. While he may be criticized for ignoring women's tremendous participation in the 2009 uprising and placing the woman (and her daughter) in traditional roles, these are still roles that most Iranians will be familiar with, namely the mother as the symbol of home and the daughter as her extension. Furthermore, traditional gender roles are part and parcel of the *javānmardi* ethic that Hichkas subscribes to and promulgates in his music. While that ethic may alienate a number of fans, its power to attract listeners by far outweighs its alienation of more progressively minded listeners, as it is deeply rooted in Iranian culture.[54]

"As I was on the plane to Kuala Lumpur [in early 2010], the kids put 'A Good Day Will Come' on YouTube," Lashkary told me. But he was determined to return. In the 2009 documentary *No One Knows About Persian Cats*, the only musician who had seemed intent on staying in Iran was Hichkas. After a music agent keeps trying to convince him to emigrate, Hichkas says to the agent: "What do they call what we sing? They call it *Rap-e Farsi*. OK? What's Farsi for? It's for right here." Hichkas called his next collaborative compilation album "*Anjām-e Vazifeh*" (Tour of Duty), a term that is applied to military service in Iran. In the track "Tour of Duty" itself, he pronounces his devotion to Iran, saying "Iran is beautiful, even from behind bars," raps about how he's under the state's magnifying glass with the clear potential for imprisonment, but then emphasizes that his departure from Iran is not out of fear but is a "tour of duty." "I haven't left forever," he told a large crowd at a London talk, "I've just come to open channels for the kids (rappers) in Iran, meet the world's best rappers and see what they're worth, and make connections for Iran."[55] He told me he regarded it as his obligation to go back to Iran, because "there are a lot of people out there who respect the things I say. . . . I put myself in their shoes . . . and, well, one must stay and fight injustice."

Even outside of Iran, Hichkas has refrained from making explicit political statements against the government. It is likely that this has more to do with his views about "keeping Iran's flag raised" than out of caution for his own safety in case he should return. I last met him in the summer of 2014 in London, and he was hard at work on his new album, "*Mojāz*" (Permitted), due to be out in 2016. He joked to me, "The title means that we give ourselves permission to produce whatever music we want." By 2016, Lashkary had still not returned to Iran. Despite his initial intentions, the tumultuous 2009 Green Uprising and its political consequences seem to have shattered his plans for now. Indeed, the political, social, and cultural repression following 2009 ruptured the futures not just of Lashkary but of many other young Iranians, including civil society activists, students, artists, and musicians who emigrated from Iran. Although the unrest led to the scattering of many lives, the Green Uprising presented a unifying force of a kind that was unprecedented since 1979 and within which music played a crucial role.

THE MUSIC OF POLITICS

FOR AN IRANIAN LIKE ME who was too young to have witnessed Iran's 1979 revolution but had spent many of her adult years as a journalist and academic trying to understand the events that culminated in one of the twentieth century's greatest revolutions, it was astounding to witness the 2009 Green Uprising. Astounding because so many of the slogans that were chanted and the sentiments that I heard from demonstrators actively linked back to the revolution that I hadn't had the chance to witness. From the nightly rooftop cries of "*Allah-o Akbar*" (God is great), which called forth "the defining sound of the 1978 protests against the Shah of Iran,"[1] to slogans that copied the chants of 1978 and 1979 in word and rhyme but replaced key actors or signifiers within them, the demonstrators were drawing on a shared memory—whether lived or learned—to lend greater significance to their actions on the streets. So, for example, "*Esteqlāl, āzādi, jomhuri-ye eslāmi*" (Independence, freedom, an Islamic Republic) was turned into ". . . *Jomhuri-ye* Irāni" (Independence, freedom, an *Iranian* Republic). And the word for machine guns in "*Tup, tānk, mosalsal, dige asar nadāre*" (Cannons, tanks, machine guns, are longer effective) was replaced with "*basiji*," as was the word "army" in "*Artesh jenāyat mikone, Shāh hemāyat mikone*" (The army commits crimes and the shah supports them) to update the phrase into "The *basij* commits crimes and the leader supports them." Among the slightly older demonstrators, many saw this as their chance to right the wrongs of a revolution gone bad, one that they had participated in thirty years earlier. Like the bank employee mother who told her children to find them-

selves dinner, because what she was doing was "more important for their future."[2] Or the forty-four-year-old man who showed me his veteran's ID and
said, "I was on the war front for eight years. This is not what we had a revolution for."

Leading up to the presidential elections on 12 June 2009, a great "green
wave" had formed in support of Mir-Hossein Mousavi, the opponent to Mahmoud Ahmadinejad, who at that point had served one term as president.
Mousavi, whose term as a well-liked prime minister (1981–1989) spanned the
tough war years, then disappeared from politics for nearly twenty years and
committed himself to arts and architecture, eventually becoming the director
of the Iranian Academy of Arts. The movement in his support was so strong
that many expected him to win the presidential elections. But when the results were announced, on the morning after the elections, as 63% in favor of
Ahmadinejad, thousands of incredulous Iranians emptied into the streets and
charged the government with election fraud. When Mousavi called on his supporters to join a demonstration on 15 June, about two million people filled
the Azadi Square area, and when government helicopters hovered above and
monitored the march, the crowds chanted up toward them: "Liars, liars, where
is your 63 percent?"

The Green Uprising was a unifying force that reached across space and
time. It was not just the recycled slogans that harked back to 1979 but also the
performativity of citational practices that clearly indexed 1979, mobilized songs
from Iran's early-twentieth-century Constitutional Revolution, and claimed the
even more deeply rooted Karbala paradigm to conjure authenticity and create
a connection within historical memory.[3] The movement's appropriation and
use of the color green, for example—which Iranians associate not just with
Islam but also specifically with 'Āshurā and with Imam Hossein's slaughter
in Karbala—provided potent symbolism on several levels. Like the "Allah-o
Akbar" cries from the rooftops, this appropriation traced a connection to these
precedents of social and political unrest in order to mobilize revolutionary
sentiments. However, although people had once used those Islamic signifiers
as weapons against the shah's secular government, the Green Movement reap-
propriated them away from the Islamic Republic and claimed them for its own
discourse of social and political justice. This was exemplified by some demonstrators wearing white funeral shrouds at protests, signaling their readiness
to die for their cause, and even more so by Mousavi himself proclaiming that,
in defense of people's rights, he was ready for martyrdom. In this way, higher

instances such as God, Islam, and Imam Hossein were called forth to side with those fighting the oppression of the Islamic Republic. One of the main rallying cries was "Yā Hossein, Mir-Hossein," evoking the name of the Shia Imam and the political opponent in one phrase and placing Mousavi at the center of this modern-day reenactment of the Karbala paradigm.[4] The *true* Islam belonged to the oppressed, not the rulers. Shi'ism here was activated in its capacity as a religion of protest.[5] This was a powerful reclaiming of Islamic slogans and symbols for the people, wrested away from a government that had for thirty years used Islam as justification for its undemocratic practices.

Young and old, parents and children, marched together, united across generations to express indignation at what they saw as having been cheated and to express visions for a present and a future that was politically more transparent and freer. After all, despite restrictions, elections and the voting process had until then remained perhaps the only path for Iranians to exercise their agency in deciding their country's political trajectory. The Green Uprising also seemed to unite Iranians across geography, inside and outside of Iran. While Iranians inside were busy mounting demonstrations and writing songs to support the movement, expatriate Iranians engaged by supporting them on social media and with statements and programs on satellite television programs broadcast into Iran and, in the case of musicians like Dariush Eqbali and Hassan Shamaizadeh, by writing songs of support.

Last but not least, the Green Uprising was also a unifier of sorts across politics, inclusive of early-twentieth-century Constitution-era and nationalist songs and forgiving toward leftist revolutionary songs. This was highlighted first and foremost by the Mousavi youth campaign's use of an old communist song, which came to represent the campaign more than any other. In this campaign, "Āftābkārān" (literally Sun-Workers), originally produced by the communist Fedayeen-e Khalq group in commemoration of the 1971 Siahkal Uprising,[6] was first broadcast on 23 May 2009, at Mousavi's biggest campaign event in Tehran, at Azadi Stadium, which seats twelve thousand. As the song played, it was accompanied on a large screen by video footage commemorating what one might call a genealogy of heroes for Iran's reformists: the Constitutional Revolution heroes Baqer Khan and Sattar Khan; nationalist champion Mohammad Mosaddeq; the Islamic liberation ideologue Ali Shariati; the ayatollahs Taleqani, Beheshti, and Khomeini; and then a series of the most famous martyrs of the Islamic Republic, including Mohammad Ebrahim Hemmat, Mehdi Bakeri, and Mohammad Ali Jahanara. Absent was Khamenei.

Youth members of the Campaign in Support of Khatami and Mousavi chose this song after long discussions. As one of its leading members, Fatemeh Shams Esmaeili, explained, "Several months before the elections, there was a certain apathy toward the elections and we as a group met and decided that we were going to use music to motivate people to get involved."[7] At first, new songs were written by activists inside the campaign, but according to Esmaeili, the songs did not really catch on because "none of the songs created contact with people's historical memory. We wanted the potential for people to sing along in a big place like Azadi Stadium." This song, because of its identification with communism, had been banned from state broadcast. After all, the Islamic Republic had executed many Fedayeen members in the first decade after the revolution. The new Mousavi "Sun-Workers" is an updated version of the song that differed from the original by exhibiting epic, anthem-like qualities, with heavy use of percussions. The lyrics are also sung more energetically, though still retaining the melancholy that Iranians connect to:

Gone is the winter
Spring has blossomed
The red flower of the sun has returned and driven away the night
The mountains are fields of tulips
The tulips are awake
They are planting the sun in the mountains flower by flower by flower
In the mountainside her heart is awake
Gun, flower, and grain she brings
In her heart, life life life
A forest full of stars she carries
Her lips a smile of light
Her heart the flame of passion
Her voice a wellspring
Her memory that of a fawn in a faraway forest[8]

The campaign knew that this song would create controversy. Esmaeili explained to me that there were great disagreements over the use of this song, and most objections fell into two categories. Some objected out of the concern that the song was too strongly associated with communists and hence would have negative connotations and fail to connect with people. Others, Esmaeili explained, disapproved out of moral considerations. "I said it would be on a par with Ahmadinejad taking the reformist song *Yār-e dabestāni* and turning it into his campaign song. Imagine people who associate Khosrow Golsork-hi's face with this song turning and seeing Martyr Bakeri's," she said, referring to the famous Marxist poet and activist who had been executed by the shah's regime. "Sun-Workers" was ultimately successful, however, not least because the majority of Iran's population is too young to be emotionally or ideologically invested in the original semantics of old revolutionary songs. Older partici-pants at Azadi Stadium, meanwhile, welcomed the fact that the Mousavi cam-paign was willing to appropriate this song, viewing it as a sign of the campaign's inclusionary politics. Some of the younger crowd, such as Azar, an eighteen-year-old student, also thought that it was "just cool that they dug this song out again." While Iranians in Azar's generation may have been too young to remember the song's precise political connotations, it still rang a positive bell in their reservoir of collective memory because of its renegade status. It was "cool" and subversive precisely because the Islamic Republic had unofficially banned it.

Subsequently, a good number of professional and amateur singers sang this song and posted their versions on YouTube, creating a platform to express af-finity for the song's lyrics and performing their allegiance to the ideals of the Green Uprising movement. At a protest event against Ahmadinejad's presence at the United Nations in New York in September 2009, Kiosk's frontman, Arash Sobhani, gave his own rendition of the song, introducing it with the following words: "The song we're about to perform for you . . . is a song that we've been singing for forty years, unfortunately. Forty years ago, those who were fighting against the dictatorship of that time made this song. Back then they thought freedom was near. Today we're forced to sing this song again, but today we *know* that freedom is near."[9]

The Mousavi campaign and other activists used other songs with Marxist origins, such as *"Bahārān khojasteh bād"* (May the Spring Be August), to create continuities as well. "May the Spring Be August," however, was less controver-sial because state television itself had started playing it, along with other songs rooted in leftist movements such as *"Qasam beh esm-e āzādi"* (In the Name of Freedom), after the Iran-Iraq war. Aside from songs from the 1979 revolution, Green Uprising supporters also relied heavily on Iran's century-long repertoire of freedom songs rooted in the constitutionalist movement of the early twenti-eth century, including songs such as "Bird of Dawn," or *"Hengām-e mey,"* better known in common parlance as *"Az khun-e javānān lāleh damideh"* (From the Blood of Youth Tulips Have Grown). An influential song that was first written and performed by Aref Qazvini in commemoration of youths who died in their struggles to institute a constitution and establish a parliament, it resonated with public sentiment again when the Chavosh group revived it in 1978, using Shajarian's voice, and again in 2009, when it was set to video footage of Green protests:

> From the blood of the homeland's youth, tulips
> Yes my dear, tulips, oh God, tulips, have grown
> The cypress's sorrow, the cypress's sorrow
> Oh God, cypress, yes dear, cypress, has bent the cypress
> In the flower's shadow the nightingale is hiding in grief

Songs created by the Chavosh movement in 1979, which called forth solidarity for a new dawn with songs such as "Join Our Path, Dear One" and "*Iran, ey saráy-e omid*" (Iran, O House of Hope)—famous in their renditions by Shajarian and, for the latter, by Shahram Nazeri as well—were also recruited for the cause.

But the music of the Green Uprising also pointed to a great rupture between its ethos and that of the 1979 revolution. While Islamic signifiers were employed as tactical measures to create continuity with the past and to encroach on and appropriate the state's self-professed and performed Islamic identity, Islam itself, as a discourse of justice and moral righteousness, played barely a role in the music chosen. This was in stark contrast to 1979, when Islamic signifiers had traction and were frequently used in revolutionary songs. When Islamic signifiers were employed in the 2009 protests, they were appropriated in contradistinction to the religious state and outside of the government-sanctioned realm to imply that Islam is on the side of the unjustly oppressed, in this case the Iranian people. The most subversive insinuations were the double-pronged accusations that the Islamic Republic was not truly Islamic and that the goals of the revolution had not been achieved, thereby denying both of the state's raisons d'être and discursively stripping it not only of its legitimacy, but also of its name.[10]

The campaign in support of Mousavi actively discussed using songs with an ideological connection to the revolution, but chose songs that made little mention of Islam or the Islamic Republic's founder, Imam Khomeini. There are dozens of songs that do make such mention, including famous tunes that Iranians would readily remember such as "*Allah Allah Allah,*" "*Allah-o Akbar, Khomeini rahbar*" (God Is Great, Khomeini Is Our Leader), "*Khomeini, ey Imam!*" (Khomeini, O Imam), or "*Buy-e gol-e susan-o yásaman áyad*" (The

Scent of Lilies and Jasmine Comes). In the end—considering the positive reception that the secular (and communist) "Sun-Workers" received, as well as the fact (as reported by the hard-line *Fars News Agency*[11]) that the scene of Imam Khomeini's passing, when it was shown in the campaign video screened at the stadium, failed to elicit any emotional response (in the form, say, of clapping)—the campaign's decision seems to have proved politically savvy.

In fact, the two songs that were most often intoned spontaneously at public Green Movement gatherings were part of the secular nationalist/patriotic repertoire of contention and had attained their contextual and political significance in postrevolutionary protests, especially protests for students' and women's rights. These two songs were "*Yār-e dabestāni*" (Primary Schoolmate) and "*Ey Iran*." Both of them are first and foremost hymns that conjure up a nostalgic sense of community, belonging, and unity, though each does it differently. While "*Ey Iran*," written in the nineteen-fifties, is an anthem in praise of Iran's natural riches and arts and declares the eternal dedication and sacrifice of the singer, "Primary Schoolmate" calls back to a time of childhood innocence, when all Iranians were still equal and united in their common first experiences. But the song galvanizes these tender memories in order to call for action and resistance:

> My primary schoolmate, you are with me, at my side
> The ruler[12] over our heads, you're my grief and my sigh
> Forever engraved are your name and mine, on the body of this
>   blackboard
> The baton of injustice and tyranny still hangs over our bodies
> This damned culture is full of useless weeds
> Good if good; but if bad, dead are the spirits of its people
>
> Your hand and mine must tear these curtains
> Who—if not you and I—can find a remedy for our pain?

The song was written and produced by film director and songwriter Mansur Tehrani in 1979 and was first sung by the popular rock musician Fereydun Foroughi, for a recording intended to accompany the screening of the film "From Scream to Terror." However, the new Islamic Ministry of Culture forbade the use of Foroughi's voice, and the song was ultimately sung by Jamshid Jam, although recordings with Foroughi's voice were sought after on the black market. "*Ey Iran*" and "Primary Schoolmate" both hail from the past but accrued their sentimental resonance within the antiauthoritarian and civil rights contexts of postrevolutionary Iran.

Quite revealingly, even supporters of the conservative, populist incumbent Mahmoud Ahmadinejad chose not to employ Islam-centered songs for their campaign. In fact, they tried to appropriate the resistance cachet of "Primary Schoolmate" for Ahmadinejad, first in 2005 and again in 2009. In the "Ahmadi" version, the melody of the song is maintained while the lyrics are changed to praise Ahmadinejad, completely missing the point that this song's power lay in calling for united, communal action rather than rescue by any one person:

> Your hand and mine must eliminate these discriminations
> Who, if not you and me, can solve our problems?
> He loves service and holy struggle, determined to eradicate poverty and
>   corruption
> He is in favor of science and knowledge—Mahmoud Ahmadinejad

While the song itself is strongly linked to reformists, its communitarian and anti-corruption content lent itself to the populist image Ahmadinejad nurtured for his first election. In addition, it drew a direct line to the demands of thirty years earlier, signaling that Ahmadinejad was the leader who would finally realize the "true" goals of the 1979 revolution. In the end, however, the song did not catch on for Ahmadinejad. When questioned about efforts to hijack the song for the pro-regime camp, the famous prerevolutionary pop star Dariush explained the Ahmadi song's lack of success as follows: "Our people are very smart and intelligent and they won't buy it. *Yār-e Dabestāni*, among the people, among the students, has now become a rallying cry; it's a romantic chant for solidarity, for national unity."[13]

Furthermore, the Ahmadinejad campaign failed to create any songs specifically associated with their candidate alone. At his election events, there was often anthemic music, free of lyrics, aimed at projecting a sense of righteousness and victory. The only song that was presented as a campaign video was pop singer Reza Sadeghi's "*Sādeh biyā*" (Come As You Are), about the virtues of simplicity, superimposed on images of Ahamdinejad.[14] Shortly after the release of the video and a news item on a music website about Sadeghi's potential engagement with the Ahmadinejad camp, however, the artist published a statement in which he denied working with any political camp, stating that "the dignity of the arts and artists is higher than getting involved in factional and political currents," thus robbing the song of any legitimacy for the Ahmadinejad camp.[15]

On the reformist side, however, stars from the younger generation's favorite music genre—*Rap-e Farsi*—did get involved in political campaigning. The rhythm and blues and rap singer Amir Tataloo, who until then had mostly sung shallow songs about girls and parties, performed a techno-beat-based track for Mousavi in which he struck a more serious tone:

> The uprooter of poverty and corruption—Mir-Hossein Mousavi
> We are all the youth of Iran, for your support we stand in line
> . . .
> Very green is our Iran, because Iranians stand behind it
> With our unity, we can kill any enemy
> Let's join our voices into one, like always, and sing together
> We are Iranians and Iran relies on us
> A Green Iran, our Iran[16]

The Green campaign took another decision toward "inclusivity" in posting this song on its website, "because that was what a lot of young voters would identify with; it was closer to the electoral atmosphere than old slow tunes," Esmaeili explained. At this point, shortly before the elections, the campaigning had heated up so much that even Sasy Mankan, the hip-popper already mentioned who had become famous with a lighthearted song called "*Nināsh Nāsh*," (baby talk for "dance"; see chapter 9) about guys digging girls in tight clothes with big lips and fake nails, was recruited by the campaign of the other reformist opponent, the cleric Mehdi Karoubi, to write a song for him, an episode that became the butt of jokes in election conversations.[17]

Like Ahmadinejad's campaign, state television exhibited artistic poverty as far as music was concerned. The two songs that television kept playing over and over again were "*Vatanam*" (My Homeland), by Salar Aghili, and Shajarian's "Iran, O House of Hope," both patriotic, all-inclusive songs empty of any particular political ideology. After Shajarian publicly protested against state television broadcasting his work, the IRIB was left with little to play besides "*Vatanam*," which was itself a somewhat ambiguous and tainted choice because Mousavi's campaign also made use of it. Hence, while the fledgling state media of the Islamic Republic, thirty years earlier, had had an abundance of songs with which to fuel national fervor and consolidate people behind the newborn government, in 2009 cultural poverty had replaced abundance. And certainly, to judge from their choice of music, neither Ahmadinejad's camp nor the state's own broadcasting system placed much hope in songs with explicit political

ideology. As a woman who was active in a semi-governmental musical institution in Iran explained, "Back then the artists who created those songs really
felt and believed the things they sang, and state television took those songs and
appropriated them. Nowadays, no one sings sincerely passionate songs for this
regime of their own volition. So they're left without any original songs that can
attract credibility among the people."[18]

Following Ahmadinejad's post-election "riffraff" victory speech on 14 June
of that year (discussed in chapter 3), in which he equated protestors with angry
hooligans on the losing side of a soccer match, there slowly emerged among the
people the slogan *Ān khas-o khāshāk to-yi, past tar az khāk to-yi* (That riffraff
[literally, dirt and dust] is you, what's lower than dirt is you), in reference to
Ahmadinejad himself. Within days, people at demonstrations were holding up
handwritten placards with these lines and sometimes an entire poem starting
with those lines. No one was quite sure where the poem had emerged from, but
soon thereafter, the US-based musician Hamed Nikpay turned the poem into a
highly popular song titled *"Mālek-e in khāk"* (Owner of This Land) that made
the rounds in Tehran. Other musicians gave the song their own renditions, too.
Part of the lyrics are:

> That riffraff is you
> What's lower than dirt is you
> I'm the passion, I'm the light, I'm the aching lover
> You are oppression, blind to the truth
> You're the halo without light
> I'm the fearless fighter
> I'm the rightful owner of this land[19]

Less than a month after the elections, the revered classical vocalist Shahram Nazeri also created his response to the events with a song titled *"Khas-o
khāshāk"* (Riffraff) and was widely lauded for having joined the movement. The
color green also offered endless metaphors in songs. In introducing his song
"Yeh dasht-e sabz" (A Green Valley) at the September 2009 protests in New
York, Kiosk frontman Arash Sobhani said: "For a country where seventy percent of the population is under the age of thirty, it is regrettable that twelve
men, each older than six hundred, sit in the Guardian Council and decide who
should be president." Sobhani then dedicated the song to the Guardian Council:

> The dinosaurs are all together
> The Coalition of Jurassic Park

Busy with approval and guidance, they're all crammed into a cave
They are allergic to light and sunshine
Chronic inward blindness, cerebral freezing
Consequences of the Ice Age
. . .
The imaginative counting of votes
Without the responsible officials
Distributing affection (*mehrvarzi*) through the force of the baton
Everyone saw your justice
At the end of this tunnel of horror
I see there is a light
Behind this stone wall
There is a green field

The names of those killed in the protests were also the subject of several songs, especially the name of Neda Agha-Soltan, whose brutal death by gunshot on 20 June was captured on a phone camera and distributed widely on social media, later called "probably the most widely witnessed death in human history" by *Time Magazine*.[20] Agha-Soltan became the most iconic "martyr" of the election unrest, and has been invoked in many songs. Perhaps the most popular song in honor of her and of other martyrs was "*Nedā-ye Sohrāb*" (Sohrab's Message, a play on the names of Neda and of another well-known martyr, Sohrab Arabi) by an anonymous singer with the alias "Mazdasht Gerami," who reportedly resides in Iran and produced this song from within the country. "*Nedā-ye Sohrāb*" is an upbeat flamenco-esque song that invokes lovers and martyrs:

News came that winter was ending
Silence is fleeing the dark city
Look at the feet of this earth's Azadi[21]
The most beautiful flowers are dying
News came that people are in the streets
All the lovers are gathered in the square
News came that Neda is rolling in blood
So she won't let freedom die easily
News came that June's heart is scarlet
The entire city full of fire and screams
News came that Sohrab's heart bled
Taraneh was burned by the hand of injustice

Rain, oh heavens, on this dark night
When they shower lovers with bullets
The answer to our rights is lead and pellets
But the forest doesn't die, beware lumberjack[22]

These and other martyrs became the most potent personified symbols of the brutality of the state in its repression of peaceful dissent. Designating these young people as "martyrs" had the same subversive impact as shouting "*Allah-o Akbar*" from the rooftops at night, which was done for weeks following the elections as a form of nonviolent protest. The flurry of artistic activity in support of the movement led Mousavi to acknowledge the importance of artistic creations in his second recorded address following the elections, on 18 October 2009:

> Today we are witnessing an unprecedented and exceptional degree of artistic creations produced by artistic hands and groups, none of whom are members of a factional movement but who belong to a vast social network. The number of clips and songs that we have seen produced in this time, the paintings and cartoons that have been produced, they are incomparable to any other historical period that we've had and in reality, it is they who are guiding and advancing the content of the dialogue and the movement of this big wave.[23]

There were several other rap songs besides Hichkas's track "A Good Day Will Come" that made the rounds, although none of them captured the wide national attention that "A Good Day" did. Among them were songs filled with anger. In her song "*Nakonim āb rā gel*" (Don't Muddy the Water), the female rapper "Kalameh" (an alias) equates the current regime to "Cain, Goliath, Pharaoh, and Yazid," historically evil rulers that Shia Islam, and consequently the Islamic Republic, proclaim as their antitheses and normative enemies. Her song starts with rooftop shouts of "*Allah-o Akbar*," then she goes on to call the killing of hope the biggest crime and raps "the people say no to oppression, no to censorship, no to turmoil, no to beatings and killings, no to injustice." Another young rap group, *Marze Ma* (Our Limit), touches on the same point in its song "*Sarkub*" (Repression) when it sings of people's growing awareness of the deceit of the current regime:

> Our protest is that they sold us
> They didn't even give us a chance to talk
> When ten million flood the streets
> There is a problem; it's not the youth's fault

. . .

Why did you kill?

Just so you could stay in power?

In response, I'll clench my hand into a fist and raise it to the heavens

. . .

My generation is willing to pay for justice

She is victorious who gives the message [*neda*] of freedom

The better-known female rapper Salome MC aligned her message with the ethos of the Green Movement by offering the peaceful song "*Sabz shodim dar in khāk*" (We've Grown Green on This Land), with the words:

So listen my brother, my sister

I know you are different but I love you

As long as we both aim

To build this sacred land

To make it the best place to live

So you can chant with me with one voice:

For the country's honor

We can sacrifice everything

Those who can't say it

Get out—you're not one of us

And from abroad, the group *Abjeez* chimed in their conciliatory tones with their popular song "*Biyā*" (Come), in which they call up codes of traditional Iranian honor, ask vigilantes and state forces whether they call the beatings of demonstrators "manliness," and urge them:

To God, the power of love is better than the love of power

Come for once and forever

And join the lovers and see what happens

This brings me to another deep division between 2009 and 1979: The Green Uprising was a fundamentally peaceful movement, without the militancy that the 1979 revolution glorified in image and action. This was exemplified by the difference between two Shajarian songs. In his 1978 "Give Me My Gun," Shajarian calls for armed resistance, whereas in his 2009 "Put Down Your Gun" he actively calls for a humane, nonviolent path. Those who participated in the Green Uprising caused a transformation of public space, through their very representations on the streets, that stimulated the imagination into a recognition that their world could indeed be different; different, in many ways, as represented in these very sites, namely a world that allows for freer expression, greater self-determination, and diversity, a world that is to a much greater extent feminine, more reflective of actual society. In effect, the Green Uprising constituted a counterpublic whose ethos was rooted in values of nonviolence and hope. Even at the biggest post-election rally surrounding Azadi Square on 15 June, about two million protestors walked for the most part silently and advised each other against aggressive slogans such as "*Marg bar diktātor*" (Down With the Dictator).

It was this strong foundation that allowed there to emerge, out of one of the darkest political and social periods in postrevolutionary Iran, a movement of hope, which ultimately culminated in the election of President Hassan Rouhani in 2013. The Rouhani campaign's symbol of a key pointed to the unlocking of doors and barriers to open up new vistas, and its decision to choose a color—purple—was a nod to the Green Movement. Rouhani officially named his government "the government of hope and moderation," and at his inauguration speech on 4 August 2013 called for unity and affection among Iranians, saying that his government aimed to "bring happiness back into Iranians' lives."[24] To mark Rouhani's first one hundred days in office, the filmmaker Hossein Dehbashi even produced a music video based on the president's inaugural speech that was closely modeled on Barack Obama's 2008 star-studded "Yes, We Can" video.[25] The equally black-and-white Rouhani version is titled "*Nowsafar*" (New Voyager) and features close-ups of both famous and regular people voicing Rouhani's words with evident passion and sincerity, accompanied by snippets of the president's own delivery of his speech, all accompanied by a strumming guitar. The video calls for unity and representation of all Iranians not just in words but also by incorporating people from Iran's various ethnic minorities who speak and sing along in their own languages. Quite strikingly, the clip shows men and women singing along with the words of a high-ranking cleric (Rouhani), interspersed with prominent displays of musical instruments. Rouhani's decision to feature this video on his official website signaled a welcome openness. And the conciliatory tone of Rouhani's government, in contradistinction to Ahmadinejad's often divisive rhetoric, is evident in the words highlighted for the clip, among them:

Let our hearts be cleansed of resentment
Let conciliation replace estrangement
And friendship replace animosity
Let this take root

. . .

Let the compassionate face of Islam
The rational face of Iran
The humane face of the revolution
The affectionate face of the establishment
Continue to create epics

. . .

I sincerely and humbly ask the compassionate Lord
O Lord, assist me to save thy weak servant from evils
Of arrogance and conceit, greed, avarice and envy
O Lord
O Lord, I take refuge in thee
From autocracy of opinion, haste in decision-making
Putting personal or group interests ahead of those of the public
And from shutting the mouths of rivals and critics
O Lord, help me
So I can be thy genuine servant
And a competent servant of the people

This attitude of openness and hope was also reflected in Rouhani's choice of Ali Moradkhani as the deputy of arts affairs at the Ministry of Islamic Guidance and Culture (*Ershād*). Moradkhani had been the director of music at *Ershād* for nearly fifteen years, from 1990 to 2005, and was credited with having facilitated more lenient measures in the field of music, as we saw in chapter 8. By 2014, *Ershād* had given unprecedented concert permits to formerly underground acts like the dance-pop singer Xaniar, King Raam, and even O-Hum.[26] But while there has indeed been some increased openness here and there, including one or two instances of female solo singing on official stages, there is no clear trajectory toward a more open and liberal public space overall. It almost seems like a déjà vu of the Khatami era, when a conservative backlash annulled newly gained freedoms. Following the ground-shaking 2009 protests, and now the nuclear rapprochement between Iran and the United States, conservative factions in Iran feel more threatened than ever, and this is reflected in the field of music, where progress seems to be encapsulated in the phrase "one step forward, two steps back."

For example, after fifteen years of applying for permits, O-Hum was finally permitted to give a few concerts in 2014. Enough time had passed since the band's early days that (as mentioned before) several—very excited—fans had even brought their children to the concert. The band rocked to an enthusiastic crowd in the performance space below Azadi Tower, with the watchful eyes of Imam Khomeini and Ayatollah Khamenei gazing down on the stage from their portraits above. But subsequently, the band was unable to get permits for further performances or for an album release. Finally, O-Hum frontman Shahram Sharbaf wrote an angry public letter to Piruz Arjomand, the director then of *Ershād*'s Music Office, in February 2015, just before Persian New Year, saying:

> I don't know about other musicians, but my life is only supported through my work in music (concerts and albums) and thanks to your kindness, in this moment and ahead of the New Year, I am a person who is absolutely broke, drowned in depression, sadness, hatred, and anger. All hopes and possibilities for having any income have been destroyed by your system of "come back next week."

Sharbaf then went on to request a finite ban on his work as a musician so that he could put an end to the misery of hanging in this infinite state of limbo.[27]

Unlike a lot of the pop music that is approved by the state, O-Hum's rock music had developed outside of the bounds of state control, with its own source of authenticity that resonated strongly with its audience. Conflicting sources of authority, along with the general anxiety of the cultural policymakers about forms of cultural production that are outside of their control, mean that independent sources of fun and spontaneity are viewed with suspicion and hindered. That is precisely why Rouhani's discourse of hope and happiness resonated with Iran's young population. It aligned with a new emerging ethos of a counterpublic that performs its resistance to paternalistic state control through notions of fun, hope, and joy. This conflict was on display when the state intervened and arrested seven young Iranians for producing and posting online a dance video to Pharrell Williams's song "Happy." The "Happy" kids and the public that engaged in circulating the discourse around this video were not just connecting with a global happy media moment, but were also using a politics of fun to exit the state's power paradigm and its policy of what Asef Bayat calls "anti-fun-damentalism."

Another, much larger, instance in which this counterpublic came to the fore was the mass outpouring for the funeral of the pop singer Morteza Pashaei, who died of cancer at age thirty in November 2014. It was the largest public gathering since the 2009 election protests. The people who poured into the streets were unified by a pop singer who had given them love songs, and these people—men and women, boys and girls, many young, but many also middle-aged—spent large portions of their time singing his songs together. In many ways, intentionally or not, this counterpublic was using an opportunity to manifest itself in public and come face-to-face with itself as an empowering tactic. In interviews, the participants often proclaimed that they were not political and were only there for the love of Pashaei. Still, the constitutional affects of this counterpublic, centered as it was around love and joy, ran counter to those officially promoted by state bodies. And even if none of the participants meant their presence to be a political act, their presence was politicized and brought home visually in online forums. There, people posted pictures of the many thousands attending Pashaei's funeral gatherings side-by-side with pictures of the attendees, only a hundred or so of them, at the public funeral of one of the Islamic Republic's highest-ranking politicians, the conservative cleric Mohammad Reza Mahdavi Kani, who had died a few weeks earlier.

Following the 2009 election unrest, the state had tried to broadcast its own form of controlled joy to a deeply depressed public. As a flurry of old and new protest songs was posted and consumed online, and while people were still enraged over what many believed were rigged elections as well as the deaths of over a hundred protestors, state radio countered by broadcasting ad nauseam a new song titled "*Hamehchi ārumeh*" (Everything Is Calm).[28] The song's main lyrics were:

> Everything is calm
> How happy I am!
> I pride myself, you are now with me
> . . .
> How lucky I am!
> Everything is calm
> . . .
> Everything is calm
> My sorrows have disappeared

Instantly, people converted the song's title into a cynical phrase that they exchanged in greetings, which signaled their awareness of the state's amateurish attempts to project happiness and calm into the public space. In repeating the phrase mockingly, people told each other that precisely the opposite was true: that there was no calm or quiet. As the state imprisoned dozens of students, political and civil society activists, journalists, lawyers, and reformists and held them in abysmal conditions, it was broadcasting joyous songs on the radio and allowing dozens of pop concerts to go onstage. But of course none of the political fervor of the 2009 protests, which was ubiquitous in online forums and private gatherings, was allowed in these official spaces.

Back in England after one of my last research trips to Tehran, in March 2011, I attended a concert by the Iranian band Radio Tehran, featuring King Raam, at a London club. There, onstage, Radio Tehran's lead singer Ali Azimi and King Raam collaborated on the latter's song titled "*Mā bishomārim*" (We Are Countless), and the audience eagerly joined in with the words:

> We are countless, countless
> On the path to freedom
> Awaiting the day when the shadow of oppression will be lifted and we
>   shall stand again under Iran's rainbow in memory of those who no
>   longer are and build a house for tomorrow
> We are countless, countless
> On the path to freedom

As I looked around and saw the passion with which the mostly young crowd was singing along, I instantly felt music's power to unite perfect strangers in common sentiments and aspirations. I thought back to the previous night, when, still in Tehran, I had attended a pop concert by the teen idol Benyamin (discussed in chapter 5) where he had crooned superficial words of love to a seemingly receptive audience, but where an artificial atmosphere reigned and none of the warmth and fervor of the London concert was evident. There, in Tehran, I had asked a twenty-two-year-old girl what she thought about the music and she had replied, "You know, we come here to forget our reality, to be aimlessly joyous for a night . . . it's a kind of empty joy (*shādi-ye puch*)." That feeling of doom and desperation that is so pervasive among youth in Iran had been present even at Benyamin's "happy" concert.

The state had banned joyous music for two decades, and now that the state had reversed course to allow it, in its own interest, it authorized only an innocuous "empty joy," as if it were trying defensively to occupy any space that might otherwise be taken up by real, possibly political, feelings or even just real, spontaneous joy outside of its control. Whereas the state initially regulated pop music based on "Islamic" sensibilities, it has gradually allowed musicians in this field to push the boundaries in terms of beats and diction. Because it continues to control the official musical space so tightly, it is not concerned, in these settings, about the potential subversive power of fun, which at a minimum requires some spontaneity and freedom.[29] Even though audiences always inject their own interpretations and subversions into even officially scripted and controlled spaces, they never leave the state's "power paradigm" in this tightly controlled field. In comparison to the atmosphere in Iran fifteen years earlier, when I first returned to the country and sensed an unspoken ban on any kind of joy, it seemed now as though the Islamic Republic had resolved to allow both music and some joy to exist, but only of the kinds that it could control and that served its interest. Sure, the parameters of the permissible have been shifting and have expanded, overall, from the days when music tapes were confiscated and clapping to music was forbidden. But ultimately, the kind of music and "fun" that possess the potential to freely empower and unite, the kind that I witnessed at the London concert, are still off-limits.

ACKNOWLEDGMENTS

I am grateful to so many people for their help in the completion of this work that I will most certainly fail to mention them all here. First, I would like to thank all my compatriots who gave generously of their time to help me on my quest to research and write this book, especially the four featured musicians, Ostād Mohammad Reza Shajarian, Alireza Assar, Mohsen Namjoo, and Soroush Lashkary (aka Hichkas); Ostād Shajarian, in particular, was exemplary in embodying the Persian saying "The fuller a tree with fruits, the more bent its branches" (so great and yet so humble). Each of these musicians indulged me with several interviews, often on different continents. Many others engaged in the field of music, from musicians to government officials, producers, record-label owners, professors, journalists, and others who make the music machinery go around in Iran, have helped me along this process; these include (but are by no means limited to) the 127 band (especially Yahya Alkhansa and Salmak Khaledi), Maral Afsharian, Yaser Bakhtiari aka Yas, the Barobax band, Ramin Behna, Babak Chamanara, Ali Mo'allem-Damghani, Farzin Darabi, Majid Derakhshani, Pedram Derakhshani, Khashayar Etemadi, Farhang Fatemi, Sasan Fatemi, the rapper Justina, Mehdi Labibi, Bozorg and Maria Lashgari, Mohammad Reza Lotfi, Reza Mahdavi, Sohrab Mahdavi, Pari Maleki, Jamaleddin Membari, Mojtaba Mirtahmasb, Ata'ollah Mohajerani, Abolhasan Mokhtabad, the Pop Recording Studio, Hassan Riahi, Sadeq Saba, Ramin Sadighi, Fereydun Shahbazian, Mojgan Shajarian, Ali Moradkhani, Mohammad Mehdi Mowlaei, the rapper Nazila, Mohsen Rajabpour, Kamran Rasoolzadeh, Babak Rezayi, Babak Ruhi, Mohammad Safajooee, Abbas Sajjadi, Mohammad Sarir, Kavous Seyed Emami, Behrang Tonakaboni, Ali Torabi, Milad Torabi, Hossein Tutunchian, and Mahsa Vahdat.

I would also like to thank the persons and institutions that provided the necessary framework that allowed me to conduct research and write this book. I am grateful to Walter Armbrust at Oxford University for his intellectual rigor and support from the very beginning of this project. More generally, I owe a debt of gratitude, for providing me a warm and intellectually stimulating environment that was my home for several years, to Oxford's St. Antony's College, the Middle East Centre, and the wonderful scholars and administrators there, including Julia Cook, Margaret Couling, Mastan Ebtehaj, Timothy Garton Ash, Homa Katouzian, Margaret MacMillan, Philip Robins, Eugene Rogan, and Michael Willis. I am also indebted, for the caring support that I received throughout, to Edmund Herzig at Oxford's Oriental Institute, for intellectual and general mentorship to Hamid Dabashi at Columbia University, and for comments on my work and support over the past years to Houchang Chehabi, and for comments on parts of my work to Martin Stokes. New York University's Hagop Kevorkian Center for Near Eastern Studies was my academic home for the final stretches of this book's completion, and there I am indebted to Arang Keshavarzian, Zachary Lockman, Ali Mirsepassi, Greta Scharnweber, and Helga Tawil-Souri for their kindness and support. At Stanford University Press, I owe so much gratitude to my stellar editor Kate Wahl, who is an exemplar of multifaceted competence and efficiency. I am lucky to have worked on my first book with Kate and her team, including Anne Fuzellier, Micah Siegel, and Stephanie Adams—the academic publishing dream-team. I would also like to thank my three anonymous reviewers for their useful feedback on my book. I am grateful as well for the scholarships and grants that I received from Oxford University, the British Institute for Persian Studies, and the Barnard College Alumnae Association. Lastly, I thank both the British Society for Middle Eastern Studies and the Middle East Studies Association of North America for granting me their awards for the best dissertation in Middle Eastern Studies in 2014, which further encouraged me toward the completion of this book.

   This journey would have been tough without the companionship of good friends, many of whom were instrumental in helping me with a variety of aspects of my work, whether it was grounding me in Iran when I first moved there in 2002, helping me clarify my thoughts in long conversations, finding connections to people in the field, or simply emotional support. In particular, for my time in Iran, I would like to thank Newsha Tavakolian, Thomas Erdbrink, Poupa Marashi, Cambyse Mirabedi, Nadia von Maltzahn, Ata Hosseinian, Amir Payvar, Babak Salek, Tahereh Sariban, Alireza Akhavan, Mahsa Shekarloo and Sohrab Mahdavi. I must also express my thanks to my colleagues in journalism, who were comrades in arms under often difficult circumstances. You know who you are. And I am grateful to my extended family in Iran, for all the things for which you can only rely on aunts, uncles, and cousins, such as lifts to the airport at three in the morning and warm homemade meals: thank you to the Seraj Ansari clan. Words cannot express my gratitude to Anandi Brennan, Carrie Bullmore, and Paige Heimark, three angels whose loving care of our child Delara gave me the peace of mind to accomplish this work.

   Last but not least, I owe gratitude to my close family in supporting me through this long process. My late father, Mir Ali Akbar Seyed Siamdoust, was a larger-than-life force of nature who lived by the honorable maxim of good thoughts, words, and deeds. His rapacious taste for Iran's culture and politics lit my imagination, and his hard work enabled us to lead privileged lives in which we could pursue education. My mother Hamideh Seraj Ansari's example of courage, curiosity, ambition, and rectitude has been an endless source of inspiration. She is a true *shir-zan*, without whose love and support life would not be imaginable. It is to her credit that I have such accomplished siblings, whose companionship has meant so much: my sister, Elham, and my brothers, Mohammad Reza and Hamid Reza Seyedsayamdost. I also owe thanks to my parents-in-law, David and Virginia Butters, for their generosity. Finally, I am deeply indebted to my husband, Andrew Lee Butters, whose sharp intellect helped me think through some of the harder questions in this book, oftentimes on long walks in Oxford's Port Meadow. He has grounded me; I have finally made my home with him and our daughters Delara and Leili, who have brought so much love into our life and put everything else into perspective.

Brooklyn, NY
July 2016

For my transliterations, I have followed a modified *Iranian Studies* system. The only diacritical marks used here are long *alef*, indicated by "ā"; *ayn*, indicated by " ' "; and *hamza*, indicated by " ' "; for the names of persons and places, I use only *ayn* and *hamza*. In line with the *Iranian Studies* system, I have transliterated the short "o" vowel as "o" and the long "o" (diphthong) sound as "ow," respectively. Hence, the Persian New Year is spelled Nowruz. Also, I have added the plural "*hā*" without a hyphen. Plurals of individual Persian words occurring within the English text are formed with an "s," hence the plural of *tasnif* (song) is given as *tasnifs*.

Where necessary for context, my transliteration of colloquial texts follows the Persian pronunciation. All names, Persian or Arabic, are given in their commonly used or accepted English forms, if these exist. If names of Arabic origin have an established Persian pronunciation, the English transliteration given here reflects that pronunciation, unless there is a commonly accepted spelling that appears in Webster's Collegiate Dictionary. Hence, Imam Hussein is given as "Imam Hossein," as opposed to "Emam Hossein," which would be the more appropriate transliteration from the Persian from a purely phonetic standpoint. In discussing people who had occasion to spell their own names in English, I use the spelling they preferred: hence Shadmehr Aghili and not Aqili, and Soroush Lashkary rather than Sorush Lashkari. All translations are my own unless otherwise stated.

CHAPTER ONE

1. Among these, some of the most famous were the pop star Googoosh and the classical musician Parisa. Both of these musicians eventually gave performances abroad. Googosh left Iran for good in 2000, giving her first concert in Toronto in August of that year. When she stepped onto the stage, she received a ten-minute-long standing ovation; see Azam Gorgin, "Iran: Singer Googoosh Ends 20 Years of Silence," *Radio Free Europe/ Radio Liberty*, 8 August 2000: http://www.rferl.org/content/article/1094454.html. Parisa relaunched her career in 1995 with a series of concerts in Europe; see Mozafari (2013).

2. For works on modern Iranian history and politics, see Abrahamian (1982), Ansari (2007), Dabashi (2007), Gheissari & Nasr (2006), Katouzian (2013), Keddie (2006), Matthee & Baron (2000). On the Green Movement, see Dabashi (2010), Hashemi & Postel (2011). On the subject of Islamizing Iran's polity, see Parvin & Vaziri (1992), Mirsepassi (2010).

3. For more on Khomeini's views regarding Islam's role in polity, see Khomeini and Algar (2002). On the evolving role of Islam in private lives as well as Iran's public sphere, see Adelkhah (1991).

4. *Fuqahā*, plural of *faqih*, means jurists; for Iran's constitution, see "The Constitution of Islamic Republic of Iran," Iran Chamber Society, accessed 5 July 2016: http://www .iranchamber.com/government/laws/constitution.php.

5. Decree issued following the remodeling of the Headquarters of the Cultural Revolution into the Supreme Council for Cultural Revolution in 1984; see "Matn-e Mosavvabeh-ye 5 Shorā-ye 'Āli-ye Enqelāb-e Farhangi" (Text of Resolution 5 of Supreme Council of Cultural Revolution), accessed 2010: http://www.iranculture.org/en/about/rahbar/ emam/e05.php (site discontinued).

6. In her autobiographical graphic novel *Persepolis*, Marjane Satrapi illustrates terrifying yet common experiences such as the morality police breaking into her friend's

mixed-sex private party and arresting everyone there, the brutish policing of her mother's make-up on the streets, and incursions into homes in search of illicit pop-culture goods and alcohol (2004; 2005). Such incidents were common in the first decade after the revolution but decreased somewhat during the presidency (beginning in 1989) of Akbar Hashemi Rafsanjani, whose policies liberalized the country in the cultural and political spheres. Then with the election of reformist president Mohammad Khatami in 1997, the public space opened up considerably, and people were left at greater ease in their private lives. This opening led to a backlash from conservatives only a few years into Khatami's term, ultimately resulting in the defeat of the reformists and the election of socially conservative president Mahmoud Ahmadinejad in 2005. For an account of this process, which highlights the struggles of select individual reformists, see Secor (2016).

7. For more on this process, see Golkar (2012).

8. I read this on a plaque in the staircase of the headquarters of the Supreme Council for Cultural Revolution.

9. One such martyr is Sheikh Fazlollah Nouri from the time of the Constitutional Revolution. He opposed constitutionalism at the beginning of the twentieth century and was hanged by a revolutionary court order in 1909.

10. Abrahamian (1993, 25).

11. Ibid., 32.

12. "*Ezhārāt-e emām dar mored-e barnāmehā-ye musiqi-ye rādio-television*" (The Imam's pronouncements on the matter of music programs on radio and television) in *Ettela'at* newspaper, Mordad, 1358.

13. Schirazi (1997, 241).

14. See also Youssefzadeh (2000, 57).

15. Shiloah (1995, 31).

16. Nelson (1985, 32–51).

17. These three verses are the suras An-Najm 53:59–62, Al-Israa 17:64, and Luqmaan 31:7. For a concise discussion of the Islamic debate on music in the Persianate world, see the chapter on music in Beeman (2011). See also Beheshti (1385 [2006/2007]) and Nelson (1985, 40).

18. These Islamic philosophers often wrote in Arabic, the lingua franca of the time, but I will henceforth cite the Persian versions of the names of the first two as they are used in conversation in Iran, namely without the definite Arabic article "al."

19. Shiloah (1995, 43).

20. MacDonald (1901, 220). In other words, as Charles Hirschkind explains in his work on Egypt, the "agency of music to either corrupt or edify, to distract from moral duties or incline the soul toward its performance, lay not in the sound in and of itself but in the moral disposition of the heart of the listener" (2004, 135). Ghazali and Farabi are still invoked as sources of authority by moderates who argue for the permissibility of music. As President Mohammad Khatami's minister of culture, Ata'ollah Mohajerani, related in a conversation, in arguments with conservative *marāje'-e taqlid* (Shia "sources of emulation"), he would argue that even Farabi said music was halal. One Grand Ayatollah, the late Mirza Javad Tabrizi, retorted that Farabi was interpreting the Prophet,

and so was he. Mohajerani replied that at least Farabi was only four hundred years removed from the Prophet, rather than fourteen hundred. Eventually, the conservative fifth majles (parliament) (1996–2000) impeached Mohajerani on accusations of lax cultural politics. Personal interview, Ata'ollah Mohajerani, 28 April 2011, London.

21. Irani (1386 [2007/2008], 39); see also Khomeini (1979; 1381 [2002/2003]).

22. Beheshti (1385 [2006/2007]).

23. Shiloah (1995, 43).

24. Personal interview, Mohajerani (2011).

25. Foucault and Rabinow (1984, 61).

26. The state may also bear the largest weight in other, nonauthoritarian, contexts, but the difference is that in more democratic situations, the state is to a greater extent a reflection of the people's will. On Althusser, see Vovelle (1982, 3).

27. Foucault and Rabinow (1984, 61).

28. See "Introduction: Setting the Stage" in Scheiwiller (2013).

29. Butler (2011, xxi).

30. For an elaboration on the term "repertoire of contention" as an intersection of culture and mobilization, see Tilly (1997).

31. Certeau (1984, xix).

32. Bayat (2000).

33. Bayat (2010, 18).

34. This concept is in line with Dick Hebdige's notion, developed much earlier, of "subversive practices," whereby the mods, (a subculture that started in the United Kingdom), for example, appropriated conventional establishment clothing, the business suit, and stripped it of its original connotations; Hebdige (1979, 104).

35. Scott's main argument is that against the public transcript "every subordinate group creates, out of its ordeal, a 'hidden transcript' that represents a critique of power spoken behind the back of the dominant" (1990).

36. Bourdieu (1984; 1993).

37. Kamrava (2008).

38. In his *Republic of Love* (2010), Martin Stokes shows how in modern Turkey, musical discourses on love produce political meanings. "Love provides a shared public idiom for talking about the nation and religion" in Turkey (28), and hence musical discourses on love bridge religious, ethnic, and political divides and evoke common ground. Stokes notes, "To observe at the most general level that love is in crisis in Turkey is to note a deterioration of the republic's fundamental social contract, to hint at the political violence and authoritarianism that the culture of love has licensed" (33).

39. Pretending to cry is called *tabaki* and one often sees grown men and women simulating crying at religious events. This is an old tradition that is rooted in the sunnah, whereby Prophet Mohammad is supposed to have said, "Whoever feigns crying will be rewarded with paradise." Al-Muttaqi (1998).

40. For more on the place of martyrdom and mourning in contemporary Iran and Shi'ism see Dabashi (2011); Varzi (2006); and Aghaie (2004).

41. See Armbrust (1993), who has written extensively on consumerism and the commercialization of Ramadan in Egypt.

42. For an elaboration on "polyarchy" within the Iranian context, see Keshavarzian (2005).

43. Bourdieu (1977, 192).

44. Warner (2002).

45. I'm drawing here on Benedict Anderson's coinage of the term in his "Imagined Communities" (1991), where he argues that print capitalism allowed for the facilitation of members of a nation-state, who often spoke different dialects, coalescing around a national language and coming to view themselves as part of one nation. Members of imagined communities do not and cannot feasibly know each other face-to-face, but nevertheless come to imagine themselves as members of this larger community.

46. Habermas (1962).

47. Varzi (2006, 108).

48. Some foreign films with unveiled female actors are permissible.

49. "Middle East Internet Users, Population and Facebook Statistics," Internet World Stats, accessed 6 July 2016: www.internetworldstats.com/stats5.htm.

50. "Mobile cellular subscriptions (per 100 people)," World Bank Data, accessed 6 July 2016: http://data.worldbank.org/indicator/IT.CEL.SETS.P2.

51. Eickelman and Salvatore (2002, 99).

52. Certeau (1984).

53. Ibid., 31.

54. Bayat and Herrera (2010).

55. Although I did not know Maryam before that, we happened to take a bus together from Parkway Square to Azadi Stadium and then sat next to each other at the event.

56. This was the case at the time of my last trip to Iran, in May 2014, and I am told by friends and family that such CDs still cost a thousand toman, in spite of inflation and the devaluation of the rial. This may be explained by the fact that it has become very easy for people to download music online, and hence difficult for the CD to remain economically competitive. Thanks to Mohammad Ansari and Mohammad Ali Helali for this insight.

57. Benjamin (1970, 236–237).

58. Ong (1988, 72).

59. Ong has been criticized for ascribing "physiological, psychological, and phenomenological characteristics" to listening, which ignore important issues of context and agency in the process of hearing; see Sterne (2001).

60. An illustration found on pottery at the ancient Chogha Mish excavation site on the Susiana Plain, in western Iran, shows what is believed to be the oldest image of a concert, dating back to about five and a half thousand years ago: Delougaz et al. (1996); Farmer (1938–39). For a brief history of Iranian music see Binesh (1380 [2001/2002]).

61. For surveys of Persian music see Farmer (1938–39); During et al. (1991); and Binesh (1380 [2001/2002]). In his review of the available history, Bruno Nettl (2006)

points out that there is "a rich body of philosophical and theoretical treatises about (or including) music that describe the system of modes, rhythms, and genres through history, and also discuss the moral and aesthetic aspects of music."

62. As interest in Eastern cultures and music grew during the nineteen-sixties and nineteen-seventies, and the Pahlavi regime allowed easier access to Iran, several Western and Iranian ethnomusicologists wrote expertly about many aspects of Persian classical music, from theoretical issues regarding the *radif* modal system to music's place in society. Many of these scholars continued their work on Iran after the revolution, though with some interruption. See Ella Zonis (1973); Mehdi Barkechli and Moussa Maa'roufi (1963); Mohammad Taghi Massoudieh (1968); Bruno Nettl (1987); Nelly Caron and Dariush Safvat (1966); Hormoz Farhat (1990); and Laudan Nooshin (2003; 2015). More recently, Owen Wright (2009) has written about the life of vocalist Touraj Kiaras and delved into issues of tradition versus Westernization. On Shajarian, see Simms and Koushkani (2012a). On the development of the *radif*, see also Ann Lucas (2014). Among the older generation of ethnomusicologists who developed and continued a relationship with Iran and its musicians both before and after the revolution, Jean During (1984; 1992) has written most extensively about the sociocultural and political aspects of classical music, including the impact of the revolution on classical music and issues regarding tradition and change, as well as the impact of official Islam on music.

63. Safvat (1990).

64. Khaleqi (2002).

65. See Chehabi (1999) for an explication of these genres during the first Pahlavi period.

66. Alizadeh (1998, 73–83).

67. Khaleqi (2002, vol. 1, 173–75).

68. Ibid., 173.

69. This was Gholam-Hossein Minbashian, also known as Salar Mo'azzez.

70. Sepanta (2003, 180). At the time, women were prohibited from attending concerts. Vaziri did run concerts for the wives of club members for a few months, but stopped after protests arose from certain quarters, "and so women were even deprived of this, their only source of entertainment," Khaleqi (2002, vol. 2, 196).

71. Pejman Akbarzadeh, "Ali-Naghi Vaziri," *Iran Heritage*, accessed 7 July 2016: http://www.iran-heritage.org/interestgroups/AliNaghi.htm.

72. Sepanta (2003, 179); Khaleqi (2002, vol. 2, 47–49).

73. Sepanta (2003, 214) names the most important private music schools of the time. In addition to the music classes run by Vaziri, for example, described above, and the Barbad Society founded by Esmail Mehrtash in 1926, which offered classes in both theory and practice, there were many others, most of them established and taught by virtuosos such as *tār* player Morteza Ney-Davud and violinist Reza Mahjubi.

74. Khamenei had made this statement as far back as 1996. For his latest expression of this view, see Saeed Kamali Dehghan, "Music fails to chime with Islamic values, says Iran's supreme leader," *The Guardian*, 2 August 2010.

75. Hemmasi (2010) offers insight into Iranian popular music in Los Angeles, which

shines light on the prerevolutionary pop music scene in Tehran. She also considers (2011) how Persian pop music produced in Los Angeles offers a transnational oppositional discourse to the Islamic Republic.

76. Singers who, following the revolution, created their work in Los Angeles are called *khānandeh-hā-ye los anjelesi* (*Los Angeles singers*) in Persian.

77. See, for example, Nooshin (2009b), who suggests that whereas groups like the Arian Band attracted genuine interest from audiences because of their modern styles, it was government support that explained the success of outwardly less modern singers like Assar.

78. For works on nationalism within the Iranian context, see Vaziri (1993), Kashani-Sabet (1999), Tavakoli-Targhi (2001), Zia-Ebrahimi (2016).

79. There are still only a handful of scholars who write about Iranian music within a sociopolitical context. This dearth of writing on music is not particular to Iran, however. While there has been some excellent scholarship on the subject across the Middle East, the study of music in the region has lagged behind that of the more established arts of literature and poetry and, in Iran specifically, behind the study of other arts such as film and theater. Other scholars also make this point; see for example Nooshin (2009a) and Nieuwkerk (2011). For works on the intersection between politics and music in the Middle East region see the volumes just mentioned; for work on Turkey, see Stokes (1992; 2010). On Egypt, see Danielson (1997) and Lohman (2010). On Syria, see Shannon (2009); for an examination of rock music across the Middle East, see LeVine (2008); on Iran, there are also two theses that deal with the subject, see Zahir (2008) and Steward (2013).

80. Personal interview with Dr. Mehdi Labibi, Director General of Research at IRIB Radio, 1 March 2011, Tehran.

81. The other singers portrayed in Tavakolian's series "Listen" are Azita Akhavan, Sahar Lotfi, Ghazal Shakeri, Sayeh Sodaifi, and Mahsa Vahdat.

82. Chehabi (2000, 159).

83. Again, there is not much writing on this subject. Chehabi writes about the importance of women singers in twentieth-century Iran, highlighting in particular the careers of three of Iran's most popular musicians of all time, namely Qamar, Mahvash, and Googoosh. His work underlines the existence of an authentic secular culture in prerevolutionary Iran that, he argues, both religious activists and elites who "disdained their country's popular culture and the strata that carried it" erroneously equated with a Westernized Iran, which made it possible for that culture to be banished from the public sphere after the revolution (2000, 166). The only comprehensive book on the subject is Tuka Maleki's *Zanān-e Musiqi-ye Irān* (The Women of Iranian Music), which was banned in Tehran soon after its publication (2001). Some other works with a focus on women in Iranian music are Wendy DeBano's articles on the all-female Jasmine festival held in Tehran (2005; 2009), Kamran Talattof's close study of the female artist Shahrzad, in which he also writes about the situation of women artists in modern Iran and the impact of the revolution on their lives and works (2011), and Parmis Mozafari's article on female solo singing (2012).

84. Googoosh was an icon across the Middle East, even though her songs were

nearly all in Persian. I saw her sing to a very receptive audience in Tunis on her first post-silence tour in the summer of 2000.

85. See also DeBano (2005; 2009).

86. Salome MC left Iran in 2010 for a fellowship in Japan and now resides there.

87. Ayat Najafi's documentary "No Land's Song" (2014) shows how a group of Iranian and French musicians finally succeeded in receiving a permit from *Ershād* and giving a public concert, which also included female vocal soloists, in Tehran in the spring of 2013.

CHAPTER TWO

1. The song was later published on Shajarian's album *"Sarv-e chamān"* (Strutting Cypress, 1991).

2. The poet's actual name was Mohammad-Taqi Bahar. He inherited the honorific title "Malek o-Sho'ara" (Poet Laureate) from his father Mohammad Kazem Saburi, who was the poet laureate to the court.

3. Parvin (2007).

4. Aside from the versions by Qamar and Farhad, the other popular renditions of this song are a nineteen-seventies-era performance by Hengameh Akhavan and a cover by Nader Golchin. In a political gesture, the song was even picked up following the 2009 Green Uprising by the younger folk-rock fusion musician Mohsen Namjoo in collaboration with Arash Sobhani of the band Kiosk, and together they engage in its reenactment through a contemporized rendition. Their version, more up-tempo and darker in its enunciation of the lyrics, is accompanied by riffs on a rock guitar but remains faithful to Shajarian's vocal style. Kiosk is arguably Iran's most popular postrevolutionary underground rock band, founded in 2003 by Sobhani, its lead singer. The band left Iran in 2006 and is now based in the United States. It still enjoys immense popularity among Iranians both inside and outside of Iran and goes on concert tours to Iranian expatriate hubs. Kiosk's songs are humorous but packed with political and social criticism. Initially, Kiosk sounded like an Iranian version of Dire Straits, but it has since developed a sound more its own, with the infusion of Eastern European gypsy and big band music.

5. Personal interview, 5 August 2010, Beirut.

6. Shajarian (1379 [2000/2001], 108).

7. "Shajarian, Pezhvāk-e Ruzegār" (Shajarian, Echo of Our Times), BBC Persian documentary by Sadeq Saba, 2010.

8. The term *"ostād"* is normatively contrasted in Persian with *"motreb,"* which refers to an entertainer of little social respectability.

9. Shajarian (2004a, 10). Although Shajarian has not yet written his own autobiography, there are three prominent Persian texts on his life and work that cite Shajarian as the author (out of respect to the *ostād*, one imagines, though they were in fact all compiled by various other authors) and are sometimes cited by others who write about him; one is purely in the form of a prolonged conversation with the artist, while the other two take the form of a compilation of data, interviews, critiques, and dedications to Shajarian: "Rāz-e Mānā" (Shajarian 1379 [2000/2001]); "Latifeh-ye Nahāni: Gozideh-ye goft-o-guhā va goftārha-ye Ostād Mohammad Reza Shajarian va naqd va nazarhāyi

darbāreh-ye u va āsārash" (Shajarian 2004a); and "Hezār Golkhāneh Āvāz: Mohammad Reza Shajarian" (Shajarian 2004b). My insights on Shajarian are informed by these volumes; four personal interviews with him that took place in Beirut, Tehran, and London; many newspaper and magazine articles about him or interviews with him: and conversations within Iran's music community about this master vocalist. The first biographical volumes on the artist in English, Simms and Koushkani (2012a and 2012b), were published after I had completed my chapters on Shajarian for this book.

10. The second-ranked reciter, Ali Rajabi, was eventually sent in Shajarian's place, but failed at the competition (personal interview with Shajarian, 10 October 2010, Tehran); Rajabi was accompanied by Abbas Salimi, equally ranked second, who will resurface in chapter 7 as the plaintiff against Mohsen Namjoo's "Qur'an" song.

11. Shajarian (2004a, 24).

12. During (2002, 859).

13. Beeman (1976, 7); for a study on the contribution of Jewish communities to the preservation of Iranian folk and classical music, see Loeb (1972).

14. Shajarian (2004a, 24).

15. Jane Lewisohn is responsible for creating the unprecedented Golha Project (beginning in 2005), which is an online compilation of the programs as well as other resources: http://www.golha.co.uk.

16. Another famous vocalist, Ali Akbar Golpaygani, recounts a similar story, whereby he was invited by *Golha*'s Davud Pirnia personally to come to the radio's studios to record his voice. While Golpaygani was waiting in the hallway for Pirnia, a certain Moshir Homayun Shahrdar, the chief of the music department at the radio station, walked by and asked the young Golpaygani, "What are you doing here?" When he responded, "I have come to perform *āvāz*," Shahrdar jumped at him, saying: "Go and sing *āvāz* in the cemeteries and for your uncles" (Bahmanpur 2008, 89), demonstrating the lack of interest in *āvāz* at the time in state radio. Golpaygani was highly upset and left the radio building altogether after that incident, only to return a few years later as one of *Golha*'s first vocalists.

17. Later he was asked to do another test and was essentially told the same thing again. The men who were testing Shajarian—including Ali Tajvidi, Moshir Homayun Shahrdar, and Hosein Ali Mallah—have since been named as some of the foremost protectors, in radio, of Iran's arts against foreign cultural influences, but it appears that even they could not find the resolve to employ him.

18. The *ghazal* is a form of lyrical verse that employs rhyming couplets with a refrain, typically on the theme of love, often in a spiritual or mystical sense.

19. Simms and Koushkani (2012a, 28).

20. Ibid., 30.

21. Khaleqi (2002, 209).

22. Ibid, 310. The Persian goblet drum gained more respect within Persian music in the nineteen-forties and nineteen-fifties, due in great part to the virtuosity and efforts of one master *tonbak* player, Hossein Tehrani (1912–1974).

23. Simms and Koushkani (2012a, 26).

24. For the most exhaustive academic treatment of the *tasnif*, see Caton (1983).

25. Khaleqi (2002, 310).

26. See Breyley and Fatemi (2016), where they treat the subject of the *motrebi* entertainer in the most exhaustive account written to date. See also Fatemi (2005b) for a history and analysis of the *motreb* and this art form within Iranian culture, where *tarab* is often regarded as light entertainment. Within Arab musical contexts, *tarab* is more than amusement: it is often described as a kind of ecstatic link between performer and audience in live performance. For a discussion of the negative implications of the term *motreb* in the postrevolutionary Iranian context, see Adelkhah (1991). For more on *tarab* in Arab cultural and musical registers, see Racy (2003) and Frischkopf (2001).

27. See Mahler (1973); Beeman (1976; 2011); and Shay (2000; 2016).

28. For more on these categories, see chapter 5 in Breyley and Fatemi (2016).

29. "Musiqi-ye 'āmiyāneh dar Irān: Kābāreh," Mahmoud Khoshnam, BBC Persian .com, 5 April 2011, accessed 18 March 2012: http://www.bbc.co.uk/persian/arts/2011/01/11 0405_l11_folklore_music_8.shtml (site discontinued).

30. In a footnote, Shay writes about Golpaygani: "While Golpaygani was reviled in some soi-disant elite classical circles, many Iranians praised him for saving classical music by performing it in new contexts for audiences who would otherwise never have listened to it. Reactions to Golpaygani's performances are not unlike those that criticize Luciano Pavarotti's 'popular' appearances" (2000, 86).

31. Breyley (2010); Breyley and Fatemi (2016).

32. Bruno Nettl (1975, 82) cited in Breyley (2010, 212).

33. Breyley (2010, 212).

34. Forough Farrokhzad died an early death in 1967, at the age of thirty-two, in a car accident. She is one of modern Iran's most influential poets.

35. See also Breyley (2010, 221).

36. Fereydun Farrokhzad (1974), "Mikhak-e noqreh-i," video (1:23:59) uploaded by Darieh 14 March 2012 (exact broadcast date and episode number unavailable): https:// www.youtube.com/watch?v=gWTsYSr9ZHM&spfreload=10.

37. Indeed, ethnomusicologist Bruno Nettl (1970) writes about the large variety of music available to Iranians in the nineteen-sixties.

38. Egon (manager of the Stones Throw label), "Iran: An Unlikely Treasure Chest of Funk" on NPR Music, 12 December 2012: http://www.npr.org/templates/story/story.php ?storyId=112829658.

39. Ibid.

40. See for example "Raks Raks Raks" (27 Golden Garage Psych Nuggets from the Iranian 60s Scene), Raks Discos, Netherlands, 2009; "Pomegranates," Finders Keepers Records, 2009; Koroush Yaghmaei's "Back from the Brink—Pre-Revolution Psychedelic Rock from Iran (1973–1979)," Now Again Records, 2011.

41. Bruno Nettl comments on negative attitudes toward traditional music in Campbell (1994).

42. Personal interview, 5 August 2010, Beirut.

43. Lewisohn (2008, 80).

44. Bahmanpur (2008, 98).

45. Lewisohn (2008, 80).

46. Personal interview, 17 October 2011, London.

47. The international Shiraz Arts Festival was the brainchild of the Pahlavi empress Farah and was held for eleven years, in 1967–1977, in Shiraz. It brought together Eastern and Western masters and avant-garde artists in music, theater, dance, poetry, and film. See Robert Gluck (2007); also see the documentary by Tony Williams (1969), "Sound and Trumpets, Beat the Drums."

48. Personal interview, 5 August 2010, Beirut.

49. Usually referred to as *vā'ez* in the poetry.

50. On the topic of anticlerical sentiments in Hafez, see Lewisohn (2010) and Olszewska (2009).

51. Karimi-Hakkak (1995).

52. Ibid., 253.

53. Ibid, 254.

54. Waring ([1807] 1973); "Musiqi-ye 'āmiyāneh dar Irān: Moqaddameh," Mahmoud Khoshnam, BBC Persian.com, 10 January 2011: http://www.bbc.co.uk/persian/arts/2011 /01/101214_l11_folklore_music_1.shtml.

55. Browne ([1893] 1984).

56. Milani (2008).

57. Mostofi (1998/99).

58. Shay (2000, 68). Shay, who gives a detailed discussion of *mardomi* music, criticizes performers of classical Persian music as well as ethnomusicologists for consigning Persian popular music, "whose texts are extremely authentic and, in many cases, very old, to the trash heap of whatever does not constitute 'pure' (*asil*) classical music" (62, 78).

59. See "Musiqi-ye 'āmiyāneh dar Irān: Tarānehhā-ye Motrebi," Mahmoud Khoshnam, BBC Persian.com, 11 January 2011: http://www.bbc.co.uk/persian/arts/2011/01/110111 _l11_folklore_music_2.shtml.

60. The journalist and historian Masoud Behnoud also comments on this; ibid.

61. Aside from Bahar and Aref, mentioned earlier in this chapter, these poets also included Adib-ol-Mamalek Farahani, Parvin E'tesami, Iraj Mirza, Mirzadeh 'Eshqi, and Vahid Dastgerdi.

62. For a discussion of the word "freedom" in constitution-era poetry, see Shafi'i-Kadkani (2001, 35).

63. Khaleqi (2002, 325).

64. Ibid., 327–328.

65. Chehabi (1999, 144).

66. Seifzadeh (1977, 331).

67. For more on this process in Egypt, see Lagrange (2009).

68. Sepanta (1998), using record company catalogues of the time, lists most of the recordings produced in this first period.

69. There is one exception here in those first years of recording, and that is the fe-

male singer Zari Arshak-Khan's recording of Aref Qazvini's *"Hengām-e Mey"* (Time of Wine), better known in common parlance as *"Az khun-e javānān lāleh damideh"* (From the Blood of Youths Tulips Have Sprouted), an influential song that Aref first wrote and performed at the time of the Constitutional Revolution and which resonated with public sentiment at a period when hundreds of young activists were killed.

70. William Morgan Shuster (1877–1960), a popular American figure in the later years of the Constitutional Revolution, was appointed treasurer-general of Persia by the Iranian parliament in May 1911 to help manage the country's chaotic and shaky financial situation, which was in great measure a result of heavy debts incurred by the Qajar royalty to Russian and British interests. Under Russian and British pressure and against the will of the Persian parliament, Shuster was expelled from office in December 1911.

71. Sepanta (1998, 128).

72. Ibid., 155.

73. *Motrebs* also played a significant role in offering entertainment in the first half of the twentieth century, often appearing by contract at private celebrations; see Fatemi (2005b). In other contexts where gramophone recordings were available throughout the period under discussion, the sale of these recordings was more lucrative than live concerts, as Racy has shown for Egypt (1978). This was no longer necessarily the case after the audiocassette became the primary medium of recording, as Schade-Poulson illustrates in the case of Algerian rai music (1999).

74. Hemmasi (2010) offers a short summary of the secular and religious music that was offered in both public and private settings and rightly concludes that the "forms which enjoyed the greatest participation and audience of the largest segments of urban society" were the devotional forms of *ta'ziyeh* (passion plays for Imam Hossein) and *rowzeh-khāni* (lamentations for the imams), which were not considered *musiqi* in the common sense.

75. Khaleqi (2002, vol. 1, 324).

76. Ibid., 322.

77. Ibid.

78. Ibid., 324.

79. "Musically, the *sorud* differs from all other forms of Iranian music: it is played in 2/4 and 4/4 rhythms and intended to be sung by groups" (Shay 2000, 87).

80. Sepanta (1998, 264).

81. Ibid., 266; for more on Vaziri's immense influence on Iranian music and music education, see Sepanta (1995) and Farhat (2003); for an elaboration on Vaziri's role in promoting women musicians and their entry into the public sphere, see Chehabi (2000).

82. "Musiqi-ye 'āmiyāneh dar Irān: Pishpardehhā," Mahmoud Khoshnam, *BBC Persian.com*, 18 January 2011: http://www.bbc.co.uk/persian/arts/2011/01/110118_l11_folklore _music_4.shtml.

83. On the very popular "Golha" radio program, which came later, see Lewisohn (2008, 80–81).

84. Ibid.

85. For the Pahlavi-era anthem (1933–1979) with English subtitles, see "Sorude Shah-anshahi—Iran National Anthem English lyrics," video (2:34) uploaded by Parham Azari, 10 November 2012: https://www.youtube.com/watch?v=e-j6rLuOF8Q&index=1&list=R De-j6rLuOF8Q; and for the Islamic Republic anthem, see "Islamic Republic of Iran—National Anthem—English and Farsi Subtitles," video (0:58) uploaded by Shabbir Has-sanally, 25 April 2013: https://www.youtube.com/watch?v=GMwjgg2Pl2s.

86. The lyrics to "*Ey Iran*" were written by the poet, musician, and educator Hossein Gol-Golab and the music was composed by Ruhollah Khaleqi. It was first performed in 1944 at Tehran's Military Officers' Academy and soon thereafter recorded and broadcast on state radio, at first throughout the day and then eventually at the start of Tehran Radio's early morning program, every day for about three decades, until it was banned by the Islamic Republic. It was later taken off the blacklist and allowed to be used during the Iran-Iraq war. See Hoseyni-Dehkordi (2011); Pejman Akbarzadeh, "Yeksadomin sāl-e tavallod-e Ruhollāh Khāleqi dar Radio Zamāneh," *Radio Zamaneh*, 28 January 2007: http://zamaaneh.com/pejman/2007/01/post_114.html.

87. For a video of "*Ey Iran*" with English subtitles, see https://www.youtube.com/watch?v=tsBKYMSr3YI.

88. For an academic treatment of this problematic binary, see Schayegh (2010); for a satirical treatment of the subject see Kambiz Hosseini's television program "Poletik" on *Voice of America Persian*, no. 44, 13 June 2014.

89. See Hall's seminal essay (1973) for an explication of encoding and decoding.

90. Reqabi had gone into hiding following the coup d'état, but was eventually allowed to leave the country legally, though with the agreement that he would not return.

91. There seems to be an unwritten state broadcast ban on the song, as I have never heard it on state radio or television in Iran. For more on the song, see Hosayni-Dehkordi (2004, 178–93).

92. Dadkhah (1999, 20).

93. See "Marā bebus barā-ye ākharin bār," Alireza Afzoudi, *Parand* weblog, 2006: http://parand.se/t-mara-bebeos.html (site discontinued).

94. I am grateful to Homa Katouzian, who has done extensive research on the political and cultural aspects of this period, for confirming my research on the dearth of popular "political" songs in this period.

95. Lewisohn (2008, 85).

96. Ibid., 92.

97. Mahler (1973); Beeman (1976).

98. Personal interview, 5 August 2010, Beirut.

99. Personal interview, 9 February 2009, Tehran.

100. Personal interview, 5 August 2010, Beirut.

101. See Mehdi Malak's article "In tarāneh būy-e nān nemidahad! Sargozasht-e taraneh-ye mo'tarez dar Irān" in *Majalleh-ye Hafteh*, 17 July 2011: http://mejalehhafteh.com/2011/07/17.

102. Sadighi and Mahdavi (2009).

103. See Chehabi (1999) for an elucidation of this process.

CHAPTER THREE

1. Baqi (2003). Following the revolution, Imam Khomeini ordered the establishment of the Martyrs Foundation, which had the important function of documenting the deaths of martyrs and providing financial support to their families. The files of the foundation were kept secret until 1996 or 1997, when the government brought Emadeddin Baqi on board as a researcher to sort through the files and make sense of them. However, Baqi's research resulted in numbers that were vastly lower than the numbers in the tens of thousands that revolutionaries at the time and Islamic Republic officials subsequently had listed as victims of the shah's regime. Baqi was unable to publish those results under the purview of the Martyrs Foundation, but published them in the book noted above.

2. Hamed Yousefi, "Honar-e Enqelāb" (Art of Revolution), BBC Persian documentary (19 February 2010). I also checked with Shajarian, who confirmed that the letter was in his handwriting, though his staff was not able to find the actual letter for me.

3. For more elaboration, see Amir Molukpur, "Kānun-e Chāvosh va mas'aleh-ye musiqi-ye chand-sedāyi," E'temād newspaper, 17 Azar 1387 (7 December 2008). Houshang Ebtehaj's pen name is "Sāyeh" (Shadow), which he used during the Pahlavi era as a cover and continues to use to this day.

4. Ali Ranjpur, "Mā hamisheh āmādeh-ye taghyirim: Goftegu bā Mohammad Reza Lotfi," E'temād newspaper, 7 December 2008.

5. Karimi-Hakkak (1991, 508). See also Hemmasi (2013) for a discussion of the famous prerevolutionary pop song "Pariyā" (Fairies), where she considers the new valences that Dariush's musical rendition of the original Ahmad Shamlu poem affords the piece.

6. Personal interview, 9 February 2009, Tehran. For the importance of small media, especially the audiocassette, in Iran's revolutionary processes, see Sreberny and Mohammadi (1994). For the immense commercial and technological success and influence of the audiocassette (or compact cassette) as a medium worldwide, see Andriessen (1999). For a more cultural analysis of the global impact of the audiocassette, see Manuel (1993), specifically the introduction.

7. The importance of song is evident in this case. According to credible accounts, Aslan Aslanian first read this poem out at the Goethe Institute's Shab-e She'r (Poetry Night) series, but subsequently, when Marxists were stripped of legitimacy and many were executed, Islamic revolutionaries claimed that the song had been written not for the Marxist Amir Parviz Puyan but for Kamran Nejatollahi, a university professor who opposed the shah's regime, and therefore the revolutionaries allowed the song to be disseminated. See here for one account: "Shab ast-o chehreh-ye mihan siāh-e," Abdolali Ma'sumi, Hambastegi-ye Melli, 5 February 2010: https://www.hambastegimeli.com/1944/ه-دیدگاه-l-r-sp-394475425.

8. I have translated the "siāh-e" and "siāhihā" (literally "is black" and "blackness(es)," respectively) of the first two lines here as "is dark" and "darkness" to create a sharper contrast with "illumination" in the last line of verse cited.

9. Personal interview, 5 August 2010, Beirut.

10. The prefix *mardom-* and the adjectival form *mardomi* (both from *mardom*, the standard translation of which is "people") accrued the meaning, over the course of the twentieth century, of "democratic" or "popular" within the context of Iran's authoritarian regimes. Hence, politically, the word *mardomi* implicitly juxtaposes a people with an inherently nondemocratic government, unless it is coupled with the word "government" or "rule," in which case it refers to a popular or democratic government, such as *mardomsālāri* (rule by the people), which first gained currency during the time of the Constitutional Revolution and then again prominently during President Khatami's reformist era, or *hokumat-e mardomi* (popular government; people's government). Within a cultural context it again denotes "popular" or "folk" forms and productions in juxtaposition to "official" or "canonical" works; it has similar connotations to the various forms of the root word *sha'b* in Arabic.

11. Personal interview, 10 October 2010, Tehran.

12. Sadeq Saba, "*Shajarian, Pezhvāk-e Ruzegār*" (Shajarian, Echo of Our Times), BBC Persian documentary, 16 May 2010.

13. Shajarian (1379 [2000/2001], 139).

14. Ibid.

15. Ibid., 136.

16. Ibid.

17. "Something Inside So Strong," Simon Broughton, *The Guardian*, 16 January 2009.

18. During (2005, 376). This piece was published in a special issue of *Iranian Studies* on "Music and Society in Iran," which contains several articles on the subject, including Fatemi (2005a) on music and gender; Nooshin (2005b) on rock and youth music, DeBano (2005) on women's music festivals, Youssefzadeh (2005) on regional musical traditions, and a very useful bibliography of Persian and non-Persian writing on music in Iran, compiled by DeBano and Youssefzadeh (2005).

19. A subsidiary of the intelligence ministry that is in charge of policing Islamic behavior.

20. Personal interview, 7 August 2010, Beirut.

21. Khomeini (1367 [1988/1989]).

22. Schirazi (1997, 142).

23. Ibid.

24. Shajarian (1379 [2000/2001], 141).

25. Chehabi (2008).

26. Personal interview, 17 October 2011, London.

27. Personal interview, 1 August 2011, Tehran.

28. Simms and Koushkani (2012a, 43).

29. Although the twelve million inhabitants of Tehran include a majority youth population (about seventy percent are below the age of 34), there are only a handful of halls where large concerts can be staged. They are mostly called *tālār* (hall). The most prominent of these are *Tālār-e Vahdat* (the aforementioned Unity Hall) and the smaller *Tālār-e Rudaki*, on the same grounds; *Tālār-e Vezārat-e Keshvar* (an Interior Ministry hall, which was not purpose-built for concerts); *Tālār-e Milād* on the international ex-

hibition grounds; and *Tālār-e Borj-e Milād*. There are also regular concerts at the Nia-varan Palace (in the summer, often held outdoors) as well as at the *Tālār-e Farabi* in *Dāneshgāh-e Honar* (Tehran University of the Arts). The most technologically up-to-date of the purpose-built halls, *Tālār-e Borj-e Milād*, has about sixteen hundred seats, four hundred of which are "useless," as the concert organizer M. H. Tutunchian put it, because they do not offer a view of the stage (personal interview, 21 July 2011, Tehran). There is some significance to the place of performance, as far as a concert is concerned. Some halls, such as Unity Hall and the Interior Ministry hall, tend to have a more con-servative atmosphere, and the concerts are therefore often of classical or less "poppy" music. *Tālār-e Borj-e Milād* has a more relaxed atmosphere, and a lot of pop concerts are staged there. *Tālār-e Farabi* at the University of the Arts is often the site for more alternative music.

30. During (1992, 142–143), translated and cited in Simms and Koushkani (2012a, 43).

31. Personal interview, 10 October 2010, Tehran.

32. For a copy of Shajarian's 1995 letter to Ali Larijani, then head of the IRIB, see "Matn-e Nāmeh-ye Ostād Mohammad Reza Shajarian beh 'Ali Larijani," Māhur: Far-hangi va Honari, Javad Mahur, 7 January 2009: http://mahoor66.blogfa.com/post-7.aspx.

33. Farhat (2010).

34. In addition to *"Bidād"* (Injustice, 1985), his other albums in this vein include *"Yād-e ayyām"* (Remembering the Days, 1995), *"Zemestān ast"* (It Is Winter, 2001), and *"Faryād"* (Cry, 2003).

35. For this excerpt of Ahmadinejad's speech, see "Khas Va khashak," video (1:36) uploaded by ripiman, 1 January 2011: http://www.youtube.com/watch?v=_UwM5ab-QfY.

36. Interview with Shajarian on BBC Persian TV, 17 June 2009; see "shajarian—bbc interview," video (1:52) uploaded by shajariandotnet, 18 June 2009: http://www.youtube .com/watch?v=yw4ebkifql8.

37. The official number given at the time was twenty, but human rights campaigners estimate that the true number may have been in the hundreds. See Robert Tait, "Hun-dreds may have died in Iranian clashes after poll, say human rights campaigners," *The Guardian*, 16 July 2009: http://www.guardian.co.uk/world/2009/jul/16/hundreds-feared -dead-iran-clashes.

38. Ruhollah Shahsavar Rais. *Shahryar* blog, 25 August 2009: http://simorghshah.blog fa.com/post-91.aspx.

39. Personal interview, 1 August 2011, Tehran.

40. Personal interview, 5 August 2010, Beirut.

41. Maziar Bijani, "Mohammad Reza Shajarian sāz-e sonnati-ye jadidi ebda' kardeh ast," *Kayhan* newspaper, 24 Mordad 1388 (2009).

42. *Rabbanā* (Our God/Lord) is a prayer from the Qur'an similar in content to the Christian "Lord's Prayer." Since Shajarian's recording of this prayer in 1979, it had been broadcast in Iran every year at the break of *iftar* for the entire month of Ramadan. Hence, Shajarian's superb performance of this prayer is in effect now considered a tradi-tion. According to Shajarian, it was created in 1979 when he was training *qāris* (Qur'an reciters) at state radio and sang this piece as a demonstration for students. Although

it was meant as a demonstration, the technicians recorded it, and state radio and TV decided to air it at *iftar* from that year onward. For sixteen years, it was not even public knowledge that the voice behind this national *Rabbanā* was Shajarian's (personal interview with Sharjarian, 10 October 2010, Tehran).

43. For one of many YouTube videos featuring Shajarian's *Rabbanā*, see "Rabbana," video (4:26) uploaded by Redemption, 3 November 2007: http://www.youtube.com/watch?v=H35tR9VCrPQ.

44. Piruzeh Rohaniyun, "Rabbanā-ye Shajarian pas az 30 sāl az sofreh-ye eftār-e mardom hazf shod," *Musiqi-ye mā*, 14 August 2010: http://www.musicema.com/module-pagesetter-printpub-tid-1-pid-2413.html.

45. This is the kind of tactic that de Certeau (1984) refers to as the "weapons of the weak." As I argue later in this book, virtual media have made it possible for such tactics to be multiplied and magnified to such an extent that those who use these tactics can no longer be viewed as "weak," because new media weapons can be truly powerful.

46. Seyed Hasan Mokhtabad, *Sarbāng*, 23 August 2009: http://www.day1348.blogfa.com/post-185.aspx.

47. For one such gathering with the Supreme Leader, see this report on *Basij News*, "Talāvat-e Qor'ān dar hozur-e rahbar-e enqelāb," 30 June 2014, (site discontinued): http://basijnews.ir/social/1393/04/09/index.html:id=1999891.

48. Seyyed-Mohammad Mirzamani stepped down from his post on 19 February 2013, citing health issues. Alireza Pashayi was named as his successor, but less than a year later Pashayi was replaced by Piruz Arjomand. At this writing, in July 2016, the director of Ershad's Music Office is Farzad Talebi. The frequent turnover in its director aptly reflects the instability of the office and its policies.

49. Personal conversation, 17 October 2011, London.

50. The sense that one is dealing with Scott's "hidden transcript" or Taussig's "public secret" (Taussig 1999) raises the stakes of what is uttered within a setting that is so much more than just a concert for musical entertainment.

51. Personal interview, 1 August 2011, Tehran.

52. See "Mohammad Reza Shajarian: Chandi ast haq-e khāndan dar mamlekat-e khodam barāy-e mardom-e khodam-rā nadāram," video (3:10), uploaded by Karmania Film, 5 May 2015: https://www.youtube.com/watch?v=E9a-c2TfhJY.

53. "Vezārat-e Ershād: Shajarian bāyad raftārhā-ye gozashteh-ye khod-rā jobrān konad" (Shajarian Must Make Good for His Past Behavior), BBC Persian Online, 30 December 2014: http://www.bbc.com/persian/arts/2014/12/141230_l51_ershad_shajarian.

CHAPTER FOUR

1. Khomeini (1367 [1988/1989]).

2. Sreberny and Mohammadi (1994).

3. At a commemoration of revolutionary songs held on the twenty-ninth anniversary of the revolution, in 2008, former president Mohammad Khatami's culture minister Ahmad Masjed-Jame'i said that these songs were truly from the people and came from within folk (*'ammi*), traditional (the Chavosh group), and pop music. The songs that he

was referring to here as *ʿammi* were those known as *sorud* (the anthem-like genre briefly discussed chapters 2 and 3), often performed with military band instruments such as drums and trumpets; "Golbāng-e Āzādi: Jashn-e Piruzi-ye Enqelāb-e Eslāmi, Tajlil az Padidāvarandegān-e Sorud va Musiqi-ye Enqelāb" (Cry of Freedom: Celebration of the Islamic revolution's victory, and recognition of the creators of soruds and music for the revolution), Mo'assesseh-ye Naghmeh-ye Shahr (Naghmeh-ye Shahr Institute), Tehran, 2008, DVD.

4. Ibid.

5. Some of these songs are still performed on the anniversary of Imam Khomeini's arrival at Tehran airport, on the 1st of February each year.

6. Mohammad Golriz is the brother of the famous vocalist and *Golha* performer Akbar Golpaygani, mentioned in chapter 2. Golpaygani has been circumscribed in his work since the revolution due to his associations with the prerevolutionary café-cabaret scene, but his younger brother became the voice of the Islamic Republic.

7. "*Rahbar-e kherad, amin-o hamrāh-e payāmbarān*"; see "Revāyat-e Ostād 'Golriz' az sākht-e sorud-e 'Shahid-e Motahhar' va didār bā Emām" (Ostad Golriz's Account of the Making of "Shahid-e Motahhar" and Meeting the Imam), *Fars News Agency*, 1 May 2010: http://www.farsnews.com/newstext.php?nn=8902110837.

8. Aʿzam Ravadrad in "Jāygāh-e Musiqi dar Siāsatgozārihā-ye Resāneh-ye Irān" (The place of music in the policies of Iranian media), *Pazhuheshkadeh-ye Farhang va Honar*, 26 February 2011, Tehran.

9. "Emām Khomeini goft: vaqti in musiqi-rā shenidam, geryeh kardam," *Khabar Online*, 19 September 2010: http://www.khabaronline.ir/detail/93509.

10. See "Revāyat-e Ostād 'Golriz,'" *Fars News Agency*.

11. His sister was married to Khomeini's son, Seyed Ahmad.

12. Musavi (2010).

13. This is based on Khomeini's response (1961, 198–224) in regard to the permissibility of music as a mode of earning.

14. Irani (1370 [1991/1992], 96); see also my brief discussion of *tarab* in chapter 2.

15. Ibid., 103.

16. Ibid., 112.

17. Ibid., 242.

18. I obtained this document from Dr. Mehdi Labibi, the Director General of the IRIB's Radio Research Unit.

19. Personal interview, 22 February 2011, Tehran.

20. Personal interview, 1 March 2011, Tehran.

21. See "Janjāl bar sar-e tak-khāni-ye zanān" (Turmoil over Women's Solo Singing), *VOA Persian Online*, 8 February 2015.

22. "Nazar-e rahbar-e enqelāb dar bāreh-ye āvāz-khāni-ye bānovān" (The Revolution's Leader's View on Women's Singing), *Bina News Online*, 5 March 2015: http://www.binanews.ir/news73896.html.

23. Although "Westernized" Iranian pop music was banned, the status and emigration of its makers allowed for the genre to survive and even thrive in the music studios

and television channels of Iranian exiles in Los Angeles. But the popular or *mardomi* music, which was more deeply rooted in the fabric of traditional Iranian life and often drew on archetypal Iranian stories or quotidian expressions, and whose makers were usually of local or regional fame rather than being polished national celebrities, has been disintegrating and increasingly relegated to the nostalgic memory of older Iranians. For more on the fate of this *mardomi* music, see Shay (2000).

24. See "Hediyeh-ye Emām beh Āhangarān," Institute for the Arrangement and Publication of Imam Khomeini's Works, 14 October 2014: http://www.imam-khomeini .ir/fa/n23129/.

25. Some of the faster sections of "*Shahid-e Motahhar*," for example, are similar to passages in some of the songs of the prerevolutionary vocal diva Hayedeh (such as her "*Shānehāyat*" and "*Del-e Divuneh*"), though they are still sadder.

26. *Hosseiniyehs* are religious centers (often someone's living room or basement or a converted house) where people gather to commemorate and mourn religious holidays, such as the martyrdom of Imam Hossein, whence the name *hosseiniyeh* originates.

27. Hooshang Samani, "War Musicians without Instruments," on his weblog *Musiqi Mā* (2007): http://hooshang-samani.blogfa.com/post-138.aspx.

28. See (starting at minute 4:40) "Ahangaran, Iran & The Concept of Martyrdom [Eng Subtitles]," video (9:39) uploaded by sayed3li, 30 December 2007: https://www.you tube.com/watch?v=_qmCwn3zOFM.

29. Ibid. (starting at minute 6:50).

30. Kevin Sim, "Once Upon a Time in Iran," MayaVision International Production, Channel 4 and Thirteen WNET New York joint production documentary, 2007.

31. Adelkhah (1991, 6).

32. As noted elsewhere, written documentation of these bans is hard to find, mainly because a lot of these regulations were and are, to this day, communicated to the various offices of radio and television either verbally or via paper memoranda. With time, such papers become buried in file cabinets or are discarded. As far as I know, no one has collected or compiled these regulations and memoranda. It is Dr. Hassan Riahi, who has worked in various capacities for the IRIB and other music-related offices, who told me that there were written memoranda about the ban on 6/8 time, the female voice, and other such matters.

33. See "Mo'arefi-ye Shorā-ye 'Āli-ye Enqelāb-e Farhangi" (Introducing the Supreme Council of Cultural Revolution) on the SCCR website: http://sccr.ir/pages/?current=vie wdoc&type=p&Sel=121&currentDGID=0&currentNGID=0 (accessed 26 July 2016)

34. Decree issued following the remodeling of the Headquarters of the Cultural Revolution into the Supreme Council for Cultural Revolution in 1984.

35. Conversation with SCCR Public Relations Officer Ali Mohammadzadeh, 12 October 2008, Tehran.

36. "Jāygāh, ahhamiyat va zarurat-e Shorā-ye 'Āli-ye Enqelāb-e Farhangi" (The Position, Importance and Necessity of the Supreme Council for Cultural Revolution): http:// www.iranculture.org/fa/Default.aspx?current=viewDoc&currentID=1338 (accessed 6 March 2012).

37. "Osul-e siāsat-e farhangi-ye keshvar" (The Principles of the Country's Cultural Policy), Statute number 286, 20/05/1371 (1992), Supreme Council for Cultural Revolution.

38. "Ahdāf-e Shorā-ye 'Āli-ye Enqelāb-e Farhangi," (The Goals of the Supreme Council for Cultural Revolution), SCCR website: http://www.iranculture.org/fa/Default.aspx ?current=viewDoc&currentID=1338 (accessed 6 March 2012).

39. Conversation with SCCR public relations officer Ali Mohammadzadeh, 12 October 2008, Tehran.

40. It should be noted here that while the written decisions and policies of the various government bodies and organizations are important documents as far as state policy is concerned, the Leader's speeches constitute a canon of decisions that are paramount over all else. These speeches are not written policy and stand outside the highly organizational and bureaucratic structures found elsewhere in government, but they give direction to all other decision-making processes.

41. For an extensive description of the tasks and activities of *Ershād*'s Music Office, see Youssefzadeh (2000).

42. "Mo'arefi-ye Daftar-e Musiqi, Vezārat-e Farhang va Ershād-e Eslāmi" (Introducing the Music Office at the Ministry of Culture and Islamic Guidance): http://music.far hang.gov.ir/aboutus-fa.html (accessed 6 March 2012).

43. In 2007, the founder of the music record label Hermes Records, Ramin Sadighi, took the initiative to self-publish a booklet titled "A simple guide for the music industry" to provide at least some guidance for musicians, which was otherwise utterly lacking elsewhere; see Sadighi (2007).

44. The booklet can only be obtained from *Ershād* itself: Mohammad 'Ali Shahni-Dashtgoli, "Majmu'eh-ye Qavānin, Āyinnāmehhā va Dastur-al-'amalhā-ye Daftar-e Musiqi va She'r," Mo'āvenat-e Honari, Daftar-e Musiqi va She'r, 1386.

45. http://music.farhang.gov.ir/fa/form.

46. This is one of the most unstable posts within *Ershād*, as noted in the previous chapter.

47. My information here is from the booklet as well as conversations with council members.

48. *Ershād* booklet.

49. Conversations with many musicians over the years 2002 through 2011.

50. Youssefzadeh (2000, 49).

51. Personal interview, Dr. Hassan Riahi, director of the Fajr International Music Festival 2011, 22 February 2011, Tehran.

52. News conference at the House of Artists, Tehran, 15 February 2011.

53. In 2009, the IRIB's assigned budget was 480 billion toman, which at the time was approximately half a billion dollars, and it was expected to raise another 300 billion toman (300 million dollars) in revenues, mainly from advertising.

54. Youssefzadeh (2000, 57).

55. Ibid.

56. Personal interview, Dr. Mehdi Labibi, Director of Research, IRIB Radio, 1 March 2011. Radio Ava has existed since 2008. Initially, it only broadcast a few hours a day,

then as of 2010 extended its programming to twelve hours, and since July 2011 has been broadcasting twenty-four hours a day. The programming consists mostly of traditional, folkloric, and some lighter pop music. "Pakhsh-e Rādio Āvā 24-sā'ate shod," *Hamshahri Online*, 13 Tir 1390 (2011): http://hamshahrionline.ir/details/139454 (accessed 26 July 2016).

57. Interview, Seyyed Abbas Sajjadi, director of the Tehran City Council's Music Office, 26 February 2011, Tehran.

58. Mehdi Labibi, presentation at the seminar "*Jāygāh-e Musiqi dar Siāsatgozārihā-ye Resāneh-ye Irān," Pazhuheshkadeh-ye Farhang va Honar (Research Institute for Culture and the Arts)*, 26 February 2011, Tehran.

59. "Darbāreh-ye Howzeh-ye Honari" (About the *Howzeh-ye Honari*), *Howzeh-ye Honari* website: http://www.hozehonari.com/Default.aspx?Page=6295.

60. Personal interview, Reza Mahdavi, 1 August 2011, Tehran.

61. "Khamushi: Howzeh-ye Honari motevvali-ye honar-e mote'ahhed ast" (*Howzeh-ye Honari* Is the Custodian of Committed Art) on *Siasat-e Rooz*, 2010: http://www.siasatrooz.ir/vdcg7w9t.ak9xz4prra.html (accessed 27 March 2013).

62. Website of the Islamic Development Organization: http://www.ido.ir/myhtml/sazman/sazman.aspx (accessed 26 July 2016).

63. Personal interview, Reza Mahdavi; confirmed by Namjoo.

64. Personal interview, Reza Mahdavi. The presupposition that the poetry of Hafez should be unproblematic seems to be universally held in Iran, although Hafez wrote some very critical anti-clerical poetry; see Lewisohn (2010).

65. See his bio on the *Howzeh-ye Honari* Music Center's website: http://www.musicenter.ir/Default.aspx?page=17091.

CHAPTER FIVE

1. For a recording of one such Assar concert, see "Ey Karevan by Alireza Assar—2001 concert, Tehran, Iran," video (3:14) uploaded by Reza, 7 April 2007: https://www.youtube.com/watch?v=pRN70_T2Nks

2. See "Alireza Assar -ghodsiane aseman" video (4:20) uploaded by Rebaz Ahmed, 6 August 2009, although in this recording Aghili is not featured: https://www.youtube.com/watch?v=TmYt8t6GlTo&list=RDTmYt8t6GlTo#t=0.

3. Album sale numbers are hard to ascertain in Iran, as no records seem to be kept. Scattered reports of sales appear in contemporary newspapers, but these are haphazard and little more than anecdotal. I base the statements above on my general readings as well as conversations with people in the music industry, including the producers Habib Sabour and Mohsen Rajabpour, as well as Babak Chamanara, the owner and manager of Tehran's oldest music store, Beethoven.

4. Personal interview, 8 August 2011, Tehran.

5. For elaborate descriptions of the *zurkhāneh* see Chehabi (2006) and Rochard (2002).

6. Assar explained this to me in our interview, 2011.

7. Varzi (2006, 10); Khosravi (2008, 164).

8. See Daniel Pearl, "Rock Rolls Once More in Iran as Hard-Liners Back Pop Revival," *The Wall Street Journal*, 2 June 2000.

9. "Pop music" in Iran's postrevolutionary context refers to a genre of music that is often similar in its fast tempo, lyrical themes of love and desperation, and general feel to *los anjelesi* pop music. It no longer accommodates the Islamic Republic ethos with passages of march or hymn music, that familiar revolutionary somberness, and when it first appeared in the late nineteen-nineties, it was recognized as new, though it was tamer in diction and beat than it is today; for more on the evolution of pop music in Islamic Iran, see Siamdoust (2016).

10. See also Nooshin (2005a, 251).

11. Arash Nasiri and Azadeh Shahmir-Nuri, "Interview with Fereydun Shahbazian," *Persian Art Music*, 23 Aban 1382 (2003).

12. Babak Bayat was also a seminal music composer who wrote music for prerevolutionary pop stars; after he returned to Iran in the nineteen-nineties, he continued to write music for postrevolutionary musicians. He passed away in 2006. Through both his music and his personal network, Bayat bridged *los anjelesi* and postrevolutionary pop music.

13. See for example "Parishan-Bijan Bijani," video (8:10) uploaded by sadikhah, 26 June 2010: http://www.youtube.com/watch?v=NyEqgHzjCds.

14. See for example "Nasime Sahari (by Hassan Homayounfal)," video (7:08) uploaded by pedijoon, 27 April 2009: http://www.youtube.com/watch?v=sgTBTjCbPO8.

15. See for example "Bijan Khavari, Darya," video (4:54) uploaded by mjavanian's channel, 3 November 2010: http://www.youtube.com/watch?v=x3BaYWZbELc.

16. See for example "Mehrdad Kazemi," video uploaded by Rebaz Ahmed, 6 August 2009: https://www.youtube.com/watch?v=43_3WrI5pqM.

17. Sadighi and Mahdavi (2009).

18. Personal interview, Mohammad Ali Mo'allem-Damghani, 2 August 2011, Tehran.

19. Assar is Etemadi's first cousin once removed.

20. I went to a Dariush concert in Las Vegas over the Christmas holidays of 2007 and happened to run into the singer himself, by chance, as he was leaving his hotel to fly back home. I got into conversation with him and asked him why he had left Iran. I had wondered about this, since I thought that of all the prerevolutionary pop singers, he might have been the one who would have been most able to continue his work under the new regime. In retrospect it is clear that he absolutely had to leave; that there would have been no space for his art. But I thought that at the time perhaps things might not have seemed so clear and that staying might have seemed to be an option.

21. See also Hemmasi (2013).

22. Two of the council members were Mehdi Kalhor and Fereydun Shahbazian.

23. *Mobtazal* is an oft-used term in discourse about music in Iran, used to dismiss everything that is thought to be unworthy. As Hemmasi explains, "encompassing moral, political, and aesthetic values, the term *mobtazal* implies banality, cliché, lack of creativity and worth, and cheapness, but also suggests a cultural form that disorients a listener and can promote disengagement with the world through harmful distraction" (2011, 90).

24. Personal interview, 2 August 2011, Tehran. This insight into Etemadi's story was not publicly known until April 2013, when the singer divulged it (long after our interview) in a news conference; see "Khashāyār E'temādi: Beh khāter-e shebāhat-e sedāyam bā yek khānandeh-ye los anjelesi chand sāl ejāzeh kār nadashtam," *Khabar Online*, 23 April 2013: http://khabaronline.ir/detail/288644. I assume that the reason he kept silent on the matter for nearly twenty years was that he had been concerned that airing this problem publicly, and thereby explicitly linking his voice to that of Dariush, would scar his relations with state officials. Had this factoid about his dealings with state officials been known at the time, however, it is likely that there would have been fewer conspiracy theories about the state's intentional attempts to produce pop singers with voices similar to *los anjelesi* stars.

25. Personal interview, 2011.

26. This is at the exchange rate of about 175 toman to the US dollar in 1996.

27. This included songs such as "*Khāk-e āstān-e mowlā*" (The Soil of Imam Ali's Grounds, referring to his shrine).

28. Personal interview, 2011.

29. It is said that Mo'allem convinced Khamenei that without homemade pop music, Iran's youth would be at greater risk of "cultural invasion" from abroad. Khamenei is then said to have "quietly sought the approval of top Islamic scholars." This is a detail I heard in conversation about the legitimization of pop music in Iran. See also Pearl (2000).

30. Personal interview, 2011.

31. Zeinab Mortezayi-Fard, "Gap-e Musiqiyā-yi bā Khashāyār E'temādi," *Bāshgāh-e Khabarnegārān*, 9 November 2012: http://www.yjc.ir/fa/news/4140123.

32. *Musiqi-ye fākher*, which can be translated as fine, or sumptuous, music, is an oft-repeated term in music discourse in Iran today. *Fākher* is basically used as the opposite of *mobtazal* (trite, banal) and is a blanket term used by officials to refer to music that consists of good composition and arrangement and contains lyrics that are either drawn from poetry or go beyond simplistic, earthly matters. Although it is an ambiguous term, both in reference to aesthetics and ideology, it seems to function as a sort of floating common ground among those who invoke the term.

33. See "shadmehr-doxdo.ir," video (3:34) uploaded by doxdosomaye, 15 March 2007: http://www.youtube.com/watch?v=MKg31bnWau4&feature=related.

34. Aghili's next album was banned by the IRIB, but received a permit from *Ershād*, which at the time was talked about as an astonishing development. The album is full of fast beats and 6/8 rhythms, which had previously been considered impermissible.

35. Like Shajarian, Assar insists that none of his work is political because, as he explains, "I'm not a political person because I don't have any political knowledge"; Fatemi (1381 [2002/2003], 56). Assar refers to his critical work as *ejtemā'i*, social.

36. Migrant workers from surrounding Persian Gulf countries often come to Kish to await extensions of their work visas.

37. See also Nazila Fathi, "Kish Journal; A Little Leg, a Little Booze, but Hardly Gomorrah," *The New York Times*, 15 April 2002; and Mark MacKinnon, "Where Iranians Go to Let Their Hair Down," *The Globe and Mail*, 18 October 2008.

38. The Islamic Republic had a complicated relationship with Farhad. He was a "revolutionary" singer who at the time of the shah, and especially during the revolution, recorded politically critical songs. In the first year following the revolution, state television and radio played Farhad's song "*Vahdat*" (Unity) ad nauseam. But even this stern song, which repeatedly intones the name of the Prophet Mohammad, was then banned. Farhad finally obtained an album permit in 1993, but soon despaired of the possibilities of working as an artist within the confines of the state. He released his next album in the United States, a year before succumbing to an illness in 2000.

39. Fatemi (1380 [2001/2002], 117); "Alireza Assar: Hameh chiz bā Divān-e Molānā āghāz shod" (Alireza Assar: Everything Started with Molana's Divan), *Tarāneh-ye Māh*, No. 29 (2002), 44–45; Pearl (2000).

40. Fatemi (1380 [2001/2002], 113).

41. "Ākhar-e hafteh bā Alireza Assar" (Weekend with Alireza Assar) on Alireza Assar's official website (2004); http://www.alirezaassar2.com/?p=2245 (site discontinued).

42. Pearl (2000).

43. I was not yet carrying out research for this project in the period 1999–2002, but I remember the time clearly, as I traveled to Iran for several visits lasting weeks or months at a time and ultimately moved there in 2002 to work as a journalist.

44. Fatemi (1381 [2002/2003], 59).

45. Azadeh Shahmir-Nuri, "Gofteguyi bā Alireza Assar dar ruzhā-ye pāyāni-ye sāl: Bāyād marzhā-rā posht-e sar gozāsht" (Interview with Alireza Assar at the End of the Year: We Must Put the Boundaries behind Us), *Beethoven Music Center website*, 9 Esfand 1384 (2006): http://beethovenmc.com/intv_details.asp?inid=10 (site discontinued).

46. Shahmir-Nuri (2006).

47. Azadeh Shahmir-Nuri and Mohammad Safajooee, "Nāgahān dobāreh Assār: Man oful nakardeh-am" (Suddenly Again Assar: I Have Not Declined), *40Cheragh*, 2010.

48. This criticism has found its strongest expression in what could be called a turn in the war genre in cinema, where the glorification of war and soldiers has given way to criticisms about the rehabilitation of veterans in a hypocritical and materialistic state, where those with power pay little more than lip service to the veterans' sacrifices.

49. Data obtained from *Ershād*'s Music Office in August 2011. The ministry issued 133 pop concert permits, with each permit corresponding to an average of 2.5 performances (for example, one concert permit for Alireza Assar might be valid for six nights of performances).

50. For a report on the concert, see "Rekordi keh dast nayāftani-tar shod" (The record that became even less breakable), Bahman Babazadeh, *Musicema*, 7 November 2012: http://www.musicema.com/module-pagesetter-viewpub-tid-1-pid-5942.html.

51. This is the *Vezārat-e Keshvar* hall in the Interior Ministry, which is not even a professional concert hall.

52. See "Hāj 'Abdolrezā Helāli maddāh-e ahl-e beyt dar hāl-e taryāk-keshi," video (0:18) uploaded by sansoorchi, 12 August 2012: https://www.youtube.com/watch?v=K s17a7s4U-w.

53. For a video recording of Helali's version see "Iran Shia Irani Song," video (2:16)

uploaded by abbas10000, 10 February 2007: http://www.youtube.com/watch?v=wtxOm5aySUk&feature=related.

54. See "Benyamin 85 Khatereha Memories.flv," video (2:54) uploaded by www.mohager0030.blogfa.com, 7 July 2011: https://www.youtube.com/watch?v=7ObSjZAiRCc.

55. See "Agham, imam zaman, (benyamin) with English translation," video (3:00) uploaded by mona20's channel, 25 September 2006: http://www.youtube.com/watch?v=iIcFi83dU3k&feature=related.

56. This was on Benyamin's Myspace page in 2005, though the site has since been discontinued: http://www.myspace.com/benyamin85.

57. Babak Jahanbakhsh, single, 2012.

58. Hamid Askari, *Komā 3* album, 2010.

59. Farzad Farzin, *Khāss* album, 2011.

60. Mohsen Yeganeh, *Tah-e Khat* album, 2008.

61. I was able to see this back-and-forth between Sadeghi and audience members when I attended one of his concerts in Tehran's Borj-e Milad on 22 February 2011, but know from others that this is a trademark Sadeghi audience interaction that happens at all of his concerts.

62. See Yaghmaian (2002) on what he calls "the rise of a new social movement for joy."

63. In my presentation, "The Counterpublic of Love in Iran," at the 2014 Middle East Studies Association Conference in Washington, DC, I argued that the large outpouring of people for the funeral of the young pop singer Morteza Pashaei in November 2014 was another manifestation of what I call the "counterpublic of love."

CHAPTER SIX

1. *Fālsh* is based on the German word *falsch* ("false" or "wrong"), and is used in the context of Iranian music to denote music that is out of tune. However, based on my observations, I would say it is also a normatively loaded term that some will use to denigrate music that they find to be subpar, or to suggest that the musician who plays *fālsh* does not even know the basics of notation.

2. *Na're* is a derogatory verb often reserved for the cry of equine animals.

3. Here again the verb used was *na're*.

4. I have my own notes from this session, which I attended, but have taken this quotation from "Naqd-e Album-e Toranj-e Mohsen Namjoo dar Khaneh Honarmandan," *BBC Persian.com*, 10 March 2008: http://www.bbc.co.uk/persian/arts/story/2008/03/080310_an-am-namjoo.shtml.

5. I received a copy of Namjoo's first album very early on, from someone who had worked on the recording of it and burned me a copy. He told me very strictly not to pass it on because there were hopes from the beginning that it would eventually be able to be released officially. As my friend handed me the copy, he said, "It's something else. You haven't heard anything like it before."

6. Personal interview, 1 October 2009, Treviso, Italy; unless otherwise indicated, this interview and several others conducted over the course of the following three days provide the information given here on Namjoo's life and are the source of quotations from him.

7. Khaleqi (2002, vol. 1, 316).

8. NODET runs about a hundred middle schools and another hundred high schools in Iran, and students are admitted through entrance exams. Competition is extremely stiff, as less than five percent of applicants are admitted nationwide. In the capital, Tehran, competition is the fiercest; there, less than one quarter of a percent of applicants are admitted each year. Namjoo attended the NODET middle school and the first year of high school in Mashhad; see "Tārikhcheh-ye SAMPĀD" (The history of NODET): http://nodet.net/index.php/sampad/history (accessed 27 July 2016).

9. Diazpam 10.

10. Personal interview, 4 October 2008, Tehran: Tehran University, College of Performing Arts and Music, Music Department.

11. Amir Bahari, "Goftegu bā Mohsen Namjoo—bakhsh-e avval, begard tā begardim," (Interview with Mohsen Namjoo—Part One, Let's Whirl), E'temād newspaper, 26 Farvardin 1387 (2008).

12. Musicologists and writers who are reverent toward Persian classical music even hold that this music is spiritual, and therefore only spiritual poetry should be performed to it; Shay (2000, 86).

13. Tazmini (2009, 129).

14. Khamenei speech, Kayhan, 8 Mordad 1373 (1994).

15. "Dr. Sa'id Hajjarian az Khatami miguyad" (Dr. Said Hajjarian Talks about Khatami), a blog that posts excerpts from a story originally published on ISNA (the Islamic Students' News Agency) but which is no longer available on ISNA's website itself: http://haghifam.blogfa.com/post-18.aspx (site discontinued).

16. Shakibi (2010, 150).

17. "Nāmeh-ye este'fā-ye Mohammad Khatami az Vezārat-e Ershād" (Mohammad Khatami's Ershad resignation letter), 3 Khordad 1373 (1994): http://fa.wikisource.org/wiki/نامه_استعفای_محمد_خاتمی_از_وزارت_ارشاد.

18. Khatam (2010, 217–218).

19. Tazmini (2009, 63).

20. De Bellaigue (2007, 7).

21. For a short commemoration of Abolhasan Saba, see "Panjāh sāl az dargozasht-e Abolhasan Saba gozasht" (Fifty years have passed since Abolhasan Saba's passing), Mahmoud Khoshnam, BBC Persian.com, 20 December 2007: http://www.bbc.co.uk/persian/arts/story/2007/12/071218_ah-mk-saba.shtml.

22. This biographical information is based mostly on a personal interview with Bozorg Lashgari in his Yamaha store in Tehran on 6 October 2010, as well as on a short commemorative article on the occasion of his eighty-eighth birthday, which laments that despite many years of service, the names of the likes of Lashgari have been "given to oblivion in the unkind bed of times"; see "Beh monāsebat-e 27 farvardin māh, sālruz-e milād-e Bozorg Lashgari" (On the Occasion of the 27th of Farvardin, the Birthday of Bozorg Lashgari), Mohammad-Reza Momtazvahed, 16 Ordibehesht 1390 (2011).

23. Bourdieu (1993a, 95).

24. Alizadeh (1998, 79).

25. LeVine (2008, 185–191).

26. Personal interview, 11 May 2011, Skype.

27. Marjan Sa'ebi, "Ghazalhā-ye Hafez dar Zirzamin: Goftegu bā 'Arash Mitooie' va revāyat-e musiqi-ye gheire-rasmi" (Hafez's Ghazals in the Underground), *Musiqi-ye Iranian*, 26 Shahrivar 1393 (2014).

28. Personal interview, 4 October 2010, Tehran.

29. On Iran's heavy metal and rock scene, see chapter 5 of LeVine (2008).

30. On this generation of rockers, see Robertson (2012).

31. Jasper (1997).

32. Prana7 concert, Tehran Conservatory of Music, 21 July 2011.

33. Newsha Saremi, "Bāzdāsht-e hameh hāzerān dar yek konsert-e metāl" (The Arrest of All Attendees at a Metal Concert), *RoozOnline*, 18 August 2013, now published on *Iran Green Voice*: http://www.irangreenvoice.com/article/2013/aug/18/36661.

34. "Iranian Musicians Jailed, Facing Possible Execution for Playing Metal," Robert Pasbani, *Metal Injection*, 10 February 2016: http://www.metalinjection.net/metal-crimes/iranian-musicians-jailed-facing-possible-execution-for-playing-metal.

35. "*Nahāl-e heyrat*" is drawn from a Hafez poem. O-Hum's official website can be found here: http://www.o-hum.com.

36. "The Gang of Three!" Interview by Arash Maleki published on O-Hum's website in English, May 2001: http://www.o-hum.com/data/archive/interview/O-HUM_Interview_May_2001.htm (site discontinued).

37. As I mention in chapter 5, fast beats no longer seem to be a problem now.

38. Khomeini and Algar (2002, 129).

39. "Bayānāt-e rahbar-e mo'azzam-e enqelāb dar didār-e goruh-e farhang va adab va honar-e sedā-ye jomhuri-ye eslāmi" (The Leader's Statements in His Meeting with Radio's Culture, Literature and Arts group), *Kayhan* newspaper, 5 Esfand 1370 (1992).

40. Omid Elahi, "O-Hum's First Gig in Tehran," O-Hum's website, March 2001: http://www.o-hum.com/data/archive/interview/O-HUM_Concert_Review_(1_March_2001).htm (site discontinued).

41. Arash Maleki interview on O-Hum website.

42. Amir Hamz and Mark Lazarz, *Sounds of Silence* (documentary), 2006.

43. The Beethoven Music Center is the oldest continuously operating record store in Tehran, and its young management is interested in promoting new material, both foreign and Iranian. It also promotes and sells concert tickets. Bamahang Studio, originally called Bam Studio, was established in 1997 in Tehran and was a pioneering enterprise for the production of alternative and underground music. For Bamahang Studio productions, see its YouTube page: https://www.youtube.com/user/bamahang/featured; Patu was another recording studio for alternative music. See this interview "Khāterāt-e Studio Patu" (Memories of Studio Patu) with its owner and Pejvak rock band member Amir Tavasoli, Meysam Yusefi, Nasim-e Harāz: http://www.nasimeharaz.com/magazine/viewer.php?id=1840 (accessed 6 March 2012, site discontinued). For more on one of the fixtures of new Iranian music, Ramin Behna, see his website: http://www.behnamusic.com/band.html (accessed 6 March 2012).

44. Shadi Vatanparast and Zebra, "Another Round of Music Competition," *Tehran-Avenue*, May 2005: http://www.tehranavenue.com/print.php?ln=en&id=384# (the TehranAvenue webzine has been discontinued since 2010 and the links no longer work).

45. Nahid Siamdoust, "Rock Me, Ahmadinejad!" *Time.com*, 6 June 2008: http://www.time.com/time/world/article/0,8599,1812245,00.html.

46. Personal interview, 30 May 2011, London.

47. Personal interview, 11 May 2011, Skype.

48. In Mirtahmasb's documentary *Off Beat* (2003: 36'38'), Mahdavi also explains that the Farabi Hall at Tehran's University of the Arts had required *TehranAvenue* to change the title of the event from *Konsert-e Rāk* (Rock concert) to *Hamāyesh-e Konsert-e Rāk*, where *hamāyesh* translates as "conference," lending the event "a certain academic respectability."

49. Personal interview, 11 May 2011, Skype.

50. The sexual innuendo was intended by Mahdavi.

51. Nooshin (2005b, 488).

52. Personal interview, 23 May 2011, London.

53. Please see chapter 8 for a more extensive discussion of the term *musiqi-ye zirzamini* ("underground" music).

54. This is drawn from an article that appeared in Persian on the Zirzamin website; unfortunately the link no longer works and the identifying information for the article has been lost: http://zirzamin.se/?q=node/126 (site discontinued).

55. Personal interview with Sohrab Mahdavi, 11 May 2011, Skype.

56. Ibid.

CHAPTER SEVEN

1. This and all other quotes from Namjoo are, unless otherwise stated, from my interviews with Namjoo in Treviso, October 2009.

2. For videos, see: Abdi Behravanfar and Mohsen Namjoo 2001 practice session, posted 28 December 2008: http://www.youtube.com/watch?v=POWf9qubVFU (accessed 22 September 2011, no longer available); Abdi Behravanfar and Mohsen Namjoo 2001 practice session, "*Vāq-vāq-e sag*," posted 28 December 2008: http://www.youtube.com/watch?v=eYnyYXZEmvo (accessed 22 September 2011, no longer available); Mād (Abdi Behravanfar) and Mohsen Namjoo concert in 2001, see "Shaayad," video (6:17) posted by ghobchak, 25 July 2008: http://www.youtube.com/watch?v=lj6T10uKTis (accessed 27 July 2016) ; and Mād (Abdi Behravanfar) and Mohsen Namjoo concert in 2001, see "Namjoo," video (6:10), posted by abtani2000, 1 August 2007: http://www.youtube.com/watch?v=1ENjRohyRKk&feature=results_main&playnext=1&list=PLEEE12AEF5B33F025 (accessed 27 July 2016).

3. I am thankful to Ahmet Karamustafa and Fatemeh Shams Esmaeili for their input on this translation.

4. Street performance has become slightly more possible in the years since, and one sees some presence of musicians on streets every now and then. However, musicians have always been able to earn money at private functions such as weddings, which,

while equally illegal, can be extremely lucrative. The "underground" band Barobax, which became famous with its "Susan khānum," told me that they earned upward of five thousand dollars for every appearance; interview with the band, 7 October 2010, Tehran.

5. "Arrests over Smuggling of 'Santuri' Movie," *Radio Javan*, 20 February 2008; this short report relates the arrest of Santuri bootleg vendors in Tehran, who say that *Santuri* is their most "popular smuggled item and that no other DVD sold so many copies."

6. For a good interview with the artist, see Sam Rahimi, "Santuri: Mohsen Chavoshi," interview with Mohsen Chavoshi, 19 Esfand 1385 (2007): http://samrahimi.persianblog .ir/post/81.

7. See "Mohsen Namjoo-Zolf Bar Bad," video (6:35) posted by Alireza sotakbar, 14 April 2007: http://www.youtube.com/watch?v=D99mkPYwnlU.

8. The scandal even made it into Iranian newspapers, as the government sought to prosecute and punish the source that had made the tape public. Amir-Ebrahimi maintains that she is not the person on the tape and that a jealous former fiancé had tried to ruin her life by fabricating the video. What I found most instructive about this entire episode, however, was that the government took a harsh tone towards the person who publicized the video, not towards the actress who may or may not have been the person shown in the video itself. Not just the government, but private individuals too came out in defense of the actress, criticizing the source of the tape, not the actress. The popular rapper Yas even created a song called, "*CD ro beshkan*" (Break the CD), referring to the CD of the sex video (which was easy to obtain in Tehran), asking, "Where is the honor of men in this busy city? . . . Addressing the boy: how could you be so dishonorable? What you did was worse than an acid attack."

9. "Ālbum-e Toranj-e Mohsen Namjoo montasher shod" (Mohsen Namjoo's *Toranj* Album Was Released), *Fars News Agency*, 21 Shahrivar 1386 (2007): http://www.farsnews .com/newstext.php?nn=8606210205.

10. "Vākonesh-e Ershād be enteshār-e albumhā-ye do Mohsen" (*Ershād*'s Reaction to the Release of the Albums of the Two Mohsens), *Hamshahri Online*, 24 September 2007: http://www.hamshahrionline.ir/news-32341.aspx (site discontinued).

11. On the tension between recitation and musicality see Nelson (1985). Although Qur'an reciters are trained in some of the same vocal techniques as singers, and many scholars have considered it legitimate to beautify the Qur'an in recitation, recitation has always been considered firmly distinct from singing.

12. *Sheikh* Qari 'Abd al-Basit 'Abd al-Samad (1927–1988) was a renowned Egyptian *qari* (Qur'an reciter). He was one of the first *qaris* to make commercial recordings of his recitations, which was unusual at the time since fame for reciters was not well regarded—or was even forbidden—on the grounds that the reciter might eclipse the importance of the Qur'an itself.

13. Treviso interview, 2009.

14. "Tangerine Dream: The Official Forum": http://www.tangerinedream-music.com /forum2/index_ad.php (accessed 27 July 2016).

15. This has been done in other contexts, with equally punishing consequences. In Egypt, Nasr Abu Zayd attempted this in a much more formal context, namely applying

modern methods of literary criticism to the Qur'an, and ended up having to flee the country.

16. Saman Salour, *Ārāmesh bā Diāzpam-e 10* (Calmness with Diazpam 10), documentary, 2003.

17. Amir Bahari, "Goftegu bā Mohsen Namjoo: bakhsh-e avval, begard tā begardim," (Interview with Mohsen Namjoo: Part One, Let's Whirl), *Etemaad* newspaper, 26 Farvardin 1387 (2008).

18. *Diazpam 10.*

19. The presence of complex and ambivalent emotions vis-à-vis the West is of course not limited to Iran. On the tension between tradition and Western modernity in the politics of patriarchy in Iran, see Moallem (2005); on the persistence of the West as a model for modernity in Lebanon, see Deeb (2006).

20. See "Mohsen Namjoo; Toranj, Āhang-e shomāreh 8," audio (6:00): http://www.iransong.com/song/25409.htm *(accessed 27 July 2016).*

21. Herzfeld summarizes his notion of "cultural intimacy" as "the recognition of those aspects of a cultural identity that are considered a source of external embarrassment but that nevertheless provide insiders with their assurance of common sociality, the familiarity with the bases of power that may at one moment assure the disenfranchised a degree of creative irreverence and at the next moment reinforce the effectiveness of intimidation" (1997, 3).

22. See "Mohsen Namjoo Daheye 60," video (17:45) uploaded by vhebrown, 18 May 2014: https://www.youtube.com/watch?v=EP0W79BdZBs.

23. See "Mohsen Namjoo-daheh shast (1980's)," video (8:09) uploaded by gholfali, 13 September 2008: http://www.youtube.com/watch?v=nr_raSUOfvw&feature=related.

24. On "counter-memory" see Foucault (1977).

25. Translation by Ahmad Karimi-Hakkak in Karimi-Hakkak (1991, 518); for the poem in Persian, see Shamlu (1378 [1999/2000], 781).

26. Taheri (1987).

27. "Wattoo Wattoo Super Bird" was a French cartoon series created in 1978, which was often broadcast on Iranian state television in the nineteen-eighties. The series consisted of short episodes that were intended to teach morals to children. They portrayed a black-and-white bird named Wattoo Wattoo that hailed from another planet and was on earth to help the Zwas—dumb and wasteful geese—to become better creatures.

28. "Shekāyat az Mohsen Namjoo beh ettehām-e tohin beh āyāt-e Qor'ān" (Complaint against Mohsen Namjoo on the Accusation of Insult against the Verses of the Qur'an), *IQNA Arts Group*, 6 Shahrivar 1387 (2008): http://www.iqna.ir/fa/news/1681348/ شکایت-از-محسن-نامجو-به-اتهام-توهین-به-آیات-قرآن.

29. "Mohsen Namjoo niyat va qasd-e tohin beh Qor'an-rā nadāshteh ast" (Mohsen Namjoo Did Not Have the Intention and Purpose to Insult the Qur'an), *IQNA Arts Group*, 8 Shahrivar 1387 (2008): http://iqna.ir/fa/news/1681775/ محسن-نامجو-نیت-و-قصد-توهین-به-قرآن-را-نداشته است.

30. "Pāsokh-e Abbas Salimi beh tozihāt-e vakil-e Mohsen Namjoo; In shekāyat shakhsi nist, e'lām-e jorm ast" (Abbas Salimi's Response to Mohsen Namjoo's Law-

yer's Explanations; This Is Not a Personal Complaint, It Is the Announcement of a Crime), *IQNA Arts Group*, 10 Shahrivar 1387 (2008): http://vazeh.com/n2199523/ پاسخ-عباس-سلیمی-به-توضیحات-وکیل-محسن-نامجو-این-شکایت-شخصی-نیست-اعلام-جرم-است .

31. "Nedāmatnāmeh va 'ozrkhāhi-ye Mohsen Namjoo' az mardom-e Irān" (Mohsen Namjoo's Letter of Remorse and Apology to the People of Iran), *IQNA Arts Group*, 15 Shahrivar 1387 (2008): http://www.ghatreh.com/news/nn2287376/ ندامت-نامه-عذرخواهی-محسن-نامجو-مردم .

32. The necklace has the *wa-in yakād* prayer from the Qur'an (68:51), which states, "And indeed, those who disbelieve would almost make you slip with their eyes when they hear the message, and they say, 'Indeed, he is mad'"; see "Surah al-Qalam": http://quran.com/68/51-61 (accessed 27 July 2016).

33. "5 sāl habs-e ta'ziri barāy-e Mohsen Namjoo" (Five-year Prison Sentence for Mohsen Namjoo), *Tābnāk*, 22 Tir 1388 (2009): http://www.tabnak.ir/fa/pages/?cid=55333.

34. On his album *Oy* (2009), released outside of Iran, Namjoo calls this song "Gladiators," with "*Faghih Khoshgele*" in parentheses. See "Mohsen Namjoo," video (5:33) uploaded by MohsenNamjooTV, 20 July 2009: https://www.youtube.com/watch?v=6yTW by7v5WY&feature=related.

35. The Supreme Leader is officially referred to by the title *Maqām-e Mo'azzam-e Rahbari* (Honorable Office of the Leader), which Namjoo subverts by turning "leader" into "superiority," implying an unjust, illegitimate value system.

36. "One hundred and twenty-four thousand wives" is a reference to the number of prophets in Islam according to a hadith. *Jir-e Pamārān* is a play on the phrase *Pir-e Jamārān*, which stands for Imam Khomeini (literally, wise man or saint of Jamaran, Khomeini's residence in the north of Tehran). *Jir-e Pamārān* doesn't mean anything but ridicules the term *Pir-e Jamārān*.

CHAPTER EIGHT

1. Orkut's immense popularity in Iran is well-known. This anecdotal statistic was given to me by Cambyse Mirabedi, one of the founders of one of the first Internet service providers in Iran, PARS ONLINE.

2. Mitchell (2001, 1–2).

3. I was present at this event. See also "Iran's Khatami Gets Bitter Reception from Iranian Students," *Agence France Presse*, 6 December 2004.

4. Dabashi (2007, 231).

5. Arjomand (2009, 149).

6. Khatam (2010, 221). I was also arrested by the police (though toward the fizzling end of this morality campaign period) and wrote a short article about it: Nahid Siamdoust, "A Night with the Morality Police," *Time Magazine*, 22 September 2008: http://www.time.com/time/world/article/0,8599,1842911,00.html.

7. Perhaps the most prominent images of police brutality and abuse from this period are an image in which a man in a yellow T-shirt is being forced to suck on a red toilet water can and another one showing a woman bloodied in the face from her scuffle with the morality police, on board a yellow taxi, defiantly raising her index finger. In a

book review, I explain that in this era of the mobile phone and the Internet, no sensational public event goes unreported; see Siamdoust (2011).

8. "Harandi: Āstinhā-rā barā-ye bāzsāzi-ye farhang-e 'omumi bālā mizanim" (Harandi: We Pull Up Our Sleeves for the Reconstruction of Public Culture), *Fars News Agency*, 1 Khordad 1384 (2005): http://www.farsnews.com/newstext.php?nn= 8406010451.

9. Manal Lutfi, "Iran's Underground Music Revolution," *Asharq Alawsat*, 26 May 2007.

10. "Saffar Harandi: Musiqi-ye harzeh nabāyad az Ershād mojavvez begirad" (Saffar Harandi: Dissolute Music Must Not Receive Permits from *Ershād*), *ISNA*, 22 Ordibehesht 1388 (2009).

11. Khatam (2010, 220). On the public and private sphere and music traversing these spaces, see also Siamdoust (2015).

12. Rap music, in the Iranian context, is similar to that found in other countries, whereby a lyrical and poetic voice is used for rhythmic chants against a backdrop of beats. This music is also called hip-hop in Iran. However, hip-hop denotes a larger category than rap, as it also describes an entire subculture that includes other art forms, such as break dancing and graffiti, both of which are also very popular in Iran.

13. Sreberny and Mohammadi (1994). In addition, both Sreberny and Khiabany (2010) and Dabashi (2010) suggest that the Internet is only the latest in a series of technological revolutions over Iran's past century that have brought about genuine change and revolution in the political sphere.

14. Johari (2002).

15. C. Bogart, "Chat Rooms and Chadors," *Newsweek*, 20 August 1995: http://www .newsweek.com/chat-rooms-and-chadors-182316.

16. Rahimi (2010, 41).

17. Sreberny and Khiabany (2010, 32); Alavi (2005).

18. Johari (2002, 83).

19. Sreberny and Khiabany (2010); Rahimi (2010).

20. *Internet World Stats*: "Middle East Internet Users, Population and Facebook Statistics": http://www.internetworldstats.com/stats5.htm (accessed 6 March 2012); there is no data with a more nuanced qualitative breakdown among Internet users, but clearly not all users are equally Internet-literate, so while more than half of the population may at times use services such as Skype and sites such as Facebook, only a smaller fraction will have integrated the Internet into their lives more fully.

21. Nahid Siamdoust, "Iranian Blogger Returns from Exile for Vote," *The Los Angeles Times*, 23 June 2005: http://articles.latimes.com/2005/jun/23/world/fg-iranblog23.

22. Rahimi (2010, 40).

23. As Castells (2000a and 2000b) explains the "network society," new information and communication technologies (most prominent among them the Internet) have amplified the main advantages of network associations, namely flexibility and adaptability, by allowing networks to operate in more dynamic and larger dimensions. He also argues that "the prevalence of networks in organizing social practice redefines social structure in our societies," where "social structure" is defined as the ways in which humans inter-

act in their relationships of power, experience, and production/consumption framed by culture (2000b, 695).

24. Rahimi (2011).

25. Sohrabi-Haghighat (2011).

26. El-Nawawy and Khamis (2012); see also Nate Anderson, "How Nokia Helped Iran 'Persecute and Arrest' Dissidents," *Ars Technica*, 4 March 2010: http://arstechnica .com/tech-policy/2010/03/how-nokia-helped-iran-persecute-and-arrest-dissidents/.

27. Morozov (2011). See also Kelly and Etling (2008), whose research shows that the Internet is used by groups of varying political persuasions and hence does not work only in the service of reformist tendencies, as well as the two reports by Aday et al. (2010; 2012), which demonstrate that the significance of the new media as a practical tool was exaggerated in contemporary reports on Iran's "Twitter Revolution" (the 2009 elections) and the Arab Spring, and that the new media were mostly effective as megaphones to the outside world, although this often did feed back to the inside as well, thus helping the movements indirectly.

28. Sohrabi-Haghighat (2011).

29. Kot (2009).

30. See Stokes (2012).

31. The singular popularity of Pink Floyd in Iran, to this day, requires further study. In 2006, for example, Pink Floyd's Roger Waters played a sold-out concert in Dubai to a mostly Iranian crowd, many of whom had travelled to Dubai just for the concert, and when Waters gave a concert in London in 2011, most Iranians I know attended it. Following the 2009 elections, the Iranian-Canadian band Blurred Vision did a cover of "Another Brick in the Wall" titled "Hey Ayatollah, Leave Those Kids Alone," a citation practice to which Iranians readily related. On the concepts of citationality and iterability, see Derrida (1988).

32. Personal interview with Yaser Bakhtiari (aka Yas), 6 October 2007, Tehran; personal interview with Soroush Lashkary (aka Hichkas), 27 October 2008, Tehran.

33. Interview with Hichkas, 7 April 2011, Skype.

34. See also Mohammad Mehdi Mowlaei, "Musiqi-ye zirzamini, az honar tā resāneh" (Underground Music, From an Art Form to a Medium), *7Sang.com*, 2007: http://www .7sang.com/mag/2007/12/07/editorial-underground_music.html (site discontinued).

35. Sohrabi-Haghighat (2011).

36. I downloaded these programs in 2006 and 2007 as podcasts; they are no longer available on the BBC website.

37. Sohrabi-Haghighat (2011).

38. PMC is the most popular Persian music satellite channel among viewers in Iran. Its programming consists of mostly Persian music, by artists inside and outside of Iran, but also some non-Persian music favored by Iranians, such as works by Jennifer Lopez and Shakira.

39. The shows are available on Aparat, a sort of Iranian YouTube: http://www.aparat .com/CHAARGOOSH/چارگوش.

40. This technology became even more important following the 2009 election un-

rest, as the government shut down the mobile phone networks and the Internet and jammed satellite television broadcasts. While announcements about upcoming protests were transmitted via SMS text messaging, protest songs were sent over Bluetooth.

41. Bilan, Gholami, and Menvari (2010).

42. Alireza Mohammadi, "Enqelāb-e eslāmi va movājeheh bā nasl-e sevvom" (The Islamic Revolution and the Confrontation with the Third Generation), *Markaz-e Asnād-e Enqelāb-e Eslāmi* (Islamic Revolution Document Center); see *Pegah Howzeh, 29 Ordibehesht 1386* (2007): http://www.hawzah.net/fa/Magazine/View/3814/4866/40499.

43. Kowsari (2010).

44. Babak Riahipour, "Unauthorized Stories," *Musiqi-ye Mā*, 14 November 2008.

45. Personal interview, 2 October 2010, Tehran.

46. Majid Mohammadi, "The Third Generation's Anxieties, Preoccupations, and Approaches," *Gozaar—A Forum on Human Rights and Democracy in Iran*, 5 May 2008: http://www.gozaar.org/english/articles-en/The-Third-Generation-s-Anxieties-Preoccu pations-and-Approaches.html (site discontinued).

47. Azadi Square was the site of the biggest protest, and *āzādi* means "freedom," so there is also an important play on words here.

48. See also my discussion in chapter 6 of the consequences for the *TehranAvenue* contest concert of using this term.

49. There is a play on words here: Sasy Mankan pronounces "tango" as two separate words, "tang-o," giving the double meaning of *shabhā-ye tang-o*, meaning nights on which tight clothes are worn (since *tang* in Persian means "tight"), as well as tango, i.e. dance, nights.

50. Personal interview, 7 October 2010, Tehran.

51. "Underground Rappers," BBC Persian Radio's *Ruz-e Haftom* program, 24 June 2007.

52. Ibid.

53. "Bāzdāsht-e sheytān-parastān dar konsert-e Karaj," *Alef* news agency, 12 Mordad 1386 (2007): http://alef.ir/vdcf1ody.w6dmyagiiw.html?13219.

54. Personal interview, Maral Afsharian, 9 October 2010, Tehran.

55. This stark reaction is similar to the exaggerated public reactions in nineteensixties England to the mod and rocker subcultures that Cohen (2011) terms "moral panics." However, in the Iranian case the government had a vested ideological interest in creating a panic around youths partaking in rap and rock music cultures, whereas in Cohen's work the "moral panics" were caused and sustained by a combination of factors.

56. Interviews with Ashkan Koosha and Kasra Saboktakin in "Sakkou Episode 37" on *Manoto 1 TV*, 19 September 2011.

57. See, for example, "Iran Detains Scores at 'Satanic' Rock Gig: Media," *Reuters*, 4 August 2007: http://www.reuters.com/article/2007/08/04/us-iran-concert-arrests-idUSL 0423282220070804.

58. "Shock" Documentary Program, *IRIB Channel* 3, 26 August 2008.

59. "Reasons for the Trend toward Satanism," interview with Hojatoleslam Hamidreza Mazaheri, *Jahan News*, 16 Dey 1387 (2009).

60. Ibid.

61. "Bāzdāsht-e yek goruh-e zirzamini bā khānandeh-ye zan" (The Arrest of an Underground Group with a Female Singer), *Buletan News*, 17 Āzar 1389 (2010).

62. "Bāzdāsht-e video-klip-sāzān-e goruh-e 25 Band" (The Arrest of the Video-Clip Producers of the 25 Band Group), *Gerdab.ir* (associated with the "Center for the Investigation of Institutionalized Crime"), 13 Mehr 1390 (2011).

63. "The Arrest of Team Related to Barobax," *Jahan News*, 18 Bahman 1389 (2011).

64. See, for example, the daylong seminar titled "Examination of Underground Music in Iran," held at the Center for Strategic Studies on 29 November 2010, which featured talks by some of Iran's foremost researchers on "underground" music, such as Masoud Kowsari, Mohammad Hossein Imani, Afshin Davarpanah, and Hasan Khademi.

65. Talks by Adib Vahdani, Sasan Fatemi, and others at *Mehr News Agency*'s "Second Seminar Series Investigating Underground Music," 4 December 2007: http://www.mehr news.com/fa/NewsDetail.aspx?NewsID=524484.

66. "Interview with Farid Salmanian" in *Gozāresh-e Musiqi*, No. 1, Bahman 1385 (2007).

67. *Ruz-e Haftom* program on BBC Radio Persian, 1 September 2006.

68. Babak Riahipour, "Unauthorized Stories," in *Musiqi-ye Mā*, 14 November 2008.

CHAPTER NINE

1. Ahmadi (2002).

2. Nassir Mashkouri, "Iran's Hip-Hop Movement Is an Event of Our Generation: In Conversation with Bahram," *Beshkan*, 12 January 2012: http://beshkan.co.uk/reports /8/12/01/12/1096 (site discontinued).

3. Ibid.

4. Johnston (2008); Nooshin (2011).

5. Academically, there has not been much written about Persian rap in English; more has been done in Persian. The scholars Masoud Kowsari, Mohammad Hossein Imani, Afshin Davarpanah, Hasan Khademi, and Mohammad Mehdi Mowlaei have spoken or written about rap; much of this work is in the format of panel presentations, online articles, and academic theses.

6. Johnston (2008, 102); Nooshin (2011, 106).

7. Kowsari (2009); Khademi (2010).

8. Nassir Mashkouri, "Gofte-gu bā 'Yās' rap-khān-e Irāni" (Interview with Yas, an Iranian Rapper), *Zirzamin*, January 2008: http://zirzamin.se/?q=node/688 (site discontinued).

9. Personal interview (Soroush Lashkary aka Hichkas), 27 October 2008, Tehran.

10. Bahram, "E'terāz-e hip-hop chist" (The Protest of Hip-Hop), Bahram's Facebook profile page, 26 May 2011.

11. Hamid Monebatti, "Qabl az mā hich kas nabud" (There Wasn't No One before Us), *Zirzamin*, 17 March 2009: http://www.zirzamin.se/?q=node/761 (site discontinued).

12. Personal interview (Mehrak Golestan aka Reveal Poison), 28 April 2011, London.

13. Mashkouri (2012).

14. Talattof (2011); Afary (2009).

15. Hasan Khademi, "Motāle'eh-ye moredi: vizhehgihā-ye musiqi-ye zirzamini-ye

rap-e Fārsi" (A Case Study: The Characteristics of Underground Persian Rap Music): http://mahmoodheydari.blogfa.com/post/122/مقاله-جالب-جاره-رپ-قسمت-اول (piece not dated but sometime between 2005–2008; accessed 27 July 2016); Effat Bilan, Mohsen Gholami, and Nuh Menvari, "Jāme'eh-shenāsi-ye musiqi-ye rap" (The Sociology of Rap Music), Ensānshenāsi va Farhang, 14 March 2010: http://anthropology.ir/node/4428.

16. Johnston (2008, 107).

17. One of the first such categorizations seems to be that established by the music journalist Nassir Mashkouri in an article on *TehranAvenue* titled "Musiqi-ye Hip-Hop yā kucheh-bāzāri," (Hip-Hop Music or *kucheh-bāzāri*), 2006: http://www.tehranavenue.com/print.php?ln=fa&id=610# (site discontinued). This is usually the set of categories that is used by Johnston (2008) and others. Mashkouri names four discrete categories, namely street rap, socially aware rap, commercial rap, and diaspora rap.

18. Or alternatively, "We're Not Man Enough," playing on the alternate meaning of "man" as "honorable, decent."

19. *Ruz-e Haftom* program on *BBC Persian Radio*, 1 September 2006.

20. Personal interview, 6 October 2007, Tehran.

21. This was more than a year before my interview with Yas in October 2007. By the time of my interview with him, he had received permits for four more songs.

22. *Ruz-e Haftom* program, 2006.

23. On Raha TV, which is accessible as a YouTube channel, there is an informative series titled "Nasl-e Rap" that features many of the young rappers; episode 14 of this series features Justina, whom I discuss next.

24. Personal interview, 26 February 2016, Skype.

25. Alizadeh subsequently received international attention, which led an American nonprofit organization to bring her to the United States, where she now attends a prep school in Utah. Robert Wainwright, "Afghan Teen Rapper was 10 When Her Mother First Considered Selling Her," *The New York Times*, 8 October 2015. Alizadeh is the subject of an award-winning 2015 documentary by Rokhsareh Ghaem Maghami titled *Sonita*.

26. Personal interview, 2016.

27. Soroush Lashkary (aka Hichkas) speaking at the event "Persian Hip-Hop and Alternative Music," St. Antony's College, Oxford, 2 June 2011, which I organized and moderated.

28. Monebatti (2009).

29. Lashkary later enrolled at Garmsar Azad University to study translation (from English), but eventually dropped out. Personal interview, 27 October 2008, Tehran.

30. Interview, 7 April 2011, *Skype*.

31. Ibid. I have intentionally translated Lashkary's phrase "*qabl-e mā hichkas nabud*" as "there wasn't no one before us" to more aptly reflect the double entendre in the Persian, since Hichkas, Lashkary's artist name, means "no one" in Persian. Grammatically, his sentence would translate as "Before us there was no one." Lashkary has repeated this statement in other interviews as well; see for example Monebatti (2009).

32. Interview (2011).

33. Mari Shibata, "The Godfather of Iranian Hip-Hop Wants Grassroots Change," 8 September 2014: https://www.indexoncensorship.org/2014/09/iran-tehran-hichkas-hip-hop-music/

34. Lashkary speaking at "Persian Hip-Hop and Alternative Music," mentioned above.

35. Soroush Lashkary (aka Hichkas), Talk at SOAS University of London, 28 June 2011.

36. Behzad Bolour, "Āsfālt-e Dāgh-e Hichkas" (Hichkas's Hot Asphalt), *BBC Persian Online*, 23 September 2006: http://www.bbc.com/persian/seventhday/story/2006/09/06 0923_bs_hichkas.shtml.

37. Lashkary (Hichkas), SOAS (2011).

38. Bolour (2006).

39. Interview with Soroush Lashkary, aka Hichkas, "Sakkou Episode 25," *Manoto 1 TV*, 22 June 2011.

40. Adelkhah (1999), in her description of a car salesman as one modern embodiment of the *javānmardi* code (which encompasses the *luti*), argues that this historical ethic has taken "very varied forms according to the social groups and historical contexts where it has developed" (34).

41. Adelkhah (1999, 31); for more on the term *luti* in Iranian culture, see Willem Floor, "*luti*," *Encyclopaedia Iranica*, Online Edition, 15 March 2010: http://www.iranicaon line.org/articles/luti.

42. Mohsen Zakeri, "*javānmardi*," *Encyclopaedia Iranica*, Online Edition, 15 December 2008: http://www.iranicaonline.org/articles/javanmardi.

43. Lashkary aka Hichkas at "Persian Hip-Hop" (2011).

44. Personal Interview (2008).

45. Najmabadi (2005, 2).

46. Lyrics from the first section of Hichkas's "*Mā az unāshim*" (We're of That Sort).

47. Bahram on Facebook (2011).

48. LeVine (2008, 198).

49. Floor (2010).

50. Lucie Ryzova has written about what she calls YLIMs (Young Low-Income Males) in the Egyptian context, explaining their participation in the revolution there as partly a performance of their masculinity. There are some similarities between these groups, but I would argue that as *Rap-e Farsi* demonstrates, the Iranian counterpart gives greater value to the democratic notions spelled out in the songs. Lucie Ryzova, "The Battle of Muhammad Mahmud Street: Teargas, Hair Gel, and Tramadol," *Jadaliyya*, 28 November 2011: http://www.jadaliyya.com/pages/index/3312/the-battle -of-muhammad-mahmud-street_teargas-hair.

51. Lashkary aka Hichkas at "Persian Hip-Hop" (2011).

52. For a focused discussion of issues of poverty and inequality in post-revolutionary Iran, see Djavad Salehi-Isfahani, "Poverty, Inequality, and Populist Politics in Iran," *The Journal of Economic Inequality* (2009) 7: 5–28.

53. Salehi-Isfahani (2009, 6).

54. In a conversation with a group of about a dozen young Iranians after the Hichkas

talk at SOAS in London, on 28 June 2011, several of the girls said that there was a sense of male chauvinism in his work that they found offensive.

55. Lashkary (Hichkas), SOAS (2011).

CHAPTER TEN

1. Negar Mottahedeh, *"Allah-O-Akbar,"* in *ArteEast Quarterly*, 30 October 2012, quoted in Roshanak Kheshti, "On the Threshold of the Political" in *Radical History Review*, issue 121 (January 2015).

2. See Nahid Siamdoust, "Power of the People," *Time* Magazine, 29 June 2009.

3. Michael M.J. Fischer first coined this term in his book *Iran: From Religious Dispute to Revolution* (1980) and uses it in the context of the Green Uprising in his 2010 article "The Rhythmic Beat of the Revolution in Iran." The phrase refers to the Battle of Karbala in 680 CE, in which Imam Hossein and his followers were slaughtered by the Umayyad Caliph Yazid I. Fischer defines this battle, which is mourned and reenacted by Shias during 'Āshurā, as the "Shi'ite paradigm of struggle for social justice, against the government" (513).

4. Nahid Siamdoust, "Forbidden Iran: How to Report When You're Banned," *Time Magazine*, 22 June 2009.

5. For an academic treatment of Shi'ism as a religion of protest, see Dabashi (2011).

6. In the Siahkal Uprising, on 8 February 1971, a group of communist students staged an attack on the military base in the town of Siahkal, next to the forest region of Gilan province, in the north. Thirty Fedayeen militiamen and several of the shah's guards were killed in this event; of the Fedayeen who died, twenty-nine were executed and one died under torture. Eleven Fedayeen activists were also arrested in the event.

7. Personal interview, 21 October 2009, Oxford University.

8. The video clip that was broadcast at Azadi Stadium was an abbreviated version of this clip: "sar oomad zemestoon," video (4:38) uploaded by msaeedi56, 22 May 2009: https://www.youtube.com/watch?v=RCkSCP22t-Q.

9. Kiosk frontman Arash Sobhani at a rally against then Iranian president Mahmoud Ahmadinejad in front of the United Nations in New York, 23 September 2009. A friend was present at this rally and shared her notes with me.

10. See Siamdoust (2012).

11. "Takhrib-e Mokkarrar va Terror-e Shakhsiyat-e Ahmadinejad dar Hozur-e Seyed Mohammad Khatami" (Repeated Denunciations and Character Assassination of Ahmadinejad in the Presence of Seyed Mohammad Khatami), *Fars News Agency*, 24 May 2009: http://www.farsnews.com/printable.php?nn=8803021538.

12. I'm indebted for the translation of *chub-e alef* to Homa Katouzian, who explained to me that a *chub-e alef* (or *chuq-alef* as it was often pronounced) was basically a ruler or pointer that the teacher would use at the blackboard, and occasionally use to beat students.

13. Hana Kavyanitavassot, interview with Dariush Eqbali, "Dirooz va Emroosz 'Yar-e Dabestani'" *Radio Farda*, 6 December 2008.

14. This video was sponsored by the messianic youth group *Bachehā-ye Qalam* (Children of the Pen); see "sade biya reza sadeghi Alireza 1974," video (3:14) uploaded by Alireza KB, 19 July 2009: https://www.youtube.com/watch?v=C-mtmAqdbn4.

15. See "Reza Sadeghi pishnahād-e sākht-e āhang barāy-e Ahmadinejad-rā rad kard" (Reza Sadeghi rejected the offer to make a song for Ahmadinejad), *Aftabnews*, 11 Khordād 1388 (2009): http://www.aftabnews.ir/prtjyheo.uqehxzsffu.html.

16. For Tataloo's "Irān-e Sabz" (Green Iran), see "amir tataloo iran e sabz," video (3:35) uploaded by KiaPersian4Ever, 28 May 2009: https://www.youtube.com/watch?v=wIultGdBjgk.

17. For Sasy Mankan's "*Ettehād-e Melli*" (National Unity, the name of Mehdi Karoubi's party), see "Karoubi Video Clip," video (2:23) uploaded by perushajinguy, 8 June 2009: https://www.youtube.com/watch?v=hVOocyVlr1w.

18. Personal conversation, October 2008 Tehran,; this woman requested that her name not be published because of her position with the semigovernmental organization.

19. See "Hamed Nikpay 'The Owner of This Land' (Maalek-e Een Khaak)," video (3:05) uploaded by arash, 19 June 2009: https://www.youtube.com/watch?v=HqONCJoADtQ.

20. Krista Mahr, "Top 10 Heroes; 2. Neda Agha-Soltan," *Time Magazine*, 8 December 2009.

21. "Azadi" alludes here both to the concept of freedom (*azadi*) and to Azadi Square, where two to three million people gathered on 15 June 2009.

22. For the song "*Nedā-ye Sohrāb*" see "Nedaye Sohrab Thanks To Mazdasht," video (4:59) uploaded by parstv parstv, 29 July 2009: https://www.youtube.com/watch?v=92kEBlUCQQE.

23. Video message posted on the Green campaign's Mowj website as well as on YouTube, recorded on 18 October 2009; see "First President Mir Hossein Mousavi interview October 18th 2009," video (17:21) uploaded by Mehdi Saharkhiz, 18 October 2009: https://www.youtube.com/watch?v=8UW6b13tQsA.

24. Jason Rezaian, "Rouhani Sworn In As Iran's President," *The Washington Post*, 4 August 2013.

25. Max Fisher, "Iranian President Rouhani Now Has His Own 'Yes, We Can' Music Video," *The Washington Post*, 26 November 2013.

26. For the Xaniar concert, see Thomas Erdbrink, "Singer Steps into Spotlight as Nation Changes Political Tune," *The New York Times*, 28 April 2014. I attended the O-Hum concert in Tehran on 8 May 2014.

27. This letter was published in various newspapers, including *Sharq Daily*, as well as on social media and other music sites. I saw it on O-Hum's Facebook page, published 15 February 2015.

28. See "Hamid Talebzadeh-Hamechi Aroomeh," video (3:38) uploaded by iiRaaaN / T 3 H R 4 N, 11 October 2009: https://www.youtube.com/watch?v=AoiM7AmNqG8.

29. I draw here on Bayat's (2007) articulation of the subversive powers of fun: "Fear of fun, consequently, is not necessarily about diversion from the higher powers or noble values as such but about the fear of exit from the paradigm that frames and upholds the mastery of certain types of moral and political authorities, be they individuals, political movements, or states" (455).

SELECT BIBLIOGRAPHY

Abrahamian, Ervand. 1982. *Iran Between Two Revolutions*. Princeton, N.J.: Princeton University Press.

———. 1993. *Khomeinism : Essays on the Islamic Republic*. Berkeley: University of California Press.

Aday, Sean, Henry Farrell, Marc Lynch, John Sides, John Kelly, and Ethan Zuckerman. 2010. "Blogs and Bullets: New Media in Contentious Politics." Special issue, *Peaceworks* 64 (September).

Aday, Sean, Henry Farrell, Marc Lynch, John Sides, and Deen Freelon. 2012. "Blogs and Bullets II: New Media Conflict after the Arab Spring." Special issue, *Peaceworks* 80 (July).

Adelkhah, Fariba. 1991. "'Michael Jackson ne peut absolument rien faire'—Les pratiques musicales en république d'Iran." *Cahiers d'études sur la Méditerranée orientale et le monde turco-iranien* 11 (January–June): 23–41.

———. 1999. *Being Modern in Iran*. New York: Columbia University Press.

Aghaie, Kamran. 2004. *The Martyrs of Karbala: Shi'i Symbols and Rituals in Modern Iran*. Seattle: University of Washington Press.

Ahmadi, Morteza. 2002. *Kohnehhā-ye hamisheh no: Tarānehhā-ye takht-e-hozi*. Tehran: Qoqnoos Publishing.

Alavi, Nasrin. 2005. *We Are Iran: The Persian Blogs*. Berkeley, CA: Soft Skull Press.

Alizadeh, Hossein. 1998. "Negāh-i gozar beh āmuzesh-e musiqi dar Irān." *Falsnāmeh-ye Musiqi-ye Māhur* 1: 73–83.

Al-Muttaqi, Ali. 1998. *Kanz al 'Ummal fi sunan al-aqwāl wa'l af 'āl*. Beirut: Dār al-Kutub al-'Ilmiyah.

Anderson, Benedict. 1991. *Imagined Communities*. London: Verso.

Andriessen, Willem. 1999. "'THE WINNER'; Compact Cassette. A Commercial and Technical Look Back at the Greatest Success Story in the History of AUDIO Up to Now." *Journal of Magnetism and Magnetic Materials* 193 (1):11–16.

Ansari, Ali. 2007. *Modern Iran: The Pahlavis and After*. Harlow: Longman.

Arjomand, Said Amir. 2009. *After Khomeini : Iran under His Successors*. Oxford: Oxford University Press.

Armbrust, Walter. 1993. "The Riddle of Ramadan: Media, Consumer Culture, and the 'Christmasization' of a Muslim Holiday." In *Everyday Life in the Muslim Middle East*, edited by Donna Lee Bowen and Evelyn A. Early, 335–348. Bloomington: Indiana University Press.

———. 2000. *Mass Mediations : New Approaches to Popular Culture in the Middle East and Beyond*. Berkeley: University of California Press.

———. 2012. "A History of New Media in the Arab Middle East." *Journal for Cultural Research*. 16 (2). 155–174.

Bahmanpur, Forugh. 2008. *Chehrehhā-ye Māndegār-e Tarāneh va Musiqi; Majmu'eh Gofteguhā 2*. Tehran: Enteshārāt-e Badraqeh-ye Jāvidān.

Baqi, Emadeddin. 2003. *Tavvalod-e Yek Enqelāb* [The birth of a revolution]. Tehran: Sarāyi.

Basmenji, Kaveh. 2005. *Tehran Blues: How Iranian Youth Rebelled against Iran's Founding Fathers*. London: Saqi.

Barkechli, Mehdi and Moussa Maa'roufi. 1963. *Les systèmes de la musique traditionnelle de l'Iran (Radif) avec transcription en notation musicale occidentale, par Moussa Maa'roufi*. Tehran: Secrétariat d'état aux beaux-arts.

Bayat, Asef. 2000. "From 'Dangerous Classes' to 'Quiet Rebels': Politics of the Urban Subaltern in the Global South." *International Sociology* 15: 533–557.

———. 2007. "Islamism and the Politics of Fun." *Public Culture* 19 (3): 433–459.

———. 2010. *Life as Politics: How Ordinary People Change the Middle East*. Stanford: Stanford University Press.

Bayat, Asef, and Linda Herrera. 2010. *Being Young and Muslim: New Cultural Politics in the Global South and North*. New York: Oxford University Press.

Beeman, William O. 1976. "You Can Take Music Out of the Country, But . . . : The Dynamics of Change in Iranian Musical Tradition." *Asian Music* 7 (2): 6–19.

———. 2011. *Iranian Performance Traditions*. Costa Mesa, Calif.: Mazda Publishers, Inc.

Beheshti, Ayatollāh Doctor Seyed Mohammad Hosseini. 1385 [2006/2007]. *Musiqi va Tafrih dar Eslām*. 3rd ed. Tehran: Bonyād-e Nashr-e Āsār va Andishehā-ye Shahid Beheshti.

Benjamin, Walter. 1970. *Illuminations*. London: Cape.

Bilan, Effat, Mohsen Gholami, and Nuh Menvari. 1333 [2010]. "Jāme'eh Shenāsi-ye Musiqi-ye Rap." *Ensānshenāsi va Farhang* (23 Esfand 1388 [2009]): http://anthropology.ir/node/4428.

Binesh, Taqi. 1380 [2001/2002]. *Tārikh-e Mokhtasar-e Musiqi-ye Irān*. Tehran: Nashr-e Hastān.

Bourdieu, Pierre. 1977. *Outline of a Theory of Practice*. Cambridge: Cambridge University Press.

———. 1984. *Distinction: A Social Critique of the Judgement of Taste*. London: Routledge.

———. 1993. *The Field Of Cultural Production: Essays On Art And Literature*. Edited by Randal Johnson. Cambridge: Polity Press.

Breyley, Gay J. 2010. "Hope, Fear, and Dance Dance Dance: Popular Music in 1960s Iran." *Musicology Australia* 32 (2): 203-226.

Breyley, Gay J., and Sasan Fatemi. 2016. *Iranian Music and Popular Entertainment from Motrebi to Losanjelesi and Beyond*. New York: Routledge.

Browne, Edward G. (1893) 1984. A Year Amongst the Persians; Impressions as to the Life, Character & Thought of the People of Persia, Received during Twelve Months' Residence in That Country in the Years 1887–1888. New York: Hippocrene Books.

Butler, Judith. 2011. *Bodies That Matter*. New York: Routledge.

Campbell, Patricia S. 1994. "Bruno Nettl on Music of Iran." *Music Educators Journal* 81 (3): 19–25.

Caron, Nelly and Dariush Safvat. 1966. *Iran*. Paris: Buchet-Chastel.

Castells, Manuel. 2000a. *The Rise of the Network Society*. 2nd ed. Oxford: Blackwell.

———. 2000b. "Toward a Sociology of the Network Society." *Contemporary Sociology* 29 (5): 693–699.

Caton, Margaret Louise. 1983. "The Classical 'Tasnif': A Genre of Persian Vocal Music." PhD diss. in 2 vols., University of California, Los Angeles.

Certeau, Michel de. 1984. *The Practice of Everyday Life*. Berkeley: University of California Press.

Chehabi, H. E. 1999. "From Revolutionary Tasnif to Patriotic Surud: Music and Nation-Building in Pre-World War II Iran." *Iran* 37: 143–154.

———. 2000. "Voices Unveiled: Women Singers in Iran." In *Iran and Beyond: Essays in Middle Eastern History in Honor of Nikki R. Keddie*, edited by Rudi Matthee and Beth Baron, 151–166. Costa Mesa, CA: Mazda Publishers.

———. 2006. "ZUR-ḴĀNA." In *Encyclopaedia Iranica*, online edition, accessed 27 July 2016, http://www.iranicaonline.org/articles/zur-kana.

———. 2008. "Shajarian, Mohamed Reza." In *Biographical Encyclopedia of the Modern Middle East and North Africa*. Detroit: Gale Group.

Cohen, Stanley. 2011. *Folk Devils and Moral Panics: The Creation of the Mods and Rockers*. Routledge Classics. London: Routledge.

Dabashi, Hamid. 2007. *Iran: A People Interrupted*. New York: New Press.

———. 2010. *Iran, the Green Movement and the USA: The Fox and the Paradox*. London: Zed.

———. 2011. *Shi'ism: A Religion of Protest*. Cambridge, MA: Belknap Press of Harvard University Press.

Dadkhah, Kamran M. 1999. "Myths and Facts in Iranian Historiography." *CIRA Bulletin* 15 (1, April): 20–25.

Danielson, Virginia. 1997. *The Voice of Egypt: Umm Kulthūm, Arabic Song, and Egyptian Society in the Twentieth Century*. Chicago: University of Chicago Press.

DeBano, Wendy S. 2005. "Enveloping Music in Gender, Nation, and Islam: Women's Music Festivals in Post-Revolutionary Iran." *Iranian Studies* 38 (3): 441–462.

————. 2009. "Singing Against Silence: Celebrating Women and Music at the Fourth Jasmine Festival." In *Music and the Play of Power in the Middle East, North Africa and Central Asia*, edited by Laudan Nooshin, 229–244. Aldershot: Ashgate.

DeBano, Wendy S., and Ameneh Youssefzadeh. 2005a. "Music and Society in Iran: A Look at the Past and Present Century, a Select Bibliography." *Iranian Studies* 38 (3): 495–512.

De Bellaigue, Christopher. 2007. *The Struggle for Iran*. New York: New York Review Books.

Deeb, Lara. 2006. *An Enchanted Modern: Gender and Public Piety in Shi'i Lebanon*. Princeton, NJ: Princeton University Press.

Delougaz, Pinhas, Helene J. Kantor, and Abbas Alizadeh. 1996. *Chogha Mish. I–II The First Five Seasons of Excavations 1961–1971*. Chicago: Oriental Institute of the University of Chicago.

Derrida, Jacques. 1988. "Signature Event Context" in *Limited Inc.*, edited by Gerald Graff, 1–24. Evanston, IL: Northwestern University Press.

During, Jean. 1984. *La musique iranienne: tradition et évolution*. Bibliothèque iranienne. Paris: Éditions Recherche sur les civilisations.

————. 1992. "L'Oreille Islamique: Dix Années Capitales de la Vie Musicale en Iran: 1980–1990." *Asian Music* 23 (2): 135–164.

————. 2002. "Tradition and History: The Case of Iran." In *Garland Encyclopedia of World Music*. Vol. 6: *The Middle East*. New York: Routledge.

————. 2005. "Third Millenium Tehran: Music!" *Iranian Studies* 38 (3): 373–398.

During, Jean, Zia Mirabdolbaghi, and Dariush Safvat. 1991. *The Art of Persian Music*. Washington, DC: Mage Publishers.

Eickelman, Dale F., and Armando Salvatore. 2002. "The Public Sphere and Muslim Identities." *Archives européennes de sociologie* 43 (1): 92–115.

El-Nawawy, Mohammed, and Sahar Khamis. 2012. "Political Activism 2.0: Comparing the Role of Social Media in Egypt's 'Facebook Revolution' and Iran's 'Twitter Uprising.'" *CyberOrient* 6 (1): http://www.cyberorient.net/article.do?articleId=7439.

Farhat, Hormoz. 1990. *The Dastgāh Concept in Persian Music*. Cambridge: Cambridge University Press.

————. 2003. "Vaziri, 'Ali-Naqi." In *Encyclopaedia Iranica*, online edition, accessed 27 July 2016: http://www.iranicaonline.org/articles/vaziri-ali-naqi.

————. 2010. "Khaleqi, Ruh-Allah." In *Encyclopaedia Iranica*, Vol. X., edited by Ehsan Yar-Shater. London: Routledge and Kegan Paul, 1982.

Farmer, Henry George. 1938–1939. "An Outline History of Music History and Musical Theory." In *A Survey of Persian Art from Prehistoric Times to the Present*, edited by Arthur Upham Pope and Phyllis Acherman. London: Oxford University Press.

Fatemi, Farhang. 1380 [2001/2002]. *Setāregān-e Musiqi-ye Pop-e Irān*. Tehran: Nashr-e Jāber: Nashr-e Farhang.

————. 1381 [2002/2003]. *Nām-Āvarān-e Pop-e Irān*. Tehran: Mahd-e Farhang.

Fatemi, Sasan. 2005a. "Music, Festivity, and Gender in Iran from the Qajar to the Early Pahlavi Period." *Iranian Studies* 38, no. 3 (September; *Music and Society in Iran*): 399–416.

————. 2005b. "Musique légère urbaine dans la culture iranienne: Réflexions sur les notions de classiques et populaire" PhD diss., Université Paris X-Nanterre Paris.

Fischer, Michael M. J. 1980. *Iran: From Religious Dispute to Revolution*. Cambridge: Harvard University Press.

————. 2010. "The Rhythmic Beat of the Revolution in Iran." *Cultural Anthropology* 25 (3): 497–543.

Floor, Willem. 2010. "Luti," in *Encyclopaedia Iranica*, online edition, accessed 27 July 2016: http://www.iranicaonline.org/articles/luti.

Foucault, Michel. 1977. *Language, Counter-Memory, Practice: Selected Essays and Interviews*. Translated by Sherry Simon. Edited by Donald F. Bouchard. Ithaca, NY: Cornell University Press.

Foucault, Michel, and Paul Rabinow. 1984. *The Foucault Reader*. New York: Pantheon Books.

Frischkopf, Michael. 2001. "Tarab ('Enchantment') in the Mystic Sufi Chant of Egypt." In *Colors of Enchantment: Theater, Dance, Music, and the Visual Arts of the Middle East*, edited by Sherifa Zuhur. Cairo: American University in Cairo Press.

Gheissari, Ali, and Seyyed Vali Reza Nasr. 2006. *Democracy in Iran: History and the Quest for Liberty*. Oxford: Oxford University Press.

Golkar, Saeid. 2012. "Cultural Engineering under Authoritarian Regimes: Islamization of Universities in Postrevolutionary Iran." *Digest of Middle East Studies* 21 (1): 1–23.

Gluck, Robert. 2007. "The Shiraz Arts Festival: Western Avant-Garde Arts in 1970s Iran." *Leonardo* 40 (1): 20–28.

Habermas, Jürgen. 1962. *Strukturwandel der Öffentlichkeit*. Frankfurt: Suhrkamp Taschenbuch.

Hall, Stuart. 1973. "Encoding and Decoding in the Media Discourse." Stencilled paper no. 7, Center for Contemporary Cultural Studies, University of Birmingham.

Hashemi, Nader, and Danny Postel, eds. 2011. *The People Reloaded: The Green Movement and the Struggle for the Future of Iran*. New York: Melville House.

Hebdige, Dick. 1979. *Subculture: The Meaning of Style*. New York: Routledge.

Hemmasi, Farzaneh. 2010. "Iranian Popular Music in Los Angeles: Mobilizing Media, Nation, and Politics," PhD diss., Columbia University, New York.

————. 2011. "Iranian Popular Music in Los Angeles: A Transnational Public beyond the Islamic State." In *Muslim Rap, Halal Soaps, and Revolutionary Theater: Artistic Developments in the Muslim World*, edited by Karin van Nieuwkerk, 85–111. Austin: University of Texas Press.

————. 2013. "Intimating Dissent: Popular Song, Poetry, and Politics in Pre-Revolutionary Iran." *Ethnomusicology* 57,(1, Winter): 57–87.

Herzfeld, Michael. 1997. *Cultural Intimacy: Social Poetics in the Nation-State*. New York: Routledge.

Hirschkind, Charles. 2004. "Hearing Modernity: Egypt, Islam and the Pious Ear." In *Hearing Cultures: Essays on Sound, Listening and Modernity*, edited by Veit Erlmann, 131–151. Oxford: Berg.

Hoseyni-Dehkordi, Morteza. 2011. "Ey Irān," in *Encyclopædia Iranica*, online edition, accessed 27 July 2016: http://www.iranicaonline.org/articles/ey-iran

Irani, Akbar. 1370 [1991/1992]. *Hasht Goftār Pirāmun-e Haqiqat-e Musiqi-ye Ghanāyi*. Tehran: Sāzmān-e Tablighāt-e Eslāmi, Hozeh Honari, Daftar-e Motāle'āt-e Dini-ye Honar.

——. 1386 [2007/2008]. *Hāl-e Dowrān: Negaresh-e jāme'eh-shenākhti beh musiqi az jāheliyat tā āghāz-e Abbāsiyān*. Chap-e 1. (1st edition). Tehran: Vezarat-e Farhang va Ershād-e Eslāmi, Sāzmān-e Chāp va Entesharāt.

Jasper, James M. 1997. *The Art of Moral Protest*. Chicago: University of Chicago Press.

Johari, Abbas. 2002. "Internet Use in Iran: Access, Social, and Educational Issues." *Educational Technology, Research and Development* 50 (1): 81–84.

Johnston, Sholeh. 2008. "Persian Rap: The Voice of Modern Iran's Youth." *Journal of Persianate Studies* 1 (1): 102–119.

Kamrava, Mehran. 2008. *Iran's Intellectual Revolution*. Cambridge: Cambridge University Press.

Karimi-Hakkak, Ahmad. 1991. "Revolutionary Posturing: Iranian Writers and the Iranian Revolution of 1979." *International Journal of Middle East Studies* 23 (4): 507–531.

——. 1995. *Recasting Persian Poetry: Scenarios of Poetic Modernity in Iran*. Salt Lake City: University of Utah Press.

Kashani-Sabet, Firoozeh. 1999. *Frontier Fictions: Shaping the Iranian Nation, 1804–1946*. Princeton, N.J.: Princeton University Press.

Katouzian, Homa. 2013. *Iran Politics, History and Literature*. London, New York: Routledge.

Keddie, Nikki R. 2006. *Modern Iran: Roots and Results of Revolution*. New Haven, Connecticut: Yale University Press.

Kelly, John, and Bruce Etling. 2008. *Mapping Iran's Online Public: Politics and Culture in the Persian Blogosphere*. Internet and Democracy Case Study Series. Cambridge, MA: Berkman Center Research Publication, Harvard University.

Keshavarzian, Arash. 2005. "Contestation Without Democracy: Elite Fragmentation in Iran." In *Authoritarianism in the Middle East: Regimes and Resistance*, edited by Marsha Pripstein Posusney and Michele Penner Angrist. Boulder, CO: Lynne Rienner Publishers, Inc.

Khademi, Hasan. 2005-2008. 'Motāle'eh-ye moredi: vizhehgihā-ye musiqi-ye zirzamini-ye rap-e Fārsi' (A Case Study: The Characteristics of Underground Persian Rap Music). http://mahmoodheydari.blogfa.com/post/122ل‌ول-قسمت-ه‌ر‌پ-درباره-جالب-مقاله (piece not dated; accessed 27 July 2016).

——. 2010. "Barresi-ye Musiqi-ye Zirzamini dar Irān." Paper presented at the Center for Strategic Studies, Tehran, 29 November.

Khaleqi, Ruhollah. 2002. *Sargozasht-e Musiqi-ye Irān (Seh jeld dar yek jeld); vols. 1–3*. Tehran: Mo'assesseh-ye Farhangi-Honari-ye Mahur. First published 1954.

Khatam, Azam. 2010. "Struggling over Defining the Moral City: The Problem Called 'Youth' in Urban Iran." In *Being Young and Muslim: New Cultural Politics in the Global South and North*, edited by Asef Bayat and Linda Herrera. New York: Oxford University Press.

Khomeini, Ruhollah. 1367 [1988/1989]. *Sahife-ye Emām*. Tehran: Mo'assesseh-ye Tanzim va Nashr-e Āsār-e Emām Khomeini.

———. 1381 [2002/2003]. *Velāyat-e Faqih: Hokumat-e Eslāmi* Chap-e 12 (12ᵗʰ edition). Tehran: Mo'assesseh-ye Tanzim va Nashr-e Āsār-e Emām Khomeini.

———. 1961. *Al-Makasib al-Muharrama, vol. 1*. Tehran: Mo'assesseh-ye Tanzim va Nashr-e Āsār-e Emām Khomeini.

———. 1979. *Kashf-e Asrār*. Tehran: Mo'assesseh-ye Tanzim va Nashr-e Āsār-e Emām Khomeini.

Khomeini, Ruhollah, and Hamid Algar. 2002. *Islam and Revolution: Writings and Declarations*. London: Kegan Paul.

Khosravi, Shahram. 2008. *Young and Defiant in Tehran*. Philadelphia: University of Pennsylvania Press.

Kot, Greg. 2009. *Ripped: How The Wired Generation Revolutionized Music*. New York: Scribner.

Kowsari, Masoud. 2009. "Musiqi-ye Zirzamini dar Irān." *Jāme'e-shenāsi-ye Honar va Adabiyāt* 1 (Spring and Summer):127–158.

———. 2010. "Barresi-ye Musiqi-ye Zirzamini dar Irān." Paper read at Center for Strategic Studies (29 November), Tehran.

Lagrange, Frédéric. 2009. "Women in the Singing Business, Women in Songs." *History Compass* 7 (1): 226–250.

LeVine, Mark. 2008. *Heavy Metal Islam: Rock, Resistance, and The Struggle for the Soul of Islam*. New York: Three Rivers Press.

Lewisohn, Jane. 2008. "Flowers of Persian Song and Music: Davud Pirnia and the Genesis of the Golha Programs." *Journal of Persianate Studies* 1 (1): 79–101.

Lewisohn, Leonard. 2010. "The Religion of Love and the Puritans of Islam: Sufi Sources of Hafiz's Anti-Clericalism." In *Hafiz and the Religion of Love in Classical Persian Poetry*, edited by Leonard Lewisohn, 159–196. London: Tauris.

Loeb, Laurence D. 1972. "The Jewish Musician and the Music of Fars." *Asian Music* 4 (1): 3–14.

Lohman, Laura. 2010. *Umm Kulthūm: Artistic Agency and the Shaping of an Arab Legend, 1967–2007*. Middletown, CT: Wesleyan University Press.

Lucas, Ann. 2014. "Ancient Music, Modern Myth: Persian Music and the Pursuit of Methodology in Historical Ethnomusicology." In *Theory and Method in Historical Ethnomusicology*, edited by Jonathan McCollum and David G. Hebert, 175–195. Lexington Books.

MacDonald, Duncan B. 1901. "Emotional Religion in Islām as Affected by Music and Singing (Being a Translation of the Ihya 'Ulm ad-Din of al-Ghazzali with Analysis, Annotation, and Appendices)." *Journal of the Royal Asiatic Society of Great Britain and Ireland* (April): 195–252.

Maleki, Tuka. 2001. *Zanān-e Musiqi-ye Irān* [The women of Iranian music]. Tehran: Enteshārāt-e Ketāb-e Khorshid.

Manuel, Peter. 1993. *Cassette Culture: Popular Music and Technology in North India*. Chicago: University of Chicago Press.

Matthee, Rudolph P., and Beth Baron. 2000. *Iran and Beyond: Essays in Middle Eastern History in Honor of Nikki R. Keddie.* Costa Mesa, CA: Mazda Publishers.

Massoudieh, Mohammad Taghi. 1968. *Āwāz-e-Šur.* Regensburg: Bosse.

Milani, Abbas. 2008. *Eminent Persians.* Vol. 2. Syracuse, NY: Syracuse University Press.

Mitchell, Timothy. 1990. "Everyday Metaphors of Power." *Theory and Society* 19 (5, October): 545–577.

Mitchell, Tony. 2001. *Global Noise: Rap and Hip-Hop outside the USA.* Middletown, CT: Wesleyan University Press.

Mirsepassi, Ali. 2010. *Democracy in Modern Iran: Islam, Culture, and Political Change.* New York: New York University Press.

Moallem, Minoo. 2005. *Between Warrior Brother and Veiled Sister: Islamic Fundamentalism and the Politics of Patriarchy in Iran.* Berkeley, CA: University of California Press.

Morozov, Evgeny. 2011. *The Net Delusion: The Dark Side of Internet Freedom.* New York: Public Affairs.

Mostofi, Abdollah. 1377 [1998/1999]. *Sharh-e zendegāni-ye man, yā, Tārikh-e ejtemā'i va edāri-ye dowreh-ye Qājāriyeh.* 4th ed. 3 vols. Tehran: Zovvār.

Mozafari, Parmis. 2012. "Carving a Space for Female Solo Singing in Post-Revolution Iran." In *Resistance in Contemporary Middle Eastern Cultures: Literature, Cinema and Music,* edited by *Karima Laachir* and *Saeed Talajooy,* 262–278. New York: Routledge.

Musavi, Amin. 2010. "Imam Hossein's Robe, A Refuge for Music: *Musiqiye Iranian's* Exclusive Interview with Sadeq Tabatabi." *Musiqi-ye Irāniān:* 119–130.

Naficy, Hamid. 1992. "Islamizing Film Culture in Iran." In *Political Culture in the Islamic Republic,* edited by Samih K. Farsoun and Mehrdad Mashayekhi, 123–148. London: Routledge.

———. 2002. "Islamizing Film Culture in Iran: A Post-Khatami Update." In *The New Iranian Cinema: Politics, Representation and Identity,* edited by Richard Tapper, 26–65. London: I. B. Tauris.

Najmabadi, Afsaneh. 2005. *Women with Mustaches and Men without Beards: Gender and Sexual Anxieties of Iranian Modernity.* Berkeley: University of California Press.

Nelson, Kristina. 1985. *The Art of Reciting the Qur'an.* Modern Middle East Series. Austin: University of Texas Press.

Nettl, Bruno. 1970. "Attitudes Towards Persian Music in Tehran, 1969." *The Music Quarterly* 56 (2): 183–197.

———. 1987. *The Radif of Persian Music: Studies of Structures and Cultural Context.* Champaign, IL: Elephant and Cat.

———. 2006. "Iran xi. Persian Music." In *Encyclopaedia Iranica,* edited by Ehsan Yarshater. London.

Nieuwkerk, Karin van, ed.. 2011. *Muslim Rap, Halal Soaps, and Revolutionary Theater: Artistic Developments in the Muslim World.* Austin: University of Texas Press.

Nooshin, Laudan. 2003. "Improvisation as 'Other': Creativity, Knowledge and Power: The Case of Iranian Classical Music." *Journal of the Royal Musical Association* 128 (2): 242–296.

———. 2005a. "Subversion and Counter-Subversion: Power, Control and Meaning in the New Iranian Pop Music." In *Music, Power and Politics*, edited by Annie Janeiro Randall, 231–272. London: Routledge.

———. 2005b. "Underground, Overground: Rock Music and Youth Discourses in Iran." *Iranian Studies* 38 (3): 463–494.

———. 2009a. "Prelude: Power and the Play of Music." In *Music and the Play of Power in the Middle East, North Africa and Central Asia*, edited by Laudan Nooshin, 1–31. Aldershot: Ashgate.

———. 2009b. "'Tomorrow Is Ours': Re-Imagining Nation, Performing Youth in the New Iranian Pop Music. In *Music and the Play of Power in the Middle East, North Africa and Central Asia*, edited by Laudan Nooshin, 245–268. Aldershot: Ashgate.

———. 2010. "The Language of Rock: Iranian Youth, Popular Music, and National Identity." In *Media, Culture and Society in Iran: Living with Globalization and the Islamic State*, edited by Mehdi Semati, 69–93. New York: Routledge.

———. 2011. "Hip-Hop Tehran: Migrating Styles, Musical Meanings, Marginalized Voices." In *Migrating Music*, edited by Jason Toynbee and Byron Dueck, 92–111. London: Routledge.

———. 2015. *Iranian Classical Music: The Discourses and Practice of Creativity*. Aldershot: Ashgate.

Olszewska, Zuzanna. 2009. "Poetry and Its Social Contexts among Afghan Refugees in Iran." DPhil thesis, School of Anthropology and Museum Ethnography, University of Oxford.

Ong, Walter J. 1988. *Orality and Literacy: The Technologizing of the Word*. London: Routledge.

Parvin, Manoucher, and Mostafa Vaziri. 1992. "Islamic Man and Society in the Islamic Republic of Iran." In *Political Culture in the Islamic Republic*, edited by Samih K. Farsoun and Mehrdad Mashayekhi, 80–91. London; New York: Routledge.

Parvin, Naser al-Din. 2007. "She'r-e Morgh-e Sahar." Bokhārā: Majjaleh-ye Farhangi va Honari no. 55:171-176.

Racy, Jihad. 1978. "Musical Change and Commercial Recording in Egypt: 1904–1932." PhD diss., University of Illinois.

———. 2003. *Making Music in the Arab World: The Culture and Artistry of Ṭarab*. Cambridge: Cambridge University Press.

Rahimi, Babak. 2010. "The Politics of Internet in Iran." In *Media, Culture and Society in Iran: Living with Globalization and the Islamic State*, edited by Mehdi Semati, 37–56. New York: Routledge.

———. 2011. "Affinities of Dissent: Cyberspace, Performative Networks and the Iranian Green Movement." *CyberOrient* 5 (2): http://www.cyberorient.net/article.do?article Id=7357.

Robertson, Bronwen. 2012. *Reverberations of Dissent*. London: Bloomsbury Academic.

Rochard, Philippe. 2002. "The Identities of the Iranian Zūrkhanah." *Iranian Studies* 35 (4): 313–340.

Sadighi, Ramin. 2007. *Rāhnamāyi-ye Sādeh Barā-ye San'at-e Musiqi* [A simple guide for the music industry]. Tehran: Anjoman-e Musiqi-ye Iran.

Sadighi, Ramin, and Sohrab Mahdavi. 2009. "The Song Does Not Remain the Same." *MERIP* (Middle East Research and Information Project) (12 March): http://www.merip .org/mero/mero031209.

Safvat, Dariush. 1990. *The Dastgāh Concept in Persian Music.* Cambridge: Cambridge University Press.

Salehi-Isfahani, Djavad. 2009. "Poverty, Inequality, and Populist Politics in Iran." *The Journal of Economic Inequality* 7: 5–28.

Satrapi, Marjane. 2004 and 2005. *Persepolis 1 and 2.* New York: Pantheon Graphic Novels.

Schade-Poulsen, Marc. 1999. *Men and Popular Music in Algeria: The Social Significance of Rai.* Austin: University of Texas Press.

Schayegh, Cyrus. 2010. "'Seeing Like a State': An Essay on the Historiography of Modern Iran." *International Journal of Middle Eastern Studies* 42: 37-61.

Scheiwiller, Staci Gem, ed. 2013. *Performing the Iranian State.* London: Anthem Middle East Studies, Anthem Press.

Schirazi, Asghar. 1997. *The Constitution of Iran: Politics and the State in the Islamic Republic.* Translated by John O'Kane. London: Tauris.

Scott, James C. 1990. *Domination and the Arts of Resistance: Hidden Transcripts.* New Haven, CT: Yale University Press.

Secor, Laura. 2016. *Children of Paradise: The Struggle for the Soul of Iran.* New York, NY: Riverhead Books.

Seifzadeh, Abdul-Rahman. 1977. *Koliyāt-e Divān-e Shādravān Mirzā Abu-l-Qāsem 'Āref Qazvini.* 6th ed. Tehran: Mo'assesseh Enteshārāt-e Amir Kabir.

Sepanta, Sasan. 1995. "'Ali-Naqi Vaziri: Pishgām-e musiqi-ye novin-e Irān." *Faslnāmeh-ye Kermān* (19, Winter).

———. 1998. *Tarikh-e tahavvol-e zabt-e musiqi dar Irān.* Tehran: Mahur.

———. 2003. *Cheshmandāz-e Musiqi-ye Irān.* 2nd ed. Tehran Mo'assesseh Farhangi-Honari-ye Māhur. First published 1990. Tehran: Intisharat-i Mash'al.

Shafi'i-Kadkani, Mohammad Reza. 1380 [2001/2002]. *Advār-e She'r-e Fārsi.* Tehran: Sokhan.

Shajarian, Mohammad Reza. 1379 [2000/2001]. *Rāz-e Mānā.* Edited by Mohsen Gudarzi, Mohammad Javad Gholamrezakashi, and Ali-Asghar Ramezanpur. Tehran: Ketāb-e Farā.

———. 2004a. *Latifeh-ye Nahāni: Gozideh-ye goft-o-guhā va goftārha-ye Ostād Moham-mad Reza Shajarian va naqd va nazarhāyi darbāreh-ye u va āsārash.* Edited by Zabi-hollah Habibnejad. Tehran: Mo'assesseh-ye Farhangi-Honari-ye Māhur.

———. 2004b. *Hezār Golkhāneh Āvāz: Mohammad Reza Shajarian.* Edited by Kāzem Motlaq and Mehdi 'Abedini. Qom: Farāgereft.

Shakibi, Zhand. 2010. *Khatami and Gorbachev: Politics of Change in the Islamic Republic of Iran and the USSR.* London: Tauris Academic Studies.

Shamlu, Ahmad. 1378 [1999/2000]. *Majmu'e Āsār-e Ahmad Shamlu.* First Book, Part Two. Tehran: Enteshārāt-e Zamāneh.

Shannon, Jonathan Holt. 2009. *Among the Jasmine Trees: Music and Modernity in Contemporary Syria*. Middletown, CT: Wesleyan.

Shay, Anthony. 2000. "The 6/8 Beat Goes On: Persian Popular Music from Bazm-e Qajariyyeh to Beverly Hills Garden Parties." In *Mass Mediations: New Approaches to Popular Culture in the Middle East and Beyond*, edited by Walter Armbrust, 61–87. Berkeley: University of California Press.

———. 2016. "Foreword." In Breyley and Fatemi (2016), xx–xxvi.

Shiloah, Amnon. 1995. *Music in the World of Islam: A Socio-Cultural Study*. Aldershot: Scolar Press.

Siamdoust, Nahid. 2011. "Review, Passionate Uprisings: Iran's Sexual Revolution." *International Journal of Middle East Studies* 43 (1): 155–158.

———. 2012. "Neither 'Islamic' Nor a 'Republic': Discourses in Music." In *Cultural Revolution in Iran: Contemporary Popular Culture in the Islamic Republic*, edited by A. Sreberny and M. Torfeh, 151–167. London: I. B. Tauris.

———. 2014. "The Counterpublic of Love in Iran." Paper presented at the Conference of the *Middle East Studies Association of America*, Washington, D.C., 24 November.

———. 2015. "Tehran's Soundscape as a Contested Public Sphere: Blurring the Lines between Public and Private." In *Divercities: Competing Narratives and Urban Practices in Beirut, Cairo and Tehran. Orient Institut Studies*: http://www.perspectivia.net/publikationen/orient-institut-studies/3-2015/siamdoust_soundscape.

———. 2016. "The Re-emergence and Evolution of Pop Music in the Islamic Republic of Iran: From Heavenly to Earthly Love" in Inside the Islamic Republic: *Social Change in Post-Khomeini Iran*, edited by Mahmood Monshipouri, 221–241. London: Hurst and Co.

Simms, Rob, and Amir Koushkani. 2012a. *The Art of Āvāz and Mohammad Reza Shajarian: Foundations and Contexts*. Plymouth: Lexington Books.

———. 2012b. *Mohammad Reza Shajarian's Avas in Iran and Beyond, 1979–2010*. Plymouth: Lexington Books.

Sohrabi-Haghighat, Mohammad Hadi. 2011. "New Media and Social-Political Change in Iran." *CyberOrient* 5 (1); http://www.cyberorient.net/article.do?articleId=6187.

Sreberny, Annabelle, and Gholam Khiabany. 2010. *Blogistan: The Internet and Politics in Iran*. International Library of Iranian Studies. London: I. B. Tauris.

Sreberny, Annabelle, and Ali Mohammadi. 1994. *Small Media, Big Revolution: Communication, Culture, and the Iranian Revolution*. Minneapolis: University of Minnesota Press.

Sterne, Jonathan. 2001. "A Machine to Hear for Them: On the Very Possibility of Sound's Reproduction." *Cultural Studies* 15 (2): 259–294.

Steward, Theresa Parvin. 2013. "'I Am the Brave Hero and This Land is Mine': Popular Music and Youth Identity in Post-Revolutionary Iran." PhD diss., University of Edinburgh.

Stokes, Martin. 1992. *The Arabesk Debate: Music and Musicians In Modern Turkey*. Oxford: Clarendon Press.

———. 2010. *The Republic of Love: Cultural Intimacy in Turkish Popular Music*. Chicago: University of Chicago Press.

———. 2012. "Globalization and the Politics of World Music." In *The Cultural Study Of Music: A Critical Introduction*, edited by Martin Clayton, Trevor Herbert, and Richard Middleton, 297–308. New York: Routledge.

Taheri, Amir. 1987. *The Spirit of Allah*. London: Hutchinson.

Talattof, Kamran. 2011. *Modernity, Sexuality, and Ideology in Iran: The Life and Legacy of a Popular Female Artist*. Syracuse, NY: Syracuse University Press.

Tavakoli-Targhi, Mohamad. 2001. *Refashioning Iran: Orientalism, Occidentalism, and Historiography*. New York: Palgrave.

Tazmini, Ghoncheh. 2009. *Khatami's Iran: The Islamic Republic and the Turbulent Path to Reform*. London: I. B. Tauris.

Taussig, Michael. 1999. *Defacement: Public Secrecy and the Labor of the Negative*. Stanford: Stanford University Press.

Tilly, Charles. 1997. "Contentious Politics and Social Change." *African Studies* 56 (1): 51–65.

Varzi, Roxanne. 2006. *Warring Souls: Youth, Media, and Martyrdom in Postrevolution Iran*. Durham, NC: Duke University Press.

Vaziri, Mostafa. 1993. *Iran as Imagined Nation: The Construction of National Identity*. New York, NY: Paragon House.

Vovelle, Michel. 1982. "Ideologies and Mentalities." In *Culture, Ideology and Politics: Essays for Eric Hobsbawm*, edited by Raphael Samuel and Gareth Stedman Jones, 2–11. London: Routledge and Kegan Paul Ltd.

Waring, Edward Scott. (1807) 1973. *A Tour to Sheeraz by the Route of Kazroon and Feerozabad*. New York: Arno Press.

Warner, Michael. 2002. "Publics and Counterpublics." *Public Culture* 14 (1): 49–90.

Wright, Owen. 2009. *Touraj Kiaras and Persian Classical Music: An Analytical Perspective*. SOAS Musicology Series. Farnham: Ashgate.

Yaghmaian, Behzad. 2002. *Social Change in Iran: An Eyewitness Account of Dissent, Defiance, and New Movements for Rights*. Albany: State University of New York Press.

Youssefzadeh, Ameneh. 2000. "The Situation of Music in Iran since the Revolution: The Role of Official Organizations." *Ethnomusicology Forum* 9 (2): 35–61.

———. 2005. "Iran's Regional Musical Traditions in the Twentieth Century: A Historical Overview." *Iranian Studies* 38 (3): 417–439.

Zahir, Sanam. 2008. "The Music of the Children of the Revolution: The State of Music and Emergence of the Underground Music in the Islamic Republic of Iran." MA thesis, University of Arizona.

Zia-Ebrahimi, Reza. 2016. *The Emergence of Iranian Nationalism: Race and the Politics of Dislocation*. New York: Columbia University Press.

Zonis, Ella. 1973. *Classical Persian Music: An Introduction*. Cambridge: Harvard University Press.s

63–65, 82–83, 268; *"Shabnavard"* (Night Traveler), 66, 301n7; *"Zhāleh khun shod"* (Dew Turned into Blood), 65
Chavoshi, Mohsen, 136, 191
Chert o pert, 172
Children of the revolution generation, 113, 177. *See also* Youth
Classical music, Persian, *see* Persian classical music
Classical music, Western, 23, 55–56, 59, 90
Communication technologies, 16–17. *See also* Internet; Mobile phones
Communists, 18, 265, 266, 325n6. *See also* Marxist poets
Concerts: all-female audiences, 31, 32, 293n70; as discursive community, 14, 18, 19; in early twentieth century, 54, 55; *Ershād* permits, 84, 100, 102, 135, 178–79, 186, 277–78, 311n49; at foreign embassies, 33, 74; history of public, 52, 54; mixed-gender audiences, 30–31, 32, 33; permits required, 84; private, 52, 54, 71, 74, 124, 126, 227, 315–16n4; regulation of audiences, 2, 12; rock music, 172, 173–74, 178, 229; state-sponsored, 18, 110, 280–81; underground, 18, 150 (photo), 172, 173–74, 185–88, 229–30
Confess, 174
Conservatives: cultural policies, 160, 166–67, 213–15, 277; in power, 213. *See also* Ahmadinejad, Mahmoud
Conservatory of Music, 173–74
Constitutional Revolution (1905–1911), 3, 21, 51, 54, 265, 267–68
Counterpublic, 85, 276, 278–79, 312n63
Cultural capital, 12, 128, 222, 234
Cultural intimacy, 200, 317n21
Cultural policies: of Ahmadinejad, 173, 213–15; ambiguity and uncertainty, 9, 25, 92–93, 175–76, 278; conservative, 160, 166–67, 213–15, 277; defense against Western cultural invasion, 98–99, 112, 125, 166–67, 213–14, 310n29; evolution, 1–3, 18, 28–29, 289–90n6; Islamization, 4–6; of Khamenei, 93–94, 105, 160; of Khomeini, 4, 7, 24, 98, 99, 105; organizations, 99–103; reform period under Khatami, 29, 166–71, 212–13; relaxation, 71–72; religious basis, 4–6,

12–13; repression of music, 4, 6–7, 17, 70; of Rouhani, 277; setting, 29–30; in Shah era, 24, 55–56, 60
Cultural Revolution Headquarters, 4–5, 98. *See also* Supreme Council for Cultural Revolution

Damghani, Ali Mo'allem, *see* Mo'allem, Ali
Dancing: 6/8 rhythm, 29, 214, 310n34; efforts to suppress, 2, 12; Islamic views, 7; pop music rhythms, 138
Dariush (Eqbali): cabaret performances, 46; concerts, 309n20; in exile, 116, 309n20; fans, 116; political songs, 60, 64, 116, 265; on protest songs, 270; singers with similar voices, 116–17, 119, 121, 122, 310n24
Dativ, 229
Davami, Abdollah, 39, 49, 53–54, 161–62
Dawn of Rage, 174
Death metal music, 171
De Burgh, Chris, 184, 218
Deev, *"Dastā bālā"* (Hands Up), 236, 245
Dehbashi, Hossein, 276
Delavaz, 80
Delkash, 31, 45, 114
Democracy: freedom associated with, 52; Western, 52. *See also Mardomi* (popular) term
Derakhshani, Majid, 33, 71
Derakhshani, Pedram, 172
Diaco, *"Man Kheng Shomdam"* (I'm Dopey), 228–29
Dia Prometido band, 47
Diaspora rappers, 239
Diāzpām 10, see Ārāmesh bā Diāzpām-e 10
Dire Straits, 172, 218
DJ Maryam, 33
Drug abuse, 190–91, 231
Dubai: concerts, 230, 320n21; Iranian exiles in, 229; Persian Media Corporation, 220–21, 320n38

Ebi, 47, 128, 129
Eblis, *"To masti"* (You're Drunk), 209–10
Ebtehaj, Houshang, 63
Education: Islamization, 5; National Organization for the Development of

Kabir Tambar, *The Reckonings of Pluralism: Citizenship and the Demands of History in Turkey*
2014

Diana Allan, *Refugees of the Revolution: Experiences of Palestinian Exile*
2013

Shira Robinson, *Citizen Strangers: Palestinians and the Birth of Israel's Liberal Settler State*
2013

Joel Beinin and Frédéric Vairel, *editors, Social Movements, Mobilization, and Contestation in the Middle East and North Africa*
2013 (Second Edition), 2011

Ariella Azoulay and Adi Ophir, *The One-State Condition: Occupation and Democracy in Israel/Palestine*
2012

Steven Heydemann and Reinoud Leenders, *editors, Middle East Authoritarianisms: Governance, Contestation, and Regime Resilience in Syria and Iran*
2012

Jonathan Marshall, *The Lebanese Connection: Corruption, Civil War, and the International Drug Traffic*
2012

Joshua Stacher, *Adaptable Autocrats: Regime Power in Egypt and Syria*
2012

Bassam Haddad, *Business Networks in Syria: The Political Economy of Authoritarian Resilience*
2011

Noah Coburn, *Bazaar Politics: Power and Pottery in an Afghan Market Town*
2011

Laura Bier, *Revolutionary Womanhood: Feminisms, Modernity, and the State in Nasser's Egypt*
2011